Modern Language Association of America
Options for Teaching
Joseph Gibaldi, Series Editor

Teaching Tudor and Stuart Women Writers

Edited by
**Susanne Woods and
Margaret P. Hannay**

The Modern Language Association
New York   2000

For information about obtaining permission to reprint material from MLA
book publications, send your request by mail (see address below), by
e-mail (permissions@mla.org), or by fax (646 458-0030).

Library of Congress Cataloging-in-Publication Data

Teaching Tudor and Stuart women writers / edited by Susanne Woods
and Margaret P. Hannay.
    p. cm. — (Options for teaching)
  Includes bibliographical references and index.
   ISBN 0-87352-346-6 — ISBN 0-87352-347-4 (pbk.)
    1. English literature—Women authors—History and criticism.
  2. English literature—Early modern, 1500–1700—History and criticism.
  3. English literature—Women authors—Study and teaching (Higher)
  4. Women authors, English—Biography—Study and teaching (Higher)
  5. Women and literature—Great Britain—History—16th century—
History and criticism. 6. Women and literature—Great Britain—History—
17th century—History and criticism. 7. Women in literature. I. Woods,
Susanne, 1943–   II. Hannay, Margaret P., 1944– III. Series.

PR113 .T43 2000
820.9′9287′09031—dc21   00-059440
ISSN 1079-2562

Ann Hurley's essay is adapted, with permission, from her article of the
same title in *Renaissance News and Notes* 7.3 (1994): 1–6.

Cover illustration of the paperback edition: *Elizabeth I When Princess
(1533–1603)*, c. 1546. Oil on panel. RCIN 40444. The Royal Collection.
© HM Queen Elizabeth II. Photographer: Stephen Chapman.

Printed on recycled paper

Published by The Modern Language Association of America
26 Broadway, New York, New York 10004-1789
www.mla.org

For our brothers,
to Samuel Woods
and
in memory of Kenneth H. Patterson

Contents

Part II: Selected Authors

Part II: Models for Teaching

Teaching Specific Texts

Part IV: Resources for Further Study

Margaret P. Hannay and Susanne Woods

Introduction

Why study the writings of early modern women? Since they have languished in obscurity for the last century, at least, why should they be gaining so much attention today? Perhaps the first reason is the search for a usable past. Virginia Woolf famously sought a female tradition when she looked on the shelves "for books that were not there" and lamented that "nothing is known about women before the eighteenth century. I have no model in my mind to turn about this way and that" (68–69). Margaret Ezell has demonstrated the impact of Woolf's lament on subsequent scholarship (*Writing Women's Literary History*), yet the irony is that Woolf, though she did not know it, was surrounded there in the British Library by the works of early modern women in manuscript and in print (Hannay, "Constructing"). Thus each generation of women writers in the English language has seemingly started anew, inventing again its own arguments for legitimacy. Listening to voices that have long been silent provides a foundation on which younger generations of women can build. As they reclaim their heritage, our students are intrigued, angered, delighted, and sometimes empowered by these early writers.

A second reason is the search for a more fully realized past. Cultural histories now seek to include all persons, regardless of sex, race, or social class. Once the issue of inclusiveness has been raised, it becomes obvious that any account of the tradition of writers in English must speak of all writers, not just male writers. As conscious as we are today that our readings are colored by our subject positions, we can still make an effort to reconstruct the past as fully as possible. Teaching Edmund Spenser's *The Faerie Queene* is a richer experience when one also teaches Mary Wroth's *Urania*; teaching Ben Jonson's "To Penshurst" is complemented by teaching Aemilia Lanyer's "Description of Cooke-ham," a country-house poem that may have preceded Jonson's. Such pairings need not descend into essentialism, as both Gary Waller and Paula Loscocco demonstrate in this volume, but they can provide a deeper understanding of both paired texts. We can celebrate "Eve's Apologie" while continuing to love *Paradise Lost*.

The intent of this volume is to present current scholarship on the writings of Tudor and Stuart women in a form that will be useful for teaching, giving background on women's lives and women's texts, presenting newly canonized authors, providing models for teaching, and listing resources for further study. By *Tudor and Stuart* we mean roughly the period from 1500 to 1700, although technically the Stuart period ended with the death of Queen Anne a decade later. We found it impossible to fit these women writers precisely into traditional periodization; the authors discussed here wrote primarily before 1700, and most of them before 1680. "Tudor and Stuart" nonetheless seemed the most descriptive title. Other period designations might be "the long Renaissance" or, more common in recent years, "the early modern period," a term used by many essayists in this collection. *Women* should be unambiguous. Although there have been some cross-gendered attributions (Harvey), the essays in this collection focus on texts generally accepted as written by women.

The initial difficulty a teacher may face in introducing works by

Tudor and Stuart women is that the world they inhabited was so different from our students' world of the Internet and shopping mall, where religious tolerance, racial consciousness, and enhanced opportunities for women are accepted ideals. Students need to know what obstacles early modern women faced and also how they overcame them. Many of these women protested against injustices toward themselves and other women, but none of them, even the religious martyrs, would have defined themselves primarily as victims. They may have lived under gender restrictions that we would find intolerable, but those restrictions were simply part of the world they inhabited, like the equally tight restrictions on behavior according to social class, which were protested by Lanyer, among others.

Women in early modern England were subordinate to men by generally accepted definitions of natural, divine, and statutory law. For most of this period they were considered to be not a separate sex but an inferior version of men. Their cold and moist natures, according to contemporary medical theory, prevented their sexual characteristics from being expressed outwardly, and their genitalia were thought to be a reversed and interior version of the male penis and testicles. Although this view changed among medical men over the course of the seventeenth century, it changed more slowly in the popular imagination and in the perception of gender (Fletcher 30–43).

As with women's bodies, so with their natures. Thomas Elyot, in his popular educational treatise *The Boke Named the Governour* (1531), expressed the received commonplaces: "A man in his naturall perfection is fiers, hardy, stronge in opinion, covaitous of glorie, desirous of knowledge, appetiting by generation to bring forth his semblable. The good nature of a woman is to be milde, timorous, tractable, benigne, of sure remembrance, and shamfast" (xxi). These characteristics also established what were considered natural social roles. According to Thomas Smith in his *Commonwelth of England* (1583), men are responsible for activities in the world, while women are responsible for the household, "to keep everything at home neat and clean" (C2). A woman's domain, like her sexual characteristics, was interior.

Religion reinforced gender distinction, both restricting and empowering women (see, this volume, King, Dolan, and Hobby; Trill). The belief in women's inferiority, particularly their moral inferiority, was grounded in the Genesis account of the temptation of Adam and Eve. Juan Luis Vives memorably phrases the commonplace: "For Adam was the fyrst made, and after Eve, and Adame was not betrayed, the woman was betrayed in to the breche of the commandement. Therfore bycause a woman is a frayle thinge, and of weake discretion, and that may lightly be disceyued. [W]hiche thinge our fyrste mother Eve sheweth" (qtd. in Benson 178). This interpretation was evidently internalized by most women, like Dorothy Leigh, who said that "we must needes confesse that sin entered by us into our posterity" (B5). Mary, however, served to redeem her sex as well as mankind through the birth of Christ (Fletcher 380; see also Klein 287–302). The standard interpretation of Eve's significance was contested by some women, notably Aemilia Lanyer in her "Eve's Apologie" and Rachel Speght (see relevant essays in this volume), who admitted that woman sinned first and "yet we find no mention of spiritual nakedness until man had sinned" (*Mouzell* 15). Like Lanyer, Speght argues that Eve's intentions in sharing the apple were loving. (For additional readings on Eve, see Keeble 1–13.)

Women were constantly reminded of their inferiority in conduct books, pamphlets, sermons, and liturgy. Some men even followed the patristic writers in questioning whether women had souls, questioning whether they were fully human, yet few went to that extreme. Catholics celebrated nuns, believing that by remaining virgins and devoting themselves to God, women had a way to overcome (most) of the inferiority natural to their sex. Protestants celebrated the godly wife and mother, praising her as the helpmate of her husband and giving her authority over children and servants.

Natural law was thought to derive from divine law, and both were used to support women's statutory inferiority: "the common law [. . .] shaketh hands with divinity" (Keeble 146; *The Lawes Resolution* 4). Single women were subject to their male relatives. A married woman had no existence apart from her husband; she was legally a "femme covert," covered by his identity (Erickson 24).

When man and wife became "one flesh" (Gen. 2.24), the one they became was the man. As the sermons and polemical literature of the period insist, the role of the woman in home, church, and society is to be "chaste, silent and obedient" (Hull, *Chaste* 1; see also selections in Klein).

How were these cultural ideals imparted? Our students, engrossed in their own educational process, are curious about what early modern girls learned and how they learned it (see Hobby, *Virtue* 190–203; Jardine, *Still Harping* 37–67; M. King 164–88; Hilda Smith, "Humanist Education"; Stock 29–104; Wiesner 117–37). We might begin by explaining about humanist learning and how it was, and was not, made available to women. We might assign brief excerpts from Thomas More and Vives, for example, and Pamela Benson's nuanced reading of the differences between them. More believes that the primary benefit of education is spiritual, providing the student with the ability to live a truly Christian life. He praises education for the female student "for providing her with spiritual and moral autonomy, that is the ability to know what is right, rather than with the reinforcement of the outward form of chastity" (qtd. in Benson 158). For More, who believes that the highest life is lived in retirement from the world, "women are in an enviable position" (166). In contrast to More's emphasis on independent judgment, which may challenge the values of society, Vives sees education as teaching rules and conformity to societal values, and he is therefore more restrictive to women. Men act in the world, and so their "preceptes" are "innumerable"; women, who must live privately, "hathe no charge to se to, but her honestye and chastity" (qtd. in Benson 173). Yet Vives's prescripts could themselves encourage independent action for women, since his exemplars of virtuous women counter his explicit arguments for silence. Furthermore, his words were translated into English by Richard Hyrde, a member of More's household, who frames the work with a translation praising Queen Katherine "for the gracious zele that ye beare to the vertuous education of the woman kynde of this realme" (qtd. in Benson 179). Hyrde defends Margaret More Roper's learning in a preface to her translation of Erasmus, arguing that learning teaches virtue (Aughterson 173–74). In Tudor England aristocratic women were increasingly learned in keeping with the humanist ideal: Mary Tudor, Lady Jane Grey, Margaret More Roper, the Cooke sisters, Queen Elizabeth, and Mary Sidney were all educated with the humanist stress on language, rhetoric, and literature. They were expected to study modern languages (particularly French and Italian, although Queen Elizabeth also knew Spanish) and the learned tongues—Latin, probably Greek, and possibly Hebrew. Their texts would be the classics and religious works.

Class was a determining factor in education, which was viewed as training that would allow a woman to perform well the tasks appropriate to her station; there was thus considerable conflict between women seen as an ontological category and the actual duties of specific women (Jordan, "Renaissance Women"). Aristocratic girls might stay for extended periods with an aunt or grandmother, but they did not normally attend school, even if their brothers did. Mary Sidney and her sister Ambrosia, for example, studied at home while their brothers went to Shrewsbury School and then Oxford. They had various tutors, including "Mistress Maria, the Italian" and a Mr. Lodowick, possibly Lodowick Bryskett. The education of the five Cooke sisters was supervised by their father, Anthony Cooke, the tutor of Edward VI (Lamb, "Cooke Sisters" 108). Sir Thomas More supervised the tutors, such as William Gonell, who oversaw the education of his children (Benson 158). Elizabeth Joscelin was taught by her grandfather, William Chaderton, bishop of Lincoln (*Mothers Legacie* 3–4). Anne Clifford studied with her governess Anne Taylour and the poet Samuel Daniel; she thought so much of her tutors that she included their portraits in the *Great Picture* she had painted (Clifford, *Diaries* 97–99; Spence 12–17). Royal women studied with the most prominent educators of their day: Mary Tudor with Thomas Linacre and Vives; Lady Jane Grey with John Aylmer; and Elizabeth with Roger Ascham, author of *The Schoolmaster*, as Janel Mueller discusses ("Tudor Queen"). Fathers sometimes disapproved of an academic education for women. Sir Ralph Verney, for example, discouraged his daughter in her desire to learn

Latin, Greek, and Hebrew, telling her to be content with studying the Bible (in English) and the catechism (M. King 186).

Most children were given rigorous religious instruction. In the Protestant household this would include daily Scripture reading, prayers, and psalm singing, with strict church attendance on Sundays. Grace Sherrington Mildmay's diary, for example, records a religious upbringing with a beloved governess who taught with gentle wit. Mildmay's reading emphasized the Bible, Thomas à Kempis's *Imitation of Christ*, and Foxe's *Acts and Monuments*, as well as instructional works on medicine like Turner's herbal (Pollock, *Faith* 25–29). In the Catholic household this instruction would include daily attendance at mass, where possible, as well as prayer, meditation, and sometimes penitential practices, though they were rarely as extreme as those recorded by Luisa de Carvajal y Mendoza (Cruz; E. Rhodes). Each day both Protestant and Catholic children would kneel to receive their parents' blessing.

Most women, like most men at the beginning of the sixteenth century, were illiterate, although they might be skilled in crafts or in agriculture. The Protestant Reformation, with its stress on the primacy of the Scriptures, encouraged reading for all. Martin Luther, Philip Melanchthon, Johann Agricola, and Martin Bucer all advocated schools where girls would be taught to read. Girls of the lower ranks might spend a few years studying in local elementary or "dame schools," where the curriculum stressed practical skills—basic reading (more rarely writing), Christian doctrine, and household skills such as spinning and weaving. The Counter-Reformation also emphasized education, so that Catholic girls in Europe might learn such skills in convent schools, particularly those established by the Ursulines. In the seventeenth century a few of the more advanced Catholic schools on the Continent, like the schools established by Mary Ward and by Jacqueline Pascal, offered a secondary education including Latin (M. King 169–72; Wiesner 121–24). Girls of the middle class might be fortunate enough to study at one of the first boarding schools for girls: Ladies Hall at Deptford, established 1617, was a particularly fine school (Fletcher 368–70). Later in the seventeenth century Quakers also set up boarding schools for girls (M. King 171). Strong advocates for women's education, like Anna Maria van Schurman in the Netherlands, author of *The Learned Maid; or, Whether a Maid May Be a Scholar?* (trans. 1659), were echoed in England by Bathsua Makin's *Essay to Revive the Antient Education of Gentlewomen, in Religion, Manners, Arts and Tongues* (1673) and Mary Astell's *A Serious Proposal to the Ladies* (1694). Thus, toward the end of the seventeenth century, women turned the debate about women from their nature to their nurture. Margaret Cavendish, duchess of Newcastle, bemoaned the lack of a good education, "which seldom is given us," and compared women's plight to that of an earthworm or a bird in a cage (Hobby, *Virtue* 190; Kramer). Women are "education's more than nature's fools, / Debarr'd from all improvements of the mind, / And to be dull, expected and design'd," as Anne Finch memorably phrased their predicament (Fitzmaurice, Roberts, Barash, Cunnar, and Gutierrez 337; "The Introduction"). Similarly, Makin defends education for women, for "Learning perfects and adorns the soul" and will lift them above petty concerns with dress and makeup (Aughterson 188).

Aristocratic women in the early modern period, as in Jane Austen's day, were expected to bring beauty into the home and were therefore expected to study music and needlework; seventeenth-century boarding schools typically also stressed these feminine accomplishments. Elizabeth Tudor and Mary Stuart were both noted for their playing of the virginals, a precursor of the piano, and Mary Wroth and Anne Clifford were so proud of their music that both chose to be portrayed with lutes. Protestant women of all ranks sang psalms in the household and in the church services, usually to the tunes of Thomas Sternhold and John Hopkins, and Richard Rowlands urged Catholic women to sing his metric psalms (A1). Elizabeth Grymeston did sing Rowland's *Odes: In Imitation of the Seaven Penitential Psalmes* as her evening meditation (Grymeston, F1–H1).

All ranks of women were involved in cloth production, considered appropriately female from the time of Homer, who famously portrayed Penelope weaving (and surreptitiously unweaving) a shroud. Thomas Moffet's charmingly witty *Silkewormes* was written primarily for women aristocrats who made a hobby of silk production; women of lower ranks like "hursts widdow" and "Robinsons wife" were more likely to be employed in the wool trade, spinning, weaving, and sewing (Hannay, *Philip's Phoenix* 113). Needlework was an essential skill for all women, although the more wealth a girl could expect, the less practical and the more ornamental was her sewing. Queen Mary Stuart, for example, spent much of her time working on magnificent needlework with Bess of Hardwick, the wife of her jailer (Swain; Frye and Robertson). Apparently girls learned to sew in the large chamber, where the women of the household took turns reading aloud while the others embroidered. Despite constant admonitions of clerics to read only godly works, women often read poetry and romances aloud together. Philip Sidney's *Arcadia*, for example, was written for his sister Mary and includes (in the *Old Arcadia*) explicit addresses to an audience of "faire ladies" (Lamb, *Gender*). As Mary Ellen Lamb notes in this volume, romances became known as a woman's genre. Nevertheless, most works for women were either devotional or practical guidebooks (Hull, *Chaste*).

Girlhood was often a happy time. Except in the most severely religious households, girls could have many amusements—watching plays, listening to musicians and minstrels, attending fairs and family gatherings. Among sports activities were archery and horseback riding, while daily life for all but the wealthiest would include long walks in the countryside or city. Church services, though they might involve long sermons, also provided a chance to visit with friends and relatives. Sisters were often very close, studying and playing together, and even dressing alike. Penelope and Dorothy Devereux are portrayed in identical dresses in a portrait at Longleat, and the Sidney account books record that Ambrosia's dresses were made like "Mistress Marie in all poynts" (Hannay, *Philip's Phoenix* 25). In an age that valued companionship more than solitude, girls typically shared a bed with a sister or cousin. Anne Clifford records as her mother's most severe punishment making her sleep alone; fortunately, her cousin Frances crept in to stay with her, "which was the first time I loved her so well" (Clifford, *Diaries* 25). Yet her mother's perceived severity did not diminish Clifford's devotion to her mother, which is evident in her diary and in the monument she built to mark the last place she saw her. Mother-daughter friendship is also apparent in the double portrait of Mary Sidney Wroth and her mother, Barbara Gamage Sidney. Aristocratic young women developed close friendships if they served together at court, like Wroth and her cousin Philip's wife, Susan de Vere, countess of Montgomery, to whom she dedicated the *Urania*. Young women of the middle and lower classes also worked together in various capacities, developing close friendships satirized in depictions of "gossips." Such female friendships enriched their lives. For aristocratic women, who spent much of the year on widely scattered country estates, the highlight of the court season was visiting female friends and relatives in London, as Anne Clifford and Margaret Hoby note in their diaries. The warm, and sometimes turbulent, relationships of mothers, aunts, sisters, cousins, and friends are appealingly portrayed in Wroth's *Urania* (Naomi Miller 182–233).

Women's earliest years were shared with their young brothers, who wore dresses and stayed with women until they were "breeched," or given pants to wear, at about age six. Considerable tension was inherent in the transition of boys from female to male domain (Fletcher 297–321). Robert Sidney, for example, told his wife that she could raise her daughters, but he knew how to raise sons; underlying his statement is the prevalent fear that boys would be made effeminate by too much contact with women. Once a boy was breeched, he might see his sisters, and even his mother, only rarely. Latin was often used as a discipline to instill manliness, with the corollary that few girls learned this language of the church, court, and government. Queen Elizabeth's own example had encouraged humanist scholarship for women of the highest ranks; in the Jacobean period, when the king mocked learned women, more women were literate, but few were scholars. As Richard Braithwaite explained, a proper woman should not desire "the esteem of any she-clerks; she had rather be approved by her living than learning" (Fletcher 368). Granddaughters of learned Elizabethan women might be permitted to study only religious devotion and practical skills—music, needlework, housewifery, and basic reading and writing in English.

A girl's education was primarily intended to prepare her for marriage. A few Catholic girls, like the daughters of Elizabeth Cary and of Katherine Bedingfield, did rebel against that cultural expectation by choosing life in a convent, although the choice meant exile on the Continent (Rowlands 166–74). Alice Thornton may speak for many wives when she looked back nostalgically on her single life as a carefree and happy time; Thornton's mother convinced her that it was her godly duty to marry, much against her will. Some clerics said that the "good wife" must be obedient, even to a cruel husband, and never show displeasure, even in her facial expression, no matter what he did (Ezell, *Patriarch's Wife* 36–61). Other clerics stressed the need for mutual love and support as companionate marriage became accepted as the ideal. The contested nature of marriage advice is presented in the dialectic of Edmund Tilney's dialogue *The Flower of Friendship*. "Marriage was too important to be left to the contracting parties" (Amussen 108). All believed that falling in love could be dangerous. Young people carried away by lust (as their elders saw it) would be unlikely to make wise marriages, so it was important, particularly for young women, to obey one's parents in the choice of a marriage partner. The effects of arranged marriages on women could be disastrous, as is shown by the multiple stories of enforced marriages in Wroth's *Urania* or by Clifford's accounts of her own marriages. Some marriages, however, turned out happily, such as those recorded in the affectionate letters of Dorothy Osborne, in Lucy Hutchinson's *Memoirs of the Life of Colonel Hutchinson*, or in the passionate poems of Anne Bradstreet to her husband. The percentage of unhappy marriages does not seem to have been markedly different than in our own day, and women's lives were intertwined with those of their fathers, brothers, husbands, and sons.

Boys were trained to run the government and the church, to fight wars, conduct business, or make crafts. Girls were trained to run a household. How much manual work they did and how much of their position was administrative depended on their wealth and the size of the household. Even Queen Elizabeth checked the household accounts, although it was officially the duty of her lord chamberlain. The countess of Pembroke held an administrative position supervising some two hundred servants who worked on three major estates and at Baynards Castle, in London. She gave orders to the head servants, who supervised their own bureaucracy. Margaret Hoby, whose husband had a smaller estate at Hackness, not only supervised her maids but also worked with them in making candles; she oversaw the haying, received the grain, and paid servants their wages. Women of lower ranks would do their own work in the house and on the farm, although all but the poorest were assisted by at least one servant. Isabella Whitney eloquently set out the duties and pitfalls of a life in service (A. Jones, "Maidservants").

All women were expected to have some medical knowledge, although the richest would have a resident doctor available as well. Gervase Markham explains in *The English Housewife* (1615) "that sith the preservation and care of the family touching their health and soundness of body consisteth most in her diligence, it is meet that [the housewife] have a physical kind of knowledge; how to administer many wholesome receipts or medicines" (8; see also Hunter). His manual therefore begins with basic medical instruction. A woman's medical duty might extend to the care of servants and local people, as recorded in the diaries of Hoby and of Mildmay. So accepted was the necessity for basic medical training that Makin, reputed to be "a good Chymist" herself, used it to justify scientific study for her female students. Quoting the familiar description of the virtuous woman from Proverbs 31, she cleverly argues that a woman "could not look well to the wayes of the Houshold, except she understood Physick and Chirurgery" (300; see also Teague, *Bathsua Makin*). Women also supported one another through childbirth, a frightening experience; many of them knew someone who had died as a result of giving birth. Alice Thornton's account of her sister's death is particularly vivid. Some women, like Elizabeth Joscelin, had a premonition of death and left instructions for their husband and child, should they die. Women, used to the care of midwives, were distressed by the growing professionalization of gynecological care under male physicians, and some argued for better training for midwives instead. Jane Sharp wrote *The Midwives Book* (1671) in clear, simple English to serve as a replacement for the physicians' manuals in Latin, and Elizabeth Cellier eloquently advocated the establishment of a college for midwives (Otten 178–79, 206–11).

Children were treasured. The death rate for young children was very high, but that fact produced great anguish rather than the indifference assumed by some modern historians. Some of the pain was turned into poetry, so that poems mourning the death of a child became almost a genre, written not only by male poets like Ben Jonson but also by Katherine Philips, Anne Bradstreet, and other mothers. Parents were taught that the child's death was God's will, but the very insistence of the instructions not to grieve too much reveals how deep was that grief.

The average woman, of whatever rank, lived a life focused on her family and her household, but women's experience of the world varied widely. Geography was almost as large a factor as gender. A girl growing up in a rural area would know little of the world beyond her village, although if she was part of an aristocratic family or served in such a household, she would probably migrate between the country house and London, following the court schedule. A girl growing up in London would meet a much wider array of people. Perhaps she would even catch a glimpse of Pocahontas (Lady Rebecca) when she was in London or see the ambassadors who came from Japan or one of the first African slaves brought to England. She might be more likely to know a *conversus* (a converted Jew, like the renowned scholar John Tremellius), although before 1655 it would be rare if she met someone openly practicing the Jewish religion, as Cellier later did when she conversed with "a learned Rabbi" (Otten 207). An educated girl might read recent accounts of New World explorations or the fabulous voyages of Marco Polo or John Mandeville. She might travel to the Continent (or even the New World) if prompted by religious persecution, as Anne Lock was, or by her father's professional duties, as Wroth and perhaps Aphra Behn were. She would be taught, however, that Christianity was the only true faith, that European culture was superior to all others, and that "fairness" was the mark of beauty (see Hall and Kennedy, this volume). In an age with much less global interaction than our own, only the most traveled achieved Aphra Behn's cultural relativism, when she observed that the "Negroes of Guinney think us as ugly, as we think them" (Folger Collective on Early Women Critics 26). It took an ability to imagine the perspective of another people in order to imply such a radical critique of the standard Petrarchan beauty, with her proverbial alabaster skin and golden hair.

Early modern English women thus lived in a world immensely different from that of our students—more religious, less cosmopolitan, and more authoritarian in terms of gender and class. Despite these insistent restraints, many women found scope for activity and expression (Erickson 8–11), and Englishwomen were generally thought to have more freedom in practice than their Continental sisters. They could inherit in their own names both property and titles, a fact that Bishop John Aylmer used to counter John Knox's attack against women rulers:

> If it were unlawfull (as [Knox] would have it) that that Sexe [i.e., female] should governe: yet it is not unlawfull that they should enherit. [. . .] And in this point their enheritaunce is so lynked with the empyre: that you cannot pluck from them thone without robbing them of the other. [. . .] If nature has geven it them by birth: how dare we pull it from them by violence? if God hath called them to it either to save or to spille: why should we repine at that which is God's wyl and order?   (B2v-C1)

Though Catherine Willoughby Brandon, the dowager duchess of Suffolk, could not pass on the Suffolk title after the death of her two sons by the duke, Charles Brandon, nonetheless as heir to the Willoughby title she was able to pass the title Lord Willoughby to a son by her second marriage to a gentleman commoner (Goff 318).

Widows were entitled to their inheritance, and a judicious series of marriages might even make a woman rich (Erickson 198). The most famous Elizabethan example was the countess of Shrewsbury (known as Bess of Hardwick): "Married four times, Elizabeth

[Hardwick] increased her wealth and position with every husband, moving from the status of a mere gentlewoman in her youth to that of countess in her last union with George Talbot, sixth Earl of Shrewsbury" (Warnicke, *Women* 130). Unfortunately, a woman might as easily die in childbirth or from any of the great number of diseases, from smallpox to the bubonic plague, that afflicted the period, and even when she lived, the law remained staunchly on the side of male primogeniture in most situations.

If contemporary observers are to be believed, however, social practice gave Englishwomen considerably more opportunity for agency than their legal situation permitted (Fletcher 3–4). It is impossible to know the extent to which women actually exercised authority, but in two arenas, at least, there is strong evidence that they had considerable autonomy: in negotiating marriages for their children and in household administration (see Ezell, *Patriarch's Wife*). In negotiating marriages, particularly among the higher classes, a woman might expend a great deal of literary effort writing letters to persuade and negotiate with the parents of a preferred suitor or potential daughter-in-law; in household administration, she might set down her directions for running the household or leading a godly family life. Within the traditional realm of her household leadership, then, a woman might collect a wide range of texts in manuscript (see Clarke, this volume), or she herself might become a writer on household matters (see Miller, this volume).

But under what circumstances might she be allowed to express herself publicly, whether through print or manuscript circulation (see Wall, this volume)? One arena for women's publication in print, translation, appears to have been unobjectionable. A second arena was religious writing, generally tolerated, and a third was belles lettres, more problematic.

Translation

Translation occupies an important but ambiguous place in early women's writing. On the one hand, it was one of the most important activities of the New Learning, with the technique of double translation at the core of sixteenth-century classical education (Ascham 3–5). Both classic and modern translations were recognized as much by the name of the translator as by the original—for example, Thomas Hoby's *Courtier* (1561), Arthur Golding's *Metamorphoses* (1565, 1567), and Sir John Harington's *Orlando Furioso* (1591). These achievements were sufficient to assure the translators a place in English literary history; they are still singled out for independent citation—for example, in C. S. Lewis's *English Literature in the Sixteen Century* (646, 650, 653) and in Hyder Rollins and Herschel Baker's *The Renaissance in England* (522, 539, 561).

On the other hand, while permitted to exercise their learning in apparent homage to male authors, women inevitably take second billing. Lady Ann Bacon's very influential translation of Bishop John Jewel's *Apologie; or, Aunswer in Defence of the Church of England* (1562) is cited under Jewel in both Lewis (656) and Rollins and Baker (168), though Lewis concedes that "Anne Lady Bacon who translated [Jewel's] *Apologia* [. . .] deserves more praise than I have space to give her. [. . .] If quality without bulk were enough, Lady Bacon might be put forward as the best of all sixteenth-century translators" (307). Yet Hoby, whose style Lewis dismisses (306) and whose output as a translator is no more than Lady Bacon's, receives a separate bibliographical paragraph in Lewis's canonizing appendix, and Lady Bacon does not.

Despite this dismissive tradition among English literary historians, women were generally permitted to exercise their literary art as translators of matter both religious and secular. As Anne Lock, friend of John Knox, famously put it in the preface to her translation of Jean Taffin's *Of the Markes of the Children of God* (1590), "Because great things by reason of my sexe, I may not doe, and that which I may, I ought to doe, I have according to my duety, brought my poore basket of stones to the strengthening of the wals of that Jerusalem, whereof (by Grace) we are all both Citizens and members" (*Markes* 77). Mary Sidney, countess of Pembroke, played an influential role in authorizing translation as a legitimate enterprise for women. Her high social status and sisterly piety gave her *Psalmes* particular validity and appeal, and her service to European Protestantism was an accepted backdrop to her translation of Robert Garnier's *Antonius* and Philippe de Mornay's *Discourse* (see Hannay, this volume). It is not surprising that one of the first theoretical treatises about translation should come from a woman writing almost a hundred years later, Behn. The gist of her small treatise, prefaced to one of her own translations, has since become a commonplace: translation is an art form. The translator's language is inevitably the translator's, rich and effective in its own way and having its own idiom. The selection and order of language, whatever is being conveyed (an idea in the head or a passage of French on the page), are a fine art properly attributable to the one who has done the work and communicated the energy of the experience through language. While we continue to honor Corneille's *Pompée* and to acknowledge that his forming imagination lies behind Katherine Philips's *Pompey*, her work of translation remains a genuine and important contribution to English letters and stage history.

Religious Writing

Religious writing was the most acceptable literary activity for women, particularly if they transcribed or transmitted the words of male writers. The least original work was to transcribe sermons from memory, as Thomas Goad claimed Elizabeth Joscelin routinely did (Joscelin A3; "The Approbation"). Other women, like Anna Cromwell Williams and Elizabeth Jekyll, included sermon notes in their miscellanies, as Elizabeth Clarke notes in this volume, and Elizabeth Middleton compiled notes from her religious reading to present as gifts to other women. In addition to such compilations women might write spiritual journals, constructions of life stories, such as those kept by Margaret Hoby and Alice Thornton, as Elaine Beilin discusses in this volume.

Religious persecution could empower women, as John King argues in "Writing Religion" in this volume. Anne Askew and Lady Jane Grey spoke out strongly; under torture and the threat of impending execution, they had little to lose, like other Protestant martyrs whose words were recorded by John Foxe or John Bale.

Katherine Parr's *Lamentacion of a Sinner* was also strongly Protestant in doctrine (J. King, "Patronage" and *Literature* 251–52; James 189–220). Anne Lock, escaping into exile during Queen Mary's persecution of Protestants, translated Calvin's sermons and wrote an original sonnet sequence meditating on Psalm 51. Frances Dolan notes, also in "Writing Religion" in this volume, that persecution had a similar impact on English Catholic women, such as Elizabeth Cellier, who was forced to defend herself against charges of treason. Elizabeth Cary, later denounced by her husband because of her conversion to Catholicism, wrote *The Tragedy of Mariam* about a persecuted wife, and one of her daughters presented her mother's biography as a saint's life. Even more notable was Luisa de Carvajal y Mendoza, a Spanish noblewoman who came to England as a Catholic missionary; because she was a woman, she was not suspected of treason (Wiesner 197; Cruz). Later in the seventeenth century, Quakers and other nonconformists also wrote boldly for their faith, as Elaine Hobby demonstrates in "Writing Religion" in this volume. Although their specific religious beliefs varied, each of these women was empowered to write by the conviction that she spoke God's words. Such religious partisanship justified public writing. Private, devotional writing was also considered a godly activity. Elizabeth Grymeston collected prayers and psalm meditations, later published by her son Bernye. Other religious meditations were included in miscellanies kept by women, as Elizabeth Clarke relates in this volume. Anne Wheathill's *A Handfull of Holesome (Though Homelie) Hearbs* (1584) was evidently the first collection of prayers published by a woman for women (Atkinson and Atkinson), although prayers and meditations by women had been included in Thomas Bentley's massive *Monument of Matrones* (1582).

Godly women could also write books of instruction, as Naomi Miller discusses in this volume, so long as that instruction was said to be intended solely for their children and so long as the authors died before their work was printed. Nevertheless, Elizabeth Joscelin's *The Mothers Legacie to Her Vnborn Childe* includes a letter telling her husband how he ought to raise and educate their child should she die in childbirth.

Psalm meditations notably provided an opportunity for poetic composition, because all Jews and Christians were encouraged to meditate on the Psalms. Though sung psalms were increasingly identified with the Protestant movement, both Catholic and Protestant women wrote poetic versions of psalms, including Queen Mary Stuart; Anne Touchet Blount; and Elizabeth Stuart, queen of Bohemia. When Anne Lock wrote a sonnet sequence on Psalm 51 and the countess of Pembroke wrote poetic paraphrases of the Psalms 44 to 150, they raised the genre to belles lettres.

But Is It Literature?

Women have less authority and less of an early tradition among those whom Philip Sidney called "right poets" (*Defence of Poetry* 80), that is, authors of secular fiction. Since what we usually think of as (male) canonical writings most often fall into this category, teachers and scholars of early women's writing may find themselves defending both the categories of women's writing and its quality. As Pamela Benson points out in this volume, early modern Englishwomen provide a much smaller corpus of "literary" publications than their Continental sisters (see also Stortoni). Poems, plays, and fictional narratives do exist for the period, however, and as the essays on Pembroke, Wroth, Lanyer, Cary, Cavendish, Philips, and Behn in this volume all attest, the works of these authors are not only teachable as sociohistorical context but also rich in the wit, complexity, and depth of experience that we associate with successful literature.

Two charges have been made against writing by early modern women, however, and they are worth a pause. The first, addressed by many of the essays in part 1, is that women's writings are not literary; they are "merely" historical, domestic, or religious. The simplest response is that we have held no such generic test for men's writings. If writing is lively, it continues to be interesting, whether it is a letter, essay, history, or sermon. The hidden issue, most often, is the lingering assumption that what women do with their lives is de facto less interesting than what men do. This judgment might result from the persistent valorizing of the public over the private sphere, although if women enter the public arena, it is equally assumed that they will not be as good at writing as the men. The essays by Elaine Beilin and by Naomi Miller largely answer those interwoven objections.

The second charge is that even literary writing by women is aesthetically inferior to comparable writing by men. Wroth has been accused of being old-fashioned, Lanyer of padding her meters, Cavendish of prolixity and incoherence, Behn of indecency. We still do not know enough either to make or to answer accusations like these. We are just beginning to learn (and teach) the genres, topics, and styles of half our heritage. We know that women were educated differently and that they generally had far less practice in writing than their male counterparts (though perhaps more than we have assumed; see Lamb, this volume). Do those facts themselves make women's literary output less interesting or valuable? Finally, most of us teaching this new material were educated in a tradition that barely noticed it, if at all. We know how to read the male writers and have a level of familiarity and comfort that surely contributes to our occasional bewilderment when we meet new and different voices from the early modern period. We may have to wait for our students to develop a level of sophistication with this material comparable to what we bring to the more traditional canon.

This book provides one basic step toward that sophistication. Along the way, it invites teachers and students to question assumptions, categories, boundaries, and limits of all kinds and to share our pleasure in this new learning.

Part I

Women's Lives and Women's Texts

Mary Ellen Lamb

Constructions of Women Readers

*It is all one for a woman to pen a story, as for a man to ad-
dresse his story to a woman.*

—Margaret Tyler

In her preface to Diego Ortunez de Calahorra's *Mirrour of Princely
Deedes and Knighthood* (1578), Margaret Tyler justifies her translation of a chivalric romance by stressing the connection between
writing and reading: a culture that permits men to dedicate romances to women readers cannot then forbid women to write romances. Tyler's defense foregrounds the significance of women's
reading as a condition of their writing. While writing generally represents a response to the reading of texts, whether in the form of as-
similation, imitation, reformulation, or refutation, this connection
between writing and reading had particular significance for early
modern women. First, women's writing was limited by the fewer
numbers of women who had access to literacy at all, though there
may have been more access than previously believed (Cressy 145;

Chartier 115–16). In addition, as this essay argues, women's access to particular genres—including romances such as the *Mirrour of Princely Deedes and Knighthood*—was also affected by exaggerated portrayals or constructions of women readers circulating within the early modern culture. While often verging on caricature, these constructions influenced the kinds of books available to actual women by rendering what women read, or even if women read at all, an issue subject to gender ideology (Margaret Ferguson, "Room").

Earlier in the century, Juan Luis Vives had forbidden women to read precisely the kind of romance translated by Tyler. This essay begins by exploring the ways in which Vives represented women's reading, unlike men's reading, according to a sexual binary, distinguishing chaste women readers of pious books from promiscuous women readers of "frivolous" romances or love poetry. Instead of reflecting actual women readers, these constructions performed an ideological task: to limit not only what women read but also the kinds of reading women enacted. As this essay argues, reading approved books was, in theory, to reproduce texts within women's minds, keeping them in conformity with patriarchal culture. By rendering women unchaste, reading transgressive texts placed women's thoughts outside the bounds of mainstream culture. Either way, whether of chaste replicators or promiscuous deviants, these constructions were designed to deny women the independent subjectivity that lies at the core of authorship. By invalidating in advance any independent meanings women might derive from their readings, these constructions represented a strategy for excluding women from discourse. The range and numbers of women who succeeded in writing, in manuscript as well as printed works, demonstrate that this strategy was not completely successful. In fact, Elaine Hobby has aptly discussed how women writers sometimes managed to transform even "proscriptions into a kind of permission" (*Virtue* 7).

By the late sixteenth and early seventeenth centuries, constructions of women readers began to change, in large part due to the rise of a newly lucrative publishing industry. Women readers exerted a formative influence on this book trade. According to Suzanne Hull, books addressed to women readers reached a peak between 1570 and 1640, when 85% of the 163 books in 500 editions addressed to women were published (*Chaste* 1). To exploit a lucrative female market, writers and printers needed to construct images of women readers flattering enough to sell books to them. To address women as active readers meant imagining their ability to respond to texts, to produce meanings from their reading, to criticize the texts they read. But even a reluctant or partial recognition of independent subjectivity empowering women as consuming agents in the book trade was a threat to early modern gender ideology. This recognition complicated both pious and promiscuous constructions of women readers. Like the women playgoers described by Jean Howard, women readers of both kinds were "licensed to look—and in a larger sense to judge what they saw and to exercise autonomy—in ways that problematised women's status as object within patriarchy" (79).

———

A popular conduct book reprinted throughout the sixteenth century, Vives's *Instruction of a Christen Woman* (1529?) provides an influential example of the cultural tendency to create a binary division between chaste and promiscuous readers (Holm; Wayne). According to Vives, reading the wrong kinds of books placed women in spiritual and even sexual danger. Reading books "to kepe them selfe in the thoughtes of love" endangered women's "honesty" (G4) or chastity, the single source of their moral and social value. It was better that women lose their eyes and ears than read of "mennes love and glosyng wordes" (E3v). Specifically warning women to avoid reading books of "wanton luste" (E4v) such as chivalric narratives and Ovid's books of love, Vives recommended that women guard their chastity by limiting their reading to church fathers and carefully selected classical works. To guard against the independent production of meaning even for these virtuous books, Vives advised that a woman should not "folowe her owne judgement" in interpreting her reading but ask "counsayle of some wyse and sad men" (F2) (Noakes, "On the Superficiality" 347 and *Timely Reading* 96–97). In Vives's work, there is little middle ground between promiscuous women readers of books of love and chaste women readers whose readings of virtuous books replicate only those meanings approved by male advisers.

As a former tutor to Margaret Roper, the learned daughter of Sir Thomas More, Richard Hyrde was a more enthusiastic advocate for women's education. In his preface to Roper's *A Devout Treatise upon the Pater Noster*, a translation of Erasmus's *Precatio Domini*, Hyrde confines his discussion to women who only increase in virtue through the reading of sober Latin authors (Verbrugge; McCutcheon). Roper serves as a primary example: her "vertuous conversacion / lyvyng / and sadde demeanoure / may be profe euydente ynough / what good lernynge dothe" (a4v). Instead of threatening her husband's authority, her learning benefits her marriage, allowing her to provide "suche especiall conforte / pleasure, and pastyme" (b1) to her husband as cannot be imagined by the unlearned. Hyrde describes the promiscuous woman reader as a figment of the imagination of other writers, who fear the consequences of educating the "frayle kynde of women" vulnerable to the persuasions of surface "eloquence / where the mater is happely somtyme more swete unto the eare / than holsome for the mynde," so that they are encouraged to "that vice / that men saye they be to moche gyven unto of their owne nature alredy" (a2). On the contrary, Hyrde claims, reading serves as a way to prevent even the "pevysshe fantasyes" that occupy women's minds while sewing or spinning:

> Redying and stydeing of bokes so occupieth the mynde / that it can have no leyser to muse or delyte in other fantasie / whan in all handy werkes / that men saye be more mete for a woman / the body may be busy in one place / and the mynde walkying in another and while they syt sowing and spinnying with their fyngers / may caste and compasse many pevysshe fantasyes in theyr myndes.   (a4)

While Hyrde's preface defends women's education, his representation of reading as thought control shares a sense of the threat posed by women's independent subjectivity—their "pevysshe fantasyes"—within the culture.

By the end of the sixteenth century, various developments—

especially the rise of Protestantism and the increasing influence of the publishing industry—rendered the earlier binary division between women readers more complex (Eisenstein 148–86; Chartier 125–27, 130–34). New versions of the chaste as well as of the promiscuous woman reader emerged to empower women's reading in ways that conduct books had not predicted. The new versions never completely replaced the older constructions. Instead, they coexisted in uneasy resolution to create a much more complicated discursive field. Within its contradictions, unreconciled impulses opened points of accessibility to women as authors.

While women readers of pious works no doubt were still considered chaste, their chastity no longer consistently signified thought control or even necessarily submission to male authority. By the early seventeenth century, William Heale delineated a stereotype of religious women readers as domineering or even shrewish in their relationships with their husbands. Reading religious works had empowered rather than contained these women, whom Heale criticizes as "too too holy women-gospellers, who weare their testament at their apron-strings" for catechizing and even preaching to their husbands (35–36; see Kusunoke). Even William Gouge's fairly conservative *Of Domesticall Duties* allowed a wife's noncompliance with her husband's demands because of "scruples" for religious or moral reasons, at least in matters of "no great consequence":

> *Objection*: What if an husband upon his knowledge observe his wife to be erroneously scrupulous, and to misinterpret the misapply the word of God which she maketh the ground of her scruple?

> *Answer*: He must first labour to resolve her conscience by a plaine discovery of her error.

Gouge advises that if the husband cannot convince her, then when possible he "ought [. . .] to forbeare to presse her conscience" (376–77).

Elsewhere in *Of Domesticall Duties*, Gouge stresses repeatedly the subordination of wives even to unworthy husbands. R. Valerie Lucas speculates that this emphasis on women's willing subjection suggests a culture disturbed by the presence of nonconforming wives (232). Akiko Kusunoke has claimed that disobedience, at least in religious matters, may have been in fact a direct result of the Puritan emphasis on the individual conscience, which encouraged women to develop "a sense of self in relation to God" (188). This development of an individual self was reinforced by the act as well as the content of private reading. According to Roger Chartier, the privatization of reading was "undeniably one of the major cultural developments of the early modern era" (125). Liberating readers "from the control of the group," silent reading made it possible "to cultivate an inner life" (116). Thus, women who read religious texts silently at home were perhaps more rather than less likely to disagree with their husbands, especially about matters concerning their souls.

Going through thirty-five editions by 1695, Philip Stubbes's unusually popular *A Crystall Glasse for Christian Women* (1591) attempted to mediate the possible strains caused by the zealous learning of Protestant women readers within the power dynamics of a hierarchical marriage. His representation of the life and death (after childbirth) of his young wife, Katherine, works hard to reconcile the tensions between the autonomy of his wife's individual spiritual life and her absolute reliance on his interpretations of her reading. Her reading sets her off from her female neighbors, who reveal their superficiality in their criticism of it, which is described as a private act: "Mistress *Stubs*, why are you no more carefull for the things of this life, but sit alwayes poring upon a Book, and reading?" (A3). Her reply constructs her reading as a religious retreat into a private self removed from the world: "If I should be a friend unto this world, I should be an enemy unto God, for God and the world are two contraries" (A3–A3v).

On the surface, her development of a private inner self does not pose any difficulties in her proper subordination to her husband, for Katherine Stubbes does not draw her own conclusions from her reading. Instead, she refers questions of interpretation to his judgment. Yet in this passage, the very number of questions she asks suggests a nervousness concerning the possibility of her bringing her reading into complete conformity with his:

> She would spend her time in conferring, talking and reason-
> ing with her Husband of the Word of God, and of Religion,
> asking him what is the sense of this place, and what is the
> sense of that? How expound you this place, and how ex-
> pound you that? What observe you of this place, and what
> observe you of that?   (A2v)

As Katherine Stubbes dies, her spiritual subordination to her husband gives precedence to her inner spiritual voice, as she declaims,
without consulting her husband, intricate explanations of Protestant doctrine in a prose whose complexity casts doubt on Stubbes's
claim that he transcribed her exact words. She rejects her husband,
as she rejected her neighbors, as too much of this world. Repeatedly crying out, "Come quickly, Lord Jesus" and "O my God, why
not now? why not now?" (A4), she kisses her newborn child and
proclaims to her husband, "I forsake him, you, and all the world,
yea, and mine own selfe, and esteeme all things but dung" (A4v).
The creation of an authoritative self in retreat from the world
through private reading fulfilled itself in the ultimately private retreat of death.

As described by her husband, Katherine Stubbes's godly death
invests her with the authority of self and voice that are separate
from her husband's, while neatly sidestepping any threat to marital
hierarchy posed by Heale's "too too holy women-gospellers." This
sense of an authoritative separate self fostered the authorship of
original works. While Katherine Stubbes never wrote any works of
her own, other women—from Mary Sidney, countess of Pembroke,
to Eleanor Davies—found in religious literature an authenticating
discourse for their own writing (Hannay, *Silent*). The new marketing of godly books to women readers played a central role in this
development. By the late sixteenth century, texts devoted to religious concerns were pouring from the presses, and many of these
were directed to women in dedications that constructed them as independent readers rather than readers reliant on husbands for interpretations of their reading (F. Williams). It is ironic that the
religious book, which signified for Katherine Stubbes a retreat from
worldliness, had become, for the publishing industry, a profitable

commodity. Pious women readers were now influential consumers, and ultimately would become producers, of the written word.

———

In an attempt to expand into new markets, the publishing industry worked a similarly significant transformation on the promiscuous woman reader, whose transgressive sexuality had been used to discount in advance any meanings she could produce from her reading or, consequently, through her writing. Authors and printers of prose romances attempted to rehabilitate the promiscuous reader into a "fair lady," an elite and discerning gentlewoman reader whose worldliness fostered her sympathy for lovers. This new image was at first fraught with ambivalence. The sudden spate of romances, love stories, and Ovidian tales addressed to women suggests that authors and printers turned to conduct books to offer women exactly the sexually dangerous texts imagined as their true desire. George Pettie, for example, embodies Vives's worst fears in his *A Petite Pallace of Pettie His Pleasure* (1576). All twelve of his tales deal with love, and five of these derive from the scandalous Ovid. Thus, it is perhaps predictable that Pettie's construction of the gentlewoman reader was not entirely stable. She begins to merge with the sexual woman reader as, at one point, Pettie's narrator begs a kiss from his imagined female audience:

> But here hee aptly ended his talke upon her mouth, and they entred into sutch privy conference, their lips beeing joined most closely together, that I can not report the meaninge of it unto you, but if it please one of you to leane hitherward a litle I will shew you the manner of it. (137)

Convincingly described by Juliet Fleming as the story's "primal scene" (163), this kiss unites not only lover and lady but narrator and woman reader as well, as sexual and textual pleasure become one. By the end of his collection, Pettie rejects his sexual women readers, along with the writing of fiction itself (Fleming 177; C. Lucas 52–73).

As the rising genre of fiction gained respectability, so did the construction of gentlewomen readers imagined as its audience. Perhaps in part because it was addressed to Queen Elizabeth, Spenser's *Faerie Queene* was one of the first works to include a viable discursive position for women's reading. Instead of changing the sexual nature attributed to gentlewomen readers, book 3 of *Faerie Queene* revalued appropriate expressions of women's sexuality. Carefully addressing his women readers in terms of their licit as opposed to illicit sexual desire, the narrator distinguishes his virtuous readers from the lustful Malecasta, who has made sexual advances to the female knight Britomart, whom she believes is male:

> Faire Ladies, that to loue captivated are,
>   And chaste desires do nourish in your mind,
>   Let not her fault your sweet affections marre,
>   Ne blot the bounty of all womankind;
>   'Mongst thousands good one wanton Dame to find:
>   Emongst the Roses grow some wicked weeds;
>   For this was not to loue, but lust inclind;
>   For loue does alwayes bring forth bounteous deeds,
> And in each gentle heart desire of honour breeds.
>   (146; canto 1, st. 49)

First evoking the earlier construction of the promiscuous woman reader by addressing "Faire Ladies, that to love captived are," Spenser's narrator then opens a space for a proper and even heroic sexual love, which always brings forth "bounteous deeds" and engenders a "desire of honour" in "each gentle heart."

This revaluation was no doubt influenced by the anticipated reading of Queen Elizabeth, figured in her private person as Britomart (Quilligan, "Spenser's Audience"; Cavanagh 3–13). But the text extends the capacity for heroic loving beyond the queen to all women readers who harbor "chaste desires." Redeeming the courtly discourse of chivalric narratives with a Protestant approval of appropriate sexual love, Spenser offers his women readers the same sexual virtue as that achieved by Britomart. Like Britomart, who demonstrates her chastity or virtuous love in her quest to find and marry Artegall, women readers are also described as in possession of a productive rather than a transgressive sexuality.

While critics have argued that Spenser's construction of gender in *The Faerie Queene* remains highly conflicted, the textual strategy employed in this address to "Faire Ladies" succeeded in opening up a crucial position in discourse for women readers (Cavanagh; Silberman). However incomplete or ambivalent, his acknowledgment of the desiring woman subject created a discursive position for women writers. By the early seventeenth century, the constant desire of Pamphilia for her inconstant lover Amphilanthus became the primary structuring device of Mary Wroth's *Countess of Montgomery's Urania*, the first romance written by a woman in English. While the scholarship on this work—only recently made accessible to a wide readership—is still in its beginning stages, critics have already demonstrated the clear and public debt expressed in Wroth's work to Spenser (Lewalski, *Writing Women* 269; Roberts, *First Part* 741 and "Radigund"; Quilligan, "Lady Mary Wroth"; Naomi Miller).

———

Although these constructions played determinative roles in circulating perceptions of women readers in the early modern culture, they revealed little concerning the nature or practices of actual women readers. These constructions are finally only caricatures, distorted by ideological functions. Much remains unknown about women readers. Even their numbers are in doubt (for conflicting evidence, see Cressy; Spufford; Chartier). Women's autobiographical writings do, however, provide some dependable information that complicates early modern constructions of women readers, which proceed from cultural fantasies and fears.

Living quietly on her country estate in Yorkshire, the devout Lady Margaret Hoby provides a particularly useful example of an actual Protestant woman reader. Her diary, which covers the years 1591 to 1605, records a life devoted to religious exercises, including the reading of Scripture and pious works by contemporary Protestant divines. But unlike Katherine Stubbes, Margaret Hoby did not confer with her husband, Posthumous Hoby, over the meanings of her reading. In this regard, Margaret Hoby's diary reveals a central flaw in the cultural representations of the Protestant household: many husbands were simply not motivated or even qualified to attend to the religious life of their wives or of their households. To guard her reading against unorthodoxy, Margaret Hoby turned instead to her chaplain, Mr. Rhodes. In her employ as a member of her household, Rhodes did not wield the absolute authority of a Philip Stubbes. Hoby's entries record her visits to Rhodes's mother (186) and Hoby's advice to Rhodes on prospective wives (107), and these familiarities suggest something closer to a patronage relationship or even a friendship between near equals, which would open up rather than close down a discussion of her thoughts about her reading.

Hoby's reading with her chaplain was only one of several social contexts for this religious practice; through her reading she performed various other functions not imagined for Katherine Stubbes. As a zealous Protestant in an area harboring many Catholics, her habit of reading with the "good wiffes" of the neighborhood represented a public and even a political act, as she extended Protestant doctrine into the region (136, 190, 267n361). As she "hard Everill read," she trained her maid in piety as well as literacy (80, 85). In neither of these acts did she record the presence of her husband or her chaplain. Whether conducted with "good wiffes" or with Everill, reading created a basis for a bonding between women, for the forming of small female societies that counteracted rather than reinforced the relative isolation of women in the Protestant family (Schleiner 1–29).

Lady Anne Clifford represents perhaps the closest available equivalent to a gentlewoman reader. This extremely wealthy woman passed considerable leisure time listening to her servants read, primarily from secular works, including *The Faerie Queene*, which her attendant, Moll Neville, read to her 28 January 1617 (48). On 8 March 1617, Clifford lists her reading of Scripture in the same entry as gambling with her steward: "The 8th I made an end of reading Exodus with Mr. Ran. After Supper I play'd at Glecko with the

Steward & as I often do after Dinner and Supper" (*Diaries* 50).
These interactions with servants complicate the figure of gentlewoman reader by serving a deeper function than merely whiling
away time. Bonding with her attendants through reading, as
through gambling, Clifford gained their loyalties in a potentially intolerable domestic politics proceeding from her dispute with her
husband over her right to inherit land (Lewalski, *Writing Women*
125–52; Lamb, "Agency" and "Tracing"; Friedman 38–70). Living
in a household that threatened to split into factions, Clifford identified even authors as her personal partisans. In a postscript to a letter,
she describes herself as sustained in her "trubles" by Chaucer's
"beauteous sperett," which reading his works "infusses" in her
(Lamb, "Agency" 355). While Clifford's construction of her relationship with Chaucer was emotional, it was not frivolous. Unlike
Pettie's gentlewomen readers imagined as kissing narrators, she used
Chaucer's infusion of spirit to strengthen her resolve to claim her
rights as an aristocrat to inherit land. In both functions, as landown-
ing aristocrat and as reader, Clifford refused contemporary definitions of gender.

As practiced by Hoby and Clifford, reading performed an array
of functions. While private reading cultivated a sense of the private
self, reading in groups, especially in groups of women, promoted a
sense of community in which ideas could be exchanged and vali-
dated. Both kinds of reading—private and communal—enabled
women to produce meanings from what they read. Both practices
prepared the way for authorship, but for authorship of different
types. Future work on the connections between women's reading
and writing would do well to take into account not only the titles
women read but also the social circumstances in which they read
them.

Wendy Wall

Circulating Texts in Early Modern England

You presse the Presse with little you have made.
—John Davies, to the countess of Bedford,
countess of Pembroke, and Lady Falkland

In 1612 John Davies of Hereford admonished three prestigious women of his time for shying away from publication (A1r). In uncovering proof of the period's restrictive gender ideology in sermons, conduct books, political tracts, and medical manuals, scholars have gone far in explaining why Renaissance women found it difficult to appear in print. Rather than merely understand Davies's complaint to mean that women were ostentatiously absent from early modern literary history, however, scholarship has begun to use women's writing to rethink the methods and critical paradigms with which we constitute our conceptions of literary history. One of the critical lenses that beg for further refinement is our understanding of why a Renaissance author chose to circulate texts in manuscript or print, how these forms influenced the emergent category of authorship, and what role gender played in this history. What did it mean to "press the press"?

In this essay, I discuss manuscript exchange and publication in sixteenth- and seventeenth-century England, with an eye to how works by women allow us to understand more fully the conditions of writing. By surveying two women who designed their works for publication (Isabella Whitney and Aemilia Lanyer) and two women who wrote manuscript texts (Mary Sidney, the countess of Pembroke, and Katherine Philips), I chart some of the advantages and limits of the category itself of "women writers," for the points of affinity among these writers only make clear the social conditions that divided them and the different ways in which gender played a role in their stories.

Print and Manuscript Exchange

Although print had been available in England since William Caxton set up a press in 1476, it was only in the latter half of the sixteenth century that published texts became affordable enough to have a real impact on the burgeoning manuscript culture. England was slow to become interested in publication, for literary amateurism served as a sign of gentlemanly status. A sixteenth-century writer would advertise skills to a patron and circulate work for entertainment as part of service rather than a vocation. Even the most monumental volumes of poetry in the period—the 1557 *Tottel's Miscellany*, which inaugurated English verse by presenting Thomas Wyatt's and Henry Surrey's poetry; Philip Sidney's 1591 *Astrophil and Stella;* and John Donne's 1633 *Songs and Sonnets*—published their writers posthumously. Edmund Spenser's inaugural 1579 *Shepheardes Calendar*, a landmark of poetry, was published anonymously. To understand the conditions of writing in this period, we have to dispense with our modern notion of the author who signs a work and publishes a finished text for the reading public and posterity. Instead we have to think of Renaissance writing as collective, collaborative, and occasional (Saunders, "From Manuscript" and "Stigma"; Marotti, *Manuscript*; Masten; de Grazia and Stallybrass).

Writers circulated manuscripts as complete books, individual items, or correspondence. Texts on loose sheets commonly traveled through the Inns of Court (schools in which lawyers were trained), aristocratic households, universities, or the royal court. This practice meant that writing was deeply embedded in social systems such as patronage structures and that manuscripts could be fairly private (e.g., diaries, letters) or quite public (e.g., a book presented at court). Verse was commonly used to celebrate a particular occasion, compliment a recipient, or enable writers to prove the rhetorical talents they had learned from humanist educational training.

As Arthur Marotti has demonstrated, manuscript transmission carried with it certain protocols of reading that reflected basic conceptions of the text. Renaissance readers did not see the author as the central frame for interpreting a text, for instance, nor did they assume that the text was the author's property (see Orgel, "What"; de Grazia). In published collections, poems were often identified by the occasion on which they were written or by their function for readers. It was common for readers to copy poems into commonplace books (private notebooks), severing them from their place in a particular edition so as to form a new textual kinship system between them and the works of other writers. Passed from hand to hand, texts were open to inscription by readers, who amended rhyme and meter, altered lines, and added answers or responses that became part of the poem proper in its variants. An author might write several copies of a verse at the request of friends, each one slightly different; some friends might transcribe these copies of a copy (with varying degrees of accuracy) when transmitting them to other readers. Thus Renaissance poems often lived happily in multiple forms, and their meanings for their original readers depended on the contexts in which the poems were placed rather than on their authors' intentions. Poems that editors previously labeled as corrupt or plagiarized now simply are recognized as demonstrating the energy and life of a popular manuscript. The author, in this mode of circulation, felt no compunction to govern writing; rather, the poem took meaning from its placement in a text, from its function, or from its association with a particular social milieu (de Grazia; Marotti, *Manuscript*).

Regulations on publishing increased in the sixteenth century as the number of printers in England multiplied. The creation of the Stationers' Company in 1557 was a watershed event, signaling the importance of the print industry, for this company was enjoined to license publication and serve as the guild through which trade regulations could be enacted. But these regulations did not target an author's rights, as we might imagine; neither did they attempt to create a more stable printed object. Instead ordinances tended to address the economic protection of printers, labor issues, or the mechanisms for censoring seditious writing (Siebert). We might think that print would ensure textual uniformity, but we find that a single print run could produce different books, mainly because typesetters kept the press running while they made corrections. The lack of copyright or of textual uniformity was generally not perceived by Renaissance writers as a problem.

The printed text was thus not categorically different from its manuscript counterpart. Because of the increased volume it afforded, however, the press did alter the way in which people conceptualized texts. Although the average print run consisted only of about three hundred copies, publishing held out the possibility of creating new circuits of readership independent of small social cliques. The increase in the number of books addressed to women at the end of the sixteenth century, for instance, suggests that writers cultivated a female literate readership (Hull, *Chaste*). And throughout the sixteenth century, there was a growth in what we call "cheap print" forms, such as broadsheets, pamphlets, and ballads, which appealed to a less elite readership (Watt).

With regard to literary works, controversies about print were not as much about proprietary rights as about the possible erosion of the class barriers that manuscript exchange consolidated. Writers naturally worried that printing could allow anyone with ready cash to become privy to the exclusive writings of the aristocracy (Saunders, "Stigma"). The courtier John Harington declared proudly of his muse:

> Myne never sought to set to sale her wryting;
> In part her frends, in all her selfe delighting,
> She cannot beg applause of vulgar sort,
> Free born and bred, more free for noble sport. (*Letters* 320)

Fending off a marketplace that might jeopardize a closed manuscript society, Harington opted to protect the "noble sport" of writing from the "vulgar" commodification of print. Davies similarly complained that people of all social standings mixed in the marketplace: "[G]reat Hearts doe scorne / To have their Measures with such Nombers throng'd, / as are so basely got, conceiv'd, and borne" (A1v). To publish was to become part of the common "throng" or crowd, where illegitimate and legitimate verse mingled indiscriminately.

Given the rate of literacy and the select readership of literary works, the press had little chance of wreaking the social havoc that these writers feared; nevertheless it did foster new ways of identifying texts, since it required that they travel far from the social site in which they were written and solicit a new community of readers. While writers from earlier periods had struggled to develop a viable persona, the growth of the print industry and its attendant stigma put English Renaissance writers in the largely new position of devising cultural authority for the living publishing author and challenging the prestige of literary amateurism.

When writers sought to make their works available to a wider readership, they thus had to reshape the period's foundational ideas about authorship and books. One tactic they used was to advertise the text's "true" placement in circles of private exchange, a tactic developed largely through dedications, answer poems, and commendatory poems. But writers also found it imperative to negotiate a place for the author within the seemingly collective dialogue of writing. Although manuscript circulation flourished throughout the sixteenth and seventeenth centuries, writers tapped into the possibilities offered by print to develop alternative writing practices that helped to institutionalize literature.

When we discover that women were reluctant to "press the press," that women's works were often printed posthumously, or that Lady Mary Wroth, famed niece of Sir Philip Sidney, disclaimed ever wanting her monumental *Urania* to be printed—we have to be careful not to leap to the conclusion that a restrictive gender ideology was the central obstacle women writers faced. Prominent writers such as Philip Sidney and Donne never sought out the press, and hundreds of male writers published anonymously or aired their reluctance to appear in print. This does not mean that gender made no difference in how writers presented their work. Even in Davies's injunction for aristocratic women to publish, we hear echoes of the combined gender and class issues that made it difficult for women to claim a public text rhetorically. In Elizabethan slang, "pressing" was the man's role in sex, and being pressed meant to play the "lady's part." Shakespeare's *Merry Wives of Windsor* testifies to this widespread pun when Mrs. Page protests that the naughty Falstaff attempts to seduce housewives by putting them in the "press" and cheapening them to common sexual-textual circulation (2.1.73–77; *Complete Works*). In his introduction to the 1604 *Daiphantus*, Anthony Scoloker also teased out the bawdy implications of being "pressed" when he mocked an author's feigned and artful reluctance to appear in print: "He is a Man in Print, and tis enough he hath undergone a Pressing (yet not like a Lady) though for your sakes and for Ladies', protesting for this poor Infant of his Brain, as it was the price of his Virginity borne into the world in tears" (A2v). Although Scoloker made visible the pun that he then disclaimed—the author is pointedly not "pressed like a Lady"—he highlighted the popular convention whereby both writer and publisher playfully branded publication as a sexual indiscretion. Davies's plea for women to "press the press" unwittingly hinted at the language certain to deter them from public writing.

Many of the strategies that male writers used for negotiating a viable conception of authorship were simply not available to women.

In his introductory addresses to *The Posies*, George Gascoigne, for instance, legitimated his text as the product of a reformed prodigal. The epic poet Spenser defined himself as a courtly shepherd who inhabited and then renounced the role of pining lover. In prefaces to numerous sonnet sequences, publishers punned on their titles— *Delia, Phillis, Chloris, Fidessa* —so as to personify their books as the idealized women of Petrarchan love. The publisher of Thomas Sackville and Thomas Norton's influential play *Gorboduc* (1570) employed a related strategy when he described the text as a "faire maide" who was raped and cast out to the reading public before being rehabilitated by the responsible printer capable of redressing her "shame" (Norton and Sackville A2r). And Samuel Daniel protested that his "private passions" (a 1592 sonnet sequence) were "betraide" to print readers when his muse was "thrust" "rawly" into the world (*Delia* 9). Texts strangely became figured as wanton maidens and "secrets" unwillingly displayed to voyeuristic readers (see W. Wall, *Imprint* 169–226). The goal of such rhetoric was to transfer the stigma of print into a titillating sexual infringement and thus create a recognizable role for author and commodity; one effect was the gendering of both the emergent author and the reader as male.

Women and Authorship

If popular models of authorship were not available to women writers, how did women writers go about "pressing the press"? Scholars have readily identified the most general obstacle to female authorship as the sexualizing by Renaissance discourse of a woman's appearance in public. The humanist court educator Jean Luis Vives wrote, for instance, that "it neither becometh a woman to rule a school, nor to live among men, or speak abroad, and shake off her demureness and honesty: [. . .] it were better to be at home within and unknown to other folks, and in company to hold her tongue demurely and let few see her, and none at all hear her" (C6). While the results of male education were expected to materialize in public life, female education was designed to promote private virtue. A woman's public appearance could damage her sexual reputation, and chastity was the centerpiece of her social standing. If we couple the prescriptive advice that a woman be "chaste, silent, and obedient" with general attitudes about women's intellectual deficiencies and women's limited access to education, we see how difficult it was to conceive of female authorship (see Beilin, *Redeeming*; Lamb, *Gender*; Hannay, *Philip's Phoenix*; A. Jones, *Currency*; Ong; Stallybrass; Waller, "Struggling").

Isabella Whitney and Aemilia Lanyer offer interesting test cases for us to see how female writers shaped a conception of authorship in print. The first Englishwoman to publish a secular text, Whitney was born to a family of the minor gentry, and thus she did not have access to the elite coteries that circulated manuscripts for entertainment or education. Instead she left Cheshire for London and, finding herself unemployed, secured a publisher, Richard Jones, to print two texts for a London audience.

We can see in Whitney's second publication, *A Sweet Nosgay* (1573), how she styled herself as author. This heterogeneous text consists of three parts: 110 versified adages, a poetic epistolary exchange in which Whitney laments her loss of position to family and friends, and a concluding verse cast as a will and testament. Her primary strategy was to embed her Tudor moral verse in a set of texts that accentuated the work's function and social milieu. Her invocation to family and friends served as a middle-class version of the patronage networks that marked elite writing. In this way, the printed text conjured up the comforting idea of a circle of friends as its ideal readership even though the text sought an audience clearly beyond that scope. In her dedication to George Mainwaring, for instance, Whitney named the text as recompense for a previous act of generosity; thus print readers became part of a social circuit of exchange elasticized to incorporate the book commodity, and the printed text formed a continuum with the intimate and collective codes of manuscript writing.

But Whitney departed from manuscript conventions by creating a unifying metaphor for the text that foregrounded its author. Presenting her work as a medicinal recipe (a "sovereign receipt"), she introduces herself as a good housewife protecting herself and read-

ers by warding off the general spiritual, economic, and physical disease of the culture. In one letter, she writes, "Had I a husband or a
house / and all that 'longs thereto / My self could frame about to
rouse, / As other women do; / But 'til some household cares me
tie, / My books and Pen I will apply" (*Nosgay* D2). Her other comments, however, designate her writing as the fulfillment of domestic
labor rather than its surrogate. Renaissance housewives of all ranks
were enjoined to maintain a kitchen garden and distillery so as to be
able to attend to the bodies of family and friends. Whitney seemingly discharges this role textually by gathering poetic "flowers"
from the intellectual "garden" of Hugh Plat, a famed Elizabethan
writer, inventor, and expert on household economy. Fashioning
poems from his truisms, she creates a curative "nosegay": "For these
be but to keep thee sound," she tells her readers, "which if thou use
them well: / (Pains of my life) in healthy state / thy mind shall ever
dwell" (A7v). She thus invites readers to imagine her authorship as
the extension of domestic work and her text as a book for handy
everyday use. Instructing readers that her text is "for thy health, not
for thy eye," she emphasizes the utility rather than the aesthetic
value of her work.

In the concluding poem, Whitney assumes the role of dying cit-
izen uttering a poetic farewell, and thus she alters the metaphor of
disease in a way that modifies her relation to text and reader. Her
versified will dramatically differs from a real testament because she
leaves items to London that she cannot possibly own: shops, gal-
lows, streets, urban institutions (see "Wyll"). Through this tactic she
extends her intimate network of friends to a broader community of
urban readers and buyers; her claim for poetic authority ironically
rests on her disenfranchisement from any real material property except her "willing" mind and her book. From an imagined dispposses-
sion, she presents a curious image of authorship, one that enables
her to claim her book in the moment that it passes to her "beneficiary," the book purchaser. In this way, she injects the marketplace
into a circuit of social exchange and foregrounds the troubled issue
of the text as property.

Vives's injunction against women's appearing in public could hardly endanger Whitney's social standing, for Whitney had no elite status to lose by soliciting common readers. Instead print offered her a means for reaching a wide audience and thus increasing her chances of finding employment. Although removed from the milieu of aristocratic households, Whitney still had to contend with the fact that contemporary texts were conceptualized in manuscript terms. It is striking that she capitalized on the characteristics of manuscript circulation (exchanged letters) in order to revise paradigms for understanding authorship and the book commodity.

Thirty-seven years after Whitney's *Nosgay* appeared to London markets, Aemilia Lanyer published a quite different religious work, entitled *Salve Deus Rex Judaeorum* (1611). Unusual because it was addressed solely to female readers, this affordable quarto text couched a defense of women within the narrative of Christian redemption (Beilin, *Redeeming*). The *Salve Deus* consists of nine dedicatory poems, a 1,056-line poem on Christ's passion, a spirited defense of Eve, and the first country-house poem published in England. Like Whitney, Lanyer generated a fictional community of readers through dedications and prefatory poems; but while Whitney addressed a middle-class urban audience, Lanyer wrote to the most notable women in the realm, including Queen Anne, Princess Elizabeth, Arbella Stuart, and Ann Clifford. The points of affinity between these dissimilar texts are that both considered a social network to be the appropriate site of reception for a printed book and both attempted to alter the collectivity of manuscript writing so as to highlight the role of author.

Married to a court musician, formerly mistress to the courtier Lord Hunsdon, and possibly descended from a Jewish family, Lanyer lived on the fringes of aristocratic culture. Capitalizing on that association, she devised two tactics for defining the book commodity within courtly circles: first, she suggested that women occupy a privileged relation to Christian piety and thus that gender overshadowed the status line that divided her from her dedicatees; second, she presented her religious subject matter as authorizing her foray both into print and into elite society. Writing to the countess of Cumberland, Lanyer noted that "[Christ's] high deserts invites my lowely Muse / To write of Him, and pardon crave of thee / For Time so spent, I need make no excuse, / Knowing it doth with thy faire Minde agree" (62). Combining gestures of humility before Christ and aristocratic women throughout, the poem opens with a dedication to Queen Anne:

> Vouchsafe to view that which is seldome seene,
> A Womens writing of divinest things:
>   Read it faire Queene, though it defective be,
>   Your Excellence can grace both It and Mee.   (3)

Lanyer's divine subject and the grace of her readers excuse the text's defects and its presumption, for her book is, as she later states, "blest by our Saviours merits, not my skil" (41). The *Salve Deus* thus transformed book buying into an act of devotion and a sign of gentility.

Lanyer published in order to join an elite community of virtuous women stretching from biblical tradition to contemporary aristocrats, all of whom embodied Christian values better than men (Lewalski, *Writing Women*; Beilin, *Redeeming*; Krontiris). Readers could prove their Christian charity by accepting the book and its author, both of which Lanyer associated with the humility of Christ: "[S]pare one look," she writes slyly to Lady Arbella, "Upon this humbled King, who all forsooke, / That in his dying armes he might embrace, / Your beauteous Soule" (17). As Ann Baynes Coiro has noted, Lanyer's critique of social hierarchy put her at odds with the elite enclave that she addressed. "All sprang but from one woman and one man, / Then how doth Gentry come to rise and fall?" Lanyer writes (42). But raising the specter of gender helped her bridge the social differences that might be exacerbated through print.

We must remember that publishing a single-authored work was exceptional (although increasingly more popular in the seventeenth century) and that an energetic manuscript culture continued to exist alongside print (Marotti, *Manuscript*). So how do we assess women who chose to write in manuscript form? Critics have been hampered by the assumption that brave women published while manuscript writers settled for a more restrictive, private, and less prestigious medium. The countess of Pembroke's *Psalmes* and Katherine Philips's poems, however, force us to revise our assessment of manuscripts as both "private" and the product of female modesty. Pembroke was well known at court and established as one of the primary patrons in the period. Born to a prestigious family, she had the benefit of educational training and court society. An accomplished lyricist, she translated and published three works, wrote poetry, and completed the translation of the *Psalmes* that her brother had begun (see Lamb, *Gender*; Hannay, *Philip's Phoenix*). Following the death of her brother, she edited Sidney's works for publication and presented the *Psalmes* to literary circles. Literary history has shown that Pembroke was instrumental in preserving her brother's work and establishing him as a Protestant legend. But scholars have had difficulty in appreciating that Sidney's posthumous publication offered *the* primary model for subsequent aspiring writers. In serving as what is pejoratively labeled "handmaiden" to her brother's works, Pembroke established a critical precedent for legitimating authorship. Writers such as Daniel, Fulke Greville, Spenser, and Wroth cited Philip Sidney's appearance in print in order to script their own authorial roles.

Pembroke also proved herself a significant poet in her own right, through her circulation of the *Psalmes*. Her literary reputation was attested to by numerous and diverse writers, including Donne, George Herbert, Thomas Moffet, Nicholas Breton, Spenser, Henry Constable, and Lanyer. Pembroke had little incentive to publish this work, for she had access to a readership of the highest rank. In designing her manuscript for public presentation to Queen Elizabeth, she included prefatory poems that fashioned her authorial role. In these poems, Pembroke situates herself in relation to two authoritative men, the biblical King David and Philip Sidney, and in relation to two traditions, a militant Protestantism and the collaborative writing of elite circles. By presenting her text at court, she emphasized the social importance of her Protestant-identified family and Sidney's standing in political-religious circles. With the image of Sidney's bleeding body in her preface, she casts the text as a public elegy linking her family's sacrifice to biblical themes. Her work thus confirms that our ideas about manuscripts as private need modification. Her "failure" to publish was the result not of gender restrictions but rather of her particular status and position.

Katherine Philips provides another case in point. Philips published a translation of Corneille's play *Pompey* (performed in both Dublin and London) but expressed outrage when a quarto volume including her intimate friendship poems to Anne Owen (the Lucasia poems) was published in 1664 by Richard Mariott. Philips, daughter of a prosperous London merchant and linked to both royalist and Parliamentarian intellectual circles, wrote indignantly about this publication:

> 'Tis impossible for Malice it self to have printed those Rhymes, which you tell me are got abroad so impudently, with so much Wrong and Abuse to them, as the very Publication of them at all, tho' never so correct, had been to me, who never writ a Line in my Life with the Intention to have it printed.   (qtd. in Ezell, *Patriarch's Wife* 86)

Philips went on to air her sense of violation at having her "Imaginations and idle Notions rifled and expos'd to play the Mountebanks and dance upon the Ropes to entertain the Rabble" (86). "I must ne'er show my face [in London] or among any reasonable people again," Philips remarked (85). As Margaret Ezell has argued, critics attributing Philips's protest to female modesty are hard pressed to find a mention of sexual decorum in her words. In fact, her willing translation of *Pompey*, her decision to circulate her poems widely, and the actual language Philips used in protesting this edition point to other reasons for her indignation. Her reference to the commonality of being theatrical sport, for instance, smacks of the conventional disavowal of self-advertisement, ambition, and greed expected from all writers. To rail at the vulgarity of potential critics was so common as to be almost a required feature of printed texts.

But Philips's language suggests more than a customary repudiation, for it also shows her specific concern over her text's inaccuracy and her interest in circulating this particular work in manuscript. What seemed to inspire her anxiety was not the medium of publication as much as the genre of the text printed (passionate poetry) and the fact that the pirated edition didn't properly edit out confidential allusions to the intimate lives of her friends. Why else would she be willing to publish a corrected text of the poems after this spurious edition? Rather than read her aversion to print as evidence of a restrictive gender ideology, we might note that she combines a conventional rhetoric (she "never writ a Line [. . .] with the Intention to have it printed") with a very real and new concern about authorial control over the text. Her interest in directing the text's publication positions her within a history whose ur-figure is Ben Jonson, one of the earliest writers to stake a proprietary claim to his works and edit them for the print shop (Loewenstein; Newton; Murray 64–93). Her protest provides evidence for a significant shift taking place in the seventeenth-century book as authors sought to control the text's circulation to a print readership.

It is tempting to take our critical cue from Renaissance voices proclaiming the oddity of women publishing and to see gender as the primary factor in their writing. Dorothy Leigh steers us in this direction when she writes in *The Mother's Blessing* (1636) that it is the "usual custome of Women, [to] exhort [. . .] by words and admonitions rather than by writing" (3). And Sir Edward Denny famously ranted about Wroth's published 1622 romance *Urania* by labeling her a "hermaphrodite" and urging her to follow the example of her ladylike aunt (Mary Sidney) by restricting herself to works of piety or translation (Krontiris 123–26). These statements suggest that gender was significant to a woman's textual production and reception.

But if we read these declarations carefully, we see how gender surfaces differently in each case. Were women in fact forbidden from publishing? Or did they feel compelled to limit their publication to only a few appropriate genres? Certainly female writers had an added set of prohibitions, as I have discussed, that made their authorship tricky. But we cannot take blanket statements about women's writing at face value. Leigh's demurrals, for instance, resembled the artful disavowals and caveats that numerous male writers and printers made in their works. And Denny radically misrepresented the truth when he implied that religious works and translations were culturally conservative genres. Religious topics, in fact, were considered the most potentially seditious subject matter by state censors; early print regulations were devoted almost entirely to monitoring the dissemination of theological texts, given that religion was the foundational discourse on which politics was predicated (Hinds 7). If Denny had in mind a less troubling brand of devotional literature, the contentious Psalms were the wrong text to cite as a positive exemplar. And Margaret Tyler's ardent defense of her 1578 translation of a Spanish romance indicates that not all translations were presumed appropriate for the female pen. In any case, what scandalized Denny were Wroth's allusions to his family and to court gossip. Had she avoided topical references, her *Urania* might never have provoked his ire. But Denny chose to express his condemnation of Wroth in terms of gender: her writing proved her to be a monster, which Denny imagined as the result of a collapse of gender—hermaphroditism. Instead of proving that gender was a fixed and primary category (e.g., the statement that women writers were restricted from public writing), these examples instruct critics to understand gender as a variable and relative category, one that structures numerous cultural fantasies, including those surrounding publication and authorship, and one best seen as deeply entangled with other social variables.

"Women" Writers

As poststructuralist feminists and feminists of color have argued persuasively in the last decades, the term *woman* needs to be critically examined rather than assumed (see Butler, "Acts"; hooks, *Ain't*; Crosby), especially when applied to a historical period where divisions such as class, race, and religion often cut deeper than those of gender. Do a 1630s petitioner to Parliament, a 1590s queen and an urban Tudor serving woman have enough in common to allow us to generalize about them? I suggest that the category "woman writers" can be effective if deployed in a contingent and self-reflexive manner, one that allows for what Lisa Jardine sees as a history that produces a "rupture" rather than "incremental change" (*Reading* 132). Rather than simply insert women's texts in existing histories, we can use those texts to investigate the very meaning of "woman" and the histories we have inherited. And while it has been important for current feminism to recover traces of women's opposition to patriarchal norms throughout history (Krontiris; Lewalski, *Writing Women*), we now are in a position to ask questions that elasticize our primary models. Women writers may no longer fit the pattern of heroic liberal subjects valiantly fighting patriarchy, but the trade-off is that their works allow for a more historically accurate picture of the circumstances in which gender functioned as a social force.

————

Let's look at the cases I have discussed. While Whitney thinks in terms of gender when choosing the metaphor of housewifery to construct an authorial role in the print marketplace, her self-presentation alerts us to consider what access nonelite people have to the press in mid-sixteenth century. Pembroke's *Psalmes* can be read in terms of metrical experimentation in the late sixteenth century and the tradition of Protestant writers (e.g., Katherine Parr), yet her prefatory poems invite us to look at how diverse texts use gender to cement family status. Philips's same-sex poetry can be placed in dialogue with Donne's poems about eros and the melting of individual identity; but her hesitancy to publish these poems needs to be understood as a consequence of their topical nature and original readership. Only Lanyer fits modern expectations of a woman whose female identity was central to both her self-presentation as author and her poetic interpretation of Scripture (McGrath). Lanyer labored to construct "femaleness," however, so as to rupture the more formidable lines of status and ethnicity that divided her from other court women. Ironically, her bold protofeminist text (in modern terms) was put forth in a religious work, supposedly a safer and more modest form of female writing.

"The point is not, therefore, that women's writing is different from men's," writes Tina Krontiris, "but that it has to be read differently" (23). I agree with Krontiris but remind scholars and teachers that one woman's writing has to be read differently also from another woman's writing. By placing women's writing in specific literary and cultural contexts (e.g. the Reformist tradition, the cheap-print debates, the romance tradition, urban history, agrarian reform, the history of the lyric), we are able to reflect on our own terms of analysis and understand how gender figures differently in each context. The story of the politics of manuscript and print provides one microhistory that allows us to analyze gender along a spectrum. Between 1500 and 1700, conceptions of authorship and literary texts were undergoing changes that shaped modern ideas of literary history and intellectual culture. Women writers from different classes, regions, and political and religious affiliations participated in these changes by offering curious and interesting models for authorship. Attending to the diverse ways in which they contributed to that history prevents us from reproducing a group called "women" whose salient characteristic is what Davies sadly proclaimed: their shared oppression by social norms or their collective absence from the life of the culture.

Elizabeth Clarke

Women's Manuscript Miscellanies in Early Modern England

Inevitably, in the feminist-inspired challenges to the early modern male canon over the last twenty years, a new kind of canon of women writers has emerged, to which part 2 of this volume bears witness. The retrieval of women's writing, and the infiltration of women authors into the teaching canons represented by the major anthologies, is a huge step forward. However, a glance at the new canon being produced by editors and scholars, beginning with Elizabeth I and continuing with Mary Sidney, countess of Pembroke, and with Lady Mary Wroth, reveals a catalog of women exceptional by any standards. One of the ways in which they were exceptional is that they participated in print culture, as Margaret Ezell has reminded us in *The Patriarch's Wife* (62). The study of manuscript writing offers insight into a more widespread literary practice.

Research and teaching on women's manuscripts, however, face obvious difficulties. The texts are often inaccessible, jealously guarded by librarians for whom seventeenth-century manuscripts form the jewel in the crown of their collections. Some anthologies are beginning to address the problem. The 1988 volume *Kissing the Rod*, edited by Germaine Greer, Susan Hastings, Jeslyn Medoff, and Melinda Sansone, pioneered the use of manuscript writing in courses on women's poetry and gave some indication of the range of subject matter and genre to be found in manuscript. The new anthology of women's writing, 1500–1700, "*Lay By Your Needles, Ladies, Take the Pen,*" edited by Suzanne Trill, Kate Chedgzoy, and Melanie Osborne, offers a wide range of different genres across print and manuscript. The editors' selection includes passages from Elizabeth DeLaval's Bodleian manuscript of memoirs and meditations; Mary More's manuscript protofeminist critique "The Woman's Right"; and Anne Bathurst's "Meditations and Visions," a two-volume manuscript of ecstatic spiritual experiences. Randall Martin's selection for Longman (*Women Writers in Renaissance England*) includes some manuscript material in the familiar context of so-called autobiographical writing, but the anthology would benefit enormously from the inclusion of poetry by women in manuscript.

The Perdita Project, funded by Nottingham Trent University, is producing a database guide to manuscripts in libraries around the world, offering articles on the documents and their compilers and a detailed index of contents. One of the project's concerns is the nature and circumstances of composition of manuscript writing, which demands entirely different reading strategies from those used in the study of printed works. The most problematic issue is that of authorship. Perdita has as its aim the study of manuscripts compiled by, rather than written by, early modern women. Compilation, rather than authorship of the writing in a document, was the dominant literary activity among women who could read and write. Commonplace books and miscellanies for both women and men of the period were not primarily vehicles for themselves as authors but repositories for storing examples of discourses prevalent in the culture. This emphasis on compilation is true even of the medium that Harold Love has identified as the primary method of circulating verse for women and for men in the seventeenth century, the verse miscellany (5). Such miscellanies usually sprang from an aristocratic context. Constance Aston Fowler's verse miscellany (Huntington MS HM 904) is an impressive affair, a quarto bound in contemporary sprinkled gold-tooled calf, two hundred pages long. It includes love lyrics, religious lyrics, elegies, epistles, light verse, shaped verse, songs, pastoral eclogues, encomia, sonnets, and translations from Spanish; it was probably compiled between 1635 and 1655. Authors represented include Ben Jonson, Thomas Randolph, Robert Southwell, Henry King, and Robert Herrick, in an anthology that is clearly the product of a strongly Roman Catholic literary circle (Burke 107–53). The other kind of volume typical of early modern manuscript culture, the traditional commonplace book, often kept by schoolboys and members of the universities, was explicitly a place to store examples of rhetoric. Women, excluded from the schools and from much of the classical rhetorical tradition, rarely produced commonplace books of this kind. Perhaps the closest in genre is the manuscript compiled in the early seventeenth century by Ann Bowyer, a draper's daughter and the mother of Elias Ashmole (Bodleian Lib. MS Ashmole 51). It contains poems, moral exempla, historical information, and handwriting exercises, but the majority of entries are sententious couplets of the kind often recorded in the classic commonplace book. Bowyer had a fondness for stern moralizing and copied selected passages from Geoffrey Chaucer, Edmund Spenser, Joshua Sylvester's translation of Du Bartas, Michael Drayton, and *The Mirror for Magistrates*. She also transcribed Walter Ralegh's "The Lie" and John Donne's "A Valediction Forbidding Mourning" from copies circulating in manuscript. Her transcriptions, which often alter the versions she is copying, show personal reading of and engagement with a wide variety of texts. Victoria Burke, postdoctoral researcher on the Perdita Project, believes that even a nonaristocratic woman could engage in this way with literary culture (20–61).

It is not always possible to trace the authorship of poetry and prose written in a manuscript, and it is certainly unsafe to assume that any unattributed piece is by the compiler. Not only does the compiler transcribe poems from manuscript or printed sources, but sometimes the compiler's friends and family contribute their poems to a miscellany. The manuscript compilation by Constance Aston Fowler includes poems by her brother, Herbert Aston; her brother-in-law, Sir William Pershall; her friend Lady Dorothy Shirley and Shirley's husband, William Stafford; her father's diplomatic associate, Richard Fanshawe; her sister-in-law, Katherine Thimelby; and her father, Walter, first Lord Aston. Fowler may well have written some of the poems herself, but without firm evidence it is not possible to attribute any of this multiauthored document to her.

It is particularly tempting to attribute verse to Anna Cromwell Williams, who was called "the poetess Cromwell" according to the Victoria County History (*Victoria History* 40). Her enthusiastically royalist family adopted the surname Williams in 1660 in an attempt to distance themselves from their relative, the Protector. Her compilation, British Library MS Harleian 2311, includes poems by Francis Bacon and Francis Quarles as well as one misattributed to "Dr. Dunne." There are two poems by female members of her family, sermon notes, and other unattributed, clearly amateur pieces of poetry and prose. Some of the prose meditations are almost certainly by Williams herself: they deal with problems such as lack of children, which must have concerned her particularly at the time this manuscript was compiled, when she was in her mid-thirties.

Part of the difficulty in establishing authorship is that most of the documents that survive are copies in one form or another. This fact is not surprising, as the manuscripts that were copied are the ones that were thought worth preserving. Very few manuscripts constitute the original notebooks, where the different colored inks, different hands, and different sequencing would offer clues as to the authorship and conditions of writing. Any kind of copy—even a fair copy by the compiler herself—will efface information that could be gleaned in this way. Perhaps the most misleading kind of copy is by the silent copyist, who does not draw attention to the fact that the document is a transcription. Thus the catalog of the Osborn collection in the Beinecke Library at Yale University declares that Osborn b. 221 is an autograph manuscript of Elizabeth Jekyll's spiritual journal. The journal begins in 1643, continuing with poems apparently signed by Elizabeth Jekyll and with sermon notes. The last entry is a copy of Alicia Lisle's last speech at her execution for involvement in the Monmouth Rebellion of 1685. It was with a sense of shock and disorientation that I discovered that Jekyll had been buried at Saint Stephen Walbrook in 1653. Since some of the material in Osborn b. 221 postdates her journal and since the entire manuscript is in the same hand, the whole document must be a copy. Jekyll's diary describes political and military activity in the First Civil War, motivated by an impeccable Puritan spirituality. An anonymous compiler or copyist, or both, seems to have adopted that narrative as an originating and inspiring point for dissenting activity later in the century. Rather than the spiritual diary of one woman, Osborn b. 221 is a document produced for a particular political situation in the mid 1680s, when radical printing was severely curtailed.

The implications of this unfixity of authorship for feminist research and teaching are enormous. Despite the long-reported death of the author, she and he remain alive and well on the pages of modern anthologies and university syllabi, which on the whole are organized by the names of authors. The loss of fixed names, to which can be attached life histories, is disorientating, especially as the feminist agenda has often made the life history axiomatic in demonstrations of women's resistance to patriarchy. If, as is all too likely, a poem in a manuscript compiled by a woman is actually written by a man, its use in a feminist agenda based on the biography of a woman is nonsensical. At a more sophisticated level, attempts to locate gendered differences between the practices of women and men using manuscript material are fraught with difficulty. *Kissing the Rod* includes, as a composition authored by Elizabeth Middleton, extracts from "The Death and Passion of Our Lord Jesus Christ: As It Was Acted by the Bloodye Jewes, and Registered by the Blessed Evangelists" (from Bodleian MS Don e. 17). In fact, this poem was published in 1622 by John Bullokar, the editor of one of the first English dictionaries. This reality makes irrelevant some of the scholarly annotations by *Kissing the Rod*'s editors. Worse, this mistake, repeated in Kim Walker's *Women Writers of the English Renaissance* (101–06), could foster generations of well-intentioned errors by students of women's writing. A doctoral student at Oxford University recently wrote an essay, part of her first-year assessment, on female-authored passion poems, comparing Middleton's "The Death and Passion" and Aemilia Lanyer's poem *Salve Deus Rex Judaeorum*, an obvious connection to make.

Given the difficulties and the uncertainty of this material for a feminist agenda, one could forgive a reluctance to embark on consideration of women's manuscript writing. However, if the manuscripts will not submit easily to traditional literary study, they do offer important insights into the production and exchange of writing by women in the seventeenth century. The most sophisticated manuscript that has recently come to light is a complex scribal collection of poetry and prose by Lady Hester Pulter, sixth daughter of James Ley, earl of Marlborough (Leeds Univ. Lib., Brotherton MS Lt q 32). As well as political and philosophical poems and religious lyrics, there is a separate "Booke of Emblemes" and an unfinished romance. The emblems in particular are extremely unusual. There are no illustrations, but the poems begin with images drawn from Lady Hester's own experience or her extensive reading. The morals to which the poems move are also not the conventional ones; they reflect personal, political, and ethical beliefs. It is unclear whether Lady Hester had a readership outside her own family. The middle-class Julia Palmer, however, bequeathed her autograph manuscript of two hundred devotional poems, written between 1671 and 1673, to eminent men in her Westminster merchant community, who were probably members of her Nonconformist church (Clark Lib. MS P 1745 M1 P744 1671–3 Bound). The beautiful Bodleian manuscript of prose and poetry sent to Sara Edmondes turned out to have been commissioned by Elizabeth Middleton, who may not have been able to write: the Lincolnshire vicar John Bourchier transcribed it for her.

Perhaps the most important critical issue to be enlightened by manuscript study is the vexed question of distinction between public and private realms. Manuscript writing by women has often been regarded as the most private writing that survives from the seventeenth century. Greer's introduction to an anthology that contained some manuscript poetry insisted on the private status of most of the writing in the volume (Greer 13). But, as this essay argues, manuscript writing in the early modern period cannot possibly be labeled private. Scribal publication continued to be an important social and political phenomenon alongside print culture well into the seventeenth century, and women participated in it alongside men. Their participation included attempts to influence royalty through literary culture. The Cooke sisters used their lavish production of the Bartholo Sylva manuscript in 1572 to try to influence Elizabeth to look on the radical preacher Edward Dering with favor (Schleiner 39–43). "Eliza," a woman who later published her poems as *Eliza's Babes* in 1652, sent them to King Charles in 1644 with a dedicatory poem suggesting to him that he "yield" and make peace with Parliament (23). Other volumes of poetry by women were used for political purposes. Jane Cavendish, daughter of the marquis of Newcastle, was left in charge of a beleaguered Welbeck Abbey when her father fled to Europe after the battle of Marston Moor in 1644. During this period she used her father's secretary, John Rolleston, to publish her poetry. In this activity she was self-consciously maintaining the elite royalist literary culture that William Cavendish had encouraged in the 1630s, preserving his own verse and that of others such as Ben Jonson in the aristocratic medium of scribal publication. Her "booke of verses," of which two slightly different copies survive— Beinecke MS Osborn b. 233 and Bodleian MS Rawlinson poet. 16—is a sophisticated collection that Ezell has called a significant contribution to the 1640s political project of reinforcing Cavalier identity ("To Be" 287). Cavendish's manuscript includes poems to friends and family, as well as replies to verse by Alice Egerton and Thomas Carew. Much of the poetry refers to the absence of Cavendish's father, an absence that is clearly a topos around which to express her grief for political power and her involvement in elite royalist literary culture. Her use of conventional religious tropes of female submission and dependence appears to be a subversive strategy for reinforcing Cavalier identity by her writing; it also gives voice to her sense of personal frustration.

The content of manuscript compilations surviving from the early modern period will add to or in some cases rewrite the history of women's lives and literature. Documents such as Lucy Hutchinson's "Elegies" (Nottinghamshire Archives MS DD Hu/2) or as Elizabeth Newell's anthology of poems, which were written on Christmas days over a twenty-year period (Beinecke MS Osborn b. 49), offer material for traditional literary scholarship and can easily be incorporated into the teaching anthology. However, the real contribution of the study of seventeenth-century women will be in the publication of entire manuscripts, such as Jean Klene's edition of the miscellany of Anne, Lady Southwell (A. Southwell). Klene's introduction offers a case study of one woman fully involved in literary culture up to her death in 1636, when she was the center of a literary network around Saint Mary's Church in Acton. Klene believes that two brief prose pieces by Southwell were published before 1614, one in response to the "Newes from the Very Country," by John Donne, the other in response to Sir Thomas Overbury's "Newes from Court." But although these pieces show Southwell participating in one of the games that characterized elite court literary culture, her most significant contribution to literature is clearly her manuscript work (Klene xxviii). Folger MS V b. 198 contains some nonliterary material: inventories of clothing, sermon notes, copies of receipts. But besides copies of poems by Henry King, Ralegh, and Arthur Gorges, it also contains a great deal of Southwell's own verse, mainly religious, in various genres: verse epistles, lyrics, and a major work on the Decalogue. The manuscript, which is a scribal copy, shows emendations in her own almost illegible hand, which Klene has meticulously documented. Southwell composed a sophisticated defense of poetry, which survives in the Folger manuscript as a copy of a letter to a friend (Klene 4–5). Another manuscript, British Library MS Lansdowne 740, contains a more polished version of her poetry and has a dedicatory epistle to the king: it seems to have been a presentation copy to James I (Burke 92). Klene's historicized survey of established and possible readerships, together with her tracing of the sources of transcribed poetry,

Southwell's own writings and rewritings, and the different scribal hands in the manuscript, allow invaluable access to one early modern woman's complex literary practice.

There is no space in this essay to describe the contribution to social history of nonliterary writing in women's manuscript compilations; to suggest the importance to the study of autobiography of the manuscript spiritual journal, which offers life stories in the process of construction; or to delineate the importance of recipe books, one of the main vehicles of cultural exchange, in charting networks of men and women. I hope this essay has made clear that women's manuscripts are a marvelous resource for research and teaching in early women's writing practice. Unfortunately, at the moment they are a scarce resource. In the next few years the efforts of scholars, publishers, and anthologizers to make manuscript material more available could revolutionize women's literary history.

Pamela J. Benson

Women Writing Literature in Italy and France

In sixteenth- and early-seventeenth-century England, women who wrote in secular genres and modes were rare, and those who published their works were even rarer. Among them, Anne Lock, Mary Sidney, Elizabeth Cary, Aemilia Lanyer, Anna Weamys, and Elizabeth Melville published sonnets, pastorals, dramas, dream visions, and a country-house poem, and Mary Wroth wrote exclusively on secular subjects and left a substantial body of work. No works by any of these writers were accepted into the traditional canon; all have been rediscovered by modern scholars.

Italian and, to a lesser extent, French women writers offer a striking contrast. In both countries, numerous belletristic works by women were published, and some of their works—Marguerite de Navarre's *Heptaméron* and poetry by Louise Labé, Vittoria Colonna, and Gaspara Stampa, for example—have been read and admired ever since. Although Frenchwomen's secular publications declined markedly after midcentury, Italian women participated ever more actively in the most popular secular genres; by the end of the century, many had published highly accomplished, confidently written Petrarchist and Neoplatonic love poetry, songs, dialogues on secular topics, plays, letter collections, chivalric romances, and prose fiction, in addition to religious poetry.

In this essay I sketch out a general description of Continental women's writing, discuss a few authors in detail, and suggest some of the ways in which Englishwomen's writing could have been directly influenced by Italian and French women's works. Specifically I discuss three authors from each country—Colonna, Veronica Gambara, and Stampa from Italy; Labé, Marguerite de Navarre, and the Dames des Roches from France. Some translated texts by each author are available in Katharina M. Wilson's *Women Writers of the Renaissance and Reformation* (see also Stortoni and Lillie).

Italian Women Writers

It would have been difficult, if not impossible, for a sixteenth-century Italian reader to be ignorant of women's writing. Between 1540 and 1601, the poems of Colonna, Stampa, Veronica Franco, Isabella di Morra, Laura Terracina, Laura Battiferi, Isabella Andreini, Tullia d'Aragona, and others were issued; several women published multiple volumes, and the works of some authors went into many editions. Poems by women were included in almost all of the dozens of Petrarchist anthologies published in those years. Many of these authors also published volumes of religious sonnets. In the second half of the century at least nine women published letters on philosophical and spiritual topics as well as on love, and numerous women published pastoral poetry, heroic poems on secular and sacred subjects, and pastoral drama and religious drama. Throughout the period nuns also wrote and produced religious dramas but did not publish.

Italian women writers came from various social classes and many geographical regions. Noble and aristocratic women were most numerous; among the best known in this class are Colonna (Naples and Rome), Gambara (Brescia and Correggio), Terracina (Naples), and di Morra (Basilicata). Chiara Matraini (Lucca) and Battiferri (Urbino and Florence) were upper-middle-class women. Franco

(Venice) and d'Aragona (Venice, Florence, and Rome) were courtesans, and Stampa (Venice) was a musician and perhaps also a courtesan. Andreini (Venice) was a commedia dell'arte actress.

The reception of women's writing seems generally to have been
positive. The most dramatic evidence for this is that d'Aragona was
excused from wearing the yellow veil, which would have identified
her as a prostitute in Florence, because she was an author. More pro-
saic evidence is the praise of women writers by Ludovico Ariosto and
Cardinal Bembo, the leader of the Petrarchists; both specifically
mention Colonna and Gambara. That women contributed commendatory verses to volumes of poetry by men suggests that their
reputations were high enough to make their praise desirable. That
so many women's poems were included in the anthologies suggests
that their names in the list of contributors attracted purchasers. Indeed, the tradition of including Colonna, Gambara, and others
never died out; they became canonical Petrarchists.

The format of volumes of women's poems often creates a sense
of dialogue between male and female poets and thus asserts that the
women are not marginal authors. The volumes usually include commendatory poems by male authors; poems addressed to particular
men, especially men who are poets; and pairs of poems, one by the
author of the volume and the other by a man, in which the meter,
rhyme scheme, or topics of the initiator's poem are repeated in the
response.

Unlike their English contemporaries, Terracina, Franco, d'Aragona, Battiferi, and others published their works with their full names
on the title pages and with minimal apologies, although Battiferi
protested that she did so only to forestall others from publishing
them without her supervision. Since Colonna's works were twice
published without her consent, Battiferi may be being honest here,
but of course such a disclaimer was also a traditional trope.

Three Poets

Despite their different social origins—Colonna and Gambara were
noblewomen and Stampa was probably a *cortigiana onesta* (she is
famous for her singing, her salon, and her love affair with Count

Collatino di Collalto)—Colonna's, Gambara's, and Stampa's texts are all strongly shaped by Petrarchism. All three poets represent their personal experience of love as involuntary separation and re-union and then final separation, which is death for the two noble-women and abandonment for Stampa. All three primarily wrote sonnets and employed conventional Petrarchist vocabulary and top-ics: hope and its loss, the inability of time and distance to diminish love, the contrast between the lover's bleak state of mind and the flourishing plants of springtime, the effect of the beloved's eyes, the poet in a frail boat on tumultuous seas, and the cruelty of Fortune. Colonna and Gambara also follow Petrarch in expressing spiritual thoughts in response to their beloved's death. Colonna is best known for her poetry memorializing her husband, but she also left a substantial body of religious poetry, her Petrarchist *Rime spirituali*. Both she and Gambara wrote poems about contemporary politics, as did Petrarch.

For most of the century Colonna was the most frequently pub-lished Italian woman, though she did not approve the publication of her works. She was the standard against which others measured themselves. Gambara wrote a sonnet in praise of her (K. Wilson 59; sonnet 2 [Wilson's numbering]). No single volume was devoted ex-clusively to Gambara's poems; most of her sixty-seven poems were published in anthologies of poetry or songs, although some re-mained in manuscript until modern times. Stampa's *Rime* was pub-lished by her sister after the poet's sudden death; this was the only edition of her works until the eighteenth century.

Conventional as they may be in their account of the history of their love, the three poets are very different in the way they interact with Petrarch's poems and approach the issue of themselves as women poets and lovers. Colonna writes as a wife. She celebrates the accomplishments of her husband as well as his physical beauty. Al-though at first she claims that she writes only to express her pain and not to increase his fame (K. Wilson 35; poem 1), her repeated refer-ences to his valor promote admiration of him. Her language is Neo-platonic; she speaks of her husband as the sun, refers repeatedly to the image of him imprinted in her heart, and says he draws her toward heaven. Finally she creates the impression of inconsolable loss in a long canzone in which she compares herself with legendary women deprived of their husbands by desertion or death and asserts that her sorrow is the longest lasting. Midway through her career Colonna underwent an intensification of religious feeling; most of her poetry was written after this conversion and is on religious topics. A number of poems address Mary or are about her experience as mother of God, and many are meditations prompted by imagining Christ on the cross from a woman's point of view and have similarities to passages on the same topic in Aemilia Lanyer's *Salve Deus Rex Judaeorum.*

In her love poetry, Gambara almost never calls attention to her identity as a woman; rather, she speaks in terms applicable to both sexes. There are no blazons, no poems on the sexual hierarchy, and the only poem about physical desire is a madrigal (K. Wilson 58; madrigal 2), a form that conventionally was used for more risqué material. Her political poetry, however, does engage with the issue of gender. In some poems she represents herself as speaking for other women; she assumes the women's voices and addresses their husbands in order to express the women's pain at separation and anxiety about their husbands' well-being. Gambara writes what the women would say if they had her ability with words. These sonnets may have had a practical purpose. For example, "There where the lovely Sebeto now adorns both its banks with grass" ("Là dove or d'erbe adorna ambe le sponde / il bel Sebeto") may have been included in a letter asking an aristocrat for a position for her son. If so, she would seem to have hoped to touch the man by invoking his wife's concern. Gambara's poems on contemporary political topics echo the tone of Petrarch's laments about the condition of Italy, but they often expressly gender her desire for peace. For example, in the person of "La bella Flora," Gambara reproaches Florence's citizens for not ending a war.

Stampa's *Rime* begins with the very words with which Petrarch first addressed his readers, "Voi ch'ascoltate" ("You who listen"). Her second sonnet explains that she fell in love at Christmas (Petrarch fell in love at Easter). She includes anniversary poems, as did

Petrarch, and numerous poems are variations of his, but Stampa's have an immediacy lacking in Petrarch's. When her lover is absent on a military mission, she worries that he thinks of her only when he is near her, or she complains that eight days have passed with no letter from him (K. Wilson 17; "Send Back My Heart"). Whereas Petrarch reproaches himself for desiring temporal and secular goods—a woman and fame—Stampa straightforwardly reveals her joy in her sexual relationship with Collalto when she praises night for restoring him to her arms (K. Wilson 17; "Night of Love") and repeatedly hopes that her poetry about him will bring her fame. Petrarch fears that he has long been a subject of gossip; Stampa happily imagines envious women wishing they had her good fortune. Stampa's imitation of Petrarch's *Canzoniere* audaciously reshaped his male voice, amatory experience, and poetic persona.

French Women Writers

The sixteenth century began auspiciously for women writers in France with the publication of works by several authors, two of whom are among the best known of all French women writers. Texts by Christine de Pisan were published in 1497, 1500, 1503, 1511?, 1519, 1522, and 1536; Marguerite de Navarre published religious works in 1531, 1533, and 1547—the 1547 volume included several plays—and her collection of stories, the *Heptaméron*, was issued in 1558. Helisenne de Crenne's invective letters and the romance that she claims is based on her life and loves first appeared in 1538 and 1539, respectively, and were republished frequently until 1560. All these volumes except the *Heptaméron* were written in genres that were more medieval than Renaissance. With the publication of Pernette du Guillet's *Rymes* in 1545 and Labé's *Œuvres* in 1555, French women writers seemed to be entering into full competition with their Italian contemporaries. However, despite du Guillet's publisher's and Labé's own appeal to women to make French women writers the equals of the Italians, almost no one followed their example and wrote on secular topics in bellettristic genres. With the exception of the Dames des Roches, the women who published poetry in the second half of the century—Anne de Marquets, Georgette de Montenay, Marie de Romieu, and many others—wrote on religious and moral topics.

Three Authors

Marguerite de Navarre resembles both Mary Sidney and Mary Wroth. Her social position as sister of Francis I made her the most prestigious of all the women writers of the century and the least concerned with the conflict between her sex and the act of publication. She produced her miracle and morality plays with ladies of her court as actresses. Though the content of these plays is not similar to that of the court masques in which Wroth acted or that of *Love's Victory*, which Wroth wrote, the involvement of both authors with court dramatic spectacles invites comparison. Marguerite's most popular and influential work was the *Heptaméron*, published posthumously. There has been some dispute about her authorship of it. The first edition did not cite her as the author; the second, rearranging the tales and adding some, cited her as the author, as do several surviving manuscripts. Most scholars accept Marguerite's authorship.

An imitation of Boccaccio's *Decameron*, the *Heptaméron* includes stories and the storytellers' discussion of issues raised by them. The great majority of the stories are about sexuality and male-female relations—lustful murders, rape and attempted rape (especially by clerics), forced marriages, socially inappropriate marriages, and infidelities by both husbands and wives. The storytellers are particularly interested in spirituality, moral philosophy, and Neoplatonism, and they use the stories as a means of rethinking relations between the sexes. The book as a whole creates the impression that human nature is corrupt and peace of mind lies only in faith.

Labé's reputation rests on contemporary praise of her singing, flute playing, and person and on the single book that she published, *Œuvres* (Labé). It contains a dialogue in which Folly and Love argue and Mercury and Apollo present extensive defenses of their respective clients; three love elegies; and twenty-four love sonnets, in which the influence of Petrarch mixes with that of the *Greek Anthology.* Some account for Labé's artistic skills by arguing that she was a *cortigiana onesta,* just as Stampa probably was; others suggest that she was a respectable middle-class woman. Whatever her social status, her writings resemble Stampa's in the confidence with which they present female experience as a suitable topic for poetry and in the originality with which they reshape Petrarch's voice and experience of love. Elegy 3, for example, speaks of the author's anxiety that her audience should forgive her youthful errors and echoes Petrarch's and Stampa's first sonnets, but the audience from whom she asks forgiveness is "the ladies of Lyon." As a woman, she both hopes for understanding from women and hopes to enlighten other women and help them understand their own experience. In the sonnets she speaks of the physical and emotional desire her beloved's beauty provokes in her (K. Wilson 150–51; sonnet 2) and of the desirability of dying in his embrace (155; sonnet 13), among many other traditional love sonnet topics.

The moderate feminism of the mother and daughter Madeleine and Catherine des Roches is typical of late-sixteenth-century Frenchwomen's writing. They insist on the compatibility of learning, writing, and publishing with chastity and woman's traditional domestic role (K. Wilson 244–45 ["Epistle to My Daughter"] and 249–50 ["To My Distaff"]). Catherine's dedicatory letter to her mother defines the difference between her writing and that of Labé. Defending her choice of love as a topic, she claims a woman's right to write about things she has not directly experienced, in terms similar to those of Margaret Tyler in her dedicatory letter to *The Mirrour of Princely Deeds and Knighthood.* Catherine says that her sonnets are not the result of lived experience inappropriate to a woman but are products of her imagination, just as a portrait of a perfect king would be. Mother and daughter were celebrated participants in the literary scene of their day and show the influence of the Pléiade in their choice of genres—Madeleine wrote odes and sonnets, Catherine a "Hymn to Water" and a double sonnet sequence composed of an exchange between two fictional lovers. As in Wroth's *Pamphilia to Amphilanthus,* the chaste female voice in these sonnets struggles with the challenge of an unfaithful lover. The sequence is preceded by a prose dialogue in which the lovers discuss Neoplatonic issues. Catherine also published allegorical and mythological dialogues (K. Wilson 254–56; "Iris and Pasithee"), parts of a masque of Amazons (248–49), and a one-act *Tragicomédie de Tobie.*

Continental Models Available to Englishwomen

There are two ways in which Italian and French women writers of belles lettres could have served as models for English women writers. First, their texts may have served as models for imitation. Second, the celebration of them in such popular works as John Harington's translation of Ariosto's *Orlando Furioso*, in which both Colonna and Gambara are lauded, might have led Englishwomen to imagine the possibility of emulating their accomplishments. No hard evidence to support either possibility has yet been found.

In theory any published work by an Italian or French woman writer was available to her English counterpart who was literate in Italian or French, but information about which books were physically present in England is limited and discovering who among the English women writers had access to these books is extremely difficult. Veronica Franco's name appears on John Florio's list of the books he consulted in writing his entries for *A Worlde of Wordes* (1598); the first printed catalog of the Bodleian Library at Oxford (1605) includes volumes by Colonna and d'Aragona, and the second edition (1620) adds Andreini's *Lettere.* These books may have been available to English women writers—Lanyer may have known her fellow Italian Florio, for example—but so far there is no tangible evidence, and no English woman writer of belles lettres mentions having heard of any Italian or French women writers, let alone reading them. By contrast, Continental women crossed national boundaries. Colonna sent a manuscript of her poetry to Marguerite de Navarre, and Catherine des Roches included the Italians Laura

Terracina, Olimpia Morata, and Hippolyta Taurella in a list of female poets (K. Wilson 238). Given the availability of the fame of Continental women writers, the lack of such references in the works of Englishwomen is notable.

Indeed, English women writers seem to have avoided associating themselves with contemporary Continental women, even though male English authors put them in this context (Harington's *Furioso* is the most obvious example; in a note explaining Ariosto's praise of Colonna, he singles out the Russell sisters as young Englishwomen who overgo their Italian competition). Those Englishwomen who create a sense of a female community in their works restrict themselves to England or to the past. Lanyer's dedicatory letters connect her with a female English intellectual and social elite, and Wroth's exemplary female poet is Sappho. Marguerite de Navarre is a partial exception; her social position and interest in reformed religion seem to have exempted her from the stigmas of foreignness and gender. The future Queen Elizabeth translated her *Miroir de l'ame pecheresse*, and the French writer's death was commemorated in volumes of verse by Anne, Margaret, and Jane Seymour (*In mortem Divae Margaritae Valesiae Navarrorum Reginae. Hecatodistichon* [1550] and *Le Tombeau de Marguerite de Valois* [1551]). Yet, although most of the English belletrists knew French and although stories from the *Heptaméron* were available in translation from midcentury in *Painter's Palace of Pleasure*, no certain influence has been noted, though Josephine Roberts notes a possible minor connection in the *Urania* (*First Part* xxxvi).

This essay presents a portrait of contrasts and isolation: Continental women accepted and praised as writers in numerous secular genres and modes, and Englishwomen, with a few notable exceptions, constrained and generally restricted to religious writing; Continental women aware of themselves as part of a network of writing women, and Englishwomen cut off. But the comparative study of women writers is a very new field, and it is quite possible that further research will reveal more direct connections between English writers and Continental ones. It is in any case certain that English women authors became more lively and forceful participants in the literary scene. By the end of the seventeenth century Katherine Philips, Margaret Cavendish, and Aphra Behn equaled the sixteenth-century Italians in the rich variety of their production.

Elaine V. Beilin

Writing History

In her preface to her book about her husband, *The Life of the Thrice Noble, High, and Puissant Prince William Cavendishe*, Margaret Cavendish acknowledges that "Many Learned Men, I know, have published Rules and Directions concerning the Method and Style of Histories"; nevertheless, she intends to follow her husband's advice not to use a learned assistant but to write "this History in my own plain Style without elegant Flourishings, or exquisit Method, relying intirely upon Truth" (b2v). Cavendish's words illuminate some contexts in which a woman wrote history: her family connections influenced both the subject matter and the conditions of publication, she acknowledges that history writing is defined by men, and she professes to shun their "Rules" while yet adopting conventional historiographical elements like the rhetoric of "Truth." Arguably, the very number of rule makers and their often conflicting "Directions" prompted novices to write history in their own way.

Between 1500 and 1700, history was constantly being redefined in varying relations with truth, poetry, and romance. Like

Cavendish, some writers follow the Baconian precept that poetry is not truth and can only produce "feigned history" (Bacon, *Of the Proficience* 203); others follow Philip Sidney's thinking (*Defence of Poesy* 224–26), arguing that poetical histories are the truest. Historians may disagree about the acceptability of imagined speeches and idealized figures, but all agree that history teaches through example. Many historians allow a clearly religious purpose, admit the historicity of the Bible, and inscribe open or coded political positions as part of the struggle to represent the truth.

Women were deeply engaged in the historical discourses of this era, producing historical works in many different genres, with a wide range of purposes, styles, and political positions. Women writers read histories, both ancient and modern; they pondered current epistemological and generic issues such as the distinctions between fact and truth and the relations of history and poetry; they used history to argue causes or to issue warnings; they studied individual lives, including their own, for evidence of the hand of God or human desire; and they dissected family life, public and private actions, local and national government to represent the relations between the individual and the community. In the mid-seventeenth century, radical female petitioners depicted their historical moment to advocate change, urging Parliament to complete the revolution, to release political prisoners, and to raise "fundamental questions about the way in which England should be governed" (Hobby, *Virtue* 16–17; Higgins).

Women contributed to the writing of British history, although the scale and focus of their work differs from that of the most prominent male historians. Extensive national histories such as those of John Foxe, Raphael Holinshed, or Clarendon (Edward Hyde) required access to eyewitnesses, documents, libraries, and collaborators. Sir Robert Cotton's great library enabled numerous male historians to accomplish their tasks (D. Woolf 106), and organizations like the Society of Antiquaries provided a collegial, political, and literary center. A work of national scope by a woman does not appear until Catherine Macaulay's multivolume *History of England* (1763–83), yet long before, women were using available sources to produce smaller pieces of that national narrative (Davis 154–55). For instance, that Anne Bradstreet's father, Thomas Dudley, owned histories by Livy, William Camden, and many others perhaps influenced her *Four Monarchies* and her poems on British history (E. White 386–87). Lucy Cary, Elizabeth Cary's daughter, writes that her mother read "history very universally" (L. Cary 268; see Wolfe). And Lucy Hutchinson indicates an oral source for her research on the Hutchinson family: "I spoke with one old man who had knowne five successions of them in these parts" (15).

In this essay, I suggest some useful categories of history writing by women to illuminate their circumstances, their sources, and their adaptation of particular genres. I have chosen four: ancient history, religious and ecclesiastical history, romance, and life writing. Romance is included because its contentious relation to history was of particular use to women writers. Again Cavendish articulates the generic problem: "Romancy is an adulterate Issue, begot betwixt History and Poetry [. . .]. History [. . .] if it be a lie made from truth it is Romancy" (*World's Olio* 9). Although each category is complicated by cultural contexts and each contributes to the larger national history, life writing is by far the most complex and voluminous.

Ancient History

Women's readings of ancient history produced an epic poem and three plays. Bradstreet; Mary Sidney, countess of Pembroke; Elizabeth Cary; and Katherine Philips apparently turned to the ancient world for political models relevant to their present. Bradstreet's historical epic, *The Four Monarchies*, contains over 3,500 lines in heroic couplets on the Assyrian, Persian, Greek, and Roman monarchies. Probably drawing on Walter Ralegh's *History of the World* (E. White 235–36), Bradstreet composes repeated examples of tyrants like Ninus, who "for a god his father canonized" and oppressed his own people and neighboring countries (*Four Monarchies* 74; lines 53–64). The moral and spiritual bankruptcy of pagan monarchies involved in wars, torture, and desecration seems to be a historical club Bradstreet uses to beat Stuart absolutism and divine right. And if she apologizes ("To sing of wars, of captains, and of kings, / Of cities founded, commonwealths begun, / For my mean pen are too superior things" ["Prologue" 15; 1–3]), yet she asks "men" for her place as a historian: "Preeminence in all and each is yours; / Yet grant some small acknowledgement of ours" (16; 43–44).

Interest in the years of the Roman Empire from Julius Caesar to Augustus produced three works: the countess of Pembroke's translation of Robert Garnier's *Antonius* (1592); Cary's *Tragedy of Mariam* (1613), derived from Thomas Lodge's translation of Josephus's *Antiquities*; and Philips's translation of Pierre Corneille's *Pompey* (1663). In each, history is also a powerful political drama and a means to discuss issues relevant to England—the relations of an absolute monarch to his subjects and the expansion of empire. Cleopatra dominates both *Antonius* and *Pompey* and looms offstage in *Mariam*, suggesting the continuing attraction of the complex erotic and political questions surrounding female rule (see Patton, this volume). Further, Cary's treatment of Herod, Mariam, and Salome probably recasts Henry VIII's divorce from Catherine of Aragon and his marriage to Anne Boleyn, representing a crucial moment of the English Reformation and Catholic resistance; the play thus requires much more than a "simple historical decoding" (Weller and Ferguson 34).

Religious and Ecclesiastical History

Women writers' contributions to religious and ecclesiastical history include representations of sacred history and a long record of dissent that creates an invaluable body of local and national history. Aemilia Lanyer's and Alice Sutcliffe's sacred histories make an interesting contrast: Lanyer lodges women's spirituality at the center of her Passion poem, "Salve Deus Rex Judaeorum" (1611), writing a defense of Eve and praise of the Virgin Mary, whereas Sutcliffe condemns Eve in "Of Our Losse by Adam, and Our Gayne by Christ" (164).

Women's religious dissent—as Reformers, Puritans, Catholics, Quakers, and Fifth Monarchists—stimulated a tremendous outpouring of texts recording the spiritual and political conflicts inherent in their challenge to established state religion. Anne Askew's *Exami-nations* (1546–47) narrates the beginnings of the English Reforma-tion in her account of her interrogations for heresy by the lord mayor of London, Bishop Bonner, and Henry VIII's council at Greenwich: Askew renders details of time, place, and identity in dia-logues that represent some of the central controversies related to the establishment of Protestantism. Later, the Puritan resolution to complete the Reformation inspires Anne Dowriche's 2,400-line poem *The French Historie* (1589), a work that exemplifies the making of history from zealous politics and religion. Dowriche's noncon-formism and the probable influence of Huguenot antimonarchical thinking shape her history of the recent French religious wars as a paradigm and a warning for England (Beilin, "Some"). In her pref-ace, Dowriche claims poetry as the best medium to depict "singular examples" of virtue and vice (A3v) and, like Bradstreet, places con-temporary politics within a providential and scriptural history of the punishment of tyrants and persecutors of the godly.

In the seventeenth century, Katherine Evans and Sarah Cheev-ers, authors of *This Is a Short Relation of Some of the Cruel Suffer-ings*, are two of the many women who continue the history of dissent, detailing Quaker persecution, including interrogations, bridling, beating, and imprisonment (Hobby, *Virtue* 36–49; Ezell, *Writing* 132–60). In *The Cry of a Stone* (1654), the Fifth Monar-chist visionary Anna Trapnel attacks Oliver Cromwell, her former hero, as a "backslider": "he would be ashamed of his great pomp and revenue, whiles the poore are ready to starve" (50); and she nar-rates her trip to Cornwall, her trial, and her imprisonment in Bridewell in her *Report and Plea* (1654). Margaret Killin and Bar-bara Patison reveal the wrongs of "corrupt Magistrates" at Exeter Prison (2). In these and many other texts from the 1640s to 1670s, women writers represent women's increasingly active participation in local and national public life, a phenomenon that contributed to and derived from the religious and political upheavals of the Civil War, the Commonwealth, and the Restoration. The narratives of radical sectaries were indeed "public documents with a social pur-pose" (Graham et al. 3). The field also extends to works written on the Continent, to manuscripts, and to texts preserved only in later editions. One such preserved text is that of Catherine Holland, a nun and reader of church history whose "divided family heritage, and [. . .] upbringing in Holland during the English Civil War, give her a clear sense of the microcosmic relation of her personal struggle to the public historical one, each about legitimate rule" (Grundy 131).

Romance

Romance, or Cavendish's "lie made from truth," exposes significant issues about historical narrative and women writers' adaptation of genre. Romance may be construed as narrative with the scope of national history and with, as Annabel Patterson argues, "ideological content, whose very fictionality held an interesting and provocative relation to its engagement with history" (24). Arthur Kinney convincingly argues that Philip Sidney's *Arcadia* develops from his reading of Xenophon, Thucydides, and contemporary Protestant historians and that "history as a means of coordinating various (and sometimes opposing) levels of conceptualization gives to Sidney [. . .] a new and vital means by which to bring past life and present poetry into close and provocative conjunction" (298). *Arcadia*, writes Kinney, "translated the antique past into the present's most pressing needs through the medium of verisimilar history" (311; see also McKeon, esp. chaps. 1 and 3). Analyzing the relations of history and romance in works by Mary Wroth, Aphra Behn, and others suggests how women could encode and develop ideas about recent history, the present polity, and a desired future. Wroth's *Urania* (1621) might be read as a roman à clef, but beyond the masquerade it can also be read as a series of fictional histories in which Wroth develops her ideas on foreign policy, government, and the relations of ruler and subject, drawing on history, politics, and contemporary issues for her events, characters, and discourses (Beilin, "Winning"). Josephine Roberts has argued that *Urania* inscribes the Bohemian crisis, the dangers of an imminent European war, James I's alleged peacemaking, and Wroth's espousal of internationalism with the crowning of Amphilanthus as king of the Romans (*First Part* xxxix–liv). In their play *The Concealed Fancies* (c. 1645), Lady Jane Cavendish and Lady Elizabeth Brackley situate the action at the castle of Ballamo, besieged by parliamentary troops, a version of the siege of their home, Welbeck Abbey. Here and in their other writings, they depict wartime conditions and the reponses of a royalist family (Ezell, "To Be" 285; Wiseman 162–63).

Behn's prose fictions and plays make complex use of history. In an early work, *Love Letters between a Nobleman and His Sister*, Behn figures closely the careers of Lord Grey of Werke, who was part of the Rye House Plot against Charles II, and his lover, Lady Henrietta Berkeley, following them when Grey became Monmouth's captain of horse during his rebellion against James II. Ellen Pollak suggests that the work may be cast as a love story because Behn understood "the greater acceptability for a woman of the role of romance historian over that of political poet" (152; see also Duffy, Introduction vii–ix; Ballaster). *Love Letters* is generically complex, providing speeches and verisimilar actions for historical figures in what Janet Todd calls "a heady mixture of history, propaganda, journalism, letters, farce and romance" ("Who" 200). Behn treats the Exclusion Crisis in *The Young King* and part 2 of *The Rover* (S. Owen); the Popish Plot in *The Feign'd Curtizans* (A. Shell); and Nathaniel Bacon's war on Native Americans in Virginia in *The Widow Ranter* (Hendricks, "Civility"). History and romance also unite in Mary Carleton's *An Historicall Narrative of the German Princess* (1633) and in her revision, *The Case of Madam Mary Carleton* (1663).

Life Writing

Life writing provided a vehicle for exemplarity, for the writer's commentary on the present, and for the writer's ideals (Hampton 3–8; McCrea), although it also raised generic and theoretical issues that greatly occupied seventeenth-century historians. Many followed Tacitus, from whom William Camden learned "that the principal Business of Annals is, to preserve Vertuous Actions from being buried in Oblivion, and to deter men from either speaking or doing what is amiss" (7). Judith Anderson's analysis of early modern life writing clarifies that works like Thomas More's *History of King Richard III* "had the status of a valid historical source" for sixteenth-century historians (76) and that factual errors or idealized and demonized characterizations call for careful decoding rather than rejection as history. For women writers, autobiography, family history, and panegyric verse were primary means to construct both past and present and to contribute to a narrative of national history. Relevant here is Michael McKeon's argument about narrative explanations of the "sociohistorical condition of status inconsistency":

> Very often this explanatory analysis will entail a specification of a complex set of circumstances on the "macrohistorical" level, a synecdochic operation that consists in reducing or concentrating it into a simpler, "microhistorical" narrative structure. And on occasion we can even watch contemporaries laboring to explain large, public macrohistories by quite self-consciously distilling them into the smaller, more accessible, private microhistories of individual and familial life that are to us recognizably "novelistic." (215)

In autobiography, women fashioned an identity, "their relations with other people and their actions within a social world of contemporary events" (Rose, "Gender" 247). To explain this world they wrote letters, diaries, and memoirs to analyze public events and figures in relation to their own experience; even texts dedicated to the writer's children might still be intended for wider commemoration or advocacy. The work of Grace, Lady Mildmay, and of Lady Anne Clifford exemplifies ways in which individual history may also encode macrohistory. The Mildmay manuscript volume contains a dedication to Mildmay's daughter, a sixty-page autobiography (c. 1617), then more than nine hundred pages of meditations written over fifty years (Martin, "Autobiography" 33–35; Warnicke, "Journal" 56–57). Mildmay describes her education by a "very, religious, wyse, and chaste" governess (45) and her devotion to her occupations as a household and estate manager, medical specialist,

meditator, and educator of her daughter. Her focus is simultaneously private and public in her "owne observation" of her father-in-
law, Sir Walter Mildmay: she praises his eloquence, "which
proceeded from a cleere judgement and true grounded discerning of
whatsoever he spake of," exemplifying him as a virtuous and godly
family man and as a great Elizabethan public servant who loved the
people and selflessly served the queen as chancellor of the exchequer
(50–52). The contentious settling of family estates occupies her, as it
does Margaret Beck in her *The Reward of Oppression, Tyranny, and
Injustice* (1655), in which Beck recapitulates a cynical history of the
monarchy to argue fervently the claim of her son to the duchy of
Lancaster. But most thorough in her research and in her collection
of genealogical records to support her court case, and most resolute
in establishing the truth, is Clifford, whose dedication to family history permeates her diaries and the accounts of her own life and her
parents' lives (D. Clifford x–xiv; Lewalski, *Writing Women* 125–51).
Clifford memorably represents her social roles, her intellectual life,
her actions ("the Civill Warres being then very hott" [*Diaries* 95]),
and her anti-Cromwellian politics ("Let him destroy my Castles if he
will, as often as he levels them I will rebuild them" [101]).

The Civil War was indeed a defining moment for life writing.
Whether "social chaos" opened new roles for women (Rose, "Gender" 247) or whether extraordinary experiences provided material
and "acted as stimulants to self-discovery" (Delany 159), autobiographies narrate social, political, and religious histories of the nation. In *A True Relation of my Birth, Breeding, and Life* (1656),
Cavendish writes "to tell the truth," to establish her identity, but
also to narrate "these unhappy Wars" that ruined both her royalist
families ("True Relation" 375). Lucy Hutchinson actually situates
her autobiography (c. 1664–65) within a brief national history,
rooting her idealized family in a paradisical, glorious Britain. She
grounds her parliamentary politics in the "Norman yoke" theory
that the monarchy continues the usurpation of ancient British liber-
ties by William the Conqueror (C. Hill, *Puritanism* 50–122) until
the people resist and "popular liberty" is restored (Hutchinson
280); her own life delineates the Civil War, "wherein I have shar'd

many perills, many feares, and many sorrows, and many more mer-
cies, consolations, and preservations" (281). In 1677–78, Anne,
Lady Halkett, wrote her memoirs of her early life and experiences in
the Civil War, including her role in liberating the duke of York from
Saint James's Palace in 1648 (Halkett and Fanshawe). Another royalist, Ann, Lady Fanshawe, wrote her memoirs in 1676, recording a
life filled with public actions, travel, and politics. Alice Thornton
began her *Book of Remembrances* after 1668, expanding it later into
what we now know as her *Autobiography*, a remarkable version of
Civil War history that explains the times through her own experiences and those of her royalist family. Mary Rich, countess of Warwick, wrote her memoirs of her life as a devoted mother and great
lady allied to one of the most politically powerful parliamentary families (see Mendelson 62–115).

In their family histories, women writers consistently express the
highest religious and political ideals, either through exemplary figures or symbolic narrative. For example, in *The Lady Falkland Her
Life* (c. 1655), Lucy Cary includes a history of Elizabeth Cary, the
extended Falkland family, court politics, Ireland, religious disputa-
tion, and recusancy. The author, one of Elizabeth Cary's daughters,
who became a nun, interweaves painstaking detail and symbolic
episodes—such as the apparent deathbed conversion of Lucy's violently anti-Catholic father—to write a history of Catholic-Protestant
political and theological struggle as it was mapped by her family,
particularly her mother, the exemplary convert (Weller and Ferguson 2). Devotion appears to motivate Cavendish to depict the exemplary virtues of her husband in her influential *Life* of him, a "short
History of the Loyal, Heroick and Prudent Actions of my Noble
Lord" (c2; see Mendelson 61). She intends her history as a correc-
tive to others who have written about the Civil War "with but few
sprinklings of Truth." Indeed, the *Life* is extended praise of William
Cavendish as the ideal subject, courtier, and warrior; all his intentions and actions are excellent, and only the treachery or incompe-
tence of others accounts for his military, social, and financial failures.
The history of the parliamentary side of the Civil War appears in
Hutchinson's *Life of John Hutchinson* (*Memoirs*), a detailed account

of Hutchinson's role and an absorbing, carefully written chronicle of public events. John Hutchinson represents the ideal characteristics of his political and religious ideology—he is a pious, dedicated antimonarchist, ready to face down the king himself and to sign the warrant for Charles's execution.

Women also wrote noble lives to articulate political ideology and historical truth in elegies, occasional poems, and panegyrics. In her *Chaine of Pearle; or, A Memoriall of the Peerles Graces, and Heroick Vertues of Queene Elizabeth, of Glorious Memory* (1630), Diana Primrose composes ten "pearles," each one symbolizing a virtue, such as religion, chastity, or clemency. She may have consulted Camden's *Annales,* for the poem refers to the years from Elizabeth's accession in 1558 to the Armada in 1588; it may also imply criticism of Charles I's rule (Greer, Hastings, Medoff, and Sansone 83). In Bradstreet's poem "In Honour of That High and Mighty Princess Queen Elizabeth of Happy Memory," the queen's reign transcends its representation in "Camden's learned history" (*Works* 195; line 25) and the poet asks, "Was ever people better ruled than hers?" (196; line 46). Philips expresses her ardent, idealistic royalism in numerous poems that characterize Charles I and members of the royal family and that celebrate the Restoration. Her poem "The Princess Royall's Returne into England," for instance, represents the significance of the event, praising the Princess Mary's active role in preserving the monarchy and her "generous care / Which did your glorious Brother's troubles share" (*Poems* [1990] 77; lines 13–14). Behn's poems on the death of Charles II, on the coronation of James II, and on Queen Mary's arrival in England represent godlike monarchs and the nobility returning Britain to its glory days: "And now the ravisht *People* shout a new!" (*Poems* 188; see Fitzmaurice, Roberts, Barash, Cunnar, and Gutierrez 319–22; Williamson 280–82). Elizabeth Singer Rowe's poem "Upon King William's Passing the Boyn" celebrates the "*Hero and the King*" who exemplifies military valor and greatness (110).

———

Studying women writers' multivocal constructions of past and present indicates once more how fully they participated in their culture. From Isabella Whitney's representation of London's streets and people in her "Wyll and Testament" (1573) to Bathsua Makin's argumentative use of the history of educated women in her *Essay to Revive the Antient Education of Gentlewomen* (1673), women's history writing represents daily life and public events and articulates their vision of the nation.

John N. King, Frances E. Dolan, and Elaine Hobby

Writing Religion

Early Protestantism

The Monument of Matrons, Containing Seven Several Lamps of Virginity (1582) is an excellent text to cite in teaching religious writings by early English Protestant women. Dedicating that text to Elizabeth I, Thomas Bentley, a law student in quest of court patronage, compiled what may be the "earliest unrestrained celebration" of her "perpetual virginity" (Collinson 105). It appeared in print shortly after the breakdown of Elizabeth's final round of marriage negotiations. The seven lamps (parts) of that massive compendium offer a panoply of prayers, meditations, precepts, and examples for virtually every occasion in the life of woman from childbirth through death.

One may initiate classroom discussion quite effectively by showing slides of the intricately carved woodcut borders of the title pages of the first five lamps (reproduced in J. King, *Iconography*), which liken Elizabeth and two other writing queens, Marguerite de Navarre and Katherine Parr, to scriptural types for the "true" church such as Eve, Deborah, Bathsheba, Queen Esther, Judith, the Virgin

Mary, and the Five Wise Virgins who filled their lamps with oil in expectation of the apocalyptic wedding feast (Matt. 25.1–13). Although those elaborate title pages confer an establishmentarian cast on Bentley's anthology of Elizabethan prayers and meditations, it actually contains texts composed or translated by genteel, aristocratic, or royal women who faced exile, imprisonment, torture, or execution because of their outspoken Protestant views. Texts contained in the *Monument* generate important questions concerning female authorship, the political and religious agency of women, and the material circumstances of production of devotional texts by, for, and about sixteenth-century Englishwomen at a time when the nature of England's official religion was by no means clear.

In her youth, Elizabeth Tudor was a marriageable princess of dubious legitimacy born to Anne Boleyn, the first of Henry VIII's three Protestant consorts. Before Elizabeth became queen, she witnessed abrupt swings in religion between "papistry" and moderate or radical Protestantism. Implementation of a Protestant religious settlement was precarious at best during years when the heresy hunt that swept Anne Askew to her martyr's pyre also threatened Katherine Parr, the monarch's sixth and final spouse (1545–46); when Edward VI, a sickly boy who advocated radical Protestant beliefs, maintained a tenuous grip on authority (1547–53); and when his Roman Catholic half sister, Mary I, apparently yearned to execute her hated half sister, Princess Elizabeth, during a reign (1553–58) notable for the deaths of hundreds of Protestant martyrs whose stories fill the pages of John Foxe's *Acts and Monuments*.

Bentley's gathering in lamp 2 of "diverse godly prayers made by sundry virtuous queens, and other devout and godly women" centers on *A Godly Meditation of the Inward Love of the Soul towards Christ*, a translation of Marguerite de Navarre's *Le miroir de l'âme pécheresse* (1531) made by Elizabeth Tudor as an eleven-year-old princess. She wrote the autograph manuscript, entitled "The Glass of the Sinful Soul" and bound in her own hand-embroidered covers, as a 1544 New Year gift to Katherine Parr. It demonstrated her learning to the stepmother who commissioned Protestant tutors such as John Cheke and Roger Ascham to educate Prince Edward,

Lady Elizabeth, and Lady Jane Grey at the royal court late in Henry VIII's reign. Elizabeth's few mistranslations, notably her rendering of *Père* as "Mother," invite psychobiographical speculation about whether her work subtly blames Henry VIII for ordering the execution of Anne Boleyn (M. Shell 108–09; Prescott). The generalized meditations in Elizabeth's "Glass" do not contain Protestant doctrine per se, but the masculine voice in the "Epistle Dedicatory" and "Conclusion" of the printed edition, *A Godly Meditation of the Christian Soul* (1548; M. Shell 83–102), demonstrate how the editor, John Bale, converted the text into a document compatible with the radical Protestant climate of Edward VI's reign.

Bentley's placement in lamp 2 of two texts by Katherine Parr— *Godly Prayers and Meditations, Wherein the Mind Is Stirred Patiently to Suffer All Afflictions Here* and the *Lamentation of a Sinner*— compliments Queen Elizabeth as the spiritual descendant of a queen consort with advanced Protestant views. Queen Catherine positioned herself with finesse in a court dominated by a cruel spouse remembered for executing two spouses, Anne Boleyn and Catherine Howard. Originally published in 1545, near the end of Henry's life, *Godly Prayers* consists of rewritten excerpts from an English translation of book 3 of Thomas à Kempis's *Imitation of Christ*. In keeping with the prohibition on the dissemination of Protestant ideas in the Act of Six Articles (1539), *Godly Prayers* is a noncontroversial document influenced by the *devotio moderna* rather than by Lutheran theology (J. King, "Patronage"; Mueller, "Tudor Queen" and Introduction).

Published only two years later, *The Lamentation of a Sinner* (1547) is in keeping with the temper of Edward VI's reign, when advanced Protestant theology ran rampant. William Cecil edited it for publication at the behest of the duchess of Suffolk. (He eventually served as chief minister to Queen Elizabeth.) Under the influence of William Tyndale, Hugh Latimer, and Thomas Cranmer, fundamental Protestant principles of faith alone, grace alone, and Scripture alone permeate a conversion narrative that exemplifies the "Protestant paradigm of salvation"—election, calling (vocation), justification by faith, adoption, sanctification, and glorification

(Lewalski, *Protestant Poetics* 13–23)—in the form of highly personalized, free-flowing meditations like the following: "I forsook the spiritual honoring of the true living God, and worshipped visible idols, and images made of men's hands, believing by them to have gotten heaven." Publication of a confession of faith by a queen consort was utterly lacking in precedent. In a conversion narrative filled with pious meditations, Catherine speaks in a voice unique among English queens.

According to Foxe's *Acts and Monuments*, King Henry's last queen was at risk of going to the headsman's block for keeping forbidden Protestant books in her privy chamber. Foxe implicates Bishop Stephen Gardiner, leader of the conservative faction, with attempting to entrap Katherine Parr at the time of the Anne Askew affair in connection with what appears to have been a coterie manuscript of *The Lamentation of a Sinner*. The muting of gender indicators in Cecil's edition may be in keeping with Foxe's account of Catherine's submission to her king and husband as a wife who fulfills the stereotypical obligation of chastity, silence, and obedience, by contrast to the loquacious disobedience of Askew, whose *Examinations* were edited for publication by John Bale in 1546–47.

Bale gained access to Askew's manuscript account of her two judicial examinations and condemnation for heresy through channels related to those through which he received a manuscript of Elizabeth's "Glass." That radical cleric, whose tracts remained under ban until Henry VIII's death in January 1547 and again during the reign of Mary I, edited the Askew and Elizabeth manuscripts for publication at a safe haven in Germany. Yet again we encounter a link to Bentley's *Monument of Matrons*, because lamp 2 incorporates "The Prayer of Anne Askew the Martyr, before Her Death" among "Certain Prayers Made by Godly Women Martyrs" (146–48). Askew's *Examinations* gained great currency when Foxe included it in the *Acts and Monuments*.

No teacher can go wrong in using *Examinations* as a vehicle for considering early feminism, because of clearly drawn gender conflict and a host of fascinating issues related to Reformation theology, transmission of texts, Protestant martyrology, the education of

women, and narratology. By contrast to the obliquity of Parr's publications, Askew openly flouted Pauline strictures against female
preachers and goaded Henrician authorities by employing a variety
of sarcastic devices including rhetorical questions, ironic similes, and
gestures to attack transubstantiation, the Mass, and auricular confession.

The Tower of London texts by Lady Jane Grey, the queen who
reigned for nine days between Edward VI and Mary I, is the final set
of royal writings in lamp 2. Of particular interest because of their engagement with distinctively feminine iconography (e.g., the Five
Wise Virgins cited in Jesus's parable), these writings include a pre-
execution prayer, an exhortation to her sister written in a New Testament, devotional verses, and a version of Psalm 51 spoken as a
prayer prior to beheading. Foxe's *Acts and Monuments* assimilates
the contents of *An Epistle of the Lady Jane to a Learned Man*
(1554?), the tract in which her writings were published as a propa-
gandistic attack on the Catholic regime of Mary I.

Lady Jane shares the antipathy of Parr and Askew toward transubstantiation, the Mass, and what she regards as the physicality of
Roman Catholic worship. Common assumptions about the supremacy of the Bible and its poetic texture underlie these writers'
use of a plain style to apply scriptural tropes and figures to contemporary religious controversy. As an example of sixteenth-century
prose style, Lady Jane's writing bears comparison with that of Parr,
which is notable for its "ejaculatory, antithetical, and parallel constructions whose chief precedents lie in the Pauline epistles"
(Mueller, "Tudor Queen" 22).

What alternatives existed for early Protestant Englishwomen
other than the subterfuge of Parr, the flirtation with beheading of
Lady Elizabeth, the fatal outspokenness of Askew, or the polemical
fervor of Lady Jane Grey? While martyrs' pyres smoldered throughout England, Anne Lock followed John Knox to exile in Geneva
during the reign of the queen who is generally remembered as
Bloody Mary. Lock's set of sonnets for each of the twenty-one verses
in Psalm 51 plus five introductory sonnets appeared in print at the
outset of Elizabeth I's reign (*Collected Works* 62–71). As the first

sonnet cycle printed in English, this forerunner of the Elizabethan sonnet vogue stamps an amatory poetic mode with Calvinistic spirituality. Three years before John Day published Foxe's *Acts and Monuments*, he appended Lock's versification of Psalm 51, "Meditation of a Penitent Sinner," to what is presumed to be her translation of Calvin's *Sermons upon the Song That Hezekias Made after He Had Been Sick* (1560). Recitation of that psalm was a conventional element at the execution of Lady Jane Grey and scores of martyrdoms in the *Acts and Monuments*. Lock presumably dedicated the Calvin volume to the duchess of Suffolk, an associate of Parr who went into exile and patronized Protestant ideologues like Hugh Latimer (see Roche 155–57; Hannay, "Unlock My Lipps"; J. King, "Patronage"). Only two copies of that publication survive. In contrast to the freely flowing meditations of Parr's *Lamentations of a Sinner*, Lock casts her meditation on original sin and the unworthiness of the soul in the long-standing tradition of the Seven Penitential Psalms.

We are at a fortunate point in the study of early modern women. After hundreds of years of inaccessibility and neglect, a library of texts by early women writers is being republished. *Women Writers Online* has posted lamp 2 of Bentley's *Monument* on the World Wide Web. The Bodleian Library tightly restricts access to what the keeper of manuscripts has termed "one of our most precious possessions" (Scoufos), but teachers who compile course packets may include a facsimile of MS Cherry 36 in Elizabeth's legible italic hand (reproduced in M. Shell). Teachers may thus address questions concerning manuscript culture without the headache of introducing classes to Tudor secretary hand. Critical editions of writings by Katherine Parr and Elizabeth I are in progress. Askew's *Examinations* is now available in both a paperback classroom edition and a facsimile text. The Renaissance English Text Society has published an edition of Lock's writings. The availability of religious writings by Elizabeth, Parr, Askew, Grey, Lock, and other women should transform the teaching of sixteenth-century English literature during the twenty-first century.

John N. King

Roman Catholic Women

Scholars often dismiss Catholic women as too medieval to participate in the early modern period; if they are discussed at all, it is as
leftovers and afterthoughts. I want to challenge the assumption that
Protestantism, progress, and print all went together. Despite the still
widespread stereotype that Catholics finger rosary beads, gaze at
stained glass windows, and are fettered by superstition and an inability to read, Catholics, including women, wrote many texts that
should be included in discussions of early modern literate culture. In
our syllabi we need to include texts by Catholic women writers such
as Elizabeth Grymeston and Elizabeth Cellier; we need to be sure
that we do not erase the conversion and complex religious identity
of Elizabeth Cary, the one Catholic woman who does make it into
our syllabi; we need to interrogate rather than perpetuate the religious biases shaping so many early modern discourses and to include
some defenses of Catholicism, and particularly of Catholic women,
among all the attacks; we need to take seriously the slights about
"popery" that we encounter everywhere in English texts and to discuss with our students why *papist* is an insult in early modern England. Regarding "Romish" or "papist" women, who were, for their
contemporaries, a category problem, rethinking the assumptions
and associations that we bring to our study of women is as important as adding more women to our syllabi.

Who, then, were these Catholic women who were, disturbingly,
more English than they were "Roman"? Drawing on xenophobia
and nascent nationalism, as well as on religious fervor, Protestantism
defined itself in protest against the old, idolatrous religion in need of
reform. It also deployed misogyny to animate attacks on female objects of worship and on an iconography rich in positive images of
femininity (Diehl; Sanders). Most of all, it required English Protestants to repress the origins and history they shared with their
Catholic neighbors, family members, and ancestors, to impose difference on those who were largely the same. In a wide range of texts,
from legal statutes, acts of Parliament, and accounts of treason trials
to ephemeral pamphlets, ballads, and broadsides, from woodcuts to

plays and poems, Protestant culture expended extraordinary effort to insist that Catholics were both other and inferior. Undermining Englishness and Protestantism by not being different enough, English Catholics unsettled the nation's relation to its past and, with their allegiances divided between England's sovereign and Rome's pope, blurred the distinction between the English and foreigners, loyal subjects and traitors. Labeling the religion "popery" and its adherents "papists," common parlance emphasized the compromised loyalty of Catholic subjects, all of whom experienced the divided duty we tend to associate with women torn between father and husband.

Since Catholics were woven into families and communities and prominent at court, the threat they presented was precisely that they could not be readily separated out and assigned to a category. Catholics were both highly influential (especially at court, where they were literally in bed with Stuart monarchs) and oppressed (the victims of legal penalties and local prejudices and blamed for everything from plotting to blow up monarchs to setting London on fire). The minority in England, they had previously been the majority, and they continued to be the majority in the countries England feared most: France, Italy, and Spain. There were far more Catholics in England than there were Jews, Africans, Moors, or Turks, yet the compatriots of Catholics found them much harder to recognize. Perhaps because of their greater but less visible presence in England and their problematic status as natives, Catholics provoked more prolific and intemperate visual and verbal representation and more elaborate and sustained legal regulation than any other group.

Legal attempts to mark as recusants people who excused or withheld themselves from Church of England services were not particularly successful. Recusants were not only those who refused to attend their parish church but also those whose absence was observed and prosecuted and who, in the face of accusation or conviction, refused to conform. "Church papists" conformed outwardly and occasionally, while maintaining observance of their Catholic faith in private; they were subject to censure but not to the laws.

Those whose neighbors chose not to pursue them were also safe. Since recusancy was more about the public enactment of belief than the belief itself or private practices, many residual beliefs, inclinations, and observances persisted invisibly beneath the law's scrutiny. While repeat offenses accrued ever stiffer penalties, conformity could, in a moment, reverse this process. Thus recusants were a smaller, constantly shifting subset of Catholics; many who viewed themselves as Catholic might not have been recusants. Furthermore, just as all Catholics were not recusants, all recusants were not Catholics; there were other religious dissidents who refused to attend Church of England services.

Some women, mostly unmarried or widowed, were convicted and fined as recusants. Married women's husbands might be penalized in a variety of ways for their wives' recusancy; for instance, they might be charged ten pounds a month, half of what they'd pay for their own recusancy, or they might be denied civil promotion and appointment. Such coercions, however indirect, put recusant wives under considerable pressure to conform. Some women, married and unmarried, were imprisoned, occasionally for extended periods. The few who were executed as recusants (most under Elizabeth, none under the Stuart kings) received that punishment for harboring priests (Marotti, "Alienating"). Recusant women paid a high price for their refusal to conform, but they left more records than the women who escaped prosecution. However, *recusant* is too narrow a term to accommodate the many people who did not wholly embrace the Reformation or the Church of England.

Conversions to Catholicism further muddied the waters. Conversions became especially fashionable in anticipation of Prince Charles's marriage to the Spanish infanta, which was never realized, and then in response to Charles's marriage to Henrietta Maria, a French Catholic. Aristocratic and court ladies were viewed as especially susceptible to conversion (Questier). According to contemporaries, they were drawn by the desire for influence in an openly Catholic court circle; by their weakness and irrationality, the same qualities that made Eve vulnerable to Satan and that made women more likely than men to become witches; by their vanity, sensuality, and delight in trinkets and toys.

The notion that women were more drawn to Catholicism than men were often corresponded to the notion that women were illiterate and unlearned. Their ignorance made them loyal to a religion that coddled their incapacities or, if they were converts, vulnerable to one that took advantage of their weakness. Some historians still suggest that Catholicism appealed to women because it was congenial to their illiteracy. John Bossy, for instance, argues that many women clung to Catholicism in reaction against the Anglican Church's emphasis on literacy as "a condition of salvation," an emphasis that placed most of them at a disadvantage (158). Many other historians tacitly accept that Catholic women were neither readers nor writers. Yet Patricia Crawford's statement "religious writing of various kinds was the most important area of publication for seventeenth-century women" was as true for Catholic as for Protestant women ("Writings" 221). Many Catholic women must have been resistant readers of anti-Catholic discourses. They also must have read the numerous Catholic texts available in England. Many converts, such as Cary, read their way into Catholicism. Margaret Clitherow took her imprisonments for recusancy as an opportunity to learn "to read English and written hand," read spiritual books, and learn "our Lady's Matins in Latin" to the end that she might someday take on a religious habit, although she was married and a mother (Mush 375, 394; see Matchinske, *Writing* 53–85, and Marotti, "Alienating").

If Catholics' resistant readings cannot always be documented, their resistant writings are surprisingly profuse. Yet the Pollard and Redgrave short-title catalog and the Wing short-title catalog do not include many Catholic texts written in English and intended for English audiences but printed secretly or printed abroad—most often at Douai or the English Jesuit College at Saint Omer in the Spanish Netherlands but also in Amsterdam and Louvain—and smuggled into England. For a more thorough listing, one must turn to references such as Allison and Rogers's *The Contemporary Printed Literature of the English Counter-Reformation between 1558 and 1640* and Thomas H. Clancy's *English Catholic Books, 1641–1700*. The online *English Short Title Catalogue* is attempting to bridge this divide by including all works printed in English anywhere in the world. This project is an important step forward, since works printed in English for Catholic readers constitute "a corpus of writings far larger than those of the Baptists and Quakers and second only to the established church" (Hibbard 13). Keeping track of Catholic book production in English, abroad and at home, can be difficult, not only because our research tools are biased but also because many Catholic books of the period lack an imprint or sport a false one. For Catholic readers, these books were expensive and difficult, even dangerous, to get hold of, since owning or trading in Catholic books or ritual objects was against the law. Engaging in the clandestine book trade might even be fatal: some Catholic stationers were executed on charges of treason for printing and distributing seditious texts (Rostenberg 22, 39, 43, 203).

Women played important roles in keeping, preserving, and circulating family and convent records and devotional materials in manuscript; they also participated in every aspect of this Catholic print culture. Some who knew Latin translated texts into English to make them more readily available; others acted as patrons for texts; still others harbored secret presses in their homes, smuggled Catholic books over from the Continent, and engaged in printing and selling Catholic books in England (Rostenberg 22, 24, 26, 101–07, 116, 204). Elizabeth Cellier offers an excellent example of Catholic women's multiple engagements with print culture. In connection with the Meal Tub Plot, an aftershock of the Popish Plot, Cellier, a midwife, was tried for treason in 1680. Like all treason defendants before 1696, she had to represent herself; unlike most, she secured an acquittal. Cellier then wrote a self-justifying account of her trial, *Malice Defeated; or, A Brief Relation of the Accusation and Deliverance of Elizabeth Cellier*. She had this text printed for her, despite the Privy Council's attempts to seize sheets while they were in press, and she sold it from her house on Arundel Street. *Malice Defeated*, like other extant accounts of the trial, demonstrates the controversial nature of Catholic writing: the Meal Tub Plot gets its name from documents found in Cellier's flour barrel, documents she claims were forged and planted; she admits to managing a Catholic intelligence network centered on Newgate Prison; there is much discussion of letters, pamphlets, incriminating handwriting, and perjured witnesses (Dolan *Whores*, ch. 4; Weil). Cellier's text is remarkable as a treason trial account written by the defendant, who is a woman, and as an outspokenly pro-Catholic text published in a very volatile political moment. It is also richly textured and highly dramatic. I've had students perform passages of dialogue as they would a play, paying special attention to how Cellier alternates between being a participant in and a commentator on the action. She did not get the last word, however. For this text, she was subsequently tried for and convicted of libel. Teaching *Malice Defeated* thus makes it possible to discuss both the extent to which Catholic women engaged in oppositional writing and the risks of their doing so.

Furthermore, teaching *Malice Defeated* and John Mush's *Life of Margaret Clitherow* in conjunction with other biographies and autobiographies of women in the period, such as the much assigned collection of seventeenth-century autobiographies, *Her Own Life* (Graham et al.), reveals how much we neglect when we wipe Catholic women off the map. These texts challenge most of the assumptions about early modern Catholic women, since Clitherow and Cellier are laypersons, married, converts, highly literate, and publically assertive. The legal struggles that bring them into public scrutiny challenge the notion that post-Reformation Catholicism was a retreat to the domestic, the familiar, or the safe.

Women also figured significantly in the production and consumption of Catholic devotional writings. The saint's life, for instance, appears to have been a feminized genre; in the late sixteenth and early seventeenth centuries, "nearly half the printed lives were about women saints and the majority of dedications were addressed to women" (J. Rhodes 18). Women also played important roles as translators, copyists (aiding the manuscript transmission of saints' lives), and consumers. Yet many students (and scholars) know little about this once popular genre, which is readily available in translations of Jacobus de Voragine's *The Golden Legend* or in popular early modern collections such as John Heigham's translation of Alfonso Villegas's *Lives of Saints*, which went through many editions and is available on microfilm. I have found that teaching an account of the life of a virgin martyr alongside Shakespeare's *Measure for Measure* enables students to take more seriously the possibility that Isabella might have compelling reasons for refusing to exchange her virginity for her brother's life or for choosing the convent over marriage. Pairing a virgin martyr's life with Christine de Pisan's *Book of the City of Ladies* positions the martyrologies in Christine's book 3 as part of a long-standing, mainstream tradition rather than as an eccentric deviation. Contrasting *The Examinations of Anne Askew* (1546–47) with both an account of a virgin martyr and Mush's *Life of Margaret Clitherow* demonstrates how Protestant writers such as Askew, John Bale, and John Foxe appropriate and transform the Catholic genre of martyrology and how gender operates differently in Catholic and Protestant accounts of the suffering female body; and it makes clear the challenges that Catholics face when they try to reclaim martyrology as a form *after* Foxe. Such a juxtaposition also facilitates discussion of how religious affiliation combines and conflicts with gender in shaping how death is construed as an enabling condition of female authorship. Mary Beth Rose ("Gender") and Wendy Wall have both argued that, when mothers address their children in writing, they often justify their speech on the grounds that they are soon to die (usually in childbirth). But do the mothers' religious affiliations and beliefs make a difference? Teaching Elizabeth Grymeston's Catholic *Miscelanea, Meditations, Memoratives* (1604) against more frequently taught mothers' legacies such as Elizabeth Clinton's Protestant *The Countesse of Lincolnes Nurserie* (1622) makes it possible to consider this question. Of course, these texts need to be presented as more than snippets if students are to engage them seriously. Megan Matchinske's work on Grymeston ("Gendering") suggests that additions made to the second (and subsequent) editions of Grymeston's work after her death substantially changed the content and addressed, even more directly than before, the situation of English recusants, especially after the Gunpowder Plot.

Considering Catholic women helps reveal the Reformation as a mixed bag for Englishwomen. In the special circumstances of post-Reformation England, married Catholic women may have gained authority and independence. If Protestantism empowered the father as priest presiding over the "spiritualized household" (C. Hill, *Society*), Catholicism empowered women as custodians of household religion. Catholic women did not look to their husbands as their spiritual teachers and leaders but turned instead to priests. Yet, in England, clergymen were few and far between. Given the suppression of the Mass (anywhere but in royal or embassy chapels in London, that is), household observance was the only kind available to most people; in many households, women motivated and facilitated clandestine worship (Rowlands; Warnicke, *Women*; Willen). Even if a priest lived in the house, he was dependent on the mistress's as well as the master's patronage and protection. Furthermore, penal laws effectively placed Catholic men in the restricted legal position of married women, constraining the men's rights to hold certain offices, to control their property and their children's educations, and to move about freely. What legal distinctions did remain between Catholic women and men often worked to empower married women, who were less liable to fines. Consequently, many English Catholic women were not clearly under either a husband's or a priest's spiritual governance. In their own households, they could dedicate themselves to piety with less interference, supervision, and restriction than nuns.

Not that all Catholic women in England married. Many remained single, as did many Protestant women. Some still became nuns, although, for the most part, they had to go abroad to do so. "Between 1597 and 1642 seventeen houses of English women belonging to eight orders were established on the continent. At least 300 young women went to join these communities" (Rowlands 167; see Guilday). Several English gentlewomen, such as Mary Ward and Lucy Knatchbull, played important roles in founding English orders or houses and in educating other women (Peters; Matthew; L. Gallagher). Ward's writings were not printed at the time, but some have been published more recently (Latz; Orchard). Evading and breaking the law, Englishwomen also helped one another ensure Catholic educations and clerical vocations for as many children as possible, smuggling them out of the country, sharing contacts and financial support. Two wonderful texts to teach regarding women's communities are the *Life* of Elizabeth Cary, which reveals the lengths to which a mother will go to get her children into holy orders and the networks of women on whom she relies for financial and moral support, and Jane Owen's *An Antidote against Purgatory* (1634), in which Owen directly addresses Catholic gentlewomen, especially widows; urges the Virgin Mary as a model of female charity; and tries to persuade Catholics of "the greater Ranke and best abilities" to finance the transportation and Continental education of Catholic children (203). Even the considerable recent scholarship on Cary focuses more on her conflicts with male authorities than on her less fully articulated, less visible alliances with women. Yet Cary's *Life*, especially when read in conjunction with a text like Owen's, provides ample evidence of Catholic women's communities. Reading the *Life* from this perspective might also open up discussion of Henrietta Maria's extraordinary role as a patron. Writers such as Margaret Cavendish and Lady Anne Halkett emphasize that their Protestantism withstood their close affiliation with the Stuart court. Still, it is significant that so many women writers of the period spent time in service to, even in exile with, Henrietta Maria.

Henrietta Maria—openly Catholic, notoriously connubial, usually pregnant—provides a wonderful contrast to Elizabeth I and a salutary reminder that discussions of Elizabeth's reign too often isolate Elizabeth as an exception (Dolan, *Whores*, ch. 3). Yet how can we understand conceptions of and reactions to queenship in general and Elizabeth in particular if we consider her out of context? Discussions of Elizabeth as author, ruler, and icon would benefit from attention to her immediate predecessor and sister, Mary Tudor, and to her rival, Mary Stuart. Both these "mischevous Maryes," as John Knox called them, were, of course, Catholic (*First Blast* Fv). Mary Stuart's letters and poems, as well as the accounts of her trial (J. Lewis), make excellent foils to Elizabeth's speeches about Mary. It is also useful to contrast Elizabeth not only to these other queens regnant but also to the queens consort who succeed her. All the male Stuarts were married to Catholics (and foreigners). While these queens did not produce many writings of their own, numerous texts survive about them, especially about the scandalous Henrietta Maria, wife of one king and mother of the next two (Charles II and James II). Discussions of queenship might include not only the works of Knox and John Aylmer, as they usually do, but also later texts, such as William Prynne's intemperate and fascinating attacks on Henrietta Maria.

Catholic women have long been viewed as spoilers, seducing and misleading Stuart kings, interrupting a Protestant succession with unseemly fertility, distracting the English nation from its march of progress. Their contribution to courses on early modern women writers might be a more positive version of this conventional role. They mess things up: organizational categories (e.g., foreign, English), neat periodizations, unquestioned assumptions.

Frances E. Dolan

Nonconformists

The year 1649 saw the beheading of Charles I, an event that marks a turning point in the history of women's published writing in Britain. In the course of the next decade dozens of women, most of them not from the upper echelons of society, broke into print (Hobby, "Discourse"; though this essay does not treat Lady Eleanor Davies, because she was an aristocrat who largely worked alone; see her *Prophetic Writings* for some comparable uses of Scriptures). In the apocalyptic fervor that linked the social upheavals of republican Britain to the "great overturning" promised in the Bible (Ezek. 21.27), such writers presented themselves as a sign that God was keeping his word:

> In the last days saith God, I will pour out my Spirit upon all flesh; and your sons and your daughters shall prophesy, and your young men shall see visions, and your old men shall dream dreams: And on my servants and on my handmaidens I will pour out in those days of my Spirit, and they shall prophesy.   (Acts 2.17–18)

The writings that rushed from the press in these years are often ecstatic and are simultaneously personal, religious, and political: as God's "weak instruments," these women authors saw their lives and ideas as embodiments of God's will for his people. Perceiving themselves as prophets—interpreters of the holy word equivalent to Old Testament prophets—pamphleteers argued for legal changes and the overthrow of all hierarchies; they told the story of their own awakening to action; they engaged in theological debate. Although the restoration of the monarchy in 1660 rechanneled their voices in various ways, it could not silence them. Indeed, as the radicals took stock of their experiences and planned a way forward, increasing numbers of autobiographies and admonitions emerged. The nonconformist sects of Quakers and Baptists reinvented themselves in an uneasy accommodation with the established church and state and went into print to define these new identities (McGregor and Reay; C. Hill, *World*; Crawford, *Women*).

All these books and pamphlets assume in their reader an easy familiarity with the Bible, which was common in that era, and they brim over with allusions to scriptural events and promises. This dimension of the texts was a crucial part of their accessibility in their own era, but today it can present an obstacle. Cracking the code, though, can be exhilarating, as it becomes clear that Anne Wentworth is using her Bible to threaten God's vengeance on her violent husband (Graham et al. 180–96), or that Hester Biddle has extensive grounds to believe that she is right to threaten to burn the universities to the ground (Hobby, "Oh Oxford"). (See also Trubowitz; Trill; Hobby, "Politics" and "Usurping".) If students are helped to understand the historical reasons for the urgency that animates these writings, their interpretation of the writings becomes a fascinating task. An alternative route into them is offered by French feminist interest in the process of signification itself, which can read prophetic writings as texts that refuse binaries and boundaries as they play joyfully with the creativity of the word (Ezell, *Writing*; Hinds; Lilley).

Although not the most numerous radical religious group in the period, the Quakers—or (Society of) Friends, as they called themselves—were the most efficient record keepers. It is probably partly for this reason that they have also been the focus of a great deal of twentieth-century research, especially over the last twenty years (Mack; Trevett; Foxton). The key Quaker convictions that the word of God could be heard by all, if they learned to listen, and that hierarchical structures were anathema to God freed female Friends to write on a wide range of topics. They protested against their imprisonment, prophesied the overthrow of governments, analyzed women's proper role in a godly society. Many also traveled throughout Britain and the world to spread God's messages and recorded their experiences of travel in print.

A comprehensive collection of early Quaker women's writing exists in *Hidden in Plain Sight: Quaker Women's Writings, 1650–1700* (Garman, Applegate, Benefiel, and Meredith). This anthology has great range, for instance including both the animated joy of Sarah Blackborow's *A Visit to the Spirit in Prison* (1658), which invites the reader to accept God and enter "the Chamber of her that conceived me" (55), and Anne Whitehead and Mary Elson's typically conservative advice to the Quaker movement twenty years later, in *An Epistle for True Love, Unity, and Order in the Church of Christ* (1680), that "Godly Women always give Preeminence" to their menfolk (492). This collection has two great strengths. First, in almost all cases it includes the entire text of a pamphlet, making it possible to analyze the range of language, tone, and concern these works span. Second, there is a series of succinct introductions, which place these pamphlets in their social and theological contexts and provide such information as is known about their authors. There is, though, no annotation on the writings themselves, and the edition follows the spelling and punctuation of the seventeenth-century originals: it is unlikely that even advanced students would be able to start their study of nonconformist women's writings here.

A way in can be found, however, through the thoroughly annotated extracts from two Quaker pamphlets included in *Her Own Life: Autobiographical Writings by Seventeenth-Century Englishwomen* (Graham et al.). Katharine Evans and Sarah Cheevers's *This*

Is a Short Relation (1662) tells the story of their imprisonment by the Italian Inquisition in Malta. In this extract, Evans's voice merges with that of the Book of Revelation as she claims, "I did hear, see, tasted and handled" (Graham et al. 124) apocalyptic events. In the Bible these events mark the end of the world; in the *Short Relation*, they are the preamble to the women's being freed from incarceration. Joan Vokins's *God's Mighty Power Magnified* (1691) sets out the author's mission around the Caribbean, including her attendance at the separate meetings of African and European Friends in Barbados (221). Vokins's use of Bible echo and parallel provides an extended example of the way in which Quaker beliefs enabled women to live entirely unconventional lives.

Her Own Life also contains annotated extracts from works by women members of the other major nonconformist denomination of the day: Baptists. Where Quakers believed that an inner Light freed silent women (and men) to write and publish, it was the Baptist practice of requiring believers to examine their lives and tell their life stories that propelled many new writers into print. Any life experience could be seen as evidence of God's special favor or his wrath and could be presented as a sign of divine intention to save or damn the believer (Keeble; Graham). As a result, Sarah Davy is able to make sense of the misery of her early life and of the freedom she finds when "the Lord was pleased" to unite her heart with that of an unnamed woman (174–75). Hannah Allen, vividly reimagining the despair she experienced when convinced God would not choose to save her, tells a story of her repeated suicide attempts as she was passed from member to member of her puzzled family (200–09). Anne Wentworth argues that she has responded to God's call in separating from her "hard-hearted yoke fellow": she has left her violent husband because he tried to prevent her from publishing her account of how "he led me in a wilderness of affliction for eighteen years" (189). The introductions and notes in *Her Own Life* offer ways to understand the cultural resonances and scriptural parallels in these narratives. Recent feminist interest in the genre of autobiography can also be mobilized in the classroom to prevent discussion from degenerating into an assertion that these women are really writing about love or depression or an unhappy marriage and that the scriptural framework used in these texts is an optional extra that can be sloughed off. Engaging with Susannah Parr's *Apology against the Elders* (1659), which describes the establishment of a new Baptist congregation, can also provoke thought. Parr argues vehemently in favor of Saint Paul's injunction in 1 Corinthians, "Let your women keep silence in the churches" (14.34) and yet still maintains her right to act and write in defense of this conservative position. It is not possible to translate these women's activities and beliefs into the terms of modern feminism; to try to do so is, in a sense, to re-silence these women, because it assumes that our modern ways of understanding their priorities are more valid than their own.

The range of interpretation of these texts and the availability of the texts themselves are both growing rapidly, as more people realize that not only the existence of these women nonconformists but also their writings are worth engaging with. I have been teaching these materials to undergraduates since 1989, and the experience is always the same. At first the students are baffled, alarmed by the extent of their ignorance and by the disorienting unfamiliarity of the generic conventions of prophecies and conversion narratives. Quickly, though, the exploratoriness of the texts and the experimentalism of their language turn the reader's confusion into puzzlement, and from puzzlement into engagement. Teaching this material is fascinating.

Elaine Hobby

Naomi J. Miller

Writing Society

In early modern terms, the notion of women writing society is a paradox: if women were to be chaste, silent, and obedient, how could they also find voices to speak, let alone write, within and of and to the society that apparently so delimited their roles? The answer lies in the malleable boundaries of those social roles for women: mothers and daughters, wives and widows, educators and friends. "Therefore let no man blame a mother, though she something exceed in writing to her children," declares Dorothy Leigh in 1616, "since every man knows that the love of a mother to her children is hardly contained within the bounds of reason" (193). Explaining the significance of her task, Leigh adds: "[M]y mind will continue long after me in writing" (294).

The wide range of writings by early modern women that address social issues and experiences offers us the opportunity to identify interconnected realms of social existence and to consider how social boundaries, rigid in theory, may be flexible in practice. In this essay, I survey a spectrum of women's writings, grouped around issues associated with society at large and society at home. In both societies, women's voices range from intimate musings in letters and diaries to assertive and even polemical engagements, not only with skeptical male onlookers but also with a welcome audience of other women. Whether confronting politics, economics, religion, the arts, and social customs at large or charting a passage of life cycles at home, from birth, child rearing, education, and household management to death, women define roles for themselves that prove to shape the very society in which they live.

Women played significant and sometimes influential roles in early modern society at large, whether involved in court politics, in economic disputes, in religious dissent, in patronage and the arts, or in social behavior that modified accepted customs. Not surprisingly, the women who proved most notable (or notorious) in these areas were those whose positions, beliefs, or practices in some way challenged or diverged from dominant social prescriptions or expectations. In short, many of the women who emerged as influential forces in early modern society were those who spoke up and whose writings survive to document their struggles.

Lady Arbella Stuart stands out in the arena of English politics; her position as a marriageable female claimant to the throne during the reigns of both Queen Elizabeth and King James accorded her actions, and her writings, considerable significance within her society. Stuart's letters offer an in-depth consideration of the social and political dynamics of power, as voiced by a ranking female member of the royal family with only limited means of economic support during her lifetime. The letters (c. 1578–1611) chart her passage from a frustrated outsider to an observant participant at the court and ultimately to an assertive woman who married against the will of her male cousin, King James, and dared to attempt an escape to France. She died in the Tower of London in 1615 after several years of imprisonment, a figure of public interest and an object of public sympathy (Steen, Introduction).

Lady Anne Clifford is another example of a strong female figure who both participated in court politics and defied an edict of the king; her diary testifies to the long course of her political and economic trials, as well as to her indomitable will. From the earliest entries in her diary, where the thirteen-year-old Anne records her impressions of the funeral of Queen Elizabeth and the accession of King James (1603), to her description of negotiations with the king fourteen years later over her claims to disputed family lands, Clifford documents her refusal to yield any ground, literally, to threats or intimidation. Unawed by James's assertions of political authority, Clifford describes her strategic decision to proceed "to the Queen's side," where Anne of Denmark warns her "not to trust my matters absolutely to the King lest he should deceive me" (*Diary* 49). Even when all the male parties in the case, including Clifford's husband, agree to submit to the king's judgment, Clifford refuses, "at which the King grew in a great chaff" (50). If James's self-vaunted authority could be reduced by a collaboration between women to "a great chaff," Clifford's diary suggests the importance of reevaluating seventeenth-century notions of women's political and economic subjection in the light of what the women as well as the men of the time wrote.

Later in the seventeenth century, the autobiographies and memoirs of Margaret Cavendish, duchess of Newcastle (1656); Lucy Hutchinson (c. 1664–65); Mary Rich, countess of Warwick (c. 1666–67); Ann, Lady Fanshawe (1676); and Anne, Lady Halkett (1677–78) give voice to women's perspectives on both parliamentary and royalist politics during the course of the Civil War (see Beilin, this volume). Throughout the period, politics and economics converge in many accounts, whether by Stuart, who was deprived of both her Scottish and English estates by her royal relatives, or Clifford, who finally received her lands not by royal decree but by the death of her proprietary male relatives, or a woman named Margaret Beck, who published a tract in 1655 entitled *The Reward of Oppression, Tyranny, and Injustice, Committed by the Late Kings and Queens of England and Others; by the Unlawfull Entry, and Unlawfull Detainer of the Dutchie Hands of Lancaster; Declared in the Case of Samuel Beck, an Infant, by Margaret Beck* [. . .] *Mother and Guardian to the Infant.* Once again, a mother's words cannot be contained.

Early modern women spoke out in their writings against religious as well as economic and political oppression, an oppression suffered most often as a result of male decrees, whether issuing from the throne, the pulpit, or the marriage bed. Anne Askew chose to convert to the Protestant faith and seek a divorce from her Catholic husband at a time when Henry VIII was persecuting Reformers, and thus she was interrogated for heresy, imprisoned, tortured, and put to death by fire in 1546. Writing her right to religious choice, Askew records her response to the interrogations in her *Examinations* (published 1546–47), which provide a striking record of a woman's response to political as well as religious controversy in early modern England (Beilin, Introduction).

A century later, in 1643–49, one of the daughters of Elizabeth Cary wrote a biography of her author-mother entitled *The Lady Falkland: Her Life*, in which she details the consequences of her mother's public conversion to Catholicism: Cary's disinheritance by her father, separation from her husband, and subsequent penury. Following her conversion, Cary apparently endured her social and familial exile with stoic independence, persevering in plans to be reunited with her children. Ultimately, she arranged for her two youngest children to be conveyed secretly to her in France, and she lived to see all four of her daughters and two of her sons converted to Catholicism. Cary's daughter observes in her biography that what Cary underwent to keep her children with her, "both from and for them, may well give them cause to acknowledge she was their mother in faith as well as in nature" (227). As a mother and as a writer, Elizabeth Cary evidently passed on to her daughter both her religious faith and her confidence with words.

A number of early modern women, including Cary, were involved in writing society in relation to the arts, whether as authors of poems and plays, as patrons of other writers, or as both. Interestingly, these female-authored writings in the arts often prove to intersect with politics, economics, and religion as well, testifying to the deeply interconnected social experiences of women. Mary Sidney, countess of Pembroke, figured as both patron and author while serving as an author-mother figure to such women as her niece, Lady Mary Wroth (Hannay, "Your Vertuous and Learned Aunt" 20–23). In her own writings, both original poems and translations, the countess addressed religious and political concerns in literary terms, even as she stayed within approved "feminine" genres (17).

Among the upper classes, many women writers found themselves connected by blood and marriage. Sidney and Wroth, for example, were related by marriage and kinship ties to Clifford as well as to Stuart. The daughters of Stuart's cousin, Sir William Cavendish— Lady Jane Cavendish and Lady Elizabeth Brackley—became poets and playwrights, while their stepmother, Margaret Cavendish, published plays, orations, and memoirs.

Aemilia Lanyer, one of the first women in early modern England to claim a professional voice for herself as an author, by publishing *Salve Deus Rex Judaeorum* (1611), frames her writings with references to many other women, including patrons, acquaintances, and friends (Woods, Introduction). Anne Clifford and her mother, Margaret, countess of Cumberland, figure in Lanyer's poetry as one of the most prominent of the mother-daughter pairs whom Lanyer addresses. Whereas patronesses of male poets were cast predominantly as objects of heterosexual desire, Lanyer's patronesses emerge as maternal and filial subjects, whose bonds with one another provide the basis for the poet's celebration of female community. When Lanyer chooses to open *Salve Deus* with a dedicatory poem not to the king but rather to Anne of Denmark, in which she questions, "[W]hy are poore Women blam'd, / Or by more faultie Men so much defam'd?" (6; "To the Queenes Most Excellent Majestie," see lines 73–78), her bold appeal to the queen's judgment fashions a direct line of communication between women that excludes the king, rather akin to Clifford's description of her receipt of the queen's advice in political defiance of the king.

Even as Cary's *The Tragedy of Mariam* (1613) probes the effects of male tyranny on women's speech and social standing, exploring a range of strategies for response, so both the publication history and the text of Wroth's romance, *Urania*, offer a wealth of social and political commentary regarding women's positions in society at large. The publication of the first part of the romance in 1621 raised a furor at court, when some of King James's male courtiers objected to the work's apparently satirical references to their private lives, forcing Wroth to withdraw *Urania* from sale only six months after it appeared. The letters that document the controversy indicate that not only Wroth's satirical subtext but also her gender and her choice of an unfeminine genre rendered her authorship unacceptable. In fact, although the topical allusions to various court scandals that mark Wroth's narrative clearly antagonized some of the powerful men at court, it is quite likely that her writing was shaped by her marginalized political position and social standing rather than vice versa (Naomi Miller; Roberts, *First Part* cv–cvi, cxvi–viii).

One of the first Englishwomen to support herself by her writings, Aphra Behn published plays, novels, poems, and translations that dared to represent such matters as politics and sex more openly than many of the writings by women that had preceded her. Behn's visit to Surinam in the West Indies apparently inspired her account of a slave rebellion in *Oronooko* (1688), while her unreimbursed stint as a spy for Charles II in 1666 led ultimately to her imprisonment in a London debtor's prison. Debts forced Behn to begin to write for money (Goreau, *Reconstructing*). Although attacked violently by critics for her bold writings until her death, Behn maintained a witty and resolute voice in commenting on women's positions in society and in the arts. That voice emerges with particular clarity in the addresses to the reader that mark so many of her writings (*Sir Patient Fancy* [1686], *The Lucky Chance* [1686]).

In addition to the writings of noblewomen and gentlewomen examined variously above, other early modern women ventured to add their voices to the challenge of writing society at large. In the arena of social custom, for example, women's behavior was expected to be regulated by directives from male-authored sermons, conduct books, treatises, and a number of openly misogynist pamphlets. In an exchange of writings that has come to be known as the controversy about women, extending from roughly 1540 to 1640, women themselves entered the fray of the pamphlet wars. Writing directly in their own defense and publishing those defenses in significant numbers for the first time, women authored pamphlets aimed at a middle-class audience living in an increasingly urban and commercial world, where social boundaries were proving more fluid than fixed (Henderson and McManus 3–4).

One of the earliest and boldest defenses written under the name of a woman, Jane Anger's *Protection for Women* (1589), is addressed not to the men whose condemnations have necessitated a defense but directly to women. Mincing no words, the author declares, "I have set down unto you (which are of mine own Sex) the subtle dealings of untrue meaning men" (184). With the publication in 1615 of Joseph Swetnam's *The Araignment of Lewd, Idle, Froward, and Unconstant Women*, a major pamphlet war erupted, eliciting eloquent responses from Rachel Speght, Esther Sowernam, and Constantia Munda (Henderson and McManus 16–17; Lewalski, Introduction). Speght may well be the first Englishwoman to identify herself by her true name as a polemicist and critic of contemporary gender ideology (Lewalski xi).

Writing society at large, the female polemicists draw in bold strokes the issues confronting so many women in the early modern period, producing a picture that complements the letters, diaries, biographies, poems, plays, and prefaces of the other women writers discussed above.

––––––

Interestingly, it is women's representations of society at home, through life cycles extending from birth, child rearing, education, and household management to death, that most dramatically testify to women's power to shape their society at large. While most of the published writings concerning childbirth in the early modern period were authored by men, women's practical influence in the birthing room remained significant throughout the sixteenth and seventeenth centuries. Networks of so-called gossip that brought local women together in a web of relationships centered on such shared experiences as the ceremony of childbirth, experiences from which men, apart from male physicians, were of necessity excluded (A. Wilson 96–97). Whereas male-authored "gossips' meeting" texts satirized female homosocial bonds as subversive of masculine authority (Woodbridge 224, 231–32), the actual meetings of women, as recorded in their letters and diaries, seem to have provided a space for shared speech apart from patriarchal constraints.

The first female-authored gynecological manual of the period, *The Midwives Book* (1671), was written by Jane Sharp, "practitioner in the art of midwifery above thirty years." Writing against a tradition that included well-known texts by such men as Eucharias Roesslin (*The Byrth of Mankynde* [1540]), Jacques Guillemeau (*Child-birth; or, The Happy Deliverie of Women* [1612]), and Jacob Rueff (*The Expert Midwife* [1637]), Sharp addresses "the Midwives of England" as "sisters," a speaking position that none of her male forebears could claim (*Midwives Book; or, The Whole Art* 5). Moreover, in the introduction to her book, she engages head-on with those who think that "it is not proper for women to be of this profession, because they cannot attain so rarely to the knowledge of things as men may" (7). Responding that "the Objection is easily answered," Sharp observes that "the holy Scriptures hath recorded Midwives to the perpetual honour of the female Sex" and argues that the art of midwifery is the "natural propriety of women," given that "not so much as one word concerning Men-midwives [is] mentioned there" (7).

In letters shared among themselves, women acknowledge the realities of childbirth, as when Lucy, countess of Carlisle, writes to her sister Dorothy, countess of Leicester (Wroth's sister-in-law), "I should be glead to hear that you wayr not with child, that you might the better pase the year" (1640). It is just such "female" discourse—confronting the practical strains and dangers of the childbearing years—that the male-authored gossips'-meeting texts attempt unsuccessfully to mock and discourage.

Within the household, many early modern women's responsibilities centered upon childbearing and child rearing, leading to a proliferation of advice books, mostly by men, with some notable exceptions. In a 1622 treatise dedicated to her daughter-in-law as an exemplary mother, Elizabeth Clinton challenges the class-bound practice of aristocratic women placing their infants with wet nurses (*The Countesse of Lincolnes Nurserie*). In urging "that every woman ought to nurse her owne childe" (6), Clinton dares to contravene socially accepted conventions of class and gender, calling on woman to recognize their shared maternal bonds across class lines.

Other early modern women found voices originating with the mother's authority in the family as a social system (Klein; Pollock, *Lasting Relationship*; Rose, "Mothers"). Addressing mothers' advice books to their offspring, these women claim the rightful maternal privilege of authority over children. Women such as Elizabeth Grymeston in *Miscelanea, Meditations, Memoratives* (1604), Dorothy Leigh in *The Mother's Blessing* (1616), and Elizabeth Joscelin in *The Mothers Legacie to Her Vnborn Childe* (1622) stress the dignity and strength that they bring to that role, not simply what they garner from it. Instead of directly opposing the authority of men, as do the female polemicists, the mothers who author advice books present their writings as a complement to fatherly authority in the family (Crawford, "Construction"). At the same time, they consistently elevate the significance of maternity from a purely physical condition to a discourse of wisdom, able to authorize female authorship. The enormous popularity of the mothers' advice books, which had a sizable female audience, indicates that the power of maternal discourse was appreciated not only by children but, more significantly, also among women themselves.

Women often played an important role in the education of their children, particularly their daughters. Extant English records document the role played at court by mothers-in-law and royal stepmothers in an educational process that commenced with the accession of Henry Tudor and continued through the reign of his granddaughter Elizabeth. From Henry's mother, Margaret Beaufort, through Maud Parr, and then to her stepdaughter Katherine

Parr, who became queen in 1543, a tradition of humanist education of girls thrived in court circles (Patton).

In the next century, the learned young Rachel Speght, who had refuted Swetnam's attack on women in her *A Mouzell for Mela-stomus* (1617), published *Mortalities Memorandum with a Dreame Prefixed* (1621), in which she opposed restrictions on women's edu-cation, confessing her own desire "to covet Knowledge daily more and more" (57). Fifty years later, Margaret Cavendish urges women in her *Divers Orations* (1662) to increase their wit by conversing "in Schools, Colleges and Courts of Judicature" (K. Jones 62). Al-though Cavendish details the difficulty of her struggle to educate herself in *Philosophical and Physical Opinions* (1655, 1663), in her *CCXI Sociable Letters* (1664) she comments on writers as diverse as Ovid, Vergil, and Shakespeare (Fitzmaurice xvi–xvii). In 1673, Bath-sua Makin observes that "a learned woman is thought to be a Comet, that bodes Mischief, when ever it appears," but makes a compelling case for her argument that "were women thus educated [. . . they] would have Honour and Pleasure, their Relations Profit, and the whole Nation Advantage" (3). Makin's list of exemplary women educated in former times includes such figures as Lady Grace Mildmay, whose autobiography (c. 1617) urges the education of young children (Travitsky 83–84), as well as Sidney, Stuart, and Cavendish.

At the end of the century, Mary Astell published two parts of *A Serious Proposal to the Ladies for the Advancement of Their True and Greatest Interest* (1694, 1697), in which she argues the case for im-proving women's education by establishing a "seminary" where young women could devote themselves to learning in seclusion from the world. Although Astell's proposal for a women's college never came to pass, her ideas exerted significant influence on her society, and she was able, with the help of her female friends, to set up a charity school for girls in Chelsea that lasted until the end of the nineteenth century (Goreau, *Whole Duty* 242–43).

Even as women wrote advice books and polemical treatises about the importance of educating their children, they were often responsible for the financial management of estates or businesses during the frequent or prolonged absences of their husbands. In fact, women who used the household as a locus of social action were enabled to demonstrate a certain measure of authority and self-definition in the domestic sphere (Heal 179, 182–83), as can be seen in the diaries and letters of women from Anne Clifford and Lady Barbara Sidney (Mary Wroth's mother), to Margaret Cavendish and Lucy Hutchinson. The final stage of the life cycle, death, paradoxically proved enabling for many early modern women, whose voices could at times achieve their greatest power at the close of their lives. In the case of Joscelin, who wrote in anticipation of the birth of her first child, her *Mothers Legacie* was all that survived her death, which came nine days after her daughter's birth. Leigh, however, appropriated not so much the literal occasion of impending death as the promise that her mind would continue long after her in writing. Counseling not only her children but also other women, she supports the existence of bonds of friendship between men and women in marriage as well as bonds of fellowship among women (301–02).

Isabella Whitney's unusual "Wyll and Testament" (1573), addressed to the city of London, effectively conveys the social diversity of the city as well as the self-reliant voice of a middle-class woman who was also a professional poet (Travitsky 117–18). The actual legacies bestowed by early modern women favored daughters over sons in no uncertain terms. An examination of wills for both women and men indicates that more than twice as many women as men left land to one daughter; with more than one child mentioned in their wills, women were more likely to leave land to one daughter than to one son. Furthermore, not only did early modern women give more authority and power in the form of land to their daughters than did their husbands, but the women were also far more likely to choose daughters, or indeed other women, as executors of their wills than were men (Amussen 34, 38, 91–94). Maternal legacies, then, existed in both word and deed, serving as lasting testaments to women's voices and positions in society.

In the early modern period, women wrote society, both at home and at large, by writing their lives, in diaries and biographies, poems and plays, advice books and polemical pamphlets, letters and wills. The interconnected fabric of women's lives, in which social existence and life cycles were daily intertwined, yielded a wealth of writings, grounded in vision as well as fact, that exhibit even today the ability to reflect and shape society.

Part II

Selected Authors

Janel Mueller

Queen Elizabeth I

Held to no less exacting standards than those imposed on her brother Edward VI as crown prince, Elizabeth Tudor (1533–1603) proved the most eminent female recipient of an early Protestant humanist upbringing in England. Her tutor was Roger Ascham, a recognized master of Ciceronian latinity and an earnest advocate of an educational plan that aimed to make learning attractive and self-regulating to future bearers of public trust in England, so that they would acquire solid Christian morality, unswerving devotion to the Commonwealth, and a thorough grounding in the pragmatic and prudential lessons of classical history and political philosophy. In *The Schoolmaster* Ascham hails Elizabeth as his best, most committed scholar (56, 87). Queen Katherine Parr, Elizabeth's stepmother from her tenth to her fourteenth year, strengthened Ascham's educational objectives through the influence on both Elizabeth and Edward of her warm personal affection and intense biblical piety. What such a Protestant humanist formation could produce has been well characterized in broader cultural and rhetorical terms by Mary

Thomas Crane: the mental address, ready responsiveness, and public authority cultivated by steeping in pithy distillations of ethical insight and political wisdom (Crane). Again and again in her writings, Elizabeth is found assessing a situation, action, or emotion in terms of the Bible verse or the classical maxim or the proverbial saying that it exemplifies; if there is no such encapsulation at hand, she just as directly proceeds to fashion the new sententia that the present occasion requires. This Protestant humanist formation also presupposed the acquisition of several languages at levels of easy fluency in reading, writing, and speaking. Here, too, Elizabeth's accomplishments are exceptional. Her literary output attests her command of English, Latin, French, Italian, Greek, and Spanish as well as her compositional success in an array of genres: the letter, private and public prayers, religious meditations, public speaking—whether formal or extemporaneous—and stanzaic and nonstanzaic verse ranging from Latin epigrams and French sapphics to such native forms as ballad meter and song verses with refrain.

Yet Elizabeth's writings remain far less familiar and less studied than the writings to and about her by John Lyly, Edmund Spenser, Sir Philip Sidney, Sir Walter Ralegh, and others (see Teague, "Elizabeth I" and "Queen Elizabeth"). Maria Perry's admirable attempt to write a biography of Elizabeth in her own words succeeds up to the 1570s, but thereafter Perry conflates Elizabeth's materials drastically and relies more heavily on contemporaries' reports of the queen's words and actions. A search for the earliest authoritative sources for Elizabeth's writings discloses quite clearly an inverse correlation between the genres Elizabeth most frequently practiced and circulated in her time and the genres for which she has gained notice in recent years (mainly from her three poems included in the *Norton Anthology of Literature by Women* [Gilbert and Gubar]). In fact, across the span of her life Elizabeth was most productive as a letter writer, next as a composer of religious meditations and prayers, next as a public speaker, and least productive as a writer of verse.

Elizabeth I: Collected Works collects her writing in four genres— speeches, letters, verses, and prayers—and groups them in four phases of approximately fifteen years each: 1544–58 (the years as

Princess Elizabeth, from her earliest extant letter to her accession to the throne), 1558–72 (from her accession to the throne to the capital treason trial of the duke of Norfolk, the first manifestly threatening intrigue involving Mary, Queen of Scots, who had taken political asylum in England in 1568), 1573–88 (years of Elizabeth's consolidation as the ranking Protestant monarch of Europe—but also of challenge and jeopardy from military actions in the Netherlands and Ireland; from the long negotiated but never consummated match with "Monsieur"—François, duc d'Alençon and then d'Anjou; from the intrigues of Mary, Queen of Scots, leading to her trial and execution in 1586–87; and from the sailing of the Spanish Armada against England), and the final period, 1588–1603 (containing much of the best of the correspondence between Elizabeth and James VI of Scotland, her successor, as well as the Cadiz and Azores expeditions; the deaths of many of Elizabeth's longtime intimates— the earl of Leicester, Sir Christopher Hatton, Lord Burghley; the Essex debacle; and the lofty retrospectives on her style and art of governance offered by her "Golden Speech" and "Last Speech").

Because Elizabeth was most prolific as a letter writer, the sheer magnitude of the collection of these primary materials presents a problem. Another problem arises because this genre encompasses not only original compositions by her, whether formal or informal, but also a huge repertoire of formulas for letter writing that enabled the official transaction of business in the sixteenth century. Concentrating on the personal or at least the firsthand (written or dictated) letters by Elizabeth, G. B. Harrison's edition collects 180 letters across the range of her active life (*Letters of Queen Elizabeth I*). But the full count of her extant letters, ones known to be signed and sent, must total at least a thousand. Elizabeth's earliest extant letter is in Italian, written in her own hand at the age of eleven (31 July 1544), to Queen Katherine Parr. Her latest is a letter in English (23 Feb. 1603), dispatched a month before her death, bearing her "sign manual"—her formal "Elizabeth R" signature—and giving Charles Blount, Lord Mountjoy, conditions for the surrender of Hugh O'Neill, earl of Tyrone, the leader of the Irish rebels. Because the letters of a reigning queen include many formulaic documents (e.g.,

land grants, military commissions, clerical and administrative ap-
pointments, safe-conduct for ambassadors and merchants), the ones
with the surest authorial pedigree are those written in Elizabeth's always distinctive italic hand. Yet even here there is an exception to
note: while her youthful Latin letters to Edward VI are in her italic,
they nonetheless read like joint exercises in classical prose composition and courtly compliment that her tutor, Ascham, may have set
her, since personal expression is kept to a minimum and elaborately
screened. Fortunately, other letters in the hand of the adolescent
and adult Elizabeth from every decade of her activity as a writer
offer rich resources for literary study. These letters reveal her self-
possession, her sharp intelligence, her capacity to declare her mind
even where she must practice courtesy, forbearance, or deference.
Notable instances of her autograph correspondence are the teen-
aged princess's letters to Edward Seymour, lord protector, on her
rumored relation with Thomas Seymour and to her sister Mary I,
again when suspected of disloyalty and conspiracy during Mary's
reign; the adult queen's sendings to François Hercule de Valois, her
last suitor, whom she addresses in her most intimate language, and
to James VI of Scotland, her successor on the English throne, whom
she upbraids sharply and instructs patiently in statecraft. Any and all
of these named sequences of letters—the best is the long running
exchange between Elizabeth and James (see *Letters of Queen Elizabeth and James VI*)—yield plentiful evidence of Elizabeth's play of
mind and sensibility, notably cast as first-person utterance. The richness of tactical interest and gender relations makes this material well-
suited to the classroom.

The edition of George P. Rice, Jr., prints seventeen speeches as
Elizabeth's compositions but often regrettably uses inferior—late,
second- and thirdhand—sources for a number of these (*Public Speaking*). *Elizabeth I: Collected Works* increases the total of Elizabeth's
speeches to twenty-two; it also presents variant versions of several
speeches that result from Elizabeth's revisions after delivering a speech
in one form or from the variable memories of earwitnesses—members of Parliament who kept journals for their constituents—who recall content and wording quite closely but may put sequencing of

material in a different order. This volume offers as well selected addresses made to Elizabeth by the speakers of the Houses of Commons and Lords so that it is evident at key points what her speeches are responding to. Such considerations—Elizabeth's revisions, variability among reporters of a speech, tracing of the dialogic interplay between parliamentary address and queen's response—command high student interest and can yield probing classroom discussion. Especially important speeches from these perspectives are those of the Parliaments of 1558–59, 1563, 1586, and 1601.

Prayers composed by Elizabeth (Clay 666–67; Brooke; Fox) total at least thirty-eight, including prayers and meditations destined for her own use in languages other than English. See *Elizabeth I: Autograph Compositions and Foreign Language Originals* for transcriptions of the original language texts and English translations of Elizabeth's contributions to *Precationes Privatae Regiae E. R. 1563* (*STC 7576.7*) and to *Christian Prayers and Meditations in English, French, Italian, Spanish, Greeke, and Latine* (*STC 6428*), an anonymously edited volume published by Richard Daye in 1569 that contains Elizabeth's only known compositions in Spanish; three short prayers; and a prayer in French, in rhymed pentameter couplets, that reflects on her sharply antithetical early life and praises God for bringing her from the Tower to the crown. Although Elizabeth never states her reasons for composing many of her religious writings in languages other than English, it is important to note that she had closely associated spiritual exercise and linguistic exercise ever since her girlhood, when as an eleven-year-old she made an English translation of Marguerite de Navarre's *Miroir de l'âme pécheresse* for Queen Katherine Parr (see M. Shell) and as a twelve-year-old presented her father, Henry VIII, with a translation of Queen Katherine's *Prayers or Meditations* into Latin, French, and Italian. When Elizabeth herself became queen, attended in every private moment by her ladies of the bedchamber, there would have been fully adult, prudential reasons why she would admit only in Latin that God had severely tried her and the people of England with her nearly fatal smallpox in October 1562 (as she writes in her "Gratiarum actio pro sanitate recuperata" in *Precationes Privatae*) or why she would use

French to accuse herself of her many and black sins ("mes pechez noirs et sanglants"), as she does in her miniature girdle prayer book in her own hand dating from 1579 to 1582 (*Book of Devotions* 24).

The following poems were composed by Elizabeth, including two in French on religious subjects ("French Verses") and two Latin epigrams. Leicester Bradner's edition credits her with six items of "undoubted authorship" (*Poems* 3–5): "Written with a Diamond on Her Window at Woodstock" ("Much suspected by me"; c. 1553), "Written on a Wall at Woodstock" ("Oh fortune, thy wresting wavering state"; c. 1553), "Written in Her French Psalter" ("No crooked leg"; 1560s–70s), "The Doubt of Future Foes" (1572), "On Fortune" ("Never think you"; before 1589), and "On Monsieur's Departure" ("I grieve and dare not show my discontent"; c. 1582). *Elizabeth I: Collected Works* denies the authenticity of "On Fortune" but enlarges Elizabeth's poetic corpus with "Hoc est corpus meum"—" 'Twas Christ the Word" (1550s); "Priere" ("O gouverneur de la machine ronde") in *Christian Prayers* (1569); "Genus infoelix vitae"—"A hapless kind of life is this I wear," answered by Sir Thomas Heneage (c. 1572); "Reginae Responsum" to Paul Melissus ("Grata Camena tua est"; c. 1577); "When I was fair and young" (1580s); "Now leave and let me rest" (1580s); "Ah, silly Pug, wert thou so sore afraid?" (reply to Sir Walter Ralegh, c. 1587); "When Greeks do measure months by the moon" (reply to Philip II of Spain, spring 1588); "Look and bow down Thine ear, O Lord" (poem on the Armada victory, Dec. 1588); "Avecq l'aveugler si estrange" (c. 1590). Teaching Elizabeth I as a poet will constructively emphasize the occasional and circumstantial character of all her writing in verse and will trace prominent features of diction, imagery, and verse craft to the pithy, sententious formulations so valued in her Protestant humanist education. These forms seem to have served Elizabeth as a preemptive defense of her poetry against the possible objection that she had too much of importance to do to trifle with writing verse.

Elizabeth's reputation as a writer has not been in any way commensurate with her renown as Good Queen Bess, the astute sovereign of England's glory days. Although George Puttenham notably and puzzlingly praises "the Queen our soveraigne Lady, whose learned, delicate, noble Muse, easily surmounteth all the rest that have written before her time or since, for sence, sweetnesse and subtillitie, be it in Ode, Elegie, Epigram, or any other kind of poem Heroick or Lyricke, wherein it shall please her Majestie to employ her penne" (63), her known literary output is sparsest in the category of verse. In her own day, Elizabeth was almost exclusively published as a religious writer, beginning with her girlish translation of Marguerite de Navarre's *Miroir*, edited by John Bale (in Wesel?) as *A Godly Medytacyon of the Christen Sowle* (1548), and continuing with her contributions to *Precationes Privatae Regiae E. R. 1563*, to *Christian Prayers and Meditations* (1569), to the first volume of Thomas Bentley's *The Monument of Matrones* (1582), and to Thomas Sorocold's *Supplications of Saints. A Booke of prayers: [. . .] Wherein Are Three Most Excellent Prayers Made by Queene Elizabeth* (1612), a third edition but the first recorded (as *STC* 22952). Among her secular compositions only her epigram to Paul Melissus was printed in *P. Melissi Mele sive Odae [. . .] Epigrammata* (1580), and her "Golden Speech" of 30 November 1601, as transcribed by A. B., saw print under the title *Her Majesties Most Princelie Answere, Delivered by Her Selfe [. . .] on the Last Day of November 1601* (*STC* 7578). Some of her shorter remarks on public occasions were put into print by Richard Mulcaster in *The Quene's Majesties Passage through the Citie of London to Westminster the Daye before Her Coronacion* (1559; *STC* 18253) and by Raphael Holinshed in *The Third Volume of Chronicles [. . .] Now Newlie Recognised, Augmented, and Continued [. . .] to the Year 1586* (1586–87; *STC* 13569).

As recorded in *Nugae Antiquae*, the memoirs of her godson, Sir John Harington, Elizabeth's personal favorite among her parliamentary speeches was that of 15 March 1576; she sent a copy to him with the note: "Boy Jack, I have made a clerk write fair my poor words for thine use, as it cannot be such striplings have entrance into parliament assembly as yet. Ponder them in thy hours of leisure, and play with them till they enter thine understanding; so shalt thou hereafter, perchance, find some good fruits hereof when thy God-mother is out of remembrance" (1: 127–28). In the seventeenth century Elizabeth was kept in some remembrance as a public speaker and a historical subject by such authors as William Camden, in *Annales rerum Anglicarum et Hibernicarum regnante Elizabetha ad annum MDLXXXIX* (1615; the English translation, *The History of the Most Renowned and Victorious Princess Elizabeth*, was done from the 1625 French translation); Sir John Hayward, who left an unfinished manuscript that has been published as *Annals of the First Four Years of the Reign of Queen Elizabeth*; and Sir Simonds d'Ewes, in *The Journals of All the Parliaments during the Reign of Queen Elizabeth*, revised and published by Paul Bowes (1682). Antiquarians of the next century republished some of her letters—notably, Thomas Hearne in his *Sylloge Epistolarum a variis Angliae Principibus scriptarum* appended to *T. Livii Foro-juliensis Vita Henrici Quinti* (1716) and Francis Peck in *Desiderata Curiosa* (1732, rev. ed. 1779)—but the most magisterial compilation in this vein was the set of three outsize folio volumes published at his own cost by John Nichols as *Progresses and Public Processions of Queen Elizabeth* (1788–1805). The earlier twentieth century would savor Elizabeth as a mistress of wit, sententious or merry, in Frederick Chamberlin's *Sayings of Queen Elizabeth* (1923). Later twentieth-century editions of her letters, speeches, and poems have already been indicated here. Queen Elizabeth I has yet to receive her full due as a writer of consummate versatility, intellect, subtlety, and erudition.

Susan M. Felch

Anne Vaughan Lock

In 1560, early during the reign of Elizabeth I, a slender octavo volume appeared in London. It was issued by the Protestant printer John Day and offered as a New Year's gift to a well-connected woman of the court, Catherine Brandon Bertie, the dowager duchess of Suffolk. This "litle boke," as it was called, was composed of four sermons by John Calvin translated from French, framed by a dedicatory epistle and twenty-six sonnets. All three parts—epistle, sermons, and sonnets—were unified by a common religious theme: the recognition of sin, repentance, and restoration through God's grace.

Such a book might now be overlooked except for two facts: the twenty-six sonnets constitute the earliest sonnet sequence written in English, and the author, Anne Vaughan Lock, was one of the earliest Tudor women writers. These two facts alone compel consideration, but the quality of Lock's writing encourages closer study. In addition, Lock's life and writings offer students an unparalleled glimpse not only into the development of the sonnet genre but also into English life in the sixteenth century as experienced by a Protestant, merchant-class woman. Her life traces a trajectory from the first days of the English Reformation under Henry VIII through the reestablishment of the Church of England after Mary Tudor's death to the strained relationships between nonconformists and established Protestants in the later years of Elizabeth's reign. Lock's major writings, both the 1560 volume of Calvin sermons and a second book published in 1590, mark out her concern with issues of national importance, particularly the continued reformation of English religious life. If nothing else, Lock complicates the notion often held by students that women in the sixteenth century were inevitably confined to a private, domestic sphere.

In 1560, when her first book was printed, Anne Vaughan Lock (c. 1534–c. 1590) was already conversant with the London world of court, commerce, and religious conflict. Her father, Stephen Vaughan, was a cloth merchant with interests in London and Antwerp who served Henry VIII as a diplomat on the Continent. Her mother, Margery Gwynnethe, worked as a silkwoman for at least two of the Tudor queens, Anne Boleyn and Katherine Parr. Furthermore, her childhood home was permeated with the "new religion" of Protestantism: Stephen Vaughan wrote letters supporting the reformer William Tyndale, who was later burned for heresy; both Boleyn and Parr, for whom Gwynnethe supplied clothes, encouraged a circle of reformers at court; Lock's tutor, Stephen Cob, was called before the Privy Council, the Court of Aldermen, and the bishop of London's chancellor to answer charges of heresy; Lock's stepmother, Margaret Brinkelow, was the widow of a radical Protestant pamphleteer and a close family friend.

Lock married the scion of another London merchant family, Henry Lock, while still in her teens and carried her family's priorities into her new household. In 1553, she hosted John Knox, the Scottish reformer, during his service as a Lenten preacher for Edward VI. When the young king died in July that year, his sister, Mary Tudor, returned England to Roman Catholicism, and Knox's popularity plummeted. Despite his change of status, the Locks extended their hospitality to Knox until he fled to the Continent, where he began an extensive correspondence with Lock that lasted over six years. Although none of Lock's letters to Knox have survived, fourteen of his letters to her are known, and from this one-sided conversation, and a few other documents, we can reconstruct Lock's life during this period. The growing persecution of Protestants by the Marian regime motivated Lock to join Knox and his family in Geneva in 1557. She was accompanied by her two young children, Henry and Anne, and a maid, though not by her husband, who may have remained in London rather than traveled to the Continent, perhaps to care for the family's extensive business interests. Despite the death of her daughter only four days after arriving in Geneva, Lock remained on the Continent for two years, returning to England in June 1559 after the accession of Elizabeth.

Lock's childhood and early adult life had already been strongly marked by Protestant beliefs, but her exile seems to have further radicalized her religious stance. On returning to London, she promptly published her first book, *Sermons of John Calvin, upon the Songe That Ezechias Made after He Had Bene Sicke, and Afflicted by the Hand of God, Conteyned in the Thirty-Eighth Chapter of Esay* (1560), assisted Knox in his efforts to bring the Reformation to Scotland, and became involved with the prominent Cooke sisters. Each of these three activities invites closer examination and provides students an opportunity to see the sixteenth century from the perspective of a merchant-class woman.

Sermons of John Calvin demonstrates both Lock's religious commitments and her wide range of learning. Students are usually surprised to discover how well educated a mid-sixteenth-century woman could be. Lock knew enough medicine to employ precise technical terms in the dedicatory epistle; enough rhetoric to structure that epistle around traditional figures and tropes; enough theology to use the old image of God's word as good medicine in a new way, by roundly criticizing the ineffective drafts of the Roman Catholic Church and promoting the new Reformation cures of faith alone (*sola fide*) and grace alone (*sola gratia*); enough French to translate Calvin's sermons gracefully and clearly; enough Latin to translate a prose version of Psalm 51 directly from the Vulgate;

enough creativity to pen the first sonnet sequence in English based on that same psalm; and enough political acumen—and courage—to urge the newly installed Elizabethan court toward Protestant piety by presenting the book as a New Year's present to the duchess of Suffolk, a woman of impeccable reputation and high visibility and herself a returned Marian exile.

That political acumen was undoubtedly visible to her friend Knox. On 18 November 1559, he wrote two urgent letters appealing for help in his rebellion against Mary Stuart. The first was to William Cecil, chief secretary of state and one of Elizabeth's most trusted counselors; the other was to Lock. Both letters bore the same message: Send money now. As students learn that Knox thought of Lock within the same frame as Cecil, they begin to understand the extent of her influence in London. I point out to them, however, that while Lock was perhaps exceptional, she was not unique; nor was Knox the only Scotsman to appeal to an English-woman. During this same time, William Maitland, Robert Melville, and James Hamilton, the earl of Arran, wrote repeatedly to Mildred Cooke Cecil, William Cecil's wife, asking her to support the Protestant Reformation in Scotland. Judging from their effusive expressions of thanks, she must have been successful in her efforts on their behalf. Certainly the Treaty of Edinburgh, signed on 6 July 1560 and negotiated chiefly by her husband and Maitland, was an important step in establishing Protestantism as the national religion of Scotland. The roles played by Mildred Cecil, and possibly by Lock, were informal but nevertheless politically potent.

This episode, which occurred when Lock was only twenty-five years old, provides students with an example of the interlocking circles of politics, religion, and friendship in early modern England. In fact, they begin to joke that Lock is only three degrees removed from anyone of importance in sixteenth-century London. Lock probably did know Mildred Cooke Cecil personally: her son, Henry, who later followed in his mother's footsteps as a poet, was educated at the Cecil home along with Peregrine Bertie, son of the duchess of Suffolk. Mildred and her three surviving sisters, daughters of Sir Anthony Cooke, a governor to Edward VI, were themselves prominent women, writers, and active supporters of the Protestant cause. Anne Cooke, wife of Sir Nicholas Bacon, lord keeper of the great seal, and the mother of Sir Francis Bacon, had her works printed by John Day, who also printed Lock's 1560 volume. Elizabeth Cooke Russell was sister-in-law to Anne Russell Dudley, the countess of Warwick, to whom Lock dedicated her second book in 1590. Lock and her second husband, the Puritan preacher Edward Dering, were good friends with Katherine Cooke Killigrew. Such associations suggest the extent of Lock's political and religious connections.

The patterns established by Lock during her twenties remained throughout her life. She continued to write poetry and translate religious tracts: one of her Latin poems is preserved in a 1572 manuscript dedicated to Robert Dudley, earl of Leicester (Cambridge Univ. Lib. MS Ii.5.37). In 1590, married to her third husband, Richard Prowse, and living in Exeter, she published her second book, *Of the Markes of the Children of God, and of Their Comforts in Afflictions*. It is a translation of Jean Taffin's treatise on suffering, prefaced by a dedicatory letter to the countess of Warwick and followed by an original poem on the benefits of affliction. Lock had retained her high profile among the nonconformist Protestants, who by this time were struggling for their existence against the established church (M. White, "Renaissance Englishwomen"). John Field, a Puritan printer, in his 1583 preface to Knox's sermon on Matthew 4 described Lock as "vertuous" and "very godly" and complimented her on being "no young scholler" in the school of Christ (Knox, *Exposition* A2r, A3r). Significantly, her 1590 volume is listed four times in Andrew Maunsell's 1595 catalog of English printed books: under its title, topic, French author, and English translator. The separate listing for "Prowse" suggests that Anne Lock's name carried weight with her contemporaries, acting as a kind of imprimatur for the translation.

Had Lock never written a single line, her life would still be of interest to students, for it is composed of the very stuff of romance—court intrigue, exile, tragedy, and friendships. Students are fascinated by the eleven-year-old Lock watching her tutor hauled before the bishop of London only ten months before Anne Askew, a member of Parr's Protestant circle and possibly an acquaintance of Lock's mother, was burned at the stake for holding similar views. They are moved by the twenty-three-year-old Lock's flight to Geneva and the sudden death of her infant daughter. They are intrigued by her relationship to Knox, by her friendship with the Cooke sisters, by her status as a merchant-class woman who dedicated her books to prominent female patrons and maintained close connections with the court.

But students are also captivated by the power of her writing, at the center of which stands her sonnet sequence composed of twenty-one sonnets that paraphrase Psalm 51 and five prefatory sonnets. The prefatory sonnets present a minidrama: a cringing narrator, oppressed by a nearly overwhelming sense of sin, is prosecuted by a personified Despair before a wrathful, but ultimately gracious, sovereign God. The psalm sonnets that follow replicate the cry of this penitent sinner as found in the biblical text. Students quickly note familiar Petrarchan conventions—the sighing narrator, the bitter roller coaster of emotion, images of sight and blindness—but the sonnets display a much broader range of genre experimentation. There are echoes of Thomas Wyatt's *Penitential Psalms*, which are not sonnets, in the general contour of the five prefatory psalms that establish the speaker's identity as well as in specific verbal echoes in the psalm sonnets. Hovering on the perimeter are all the earlier—and later—metrical versions of the Psalms, including those of Mary Sidney, countess of Pembroke (see Hannay, this volume). Lock's sonnets also incorporate a genre unfamiliar to students, that of paraphrase. Lock says her sonnet sequence is written "in manner of a *Paraphrase*," and this term had achieved some generic stability by 1560 (*Collected Works* 62). In England, it had come to mean a species of commentary particularly suited to the Protestant church. Under Parr's leadership, Erasmus's New Testament paraphrases had not only been translated into English but also turned into official church documents: every parish church was required to own a copy. Lock stretches the genre boundaries of both sonnet and paraphrase when she combines the two in her sonnet sequence. She provides a theological commentary on a penitential psalm, drawing out its national as well as personal consequences, but coats that commentary in the sweet rhetoric of poetry. It is possible to see in this audacious move the anticipation of Philip Sidney's praise of the poet as one who "giveth so sweet a prospect into the way, as will entice any man to enter into it. [. . . For h]e beginneth not with obscure definitions, which must blur the margin with interpretations, and load the memory with doubtfulness; but he cometh to you with words set in delightful proportion" (*Defence of Poetry* 92).

It is precisely these "words set in delightful proportion" to which students respond, particularly the immediacy of Lock's sensual imagery. The tears of the sinner are "distilled byrne / Sent from the fornace of a grefefull brest," while the narrator cries out, "My cruell conscience with sharpned knife / Doth splat my ripped hert" (*Collected Works* 62 [prefatory sonnet 1], 65 [psalm sonnet 5]). Such vivid imagery is also displayed in Lock's prose, particularly the well-crafted epistle to the duchess of Suffolk, which deserves as much attention as the sonnets. There students are made to feel the pain in Hezekiah's body "nowe fresing, now fryeng," to see his "gastly eyen, starynge wyth horrour" and his "white and blodles hand" reaching up toward heaven, and even to hear his gasping "unperfect soundes" (7–8). The rhetorical skill of the English writings is mirrored in the Latin poem that offers an encomium to an Italian author, Bartholo Sylva, and then puns on his name, comparing the reading of his book to a walk in a sylvan landscape (73).

As important as Anne Lock is in her own right—as reformer, poet, and translator—she is also significant for her connections with earlier and later women writers. She may have been influenced by *The Examinations of Anne Askew* as well as by Askew's metrical paraphrase of Psalm 54. Echoes of Lock's work may certainly be heard in Pembroke's and Amelia Lanyer's religious poems (Hannay, "Unlock"; Woods, "Lock"). For Lanyer, we know of a personal connection: Lock's brother, Stephen Vaughan, was a close friend of Lanyer's family and the primary overseer of her father's will (Woods, "Lock" 172–73).

Lock's writings are eminently teachable. Her poems are well suited to any course, from introductory surveys to upper-level seminars, that deals with the sonnet genre or devotional lyrics. Their vivid imagery draws on earlier religious writings and foreshadows the metaphysical poetry of the seventeenth century. Lock's literary experiments, such as combining traditional rhetorical tropes with contemporary medical and religious terms or interweaving the sonnet and paraphrase genres, help students become aware of the fluidity and flexibility of mid-sixteenth-century writing. Too often, students are exposed only briefly to Tudor literature before the 1580s and tend to read the earlier works from the perspective of the later, more settled genres. Similarly, Lock's prose and poetry together allow students to explore the rapidly expanding repertoire of the English language. Budding linguists, for instance, can track her introduction of new words into the language (e.g., *niggardly, soul-slayers, tasteless, vapoury*) and her inventive deployment of participial constructions long before they were commonly used in literary texts, while stylists can analyze her elegantly designed sentences. Perhaps most important, Lock enables students to encounter an early Elizabethan writer on her own terms as a woman who throughout her life carefully crafted her words "into an Englishe box" (*Collected Works* 5).

Margaret P. Hannay

Mary Sidney,
Countess of Pembroke

Mary Sidney, countess of Pembroke (1561–1621), was the first nonroyal Englishwoman celebrated as both a patron and a writer of belles lettres. Praised by her contemporaries not only for her feminine accomplishments in music and needlework but also for her virtue, learning, and poetic achievement, Pembroke effectively counters many of the stereotypes of early modern women held by our students. Her privileged position and her astute manipulation of gender restrictions allowed her to write, to circulate, and to print her works without apology for her gender. Queen Elizabeth was perhaps the only woman who outranked her, for Mary Sidney was the granddaughter of the duke of Northumberland; niece of Lady Jane Grey and of Elizabeth's favorite, Robert Dudley, earl of Leicester; and daughter of King Edward's friend Henry Sidney and of Mary Dudley Sidney, who nursed Elizabeth through smallpox. Henry Sidney's comparative poverty and lack of formal rank hindered the advancement of his sons, but when Leicester arranged young Mary's marriage to Henry Herbert, earl of Pembroke, her husband gave her, at age fifteen, the title and the enormous wealth that eluded Philip. Their younger brother, Robert, long in Philip's shadow, eventually did become earl of Leicester.

Pembroke's first recorded literary activities begin shortly after the death of Philip in 1586. She seems to have begun writing as an outlet for grief; the pretense that elegy was a spontaneous and artless cry made the form "accessible to writers of all ages and abilities," a safe space to practice "the components of art and the disciplines of the craft," as Dennis Kay notes (6). "The Dolefull Lay of Clorinda" appears to be her earliest extant work; it is an elegy for Sidney, who died from wounds received in the Netherlands, where English forces commanded by Leicester sought to aid the Dutch in throwing off Spanish occupation. Called a Protestant martyr, Sir Philip was honored with an extravagant funeral, with volumes of elegies published by Oxford, Cambridge, and the Dutch university of Leiden and with a stream of popular ballads and eyewitness accounts of his death. As a woman, Pembroke could not participate in the public grief, but she wrote an elegy in those "sadd tymes" and gave the only copy to Philip's friend Sir Edward Wotton; in 1594 she wrote asking for the poem back (*Collected Works* 1: 286; "Correspondence 3"). Most likely this elegy was "The Dolefull Lay," included in the *Astrophel* volume of elegies published the following year (Hannay, *Philip's Phoenix* 63–67; M. Sidney, *Collected Works* 1: 119–32). The extent of public mourning for Sidney can hardly be overstated. Depicting him as the equal of Hector and Priam, declaring that he died for his God and for his country, poets proclaimed their love and zeal, implying (in the Protestant code) that honoring Sidney was honoring God. Like "The Dolefull Lay," these elegies frequently end with Sidney's apotheosis; he dwells "in everlasting bliss" while those on earth mourn his absence (line 85). "To the Angell Spirit of the Most Excellent Sir Philip Sidney," her later poem dedicating the *Psalmes* to Sidney's memory, employs another conventional ending, the wish that the speaker could join him in heaven (*Collected Works* 1: 112).

Certainly she was devastated by Philip's death, particularly coming within two years of the rapid deaths of her daughter, father, and mother. Her three-year-old daughter Katherine had died, in 1584, on the same day her son Philip was born; perhaps the trauma of that death had brought on labor. It is no wonder that several of her literary works focus on "the art of dying" (Lamb, "Countess of Pembroke"). Her personal tragedies were overshadowed by national crisis; as she mourned family deaths, England was preparing defenses against the impending Spanish invasion. Her husband was responsible for setting up the defenses of Welsh ports, where the attack was expected, and her brother Robert was with the queen at Tilbury, where Elizabeth gave her famous "Armada Speech." At Wilton she received regular reports from Robert on the progress of the Armada, with instructions to prepare the household to flee to Wales if the Spanish came ashore. She was thus responsible for the safety of her adolescent brother, Thomas; Robert's wife, Barbara Gamage; Robert and Barbara's little daughter, affectionately called Mall (Mary Sidney, later Wroth); and her own three young children: William, who later became third earl of Pembroke and Lady Wroth's lover; Anne, who died in her early twenties; and Philip, who was created earl of Montgomery by King James and eventually became fourth earl of Pembroke.

Pembroke returned to London in a magnificent procession, after two years of mourning at their Wiltshire country estates. Claiming the role of "the sister of Sir Philip Sidney" (*Collected Works* 1: 294–95; "Correspondence 12"), she began to assert herself as his true literary heir, serving as a patron to poets who honored him, supervising the printing of his works, translating a work by his Huguenot friend Philippe de Mornay, and completing the metrical paraphrases of the Psalms that he had begun. She both helped shape the Sidney legend and was shaped by it. As William Ringler says, "there is something unbelievable" about Sidney, who was described by his contemporaries and successors as "an image of almost impossible perfection" (3). Because he never achieved his full promise, he was celebrated more for what he was than for what he did. The myth of Sidney as religious martyr and national hero preceded Pembroke's voice or patronage; she added a literary dimension to the legend, even in "The Dolefull Lay of Clorinda," which celebrates

him as a merry maker of poetry. "Angell Spirit" presents him primarily as a writer, which is a way that she can stand on the same
ground, as it were, despite her gender. That is, she cannot be a military hero, statesman, or model courtier, but she can be a poet.

Pembroke's first works to appear in print were two translations
from French, Philippe de Mornay's Christian stoic meditation, *A
Discourse of Life and Death*, and Robert Garnier's drama on Antony
and Cleopatra, *Antonius*; the works were published together in
1592 by William Ponsonby, who became the quasi-official publisher
of works by Sidney and his circle (Brennan 55–58). Garnier's *Marc
Antoine* was one of the first Continental dramas to use Roman history to comment on contemporary politics; Pembroke's translation
directly influenced Shakespeare, who adapted some of her phrasing
and elements of her characterization in his *Antony and Cleopatra*
(Spevack, Steppat, and Munkelt 475–78). Samuel Daniel wrote his
Cleopatra as a companion to her work. Others who followed her example in writing historical closet drama are Thomas Kyd, Samuel
Brandon, Sir Fulke Greville, William Alexander (later earl of Stir-
ling), and Elizabeth Cary (see Weller, this volume; May 167). One
other work was printed during her lifetime: "A Dialogue between
Two Shepherds, *Thenot* and *Piers*, in Praise of *Astrea*," a poem she
had written to honor Elizabeth, probably for presentation at the
queen's planned visit to Wilton in 1599 (Erler 41–43). It appeared
in Francis Davison's *A Poetical Rhapsody* (1602). Four works remained in manuscript: her translation of Petrarch's "Triumph of
Death," the Sidneian *Psalmes*, and her two original, dedicatory
poems in the *Psalmes*.

She frequently had her young niece Mary with her during this
period, while she was also supervising the publication of the 1593
edition of *The Countess of Pembroke's Arcadia*, the prose romance
Sidney had dedicated to her, and then the 1598 edition, which
served as his collected works. Mary Wroth was thus the first English
woman writer known to have grown up with a female role model
(Hannay, "Your Vertuous and Learned Aunt"). The love and respect
Wroth felt for her aunt is evident in her *Urania* (1621), where Pembroke is portrayed through several characters, notably the queen of

Naples, who is "as perfect in Poetry, and all other Princely vertues as any woman that ever liv'd" (*First Part* 371).

Pembroke actively participated in the printing of other works by her brother Philip and herself, but she carefully restricted to manuscript circulation the *Psalmes* that her brother had begun (he paraphrased Psalms 1–43; she paraphrased the rest of the 150, including the 22 poems of Psalm 119). She may have believed that these complex poems could be fully appreciated only by the sophisticated readers of a literary coterie (see also Wall, this volume). Her paraphrases of the Psalms are remarkable both for their scholarship and their metric variety. Using Genevan translations and commentaries as her primary resource—the Geneva Bible (1560); the Psalms translations and commentaries of John Calvin and of his successor, Théodore de Bèze; and the French *Psaumes* by Clément Marot and Bèze—she expanded her scholarship to include almost every Psalm translation and commentary available to her in English, French, and Latin; she also may have consulted the original Hebrew (Steinberg). She may have begun with the poetic French *Psaumes* as her literary inspiration (Rathmell xvii), but her use of a dazzling array of rhetorical devices and 126 different verse forms was also inspired by the poetry of Philip Sidney and Spenser (Woods, *Natural Emphasis* 169–75, 290–302; Alexander, "Five Responses" 34–41, 197–201; Hannay, "Countess of Pembroke as a Spenserian Poet"). Copied with gold ink by the famous calligrapher Sir John Davies and circulated in manuscript among a literary coterie, the *Psalmes* were celebrated by her contemporaries, including such poets as Samuel Daniel, John Donne, Michael Drayton, George Herbert, and Aemilia Lanyer (see Woods, this volume). Her poems dedicating the *Psalmes* to Queen Elizabeth ("Even Now That Care") and "To the Angell Spirit of the Most Excellent Sir Philip Sidney" evidently did not circulate with the manuscript; they are extant only in Bent Juel-Jensen's manuscript (MS J), although they were probably included in the opening leaves now missing from the authoritative Penshurst manuscript from which MS J was copied.

Despite the pernicious cultural linkage between silence and chastity that dissuaded many women writers from circulating their works, Pembroke actively cultivated a literary reputation in her mature years as she circulated her works in print and in the most elegant manuscripts. "Angell Spirit" is almost as much a meditation on her role as writer as it is a celebration of her brother. Using the conventional inexpressibility topos, she says that her words are inadequate to Sidney's praise, adding that "There lives no witt" who can sufficiently praise him (line 49). Thus she is putting herself in the company of all those poets who have praised Sidney, masking "the assertiveness of her style with the self-abnegation of her subject matter," as Beth Wynne Fisken notes ("To the Angell Spirit," 266; see also Schleiner 75–81). The portrait of Pembroke engraved by Simon van de Passe in 1618 is particularly revealing as self-presentation; dressed in the velvet, pearls, and ermine appropriate to her rank, she assertively holds out to the viewer a volume clearly labeled "Davids Psalmes." And lest the viewer underestimate the vocation thus implied, the portrait is crowned with the poet's laurel wreath. Pembroke knows how to be decorously self-effacing when writing elegy or encomium or a letter petitioning the queen, but she never apologizes for being a woman or a writer. Wroth captures her self-assertion. When the queen of Naples recites an extemporaneous poem, listeners ask for copies and give the poem the extravagant praise she expects as one "who knew when she did well, and would be unwilling to lose the due unto her selfe" (*First Part* 490).

The decline and rise of Pembroke's reputation is paradigmatic. Widely known as a writer during her lifetime, Pembroke was increasingly defined after her death as "Sidney's sister, Pembroke's mother," in the words of William Browne's familiar elegy. Such a summary privileges her family connections at the expense of her achievements. More recent studies have demonstrated that the technical virtuosity of Pembroke's *Psalmes* "makes her the first known woman to have a solid and wide-ranging, though largely uncredited, impact on the development of English poetics" (Woods, *Natural Emphasis* 175; see also Freer 73; Lewalski, *Protestant Poetics* 241–45, 300–02; R. Todd; Fisken, "Mary Sidney's *Psalmes*; Rienstra; Zim 185–210).

The countess of Pembroke is easily integrated into a wide variety of courses, because of the quality of her literary work and her prestige among her contemporaries. In my survey course her two poems addressed to Queen Elizabeth raise important political and literary issues. To introduce Elizabeth and the problem of women's rule, I begin by showing "The Marriage Game" segment of the television series *Elizabeth R.* This segment presents Elizabeth as a woman as well as a ruler, focusing on her use of marriage offers as part of her diplomacy and on her affection for Robert Dudley, earl of Leicester. That Sir Henry Sidney and Lady Mary Dudley Sidney are also portrayed in the film makes it much easier to explain the countess of Pembroke's rank and position in the kinship network. Then I show students photocopies of two holograph letters. (Pembroke's *Collected Works* makes an attempt to reproduce the visual elements, following Sara Jayne Steen's advice "to interfere as little as possible with the [. . .] [writer's] voice" [Steen, "Textual Introduction" 108n, 110].) The first letter ("Correspondence 1") was written when Mary Sidney was a bride of sixteen. Full of deletions, substitutions, blots, and smudges, probably even tear stains, it was obviously "[s]cribbled in haste," as she says (*Collected Works* 1: 285). Students immediately sympathize with a girl, younger than they, who had been just married to a rich and powerful man the age of her father. They understand why she would be upset at being caught between the anger of her husband and the anger of her uncle Leicester for a trivial matter; they are moved to see her in the process of learning to be an aristocratic wife, as she crosses out "he was" and substitutes "my lord was," the correct way to refer to her husband. If there is time, we then discuss her translation of Psalm 45, which gives advice to a young bride in a similar situation (Fisken, "Mary Sidney's *Psalmes*" 174–75). The second holograph letter we read (M. Sidney, *Collected Works* 1: 290–92; "Correspondence 9") is written to Queen Elizabeth in the year after the death of Pembroke's husband, when Pembroke is seeking a position at court for her nineteen-year-old son. Once again, students can identify with the situation, with its concern about employment prospects. They immediately notice the difference in appearance of the letters: this petition is carefully presented, with absolutely regular spacing, no deletions, and the signature in the position of utmost humility, in the bottom right-hand corner. Students are amused by the groveling language then thought decorous in such a letter, but this language raises the issue of the queen's relationship to her male and female courtiers and prepares students for the two poems by Pembroke to the queen, as well as for longer works addressed to Elizabeth, such as Spenser's *Faerie Queene.*

After we have read Elizabeth's "Armada Speech," with its emphasis on the queen's two bodies, students perform Pembroke's pastoral "Dialogue between Two Shepherds" (usually referred to as "Astrea"), which raises the same issue (she is "A manly Palme, a Maiden Bay") and also serves as an example of the encomium (*Collected Works* 1: 89–91). My students do not understand why poets are so extravagant in their praise of Elizabeth, so I wear to class on that day a reproduction of the Armada medallion from the British Library to demonstrate that people did wear portraits of Elizabeth, much like the college hats or T-shirts my students are wearing. Praising Elizabeth, particularly in the years immediately after the defeat of the Spanish Armada, was a way to celebrate England. We also look at a reproduction of the Armada portrait, which shows the storm that the English believed was sent by God to deliver them from Spanish occupation. Then we read the dedicatory poem to the *Psalmes*, "Even now that Care," which refers to that storm (lines 77–78). Like "Astrea," it uses encomium, but whereas "Astrea" addresses the ineffability of language, subverting encomium to question its effectiveness in the final admonition to "silence," the dedicatory poem uses encomium as admonition: Elizabeth is compared to the biblical King David and urged to be "active" on the Continent, that is, to intervene on behalf of Protestants in the Low Countries and in France. The poem also notes the paradoxes of Elizabeth's reign, using the image of the primum mobile, or unmoved mover, to emphasize that God has called a woman to rule:

Kings on a Queene enforst their states to lay;
Main=lands for Empire waiting on an Ile;

Men drawne by worth a woman to obay;
one moving all, herselfe unmov'd the while. (81–84)

Antonius, a source for *Antony and Cleopatra*, is appropriate for a Shakespeare course, particularly as part of a historical-political contextualization of Shakespeare's drama. Pembroke's portrayal of Cleopatra, an increasingly contested figure, can become part of a discussion of women's rule, of gender stereotypes, of conflicts between public and private duty, of motherhood, or of Roman imperialism and orientalism (see Patton, this volume; Sanders 89–137).

Pembroke's works may also be discussed in the context of the sonnet tradition or of the religious lyric. Her Psalm 73, which paraphrases both the fifth poem of Philip Sidney's *Astrophil and Stella* and the Psalms commentary of Bèze, works particularly well (Hannay, "Incorporating"). Two of her Psalm paraphrases are sonnets: Psalm 100 uses Spenser's form and Psalm 150 uses Sidney's. Her translation of Petrarch's "The Triumph of Death," in which Laura is given a voice, may be usefully discussed as a precursor to Wroth's *Pamphilia to Amphilanthus*. For a discussion of the seventeenth-century religious lyric, Donne's metaphysical verse, with its dramatic openings and argumentative structure, may be compared to the opening of Pembroke's Psalm 52 or the structure of Psalm 73; her treatment of the embryo image in Psalm 58 (lines 22–24) and Psalm 139 (lines 43–56) is virtually metaphysical. George Herbert's debt to the Sidneian *Psalmes* is more obvious (Bloch 233–35, 250–51; Freer 240; Kinnamon, "Notes"; Martz 273–79; Rathmell xviii–xix; Rienstra 288–384; Waller, *Mary Sidney* 226–27; Woods, *Natural Emphasis* 171). Psalm 88, for example, anticipates the form of such lyrics as Herbert's "Longing" and "Dullnesse," and Herbert's "Easter" echoes Pembroke's Psalm 108 (Kinnamon, "Note" 44–48).

In a consideration of women's use of religious discourse, Pembroke's Psalm 51 in rime royal can be compared with the sonnet sequence of meditations on that psalm by Anne Lock (Hannay, "Unlock"; Donawerth; see also Felch, this volume). Psalm 51 is also a vivid example of the political use of Psalms (Reid; Whitehead). If a class is looking specifically at the self-construction of the woman writer, then Pembroke's two versions of Psalm 68 work splendidly.

In the first version she includes a presentation of the women who sang before the ark as a symbol of women poets who are freed to soar like doves, in the familiar equation of flight = song = poetry. The revised version, a noticeably better poem, removes that emphasis on gender (Hannay, "House-Confined Maids"). Students can speculate on what forced her to back down, on whether the operative constraints were primarily internal or external.

While Pembroke's works can be read in the context of encomiums for Elizabeth, of the sonnets of Sidney and Spenser, of Shakespeare's historical drama, of the religious lyrics of Herbert and Donne, or of Protestant psalm translation, students may find her words most moving when they are read in the context of what she meant to seventeenth-century women writers—Lanyer's dedicatory poem, in which she seeks to become Pembroke's literary heir, or Lady Wroth's portrayal of the queen of Naples, who was "Perfect in Poetry."

Note

Pembroke's complete works are available in the two-volume *Collected Works of Mary Sidney Herbert, Countess of Pembroke*. *Antonius* and *A Discourse of Life and Death* are available from *Renaissance Women Online* and in a facsimile edition from Ashgate Press. *Antonius* is also included in two paperback texts, *Renaissance Drama by Women*, edited by S. P. Cerasano and Marion Wynne-Davies, and *Three Tragedies by Renaissance Women*, edited by Diane Purkiss. Shorter selections of Pembroke's works are widely anthologized in such volumes as the *Norton Anthology of English Literature* (vol. 1); *The Penguin Book of Renaissance Verse, 1509–1659*; and *The Longman Anthology of British Literature* (vol. 1). For additional Pembroke bibliography, see Roberts, "Recent Studies"; M. White, "Recent Studies."

Josephine A. Roberts and Margaret P. Hannay

Lady Mary Wroth

Mary Sidney Wroth was the first Englishwoman to write a full-length work of fiction, *Urania*; the first Englishwoman to write a sequence of love songs and sonnets, *Pamphilia to Amphilanthus*; and one of the first Englishwomen to write an original drama, *Love's Victory*. It is thus difficult to overstate her importance in the development of women's writing.

Students are immediately drawn to Wroth, since her biography reads like episodes from a romance and provided "a rich reservoir for her fiction," with her "multiple self-portraits" demonstrating "a continuing struggle of self-representation" (Roberts, *First Part* lxxi–ii). The story of Lindamira, for example, begins with a refraction of the dramatic wedding of Wroth's parents (Wroth, *First Part* 499). Barbara Gamage, related to Sir Walter Ralegh, was a Welsh heiress much sought for her wealth. In a struggle between the families of Herbert Croft and Robert Sidney, the Crofts convinced Queen Elizabeth to send a messenger to stop Barbara's impending marriage to Robert. The messenger conveniently arrived two hours after the wedding, so that everyone saved face. The records are ambiguous, but it would not be surprising if the young people had chosen each other, since there was ample opportunity for them to have become acquainted. The hundreds of letters that survive from Robert to Barbara testify to his genuine affection for his wife despite his other dalliances at court. Barbara's voice is largely unrepresented, but Robert's letters to her and from his agent, Rowland Whyte, so frequently mention family matters that we have many details about Mary Wroth's childhood, such as her bout with measles when she was nine; her voyages to visit her father in Flushing; her participation in the christening of her little sister, Barbara; and her frequent visits with her cousins (Hannay, "Your Vertuous and Learned Aunt" 20–24; Lewalski, *Writing Women* 244–45). As the daughter of Robert Sidney, she was the niece of Sir Philip Sidney and of Mary Sidney, countess of Pembroke, a lineage, emphasized on the title page of the 1621 *Urania*, that positions her as the literary heir of all three Sidneys. These family connections were essential to her development as a writer.

Wroth was probably born in 1587 at Baynards Castle, the London home of the Pembrokes. Her frequent visits there and at their Wiltshire estates meant that even as a child she saw the countess of Pembroke translating, writing, and publishing her own work and that of her brother Philip; being a woman writer may thus have seemed normative to Wroth (Hannay, "Your Vertuous and Learned Aunt"). She also grew up with her three Herbert cousins: Anne, with whom she later served at court and acted in Ben Jonson's *Masque of Blacknesse*; Philip, who later became the earl of Montgomery and the husband of Wroth's dear friend Susan de Vere, to whom *Urania* is dedicated; and William, who became a poet and statesman. Wroth seems to have loved William most of her life, and in her youth may have entered into a private marriage with him, a *de praesenti* contract that should have been binding but was later repudiated, as the semiautobiographical story of Pamphilia and Amphilanthus suggests. If she believed that William Herbert was her true husband, that belief would go far toward explaining her emphasis on constancy. Certainly many female characters in *Urania* are married against their will and show their chastity and fidelity not to their husband but to their first love—such as Limena, Bellamira, Lady Pastora, Liana, and to some extent Pamphilia (Roberts, "Knott").

In 1604 both entered into arranged marriages: William to the heiress Mary Talbot, daughter of the earl of Shrewsbury, and Mary to Sir Robert Wroth, a hunting companion of King James. Many versions of this story are given in *Urania*, including that of the Angler Woman who recounts her love for her cousin Laurimello; he "not once imagining my end, married another Lady, rich, and therefor worthy" (294). Knowing her love was hopeless, the speaker gave in to family pressure to marry someone else: "I liv'd an ill, and froward life with him, for some two yeares, while ignorance held me, and willfulnes lived in him," but they eventually became "good friends, and like kinde mates" (295). Other tales, such as that of Bellamira, have similarly autobiographical allusions, including widowhood and the death of an only son (389). Wroth's years as a widow are perhaps also shadowed in the unnamed lady who, after her true love abandoned her, "cover'd her misfortune with the losse of her Husband" (632). Rodomandro, king of Tartaria, appears to be a more sympathetic portrait of Robert Wroth. He died in 1614, shortly after the birth of her first child, named after King James. When the child died two years later, the estate went to her husband's male relatives, but her husband's debts stayed with her, some £23,000. Records show her repeated attempts to have the debts repealed, but she remained in dire financial straits.

It is unclear just why Wroth left the court, but *Urania* hints that it may have been because of Queen Anne's jealousy, shadowed in the stories of Bellamira and Lindamira. Even more vivid is the Queen of Design in the manuscript continuation, a character who is cruel, tyrannical, and always seeking new lovers. Amphilanthus falls into her clutches—and then a bifolio sheet is missing, destroyed by someone. Wroth eventually returned to court for Queen Anne's funeral in 1619 and subsequently received marks of favor from the king. Her contemporary reputation was clouded by the birth of her two natural children by Herbert, William and Katherine, born perhaps around 1620 (Roberts, *First Part* lxxiv–v, lxxxviii). These beloved children are shadowed in the manuscript continuation of *Urania*, particularly in the character of Fair Designe, who is evidently Amphilanthus's natural son (lxvi).

Modeled on Philip Sidney's *Arcadia, Urania* is even more complex, with a dazzling array of characters and nested stories. Students are overwhelmed by its three hundred characters, so it is essential to present material in pieces small enough to be taken in. Students might best focus on the young people in two royal families of cousins: the children of the king and queen of Naples—Amphilanthus, Leonius, and Urania (who shadow the family of Mary Sidney, countess of Pembroke, especially her son William as Amphilanthus)—and the children of the king and queen of Morea—Pamphilia, Parselius, Rosindy, Philarchos, and Philistella (who shadow the family of Robert Sidney, esp. Pamphilia as Wroth herself). Josephine Roberts would often prepare students for *Urania* with a slide show of portraits, explaining the cultural significance of Philip Sidney and telling the life stories of Wroth, Pembroke, Herbert, and other friends and family members in order to help students visualize Wroth's world and to present the social, personal, and political contexts of *Urania* (xxxix–cv). Roberts would then begin a discussion of the position of women in the seventeenth-century with the old joke that *woman* meant "woe to man." Once students had a sense of women's lives at the time, she had them analyze three brief self-referential tales that mirror Pamphilia and Wroth herself, as they show women negotiating a patriarchal culture: Bellamira (377–91), Pastora (414–20), and Lindamira (499–505).

Pamphilia has inherited her uncle's kingdom, even as Wroth seeks to inherit her uncle's literary world. Barbara Lewalski notes that Wroth "used her [Sidney] heritage transgressively," replacing heroes with heroines; transforming the genres of the sonnet, romance, and pastoral drama into "vehicles for exploring women's rather than men's consciousness"; and making those genres "resonate against a Jacobean rather than an Elizabethan milieu" (*Writing Women* 244; see also Beilin, *Redeeming* 214–17; Baer). Students can be encouraged to analyze how *Urania* reworks specific episodes from the *Arcadia*, as when Pyrocles's cross-dressing as an Amazon is transformed to Leonius's cross-dressing as a shepherdess. *Urania* also deals with primogeniture, treatment of natural children, incest, homosexuality, and many tales of love between first cousins (Roberts, *First Part* lxvii; see also Waller, *Sidney Family Romance*; Carrell 94–95). Specific parallels to court scandals provoked attacks from the duke of Buckingham and from Sir Edward Denny, who called her a "hermaphrodite" and a "monster," telling her to "repent you of so many ill spent yeares of so vaine a booke" and "redeeme the tym" by writing "as large a volume of heavenly layes and holy love as you have of lascivious tales and amorous toyes" (Wroth, *Poems* 32, 238–39; see also Wall, this volume). To defend herself, Wroth returned to Denny a bold and witty poem parodying his attack on her (31–36; Lewalski, *Writing Women* 249–51). Yet she was forced to protest that she never meant to publish the romance and to promise that she would have it withdrawn from sale. The thousands of variants in the extant copies of *Urania* indicate that her protests were disingenuous, because someone, most probably Wroth, carefully oversaw its publication (Roberts, *First Part* cxii–viii, 680–712). The manuscript continuation of the romance (part 2), extant only in one manuscript at the Newberry Library, was never prepared for publication. (Roberts did not complete her edition of this second part; Suzanne Gossett and Janel Mueller have completed it for the Renaissance English Text Society. See Wroth, *Second Part*.)

Not surprisingly, *Urania* has most commonly been read as a roman à clef (Schleiner 150–63). But while Wroth did include many allusions to the lives of her family and fellow courtiers, her work should also be read in the context of the larger historical and political events of her age. "At the heart of the *Urania* lies one of the most powerful fantasies of sixteenth- and seventeenth-century Europe—the revival of the Holy Roman Empire in the West" (Roberts, *First Part* xxxix). Reflecting King James's presentation of himself in Roman guise as the new emperor who would usher in a time of universal peace, Wroth casts Amphilanthus in the role of an emperor who unifies the Western world. The Sidney-Herbert family were strong supporters of Queen Elizabeth of Bohemia; she was James's daughter, but James refused to aid her. Wroth, at the height of this

Bohemian disaster, writes a countermyth of an emperor who becomes "Master of the greatest part of the Western World" (Wroth, *First Part* 568) and promotes peace and religious tolerance. This presentation of Amphilanthus perhaps "veils a desire for [William Herbert] to assume a more public and assertive role as leader of the Puritan faction" (Roberts xlvii), making *Urania* admonitory flattery aimed at Wroth's lover, as her aunt's earlier admonitory flattery was aimed at Queen Elizabeth (Hannay, *Philip's Phoenix* 85–96). (If Wroth was instructing Herbert on his political duty, then their relationship was rather different from what we might have guessed from Pamphilia's laments.) The first part of *Urania* ends with the triumph of Amphilanthus, who brings about an era of peace, though threatened by the Turkish powers of the East. The Newberry manuscript reflects the political crisis of an England on the brink of involvement in the Thirty Years' War, depicting armed rebellions of the people in Austria, Hungary, and Denmark as well as in Bohemia. The work thus shows both absolute monarchy as the best form of government and the increasing desires of the people, which Elaine Beilin sees as part of the debate on constitutional and absolute rule in the early seventeenth century ("Winning").

For many students the most problematic part of Wroth's *Urania* is the valorization of constancy as a female virtue, quite independent of whether or not such faithful love is reciprocated (Shaver 67–74; Beilin, *Redeeming Eve* 216–25; Lamb, *Gender* 142–93; Alexander, "Constant Works" 16–23). A general discussion of the controversy over women (Woodbridge; Henderson and McManus) might lead into the concept of male superiority, which is comically treated by Wroth when she reverses the cultural stereotype that women were incapable of constancy: "[B]eing a man, it was necessary for him to exceede a woman in all things, so much as inconstancie was found fit for him to excell her in, hee left her for a new" (*First Part* 317). Despite the presence of some constant male lovers, such as Pamphilia's brother, Rosindy, the romance focuses so much on Pamphilia's constancy that she personifies the virtue (168–70); this "heroic virtue" is "capable of transforming a lovelorn woman into a great queen, a poet, and finally, a transcendent image of divine

love" (Beilin, *Redeeming Eve* 208). Students need to be reminded
that Pamphilia's fidelity to the unfaithful Amphilanthus is, in one
sense, transgressive, for Wroth redefines constancy as fidelity to
"one's own freely chosen love. This reinterpretation of constancy asserts the right of women to select their own partners, regardless of
societal and parental authority" (Roberts lxi). Students may nevertheless respond more enthusiastically to the other primary female
character, Urania, who is seeking her true identity as the romance
opens. Raised as a shepherdess, she is eventually revealed to be the
sister of Amphilanthus and the cousin of Pamphilia. Like Pamphilia,
Urania falls in love with her cousin, but when Parselius is unfaithful,
she doesn't crumple into a heap of lamentation like Pamphilia—she
finds someone better and advises Pamphilia, "Tis pitie [. . .] that
ever that fruitlesse thing Constancy was taught you as a vertue [. . .]
those with whom it is broken, are by the breach free to leave or
choose againe where more staidnes may be found" (470). Pamphilia, like Queen Elizabeth, vows never to marry because she is
married to her kingdom, but in part 2 both she and Urania do eventually marry. In a radical revision of the romance tradition, the characters age as these dear friends raise their children to adulthood. The
emphasis on affiliation, on female friendship, and on mothering
contrasts with male-authored romances, which focus solely on romantic love and on male prowess (Naomi Miller).

   Urania can profitably be read in the context of other pastoral
romances, particularly Sidney's *Arcadia* and Edmund Spenser's
Faerie Queene (Hannay, "Trial"; Lewalski, *Writing Women* 263–96).
Allegorical episodes, such as the "Throne of Love" (illustrated on
the title page) and the "Tomb of Love," can be set beside Spenser's
"House of Busirane" episode, for example, even when there is not
time to teach the entire complexity of *Urania* (J. Miller). These allegorical episodes by Wroth, edited by Roberts, are readily available
in *Major Women Writers of Seventeenth-Century England* (Fitzmaurice, Roberts, Barash, Cunnar, and Gutierrez 129–32, 139–45). If
there is sufficient time, *Urania* can also be discussed within the context of the Continental romance tradition and its connection to
women readers (Roberts xviii–xxxix; Hackett).

Appended to the 1621 *Urania* is a sequence of 20 songs and 83 sonnets, *Pamphilia to Amphilanthus*, modeled on Philip Sidney's famous *Astrophil and Stella*, with some references to Wroth's father's poems, which are extant in only one manuscript, addressed to the countess of Pembroke. Wroth's poems circulated in manuscript prior to their 1621 publication and were praised by other poets. Jonson, for example, who read her poems in manuscript and made a copy, claimed that "Since I excribe your Sonnets, am become / A better lover and much better Poët" (Jonson 349). Wroth's entry into Petrarchan discourse was revolutionary, for she was the first in England to present fully the women's perspective. Like Gaspara Stampa, she uses the female speaker's "abandonment as an occasion for constructing a permissibly powerful poetic sequence." Women's "pastoral vocabulary legitimates the women's complaints and their desire to break free of the limits imposed on them by their social circumstances" (A. Jones, *Currency* 123). Students respond enthusiastically to discussions of Wroth's search for a female identity and authorial voice in these songs and sonnets and in *Urania* as a whole (Swift, "Feminine Identity"; Quilligan, "Constant Subjects"; Fienberg; Weidemann; W. Wall, *Imprint* 330–38; Naomi Miller 143– 81). Unlike most male sonneteers, Wroth never describes the beloved, recounts no kisses or other favors, and never promises to eternize him. His infidelity is a major character flaw; the speaker's constancy is presented "paradoxically, as the fulfillment of her own desire and determination," thus giving the woman "the Petrarchan poet's power of self-definition" (Lewalski, *Writing Women* 253, 256). The woman's voice may directly address the male tradition, as Wroth's song "Sweetest love returne againe" answers John Donne's "Sweetest love, I do not goe" (257–58). Carefully constructed in a circular pattern (Alexander, "Constant Works" 5–15), Wroth's sequence can be read in the context of Continental women's love lyrics and of Petrarchan sonnet sequences (A. Jones, *Currency* 118–54; Lewalski, *Writing Women* 251–63; Roberts, "Thou Maist" 410–12, 420–23). One of the most fruitful ways to teach Wroth's sonnets is to read them with those of Shakespeare and others in a "paratactic method—juxtaposing sonnets on related subjects, such as absence, night, lust, betrayal, or constancy," encouraging students to focus on "exploration of a divided self" (Roberts, "Thou Maist" 407, 409).

Wroth's *Love's Victory* has been less frequently studied to date, but it also repays careful attention, particularly in the context of the pastoral tragicomedy in the tradition of Tasso's *Aminta* (1580), Guarini's *Pastor Fido* (1590), and the English works of Abraham Fraunce, Samuel Daniel, and John Fletcher (Lewalski, *Writing Women* 296–307). It uses a variety of languages—of the court, of comedy, of myth and ritual, of avoidance (McLaren). It can also be studied for its presentation of "feminine self-definition" (Swift, "Self-Definition") and for its "sexual politics" (Schleiner 134–49).

Note

If time and money permit, students will be best served by using Roberts's edition of part 1 of *Urania*, with full commentary on the literary, political, social, and personal contexts; a complete textual apparatus; and indices. The volume's index of characters will be a tremendous aid to student research. A facsimile edition, with a brief introduction by Roberts, is available from Ashgate Press. *The Second Part of the Countess of Montgomery's Urania*, edited by Roberts, Suzanne Gossett, and Janel Mueller, is available from the Renaissance English Text Society / Medieval and Renaissance Texts and Studies. Book 1 of part 1 is available in Paul Salzman's *An Anthology of Seventeenth-Century Fiction*. Several episodes and twenty-five poems from *Urania* are included in *Major Women Writers of Seventeenth-Century England* (Fitzmaurice, Roberts, Barash, Cunnar, and Gutierrez 109–49). Roberts's edition of *The Poems of Lady Mary Wroth* is now available in paperback. Selections from *Pamphilia to Amphilanthus* are printed in the context of Continental women writers in "Mary Sidney: Lady Wroth" in Katharina Wilson's *Women Writers of the Renaissance and Reformation*. *Love's Victory* is available in *Lady Mary Wroth's* Love's Victory: *The Penshurst Manuscript* and in *Renaissance Drama by Women: Texts and Documents*, edited by S. P. Cerasano and Marion Wynne-Davies. Shorter selections of Wroth's works are widely anthologized in such collections as the *Norton Anthology of English Literature* (vol. 1); *The Penguin Book of Renaissance Verse, 1509–1659* (Woudhuysen); and *The Longman Anthology of British Literature* (vol. 1).

Editor's Note

Shortly before her death in August 1996, Josephine Roberts agreed to write this essay. To honor her as scholar and as teacher, the essay incorporates ideas from her published work and also from her teaching methods, as recalled by Jane Donawerth and Anne Shaver.

Susanne Woods

Aemilia Lanyer

Aemilia Bassano Lanyer (1569–1645) has some claim to be called the first professional woman poet in English. Her one volume of verse, *Salve Deus Rex Judaeorum* (1611; "Hail God, King of the Jews"), is a bid for the sort of patronage by which her contemporaries, such as Samuel Daniel and Ben Jonson, were able to support their writing and maintain connections with the nobility. Although other women had written to make money (Warnicke, *Women* 123) and some, such as Isabella Whitney (fl. 1567–72) and Anne Dowriche (fl. 1589), had published verse in their own names and developed techniques for negotiating this apparent lack of female modesty, Lanyer is the first both to claim divine calling as a poet and to seek patronage through a community of intellectual women whom she praises and seeks to represent. For this reason alone she may be of interest to students. But Lanyer is also readily accessible through the feminist wit in such passages as the "Eve's Apologie" section of the volume's long title poem, "Salve Deus Rex Judaeorum" (lines 745–840), and through the interesting comparisons she allows with more familiar and traditionally canonical male poets.

She was born in 1569 (the year of Spenser's first publication), a member of the minor gentry as the daughter of the court musician Baptista Bassano and his wife, Margaret Johnson. Her father was a native of Venice, the youngest of several brothers brought to England by Henry VIII to enrich the music of the court, and may have been of Jewish background. Her mother was an Englishwoman with ties to families associated with the Reformation wing of the English Church. Baptista died when Aemilia was seven, and her mother when Aemilia was eighteen. At some point in her childhood she was educated in the household of Susan Bertie, the young dowager countess of Kent, where she was exposed to standard Renaissance humanist texts and ideas. Probably after her mother's death, Aemilia became the mistress of the much older lord chamberlain, Henry Cary, Lord Hunsdon, Queen Elizabeth's cousin. Lanyer reported to the astrologer Simon Forman in 1597 that "the old Lord Chamberlain kept her long and she was maintained in great pomp," that he "loved her well," and that she "had been favored much of her majesty [Queen Elizabeth I]." Aemilia became pregnant by the lord chamberlain in 1592, which cost her the access to court she had so enjoyed. In October 1592 she was married to a musician cousin, Alfonso Lanyer, and gave birth to a son, whom she named Henry, a few months later (Woods, *Lanyer*, ch. 1; Lasocki 26–27; R. Prior, "Emilia Bassano").

What we know of the rest of Lanyer's life strongly suggests that she was ambitious to return to the glamour and pomp of her younger years and frustrated by the class and gender distinctions that prevented that return. There were no avenues for a woman to rise independently in the social hierarchy. While her husband could volunteer as a gentleman-soldier with the earl of Essex and develop contacts with important courtiers that included the earl of Southampton and Thomas Egerton, lord chancellor under James, Aemilia could only hope he would be knighted, so that she could rise to the rank of lady. Alfonso was never knighted, although he eventually managed to receive income from a hay-and-grain-weighing patent, a typical reward for government service (Lasocki 106–10).

A. L. Rowse has fit into this era of Lanyer's life the conjecture that she was Shakespeare's dark lady, and a few literary critics have followed his lead (Rowse; R. Prior, "Was Emilia"). Most Lanyer scholars, however, have found the idea to be merely distracting speculation supported by circular reasoning, bits of information taken out of context, and wishful thinking (Lewalski, *Writing Women* 213; Woods, *Lanyer*, ch. 1; Bevington). Lanyer may have encountered Shakespeare, whose acting company came under the protection of Lord Hunsdon (as The Lord Chamberlain's Men) after she was forced to leave the court, but it is hard to believe so ambitious a woman would have left the bed of one of the mightiest peers of the land for that of a player who was not yet even of the rank of gentleman. The major poets of the period with whom she was more plausibly acquainted include Edmund Spenser, who was at the Elizabethan court for periods of time between 1589 and 1591, when Aemilia was enjoying the queen's favor, and Jonson, who consorted with court musicians and numbered among his closest friends Alfonso Ferrabosco, who married Alfonso Lanyer's sister, Ellen, in 1610 (Woods, *Lanyer*, ch. 1).

Aemilia Lanyer's best hope of advancement lay in her friendships with Margaret Russell, the dowager countess of Cumberland, and her daughter, Anne Clifford. The countess of Cumberland, like the countess of Pembroke (Mary Sidney) and the countess of Bedford, was a well-known patron of the arts (Lewalski, *Writing Women* 95–123, 138). Spenser dedicated verse to her. Daniel lived in her household and was tutor to Clifford. At some time during the first decade of the seventeenth century, Lanyer resided with the countess and her daughter at the crown manor at Cookeham, where she apparently enjoyed patronage similar to Daniel's (see her "Cookeham," lines 1–12). Remembering how the departure of the countess and her daughter broke up this idyllic household, Lanyer complained of the differences in class and responsibilities that create such separations:

Unconstant Fortune, thou art most to blame,
Who casts us downe into so lowe a frame:
Where our great friends we cannot dayly see,
So great a difference is there in degree.
            (134; "Cookeham," lines 103–06)

Lanyer's book of poems is, among other things, an effort to bridge the gap in class by encouraging and justifying patronage support.

With the death of Alfonso in 1613, Lanyer was forced to find income to support herself and her son, who eventually became a court musician himself, married, produced two children, and then predeceased his mother. She ran a school from 1617 to 1619, when a dispute with her landlord forced her out of the building she was using. She negotiated with Alfonso's relatives over the hay-and-grain patent, eventually getting a settlement on behalf of herself and her grandchildren. When she died in 1645 (the year Milton's *Poems* appeared), she was buried in the churchyard of Saint James Clerkenwell, the parish in which her son and his family had settled in the 1620s.

Some of this background, and the portrait it gives of an ambitious woman at odds with many of the class and gender assumptions of her time, helps students understand the motive and power of the eleven dedicatory pieces that preface the long poem of the volume's title. Of these, three are particularly useful, for a variety of courses. In introductory surveys, her general prose dedication, "To the Vertuous Reader," sets a tradition of virtuous women against the disparagements of women and men who too readily accept common negative attitudes toward women. In my experience, both men and women students are delighted by Lanyer's condemnation of women who disparage other women, imitating the practice of "evill disposed men, who forgetting they were borne of women, nourished of women, and that if it were not by the means of women, they would be quite extinguished out of the world, and a finall ende of them all, doe like Vipers deface the wombes wherein they were bred, onely to give way and utterance to their want of discretion and goodnesse" (48; lines 19–24).

For a period course in which the purposes and techniques of the poetry of praise are an issue, Lanyer's dedications to Queen Anne ("To the Queenes Most Excellent Majestie") and the countess of Pembroke ("The Authors Dreame") provide rich fields for discussion. In the dedication to Anne, Lanyer begins her book by both acknowledging and overcoming the disadvantages of gender, using many of the same gestures male poets used in order to acknowledge and bridge class differences between themselves and their patrons. As Spenser approached Queen Elizabeth in *The Faerie Queene* (e.g., st. 4 in the proem of bk. 1), Lanyer asks only that the grace of the great queen overcome her inadequacies and in return promises the grace of her own gift, the long poem she presents:

> Renowned Empresse, and great Britaines Queene,
> Most gratious Mother of succeeding Kings;
> Vouchsafe to view that which is seldome seene,
> A Womans writing of divinest things;
>   Reade it faire Queene, though it defective be,
>   Your Excellence can grace both it and me. (3; lines 1–6)

As in Jonson's contemporary poems to King James (such as epigram 4, in which he praises James as a poet), Lanyer aligns her own interests with those of her royal patron:

> Behold, great Queene, faire *Eves* Apologie,
> Which I have writ in honour of your sexe,
> And doe referre unto your Majestie,
> To judge if it agree not with the Text:
>   And if it doe, why are poore Women blam'd,
>   Or by more faultie Men so much defam'd? (6; lines 73–78)

"[Y]our sexe" is also, of course, Lanyer's sex, which makes the "honour" of "*Eves* Apologie" pertain to them both.

"The Authors Dreame" is particularly useful in a course that has included the countess of Pembroke. It allows students to see the power of her example and its ability to stir and alter imaginative vision in another woman writer. In Lanyer's dream the "author" (an audacious word for a woman in this period) envisions the countess as centering classical figures of beauty, intellect, and power (including the Graces, Minerva, and Bellona) and reconciling the traditional dispute between nature and art. From Pembroke's example issues a new harmony that enables the author to offer boldly her own vision of Christ's Passion. In addition to showing clearly that women writers did have a tradition of their own, the poem is a delicate recasting of the classical figures who pervade male Renaissance humanist discourse. The Muses, for example, provide the musical background for the speaker-dreamer's vision of Minerva (who trumpets the countess's fame), then of the countess, who effectively replaces the Muses as inspiring motives:

> And nine faire Virgins sat upon the ground,
> With Harps and Vialls in their lily hands;
> Whose harmony had all my sences drown'd,
> But that before mine eyes an object stands,
>
> Whose beauty shin'd like Titons cleerest raies,
> She blew a brasen Trumpet, which did sound
> Throgh al the world that worthy Ladies praise,
> And by Eternall Fame I saw her crown'd. (22; lines 9–16)

The main poem of the volume, "Salve Deus," is at core the story of Christ's Passion told entirely from the point of view of women. It highlights the suffering of Christ as an analogue to women's suffering (Mueller, "Tudor Queen"), notably the suffering of Lanyer's patron, the countess of Cumberland, who endured an unfaithful husband and, in her widowhood, a dispute with King James over the inheritance rights of her only child, Anne Clifford (Clifford's *Diaries* provide a fascinating accompaniment to this feature of Lanyer's poem; see Beilin, *Redeeming* 191–93). The leitmotiv of the countess's suffering surrounds the central story with dedicatory language to the countess and tales of faithful and misunderstood women from history, romance, and the Bible. The story itself moves peripheral biblical characters to the center, emphasizing the wisdom of women as opposed to the malice of men, as in the warning of Pilate's wife, the tears of the daughters of Jersusalem, and the suffering of Mary, the mother of Jesus (106; line 1287).

Pilate's wife utters the "*Eves* Apologie" section, which teaches well to students in both British literature surveys and period courses.

Though it loses some force when extracted from its context (i.e., from the interwoven female points of view of the whole), this section could also be useful for a variety of other courses, from an introduction to literature, where it might show that devices of irony and wordplay are not confined to male poets, to women's studies courses, where it might illustrate an early but witty consciousness of gender injustice. Several of my colleagues have found that the "*Eves Apologie*" section teaches wonderfully in relation to Milton's Eve in *Paradise Lost*.

"The Description of Cookeham," the poem that concludes the volume, is one of the best poems in the book and the most teachable as a whole work. In 210 lines of often elegant pentameter couplets, the poem describes what Barbara Lewalski has called "a valediction by author and residents to an Edenic pastoral life and place" (*Writing Women* 234). It is the first country-house poem printed in English, although the traditional first, Jonson's "To Penshurst" (printed in 1616), may have been written around the same time. "Cookeham" can be taught separately, as a woman's vision of "an Edenic pastoral life," but it has also proved very effective when paired with the Jonson poem.

Since the conventions of the country-house poem are not immediately accessible to most of our students, I use the idea of the travelogue to try to get them to visualize the scenes as Lanyer and Jonson lay them out. I begin by showing them pictures of Elizabethan country houses (including Penshurst; Cookeham unfortunately no longer exists). Each poet has spent some time at a fine country estate and wants to share the experience. If you were operating the camera and following the narrator around, where would you go? What would you see? Where do you as narrator-director pause and comment, and where do you focus your camera? Which scenes have motion, which are close-ups? Taking it further, who is the audience for each film? If these were episodes of *Lifestyles of the Rich and Famous*, what modern company might advertise on either or both episodes?

With luck, students will see that, as with any good travelogue, the place becomes an emblem for the values of the auteur, and those values not only differ from our own time, they also differ interestingly from one another. Since the Lanyer poem is a valedictory for a lost paradise and the Jonson poem is a celebration of ongoing order, the poems allow for good discussion not only about the different viewpoints of women and men but also about the relative positions of women and men as definers of their culture.

In looking at Lanyer's extant corpus, I have found her work useful for discussing with students three major concerns of the Jacobean period: poetic authority, wit, and religion (see Silcox, this volume, for another valuable approach to Lanyer, the handling of virtue). The protective dedications to high-born patrons and the topic of Christ's Passion finesse the general issue of whether women have a right to speak publicly. Lanyer's claim that she was born to praise the countess of Cumberland ("Salve Deus" [139; lines 1457–64]) and that she had a divine calling to "performe this Worke" ("To the Doubtful Reader") makes her claim for authority more direct. Comparing these strategies with those of other women, and with those of contemporary male poets, allows students a glimpse of the period's cultural injunctions and of the various ways in which poets could challenge or fulfill them.

Lanyer's wit fits the classic Johnsonian dictum of *discordia concors* and provides a lively balance to the more famous wit of John Donne. Her principal technique is to use logic to turn traditional biases around. So, for example, women are not expected to have the learning or artfulness of men and are therefore not expected to write, yet women are generally conceded to be closer to nature:

> And since all Arts at first from Nature came,
> That goodly Creature, Mother of Perfection,
> Whom *Joves* almighty hand at first did frame,
> Taking both her and hers in his protection:
>   Why should not She now grace my barren Muse,
>   And in a Woman all defects excuse.
>   (10; "To the Queenes," lines 151–56)

Lanyer flips the usual connotations upside down: women's closeness to nature does not make them less sophisticated artists, it makes them more authentic ones. Similarly, in the "*Eves* Apologie" section of the "Salve Deus," Lanyer alters both Eve's guilt and man's boast of knowledge:

> Yet Men will boast of Knowledge, which he tooke
> From *Eves* faire hand, as from a learned Booke.
> (86; lines 807–08)

As a religious poet Lanyer challenges patriarchal assumptions about Christianity and offers a rich description of the central event of Christian belief. Her crucified Christ is the beautiful object of female gaze, a risen bridegroom worthy of the rapturous language of the Song of Songs:

> This is that Bridegroom that appeares so faire,
> So sweet, so lovely in his Spouses sight,
> That unto Snowe we may his face compare,
> His cheekes like skarlet, and his eyes so bright
> As purest Doves that in the rivers are,
> Washed with milke, to give the more delight;
>   His head is likened to the finest gold,
>   His curled lockes so beauteous to behold.
> (107; lines 1305–12)

Although she is questionably Protestant in her background and in her effort to appeal to strongly Protestant patronesses, her "sensuous baroque passage[s]" (Lewalski, *Writing Women* 234) are more reminiscent of Robert Southwell's "St. Peter's Complaint" (Southwell 75–100) than they are of, say, Fulke Greville's sonnets 86–109 (1: 135–53) or the poems of George Herbert.

Lanyer's one book has proved valuable for a variety of courses, and it will likely continue to be a rich source of material for observing and defining class and gender similarities and differences in Jacobean poetry. In addition, setting Lanyer's work alongside that of her contemporaries expands our understanding of a variety of genres, including the dedicatory encomium, the religious lyric, and the country-house poem.

Barry Weller

Elizabeth Cary, Lady Falkland

By her life as well as her writing Elizabeth Cary generated two remarkable seventeenth-century texts: her *Tragedy of Mariam* (published in 1613 but written possibly as early as 1602) and the biography of her that one of her daughters produced, probably in the 1640s. The conflicts narrated in *The Lady Falkland: Her Life* may well have more immediacy for students than those of the tragedy. Even the opening pages of this biography reveal Cary's hunger for learning and her precocious alertness to abuses of power; one of the first striking anecdotes records her intervention to rescue an old woman accused of witchcraft. Throughout her life Cary found refuge in reading and writing from domestic tyranny, poverty, and illness, but she claimed more than imaginative freedom for herself. While her husband, Lord Falkland, was serving as lord protector of Ireland and thus as an agent of Protestant conformity, Cary chose to convert to Roman Catholicism. After breaking with friends and family, she proved resilient under economic hardships and waged a lifelong struggle, first with her husband and then with her eldest son, for what she saw as the spiritual welfare of her younger children. (The biography was written by one of the four daughters who entered the Benedictine convent at Cambray in France.) The competing claims of familial affections, political allegiance, and religious conviction affected not only Cary but also her husband and children, and an unusually complex picture of aristocratic domestic life emerges from this narrative. Cary's daring choices reveal both the surprising scope of action that an early seventeenth-century upper-class woman might exercise and the costs of asserting her freedom of conscience.

It may require more effort to engage the students' interest in the tangled historical background and labyrinthine political intrigues of *The Tragedy of Mariam*, but Cary's play offers a distinctive vantage on issues of gender and power that students will also encounter in contemporary male-authored drama. Apart from the translations of French and classical tragedies by Mary Sidney and Joanna Lumley, *The Tragedy of Mariam* is the first play in English by a woman, and this fact alone will probably stimulate enough curiosity to get students past some of the initial difficulties of orienting themselves in an unfamiliar dramatic world. The unique status of *Mariam*, as an original, pre-Restoration play by a woman, would demand serious critical attention no matter what its caliber, but *The Tragedy of Mariam* shows erudition, conceptual complexity, and startling flashes of dramatic wit and power.

While Shakespeare's plays represent intimate conversations among women (e.g., between cousins, between mistress and maid-confidante), in *Mariam* it is most frequently political, rather than romantic, power that is negotiated in women's conversations—as though the scenes could accommodate not merely a single Bel-Imperia, Queen Margaret, Cleopatra, or Vittoria Corombona, but three or four of them at once. A discussion of the different ways in which Mariam, Alexandra, Salome, and Doris, as well as the submissive Graphina, interpret their sources of power or exercise the prerogatives of their respective positions should immediately foreground one of the play's distinctive features, its exceptionally broad spectrum of women characters. Allusions to Cleopatra and Augustus

Caesar's wife, Livia, also extend the array of politically consequential women who shape the world in which the play's action occurs: Cleopatra in particular is insistently evoked as an antitype to Mariam. (If the context of the course permits comparison with figures from Kyd, Shakespeare, and Webster, the discussion of women's power and agency within patriarchal structures might have an even greater scope. My supposition—and certainly my hope—is that *Mariam* will begin to be read not only in courses on women writers or women's history of the early period but also in courses that take a revisionary look at the canon of Renaissance drama.)

Mariam and Salome

Focusing on Mariam's interactions with the other characters avoids the risk of idealizing her or treating her fate as the tragedy's sole concern—in other words, of reading *Mariam* as Romantic critics and their successors have often read *Hamlet*. She is certainly the most self-aware and reflective of the tragedy's characters, but she taunts Salome not only for her parvenu status as royalty but also for her racial inferiority as an Edomite, a descendant of Esau rather than of Jacob. If Mariam feels any guilt about displacing Doris, Herod's first wife, it finds only belated expression, when she cringes before Doris's curses—much as Queen Elizabeth, Edward IV's wife, recoils from Queen Margaret in *Richard III*. Although Mariam is willing to face Herod's wrath, she also relies on the power of her beauty to protect her from ultimate consequences (4.8). None of these unappealing traits should obscure Mariam's intrepid navigation of political danger, her forthright and authoritative language (the public voice whose decorum she weighs at the play's opening), the courage with which she gambles her future for some measure of integrity, or the dignity with which she ultimately meets her death; but they do contribute to Cary's unusually multifaceted conception of a female protagonist.

The figure of Salome may well be more immediately vivid. Like other malcontents, rebels, and intriguers in Renaissance drama, Salome has more than her share of the best lines, and if class discussion flags, a few moments with Salome should give it new energy. At first approach, she is likely to seem the play's protofeminist. She proclaims her desires without hypocrisy or inhibition and acknowledges no legitimate obstacle to their fulfillment: "And for my will I will employ my wits" (1.4.295). She expresses open contempt for the Mosaic law, which restricts the right to divorce to men ("Why should such a privilege to man be given? / Or given to them, why barr'd from women then?") and asserts her pioneering disposition: "I'll be the custom-breaker: and begin / To show my sex the way to freedom's door." It's not that she's willing to pay a penalty for her innovation; she simply intends to bribe the appropriate priest ("with an off'ring will I purge my sin"), and with a cynicism worthy of Marlowe's Machiavell, she declares that "The law was made for none but who are poor" (309–12).

Later in the play Salome is not merely frank but also ruthless; nevertheless, her malevolence retains a certain charisma. She prompts Herod's murderous impulses by helpfully suggesting instruments for Mariam's destruction—while simultaneously deflating the maudlin romanticism with which Herod couples his tyranny. He raves that Mariam's perfect skin will blunt the executioner's blade. Well, then, Salome matter-of-factly proposes, how about drowning her? burning her, perhaps? Salome's detachment and the economy of her speeches, especially compared to Herod's, bring a comic rhythm to the scene.

Herod. Is't possible you can command so soon
   A creature's heart to quench the flaming sun,
   Or from the sky to wipe away the moon?
Salome. If Mariam be the sun and moon, it is [. . .].
Herod. But have you heard her speak?
Salome.   You know I have.
Herod. And were you not amaz'd?
Salome.   No, not a whit.
            (4.7.394–97, 425–26)

Salome's refusal to be dazzled by Mariam's transcendent qualities or to join in Herod's extravagance makes her exchanges with Herod seem less a dialogue about an impending execution than a satire on Petrarchan rhetoric and the lethal contradictions of male infatuation. Despite her transgressive opinions and villainous designs Salome remains conspicuously unpunished at the end of the play. Moreover, the entertaining dimension of her stage presence acts as a reminder that in *Mariam*, as in other complex literary texts, the play's sympathies and imaginative investments may not be fully aligned either with the official morality that the play sometimes voices or with the play's internal ethical hierarchy, which would certainly assign a far higher value to Mariam than to Salome. As students will no doubt point out, however, the assertive directness of Salome's speech is at odds with her actions in the plot. She operates by subterfuge: insinuating Mariam's adultery with Sohemus; coaching her brother Pheroras to betray the secrets of her husband, Constabarus; bribing or coercing her servant to say that Mariam has prepared a poison drink for Herod; and so on. The success of her manipulations depends on the continuance of male power, specifically, Herod's. Although Mariam's views less aggressively challenge the assumptions of a patriarchal order, Mariam is finally more intransigent in her dissent and more exposed than Salome to the fatal machinery of repression.

Even at the outset it is apparent that Mariam is the most introspective and self-aware of the drama's characters. However, the opening monologue, on the instability of her judgments and emotion, may make it surprising, later, that she discovers a place of self-consistency, a principled selfhood, that she cannot renounce without consequences more tragic than her death. Reading—and therefore teaching—the first scene probably presents more obstacles than reading any other part of *Mariam*, because this scene is loaded with exposition and the tragedy's historical background is at least as complex as—and less familiar than—that of Shakespeare's history plays. Still, the basic elements of Mariam's situation at the opening of the play can be stated with relative simplicity: she believes that her husband, Herod, is dead, and while Herod had killed Mariam's grandfather and brother in order to consolidate his political power, he doted on Mariam herself—but so possessively that he could not stand the idea of her surviving him and taking another husband.

This account of her position should give students enough information to analyze her contradictory feelings about Herod's death—which include relief, satisfaction, memories of his (and her) genuine affection but resentment of his attempt to ensure her posthumous fidelity, self-criticism for doubting the sincerity of others' ambivalent emotions, and so on. The monologue's labyrinth of memory, surmise, and unnameable feeling is an appropriate prologue to the play, which frequently proceeds in a tangle of subjunctives, as though no decision is ever exempt from second-guessing.

During the first half of the play the supposition of Herod's death gives freer play to the collisions of motive and temperament among Mariam, Alexandra, Salome, and Doris. Herod's return, by restoring a male figure to the apex of political authority, reimposes limits on the power to which the women can lay claim (even during this interregnum, this power remains provisional and contingent on their relation to sons, grandsons, brothers, and prospective husbands). For Mariam, Herod's reappearance marks a more definitive crisis. What she has discovered during his absence is that while she can notionally contemplate the value of his devotion—and even remember the love that her "virgin freedom [. . .] unrestrain'd" once felt for Herod—she can no longer stomach the prospect of cooperating in his fiction of a loving marriage. She must by now be inured to his fluent rationalization for killing her grandfather and to his glib expressions of regret for murdering her brother, but Herod seems unable to see the contradiction between his professions of love for Mariam and his even more powerful lust to control her destiny. He once saw his marriage to Mariam as supplementing and completing his existence; just as her dynastic prestige consolidated his claims to kingship, her beauty, intelligence, and aristocratic style ennobled his court, his domesticity, and his progeny. As his discarded wife Doris bitterly complains, he regards only his children with Mariam as truly his own. Although Herod persists in this understanding of his marriage, he now sees her life as valuable only insofar as it is coextensive with his own. If he cannot absorb her so completely that nothing of her will outlive him, death will reveal that he was her supplement and not she his.

It's not so much that Mariam defies Herod; rather, she will not play the part—of exultant wife welcoming home a triumphant husband—that his imagination has designed for her. "Is this my welcome?" (3.4.93), Herod asks, almost more perplexed than angry. Like Cordelia, Mariam runs the risk of showing regal power what it cannot command: "I cannot frame disguise, nor never taught / My face a look dissenting from my thought" (145–46). There's scorn and a touch of stubbornness in Mariam's resistance; Herod calls it "peevishness" (149), and Mariam later says she "was ever innocent, though sour" (4.8.568). She has only one subsequent soliloquy of any length, and there she describes herself as having lost a wager: she blames herself for lacking humility and relying too much on the single virtue of chastity—*chastity* meaning as much integrity, perhaps, as sexual continence or fidelity. But unlike her earlier haughtiness toward Salome, the pride she shows to Herod seals a compact with herself and sets the terms on which she will either live or die: "And therefore can they but my life destroy / My soul is free from adversary's power" (569–70).

Speech and Silence

Mariam's power in her scenes with Herod derives more from her sparing expenditure of speech than from the linguistic command she has already exhibited. Cary thus revises—or puts in an odd light—the judgment of the historian Josephus (in *Jewish Antiquities*, one of her major sources) that Mariam was found guilty of "a great and intemperate libertie in her discourse" (appendix A, 281). Even Sohemus, one of her well-wishers in the play, declares, "Unbridled speech is Mariam's worst disgrace" (3.3.183), but his share in this accusation shows the extent to which the male characters unanimously view a woman's body as something best sealed at every orifice. Constabarus tells Salome that a wife's "private conference" (i.e., conversation) with a stranger brings shame to her husband, country, and race (1.6.375–77), and the Chorus corroborates this view: "That wife her hand against her fame doth rear, / That more than to her lord alone will give / A private word to any second ear"

(3.227–29). It is unclear whether the open ear or the open mouth invites more pollution, but both are penetrable. "Her mind if not peculiar is not chaste" (3.242); the only safeguard against adulteration is the husband's exclusive possession of her thoughts. (*Peculiar* is related to *pecuniary* and thus, etymologically, to the reckoning of wealth in terms of herds: "Thou shalt not covet thy neighbour's wife, nor his manservant, nor his maidservant, nor his ox, nor his ass [. . .].") But silence too can be a subversive text: Pheroras prompts Graphina, "Move thy tongue, / For silence is a sign of discontent" (2.1.41–42), and despite the male characters' preoccupation with Mariam's "unbridled speech," it is her reticence that provokes Herod on his return.

The first line of the play ("How oft have I with public voice run on") draws attention to Mariam's speech, and the 1613 text, which ends this line with a question mark, hovers even more evidently between declaration and self-interrogation. The "public voice" of *Mariam* itself is a borderline phenomenon. Although the play is published, its authorship is simultaneously announced and veiled by attribution to "that learned, vertuous, and truly noble Ladie, E.C." (62; facsim. of orig. title page). The play is, moreover, a closet drama, meant for the study rather than the stage. Does the private performance of its text in reading constitute a public voice? (See Margaret Ferguson, "Running," for further discussion of this topic.) Whatever the particular status of *Mariam* as script or dramatic poem, it seems clear that any woman who produces writing—language that can circulate—necessarily becomes a target of the Chorus's strictures on one who "seeks to be by public language grac'd" (3.240). Cary may not have cooperated in the publication of *Mariam*, but the disseminative power of printing enlarges that of writing and ensures that the "mind" of its author, as notionally embodied in its words, can no longer be "peculiar," either to the husband of that "vertuous, and truly noble Ladie" or to the lady herself. Ostensibly Graphina is the most obedient woman in the play, just as writing (*graphein*, from which Graphina's name seems derived), in the classical ideology of language, ought to be the subordinate, ancillary instrument for enlarging the circulation of meaning. However, the silence of writing (or of Graphina) requires interpretation. When prompted, Graphina mirrors Pheroras's desires and produces the reading of her silence that Pheroras wants, anticipates, and needs. But the very narcissism of this circuit may raise questions about whether Graphina's, or any woman's, silence guards a reservoir of alternative, less patriarchally assimilable meanings.

The Challenge to Ideological Coherence

The male characters of *Mariam* struggle to extract acceptable morals from the play's events or fit its characters' motives to reassuringly familiar patterns. Sohemus is a loyal adherent of Mariam but, as noted above, an inadequate interpreter of her downfall. As a protector of Babas's sons and a generous rival to Silleus, Constabarus proves, perhaps revealingly, a better friend than husband (though one hesitates to attribute Salome's dissatisfaction to Constabarus's intrinsic qualities). He initially excepts Mariam from his global condemnation of women ("You had but one to give you any grace" [5.6.312]) but soon after seems to forget the exception ("You are the least of goods, the worst of evils, / Your best are worse than men: your worst than devils" [349–50]). The extremity of his misogynistic rhetoric proves self-disqualifying. Nevertheless, this language symptomatically displays the reflexive hostility and the sense of female otherness that uniformly environs women as diverse as Salome and Graphina.

The most ambitious efforts at generalization occur at the end of each act, where the Chorus ("a company of Jews," presumably the elders of the community) offers a commentary on the preceding scenes. These choric stanzas should certainly provide a focus for classroom discussion, not least of all because dealing with their linguistic compression and jagged transitions of thought will require collective work. They distill into a quasi-proverbial language the not always coherent attitudes of the world that Mariam—and, to a large extent, Cary—inhabits. Despite their nominal identification as Jews, the chorus members borrow their axioms indiscriminately from sources as various as Stoic psychology, Horatian praise of moderation and the simple life, Christian lessons of forbearance, aristocratic codes of honor, and an austerely restrictive version of Renaissance patriarchy. There is, in any case, a bad fit between this hybrid moralizing and the dramatized events of *Mariam*—when, for example, the choric stanzas of act 1 that castigate the appetite for variety are unexpectedly applied to Mariam rather than Salome. (See Weller and Ferguson 35–38, for further discussion.) Reading the characters and actions of the play *against* the intellectual commonplaces that attempt to contain and fix their meanings should open up a series of questions about what Cary's tragedy accomplishes. For example, What use does *Mariam* make of the tension between these general pronouncements and the play's dramatic substance? (Does it seem possible that Cary was unaware of this tension?) Does the text's ventriloquism of familiar social attitudes camouflage its dissent from their validity, or does the play seem designed more directly to falsify, if not satirize, such attitudes? Arguments about interpretative strategies for addressing the problems posed by *Mariam* should raise even larger issues of how—or even whether—to read historically.

It is hard, and maybe not even desirable, to examine the different styles of female resistance and autonomy depicted in *Mariam* without considering Cary's personal history. The complementary teaching possibilities of *Mariam* and *The Lady Falkland: Her Life* allow a rare opportunity to interrogate a broad ideological context in the light of particular women's stories, both real and imagined (though it is well to remember that *Mariam* is at least grounded in history). For once, the historical instance suggests a modestly happier, more liberating outcome than the fiction. What, Stephen Orgel asks, do such stories as Cary's tell us about patriarchy? "Ideology," he comments, "is the least certain of guides to actual behavior" (*Impersonations* 125). In the complementary modes of fiction and biography *The Tragedy of Mariam* and *Lady Falkland: Her Life* each test the gap between prescription and performance.

Barbara K. Lewalski

Rachel Speght

Rachel Speght (c. 1597–?) was the first Englishwoman to identify
herself, by name, as a polemicist and critic of contemporary gender
ideology. This well-educated young woman of the London middle
class wrote, so far as we know, two significant works. One is a tract
defending women, *A Mouzell for Melastomus* (1617), the first and
perhaps the only female contribution to a vigorous pamphlet war in
1615–20 over women's nature, worth, and role. This debate, a revival of the centuries-old *querelle des femmes*, was touched off in
1615 by an anonymous attack on women, the rambling, boisterous,
tonally confused but lively *Araignment of Lewde, Idle, Froward, and
Unconstant Women*, by Joseph Swetnam (for the *querelle* and the
Jacobean controversy see Crandall; Henderson and McManus;
Kelly-Gadol, "Early Feminist Theory"; A. Jones, "Counter-attacks";
Lewalski, *Writing Women*; Woodbridge). The immediate context for
Swetnam's tract and Speght's answer is the apparent challenge to
gender hierarchy in the oppositional writings and activities of several
Jacobean women and the responses to them, which made the

"woman question" a prominent locus of interest and anxiety during James's second decade (Lewalski, *Writing Women*).

Reading Speght's response to Swetnam's attack, as well as the later anonymous answers published under allegorical women's names, can provide a fascinating insight into the rhetorical games-manship and publication strategies but also the serious gender issues involved in such exchanges. Reading it alongside such works as the English Church's official "Homilie of the State of Matrimonie," Shakespeare's *Taming of the Shrew,* and passages on Adam and Eve from Milton's *Paradise Lost* can illuminate contemporary assump-tions about gender and marriage and the contemporary interpreta-tions of biblical texts that underly them. As well, the extensive and derogatory marginalia on the Beinecke Library (Yale) copy of *Mouzell* by a contemporary male annotator (probably Swetnam, preparing an answer to Speght) constitutes an intertextual dialogue that sheds light on early modern reader response, on the making of polemic, and on early strategies for trying to keep subversive women in their place (van Heertum; Lewalski, "Female Text").

Speght's second known work, *Mortalities Memorandum,* pub-lished in 1621, takes its title from her long poetic meditation on death. It is prefaced by a much more interesting allegorical dream-vision poem, "The Dreame," which treats her rapturous encounter with learning and defends women's education. Reading that work alongside its generic model, *The Romance of the Rose* (Lorris); alongside other women's diaries and memoirs of the period (see Beilin, this volume); and alongside Milton's *Of Education,* which proposes an ideal education for young men, offers insights into gen-dered assumptions about the self and about education (Lewalski, In-troduction xxvii–xii).

Speght was born into a religious and bourgeois family. Her fa-ther, James Speght, was a Calvinist minister and the rector of two London churches, Saint Mary Magdalene, Milk Street (1592–1637), and Saint Clement, Eastcheap (1611–37). He was also an author and had some associations with the City establishment and the guild of goldsmiths. In 1613 he published a tract arguing Calvinist positions on justifying faith and the final perseverance of the elect, based on the usual proof texts in Romans 8 (*Demonstration*); in 1615 he published an Epiphany sermon that he had preached four years earlier before the lord mayor and aldermen of London (*Day-Spring*). Rachel intimates that her mother exercised a profound influence on her life and states that her death was the stimulus for *Mortalities Memorandum*. No surviving records provide the mother's name or any facts about her life, but "The Dreame" indicates that she died sometime after Rachel completed the *Mouzell* (late in 1616) and before she wrote *Mortalities Memorandum*, completed by mid-January 1621. If she had siblings, their birth and baptismal records have been lost. Thomas Speght, the editor of Chaucer (1598, 1602), may have been a kinsman.

Speght's writings both claim and display a knowledge of Latin and some training in logic and rhetoric—a classical education rare for seventeenth-century women of any class. She cites several learned authorities, most of them probably drawn from one or more of the numerous popular anthologies or commonplace books of maxims and sayings that juxtapose classical and Christian sources (e.g., Meres, *Palladis Tamia* [1598] and Ling, *Politeuphuia* [1597], both often reprinted). Writers of all sorts relied on such collections, sometimes supplementing them from their own commonplace books, as Speght may have done. "The Dreame" suggests that she encountered and overcame many obstacles in her pursuit of learning—her own fears, the dissuasions of others, the distractions of domestic duties; the poem also allegorizes her delight in learning and the fact that some unspecified occasion forced her, regretfully, to end her studies shortly before her answer to Swetnam. She was then nineteen, by which age her formal education surely had ended, though she did not marry until four years later. Whatever its scope, her unusual classical education must have been approved by her father: it may have been conducted by him or by a tutor or conducted in one of the few schools for young gentlewomen.

Swetnam's tract was signed in the first printing "Thomas Tel-Troth"; Speght claims that she unmasked the author as the fencing master Joseph Swetnam. His prefatory epistles seem deliberately calculated to provoke responses from women or their defenders, suggesting an effort by the author and by the bookseller, Thomas Archer, to start a profitable controversy. Two years later Archer published Speght's *Mouzell* [muzzle] *for Melastomus* [black mouth]. Speght herself may have decided to answer Swetnam and then presented her tract to Swetnam's bookseller, but it is more probable that she was solicited by Archer to write this rejoinder so as to reawaken the controversy and sell more books. If so, she must have been suggested to him by family or friends, or else, at age nineteen, she had already acquired some reputation in city circles as a learned young woman. Of the eight major contributions to the Swetnam debate and the related cross-dressing controversy in 1615–20, only Speght published under her own name and insisted on her authorial identity.

Some months after Speght's treatise appeared, two other answers to Swetnam were published under female pseudonyms. The writers may be women, or (perhaps more likely) men strategically representing themselves as women, writing for other booksellers who wanted to get in on the lucrative controversy. In *Ester Hath Hang'd Haman* Ester Sowernam (punning Swe[e]tnam) adopts the persona of a mature, experienced woman who somehow has escaped all the usual categories—"neither Maide, Wife nor Widdowe, yet really all, and therefore experienced to defend all"—and who offers to improve on the inadequate answers of the young and inexperienced "maid," Speght (A2v). By contrast, in *The Worming of a Mad Dogge*, Constantia Munda praises Speght's "modest and powerful" work (16). An anonymous comedy (perhaps by Thomas Heywood), *Swetnam the Woman-Hater. Arraigned by Women*, produced in 1618 or 1619 and published in 1620, taunts Swetnam with Speght's title Melastomus (I4v). In 1620 three other tracts, also anonymous, deal with the related issue of cross-dressing: *Hic Mulier; or, The Man-Woman*, *Haec-Vir; or, The Womanish-Man*, and *Muld Sacke; or, The Apologie of Hic Mulier*. The fad of female cross-dressing had been adopted by highborn ladies as well as by such legendary lower-class roaring girls as Long Meg of Westminster and Moll Cutpurse. A cleric, Thomas Adams, wrote in 1615 that it was becoming difficult to tell men from women on the streets of London, and early in

1620 King James urged ministers "to inveigh vehemently and bitterly in theyre sermons against the insolencie of our women, and theyre wearing of brode brimd hats, pointed dublets, theyre haire cut short or shorne, and some of them stillettaes or poinards, and such other trinckets" (Adams 50).

Swetnam's tract, which went through ten editions by 1634, is a jumble of proverb lore, rowdy jokes, invective, authorities, and anecdotes and examples pertaining to women's lechery, vanity, shrewishness, and worthlessness, cobbled together from the entire tradition of misogynist writing. Some defenses of women, notably the *Book of the City of Ladies*, by Christine de Pisan (1364–1430), challenged misogynist stereotypes, offering positive images of female warriors, rulers, and scholars and exposing male bias and interest in subjugating women. But throughout the English Renaissance the formal polemic over women owed more to rhetorical convention than to ideological conviction or emotional involvement, recycling hoary arguments pro and con (Woodbridge). Most writers were participants in an ongoing game of wit played by men for their own and (they seem to have supposed) women's amusement (e.g., Swetnam A2v–A4).

Speght's tract breaks the mold of such rhetorical gamesmanship, eschewing many of the tired formulaic gestures of the *querelle* defenses (such as citing lists of good women to balance the evil examples adduced, citing authorities who praise women to counter the defamers, and overstating claims for female superiority to counter outrageous claims for male superiority). Instead, Speght undertakes to reinterpret biblical texts, supported by many cross-references in the margins in the approved manner of Protestant theological argument, so as to make the dominant discourse—Protestant biblical exegesis—yield a more equitable concept of gender. She devises a structure that allows her to attack Swetnam on particular points, as the genre and readership of such polemics required, but also to mount a serious, coherent, liberalizing critique of gender ideology. Her sometimes trenchant invective against Swetnam's logic and style is restricted to her prefatory matter and to an appended small tract, *Certaine Quaeres to the Bayter of Women*, which has a separate title page, epistle, and preface. In that little work she gives specific examples of Swetnam's grammatical errors and illogic, spicing them with invective and puns, notably on *as/ass*, pointing to Swetnam. In the *Mouzell* proper she looks past Swetnam to engage worthier antagonists, all those ministers or other commentators who find in Scripture some basis to devalue and wholly subjugate women. While her dedicatory epistle invites patronage from women of rank and power, it also reaches out to and offers to defend all virtuous and God-fearing women of every station, "rich and poore, learned and unlearned": here and elsewhere she comes close to recognizing all "Hevahs sex" as an oppressed gender in a misogynist, patriarchal society (3–4).

Throughout, Speght mounts an effective answer to Swetnam by creating a persona who is a living refutation of his charges against women. She presents herself as religious, learned, serious, truthful, eminently rational, engagingly modest, unassuming, justifiably angry yet self-controlled, and courageous in defending wronged women and their Creator. She modestly admits her youthful and female insufficiencies in learning: "I am young in yeares, and more defective in knowledge, that little smattering in Learning which I have obtained, being only the fruit of such vacant houres as I could spare from affaires befitting my Sex" (31). But she counters this modesty topos by displaying her capacity for logical argument, her knowledge of rhetoric, her ease with Latin quotations and wordplay (it may be "small Latin," but she seems in tolerably good control of it), and her range of reference beyond the Bible to the church fathers and some classical authors: Lactantius, Seneca, Aristotle, Zoilus, Livy, Pliny, Cicero, Augustine, Plutarch. She also takes pride in her ability to manage a syllogism. Though she has not studied the famous logicians directly, she can do a better syllogism than Swetnam and one that proves him damnable: "To fasten a lie upon God is blasphemy; But the *Bayter of women* fastens a lie upon God [in falsely claiming that God called women necessary evils]: *ergo*, the *Bayter* is a blasphemer" (37). Speght appears to accept the ways in which gender has restricted her access to learning, but that acceptance holds a quite subversive subtext: if her "vacant hours" of study have made her so much more learned than Swetnam with all his sup-posed masculine advantages, then her example makes the case for women's equal intelligence and equal capacity for education. Against this persona she poses her character of Swetnam based on his tract: "the very embleme of a monster" (4), a blustering, scan-dalmongering, blasphemous bully who is "irreligious and illiterate" (1), whose grammatical faults and stylistic errors reveal his abysmal ignorance and whose disjointed and contradictory arguments reveal his intellectual, moral, and spiritual chaos. Her governing metaphor for her encounter with him is unequal combat, a David battling Go-liath, or a Saint George with the dragon.

Many of Speght's arguments in the *Mouzell* proper are com-monplaces of liberal Protestant marriage doctrine and earlier de-fenses of women, but they have considerable subversive potential in pressing biblical-Christian discourse to affirm categorically the moral and spiritual equality of women. And while she admits, as she has to, those biblical texts proclaiming woman the weaker vessel (1 Pet. 3.7) and the man the "head" of the wife in marriage (1 Cor. 11.3), she pointedly refrains from justifying that headship on the usual grounds of woman's physical, mental, and moral weakness or nat-ural inferiority—spelled out in the officially promulgated "Homilie of the State of Matrimonie" and reiterated constantly in contempo-rary marriage sermons and tracts (Henry Smith 62; Whately 113, 189). By contrast, Speght subjects the term "head" to an exegesis that removes every sanction for the husband's authority from female nature itself, as created or as redeemed. Gender hierarchy is made to seem simply a somewhat anomalous social institution sanctioned in the Bible primarily to afford protection to women's comparative physical weakness. Speght also defies the often articulated precept that wives owe total obedience even to evil husbands (e.g., in Gouge 317–18), by appealing to the central tenet of Protestantism, the pri-macy of the individual conscience.

Speght develops her claims for woman's excellence through an extended examination of the Creation-Fall story from Genesis ac-cording to the categories of Aristotle's four causes. The efficient cause of woman's creation is God himself, and so "the work cannot chuse but be good, yea very good" (18). The material cause, Adam's rib, is more refined matter than the dust from which Adam himself was made. The formal cause shapes both man and woman after the image of God, leaving no basis for the usual comments about women's cold humors or imperfect bodies. Woman's final cause or purpose is to glorify God and give good counsel and companionship to her husband. Speght concludes that woman is God's best gift to man, and that "God [. . .] makes their authority equall, and all creatures to be in subjection unto them both" (18).

Her analysis also empties problematic biblical texts of damaging significance for women. The Fall story reveals Eve's good intentions and Adam's greater guilt. Paul's statement (1 Cor. 7.1) that "[i]t is good for a man not to touch a woman" refers only to the times and conditions of persecution—an impressive and potentially radical claim that culture and historical circumstances are determinants even of sacred texts. Her most radical claims are extrapolations from Galatians 3.28, that under the New Testament "male and female are all one in Christ Jesus," leading her to apply the parable of the talents to women and to conclude that "no power externall or internall ought woman to keep idle, but to imploy it in some service of God" (20). Her own act of writing this tract makes the case that some talents ask employment beyond the domestic sphere. She also challenges the pervasive formula in treatises on marital duties and in Swetnam that defines separate spheres for men and women ("He without doores, she within; he abroad, she at home" [Whately 84]), by citing examples from nature—pigeons, cocks and hens—that exhibit mates sharing all the offices and duties of life. Her epilogue concludes with a stern warning: Men who speak and write against women invite God's certain revenge for reviling his best gift and handiwork, "women I meane, whom God hath made equall with themselves in dignity, both temporally and eternally" (26). In her *Mouzell* Speght does not attack patriarchy as a social arrangement, but she does deny any essential basis for it in nature or in the spiritual order.

Speght's volume of poems, *Mortalities Memorandum*, provides further insight into her sense of self, her role as author, and the conditions that empowered her to write and publish. Her epistle describes the volume as a tribute to the women most important to her—her recently deceased mother and her godmother, Mary Moundford, wife of a prominent London physician—and as a way to assert her authorship of her anti-Swetnam tract against those who, refusing to credit female achievement, had attributed her tract to her father (45). It also disposes briskly of the gender constraints that normally kept women from publishing their writing, by appealing to unimpeachable religious motives: the desire to benefit others and the biblical command to use and not hide a God-given talent. The title poem urges, and offers itself as an example of, a proper Christian meditation on death. Though the verse is pedestrian, the poem has considerable interest as a cultural document, in that Speght makes of it a sanctioned way for a woman to instruct a Christian audience. Her experience with the market-driven *querelle* controversy may have led her to recognize the large middle-class market for books on piety, devotion, and self-analysis as an opportunity for a would-be professional woman writer (see Wright 228–96). In the allegory of Speght's long prefatory poem, "The Dreame," the stimulus for this book is another monster, an all-devouring Spenserian beast (Death) who has slain her mother; and again, as with Swetnam, Speght takes on the role of a courageous romance heroine daring to do battle with a cruel and terrible foe.

"The Dreame" is described as substantially autobiographical: "imaginarie in manner, *reall in matter*" (43). Here too the verse is sometimes pedestrian, but this dream-vision poem is enlivened by the allegorical fiction, by the dialogue of the speaker with allegorical characters, by the author's emotional engagement with sensitive autobiographical concerns, and especially by the fictional representation of a woman's obstacle-laden path to education. It cleverly plays off romance, a genre long associated with women readers, and especially off that classical romance literature, the *Romance of the Rose*, whose lover-hero is variously hindered by or helped by many personifications of courtly love psychology and social custom in his efforts to enter the delicious Garden of Love and pluck the budding rose of love. In Speght's poem the speaker, Rachel, recounts a dream that led her "[i]nto a place most pleasant to the eye," named Cosmos, where, "wanting wisdom," she finds herself suddenly amazed and disconsolate (lines 20–28). Approached by Thought, who inquires the reason for her grief and promises aid, she names her problem as "*Ignorance*"—defined very generally. Ignorance has reduced her to a brutish reliance on instinct and to solipsism: "I measure all mens feet by mine owne shooe" (line 65). Thought sends her to Age, who directs her to Experience. Experience recommends Knowledge as "[t]he onely medicine for your maladie," locating it, "[i]n *Eruditions* garden" and promising that Industry will serve as Rachel's guide (91–100). The allegory suggests that some persons of age and experience helped her acquire an education and realize its benefits.

A dialogue follows in which Dissuasion sets forth the many difficulties in Rachel's way—"As dulnesse, and my memories defect; / The difficultie of attaining lore, / My time, and sex, with many others more" (106–08)—and is answered by Desire, Truth, and Industry. Industry promises to "cut away / All obstacles, that in her way can grow" and predicts victory: "I'll make thee *labor omnia vincet* know" (122, 124; "labor will conquer all"). This allusion to Vergil's *Georgics* 1.45 plays off against the romance expectation of the familiar saying, "*Amor vincit omnia*" ("love conquers all"); it makes woman's province not love but intellectual labor and shows Speght taking considerable credit for her own industry and achievements. Truth speaks to the gender issue, claiming that the natures of men and women are alike suited to education on precisely the same basis: the equality of their intellects and the fact that God himself requires from both men and women the use of all talents. Rachel is then led by Industry to "*Instructions* pleasant ayre," where she delights in the "taste of science" and desires to "reape this pleasure more and more" (187, 195, 198). Truth then delivers a paean to knowledge, forcefully countering the familiar arguments in contemporary tracts for limiting woman's education to what is of practical use in her life: the Bible, religious treatises, grammar, handwriting, domestic skills (and for aristocrats, music, dancing, and modern languages). Truth takes the high line, arguing that the very nature of humankind makes all knowledge useful for all humans. It is Speght's most progressive argument, buttressed by numerous scriptural citations in the margins, and no doubt derives its urgency from her experience. She then reports that some "occasion" cut short her education (line 134), linking it to the duties and the obedience demanded of women in the era. She obeys but makes her dismay evident, indicating that she has not internalized or truly accepted this construction of woman's role.

Speght's later life is a virtual blank. On 6 August 1621 at Saint Mary Woolchurch haw, London, she married a minister, William Proctor, closely allied to her father in his Calvinist theology and City connections. Baptismal records at Saint Giles, Cripplegate, identify two children whose names suggest they were probably the first ones born alive: Rachel (26 Feb. 1627) and William (15 Dec. 1630); evidently the family then lived in that parish. I have found no record of other children or of Rachel Speght's death or burial. Her writing, at least for publication, seems to have ended with her marriage.

Elizabeth H. Hageman

Katherine Philips

On 10 August 1667, Samuel Pepys wrote in his diary that he went

> to the New Exchange to the bookseller's there, where I
> hear of several new books coming out—Mr. Pratts history
> of the Royal Society and Mrs. Phillips's poems. Sir Jo. Den-
> hams poems are going to be all printed together [. . .] .
> Here having stayed and divertized myself a good while, I
> home again [. . .] and betimes to bed with my wife because
> of rising betimes tomorrow. (8: 380)

The bookseller whose shop Pepys visited that day was Henry Herringman, who on 21 January 1667 had entered in the *Stationers'*
Register his intention of publishing a new edition of poems by "Mrs
Catherine Phillips." Dated with the imprimatur of Roger L'Estrange
on 20 August 1667, the book was available in Herringman's shop
by at least 16 September, when Pepys, again at the New Exchange,
"stayed reading Mrs. Phillips's poems till my wife and Mercer called
me to Mrs. Pierce's by invitation to dinner" (8: 439).

Herringman's 1667 title page announces that the author of the volume is "the most deservedly Admired Mrs. Katherine Philips, The matchless ORINDA." The book prints 116 of Philips's original poems, her translations of one Italian song, four French poems, and two heroic dramas by Pierre Corneille (*La mort de Pompée* [1644; rev. 1660] and *Horace* [1641; rev. 1660]). On the frontispiece is a classicized portrait of Philips by William Faithorne, labeled with her sobriquet, Orinda. An unsigned preface tells an abbreviated history of the book and of its appropriately modest female author. And seven prefatory poems, including one by a woman who signed herself Philo-Philippa, commend Philips's virtue and her literary skill.

As the preface says, Herringman's folio was preceded by a pirated edition of Philips's poems. This was an octavo edition of seventy-five poems published in London by Richard Marriott. On 18 January 1664, four days after he first advertised the book, Marriott announced in the London *Intelligencer* that he was withdrawing it from sale: "[W]hereas he was fully persuaded, both of the Correctnesse of the Copy, and of that Ingenious Lady's Allowance to have [the poems] Printed; [. . .] now he finds neither the One, nor the Other, according to his Expectation; which is a double Injury, [. . .] he intends to forbeare the sale of them, being not without hope, that this false Copy, may produce the true One." In three letters written soon thereafter—one to Dorothy (Osborne) Temple and two to Sir Charles Cotterell—Philips expresses deep concern over the printing of the book. As she wrote to Cotterell in the letter that was subsequently printed within the 1667 preface (and, slightly revised, in 1705 in *Letters from Orinda to Poliarchus*), the edition had made her an "unfortunate person [. . .] that must have my imaginations rifled and exposed to play the Mountebanks, and dance upon the Ropes to entertain all the rabble; and to undergo all the raillery of the Wits, and all the severity of the Wise, and to be the sport of some that can, and some that cannot read a Verse" (*Poems* [1667] A1v). Apparently convinced that the only solution to the problem was to issue a corrected version of the poems, Philips went to London that spring. She died of smallpox, however, on 22 June 1664, leaving it to others to reprint the seventy-five poems, as the 1667 preface says, "in some measure restor'd to their native Shape and Beauty" (a2v), and to add to them forty-one more poems by her and also her translations.

Nothing in the preface indicates that Philips's translation of *Pompey* was a landmark in women's literary history, that when it was performed at the Theatre Royal in Dublin in February 1663, Philips became the first woman to have a play on the British public stage. Nor does the preface indicate that the base text for the 1667 *Pompey* is the first of two quarto editions printed in 1663 in Dublin and then London by John Crooke. The preface does not explain that the 1667 *Horace* is incomplete because Philips had reached only act 4, scene 6, of her translation when she died, in 1664. Finished by Sir John Denham in time for a performance at court on 4 February 1668 and then by the King's Company at Bridges Theatre during the 1668–69 season, the Philips-Denham *Horace* was printed as a unit in the second and third editions of the folio (1669 and 1678). (In 1710, when Jacob Tonson republished Philips's writing, he used the conclusion of Charles Cotton's translation of *Horace* instead of Denham's looser version.)

Happily, some of Philips's poems are also extant in her own manuscript copies or in transcripts made by friends; her poem on John Lloyd is engraved on his funeral monument in Cilgerran, Wales; and several poems survive in settings by musicians such as Henry Lawes and Henry Purcell (for photographic facsimiles of these texts, see Applegate; Hageman, "Making"; Hageman and Sununu). Philips's poem on the arrival in England of Charles II's bride, Catherine of Braganza, was printed in 1662 on a broadside now extant in at least two copies, one at Harvard University and one at Worcester College, Oxford (Hageman, "Broadside"), and three of her poems were printed in *Poems, by Several Persons* (Dublin, 1663), a volume now owned in an apparently unique copy by the Folger Library. Other recently relocated Philips items are a copy, now at the University of Kentucky, of "A Sea Voyage from Tenby to Bristol" torn from Philips's manuscript book, which is now in the National Library of Wales, and an early manuscript of *Pompey*, transcribed in an unidentified hand and corrected by Philips (Hageman and Sununu, plates 1, 2, and 10). Happily, too, fifty-six of Philips's letters are known to have survived,

forty-eight of them in *Letters from Orinda to Poliarchus* (rpt. with
one additional letter, 1729). Materials such as these, taken together
with documents such as seventeenth-century parish records, copies
of extracts from Philips's poems and plays in contemporary commonplace books and poetical miscellanies, and allusions to Philips in
Restoration and eighteenth-century writing, provide a remarkably
detailed record of the life, perceptions, literary interests, and contemporary reputation of "the matchless Orinda."

Philips's most striking poems are the friendship poems written
to women such as Anne Owen (often addressed with the sobriquet
Lucasia), Mary Aubrey (Rosania), and Lady Elizabeth Boyle (Celi-
mena). Many are written against love poems such as John Donne's
"The Canonization." "Friendship's Mystery, to My Dearest Lucasia," for example, begins:

> Come, my Lucasia, since we see
> That Miracles Men's faith do move,
> By wonder and by prodigy
> To the dull angry world let's prove
> There's a Religion in our Love.
>
> (*Poems* [1667] 21; lines 1–5)

"Parting with Lucasia," a poem that recalls "A Valediction Forbidding Mourning," begins with similarly cheerful directness: "Well,
we will do that rigid thing / Which makes Spectators think we part"
(65; lines 1–2). Far more somber is "Orinda to Lucasia," whose
comparison of Lucasia's power and the sun's is as compelling, as
deeply serious, as are analogous lines in Donne:

> Thy absence makes my night.
> But ah! my Friend, it now grows very long,
> Thy sadness weighty and the darkness strong:
> My tears (its dew) dwell on my cheeks,
> And still my heart thy dawning seeks,
> And to the[e] mournfully it cries,
> That if too long I wait,
> Ev'n thou may'st come too late,
> And not restore my life, but close my eyes.
>
> (154; lines 16–24)

"Wiston Vault," a poem worthy of comparison with George Herbert's "Church Monuments," contrasts inept friends who commission engraved monuments—"did they not suspect his Name would fall, / There would not need an Epitaph at all" (36; lines 13–14)—with true lovers. Orinda's "Monument" (line 18), Orinda says, will be in Lucasia's heart, which, "[t]hough ne're Stone to me, 'twill Stone for me prove" (line 19).

Philips's oeuvre includes many other kinds of poems: five celebrating weddings of friends and relatives, poems on the deaths of Philips's infant son and young stepdaughter, verses to and about her husband (Antenor in the poems and letters), philosophical poems, poems commending authors such as William Cartwright and Henry Vaughan, and political poems such as two on the coronation of Charles II and the one on Catherine of Braganza mentioned above. Many of these poems are "response" poems in the sense that Mary Ann Radzinowicz uses the term in "Reading Paired Poems Nowadays." Radzinowicz argues that in each of her friendship poems Philips is in "a conversation with the elder male poet [Donne] and an individual member of her female coterie" (285). Similarly, in "To My Dearest Sister, Mrs. C. P. on Her Marriage," Philips is in conversation with earlier marriage poets (especially Spenser), with the male members of the Barebones Parliament (including Philips's own husband) who passed the new marriage law under which Cicily Philips married John Lloyd in October 1653, and of course with Cicily (under the name of Cassandra) herself.

Some of Philips's poems are gender-neutral, but many are written from an overtly female perspective. For example, the poem on Cicily's marriage outlines "Orinda's wishes for Cassandra's bliss" (26; line 8), and it includes a hope that no reader of early modern marriage poetry would expect to see addressed to a bridegroom: "May her Content and *Duty* be the same" (line 13; emphasis mine). "The Virgin" critiques the masculinist ideology of Martial's "The Happy Life," an epigram translated and imitated by early modern poets as various as Surrey (Henry Howard), Ben Jonson, Henry Wotton, and Abraham Cowley. And the speaker in "Upon the Double Murther of K. Charles I, in Answer to a Libellous Copy of Rimes by Vavasor Powell" says she is forced by Powell's assertion that Charles I broke all the Ten Commandments to move from "female" silence into the "male" voice of an outraged satirist.

Some years ago one of my graduate students wrote a wonderful term paper centering on three kisses: the "chaste, yet loving kisse" (137; line 165) of the tree in Aemilia Lanyer's "Description of Cooke-ham," the "Spirits [that] greet and kiss" (58; line 11) in Philips's "To my Lucasia," and Lady Happy and the Princess's kiss in Margaret Cavendish's *Convent of Pleasure*. Among many issues raised by that paper is the extent to which seventeenth-century women writers were aware of one another's writing or perceived themselves as united by gender even in spite of economic, religious, and social distinctions. I know of no evidence that Philips or Cavendish read Lanyer, but Lanyer's "The Authors Dreame to the Ladie Marie, the Countesse Dowager of Pembrooke" shows her allegiance to a female predecessor. Similarly, I have no reason to believe that Philips and Cavendish met or even corresponded (the Lady M. Cavendish who is mentioned in the title of one of Philips's poems is not—as some have thought—the writer Cavendish, duchess of Newcastle, but Lady Mary Cavendish, the married daughter of James Butler, lord lieutenant of Ireland). But in a letter to Cotterell of 24 December 1663 Philips recounts an anecdote about Edmund Waller's response to Cavendish's "The Hunting of the Stag" (printed in her *Poems and Fancies* [1653]). In the midst of a playful discussion of Waller's having purposefully written a poem inferior to one of her own, Philips says:

> I remember I have been told that he once said, he would have given all his own Poems to have been the Author of that which my Lady Newcastle writ of a Stag: And that being tax'd for this Insincerity by one of his Friends, he answer'd, that he could do no less in Gallantry than be willing to devote all his own Papers to save the Reputation of a Lady, and keep her from the Disgrace of having written anything so ill.   (*Letters* O7v)

Although the story may not express respect for Lady Newcastle's poem, it does show Philips's awareness that as women poets she and

Cavendish were in the same social category. She goes on to say, "Some such Repartee I expect he would make on this occasion; but I fear I have lost his Favour for ever in having twice trod in his Steps by writing on Subjects he had chosen" (O7v).

Similarly, it is clear that Cavendish was aware of herself as one in a line of literary women to be criticized, for in *Poems and Fancies* (and again in 1664 in her *Sociable Letters*) she quotes Sir Edward Denny's poem on Lady Mary Wroth when she predicts that her writing will be derided:

> I imagine I shall be censur'd by my owne Sex; and Men will cast a smile of scorne upon my Book, because they think thereby, Women incroach too much upon their Prerogatives; for they hold Books as their Crowne, and the Sword as their Scepter, by which they rule, and governe. And very like they will say to me, as to the Lady that wrote the Romancy,
>
> Work Lady, work, let writing Books alone,
> For surely wiser Women nere wrote one. (A3r–v)

Also relevant here are the two letters in which Dorothy Osborne (later the wife of Sir William Temple) criticizes *Poems and Fancies*, saying, for example, that having seen it, she is "satisfyed there are many soberer People in Bedlam, i'le swear her friends are much to blame to let her goe abroad" (*Letters to Sir William Temple* 79). And then Philips's 1664 letter to Lady Temple expresses unease over the pirated edition of her poems and also pleasure that Lady Temple prefers her translation of *Pompey* to a rival translation of the same play by Waller and four other court wits (Hageman, "Making," plates 5 and 6).

Although I have taught Philips's poetry in a sophomore-level course called Writing by and about Women from *Antigone* to *Annie John* and also in seminars in early modern women, I prefer to teach her writing in the seventeenth-century survey course, where my students and I have more time to examine it within and against its contemporary contexts. At the University of New Hampshire, Durham, English majors are required to take two courses in literature written before 1800. As a result, a few students come to my class after taking the early British literature survey or colonial American literature; most have taken our popular Shakespeare course. Wanting to have on my syllabus at least one item they will recognize by name, I include a Shakespeare play, often *The Tempest*, because it shares so many themes with Francis Bacon's *New Atlantis*, Thomas Hobbes's *Leviathan*, and Cavendish's *Blazing World*; I also include poems by Robert Herrick, Philips, and Andrew Marvell. Or we might read *Love's Labour's Lost* or *The Winter's Tale* alongside Wroth's *Urania* and conclude the semester with Aphra Behn's *The Unfortunate Happy Lady* and Cavendish's *Convent of Pleasure*. We can also study Philips's *Pompey*, which treats the aftermath of civil war and which includes two assertive female characters: Cleopatra, who seeks to regain the Egyptian throne from her brother Ptolemy, and Pompey's widow, Cornelia, who is loyal to his memory and to her own sons. *Horace*, too, would be an interesting choice, especially since its two female protagonists must choose between loyalties to state and family—and because of its interesting publication and performance history. (Students are likely to be interested also in Anne Bradstreet, who was born in England and whose first print publication was in London: *The Tenth Muse, Lately Sprung Up in America* [1650].)

Because it is difficult for students to acquaint themselves with too many authors, genres, and literary styles in one semester, I limit the course to eight to ten authors or topics and allot a week or two to each. Every time I plan the course, I make different, always painful, choices—Thomas Traherne or Herbert? the Quakers or the Fifth Monarchists?—reminding myself, however, that one of the most successful courses I have taught at the University of New Hampshire, Durham, was a seminar whose syllabus I cut in half twice before sending in my book order. If we have a week for Philips, we can read the nineteen poems I edited for Katharina Wilson's *Women Writers of the Renaissance and Reformation* and a few more that relate to other readings in the semester—"The Virgin" with Jonson's translation of Martial, for instance, or Philips's poem on Cowley's retirement with Cowley's two poems celebrating Philips.

If we have two weeks for Philips, we can study one of the plays and also a few of the letters, the letters perhaps with selections from John Evelyn's and Pepys's diaries, both of which comment on many of the same events that Philips mentions and both of which record seeing *Horace*: Evelyn at court (505) and later at Bridges Theatre (524), Pepys at Bridges (9: 420).

I arrange the syllabus in roughly chronological order, beginning with Lanyer and Jonson. The first assignment is to read Lanyer's "A Description of Cooke-ham" and Jonson's "To Penshurst" and to write a short paper on one or both of them. We then spend a whole class (we meet twice weekly in eighty-minute units) listening to all the papers read aloud by their authors—first those on Lanyer, then those on both poems, and finally those on Jonson. (I explain that we are treating the poems in the order that they were printed: Lanyer's in 1611, Jonson's in 1616.) If the class is large (I usually have between twenty and twenty-five students in the survey), it takes most of the period to hear them all. The time is, however, well spent, for as the students listen to their classmates' papers, they see how many approaches to the poems can fruitfully be taken, they see how two readers may hear two quite different voices within a single line. By the end of the class period, every student has accomplished the (sometimes frightening) task of reading his or her work aloud. Students get some immediate feedback from their classmates' and my nods, laughter, and brief words of appreciation, and they soon receive written feedback from me, since I collect the papers and write comments on them before our next meeting. The exercise establishes the class as one that will deal with issues of intertextuality; both Lanyer and Jonson, for example, locate happiness within orderly landscapes and both define themselves in terms of hospitality they have received from worthy patrons—the daughter of a court musician and the stepson of a bricklayer thus asserting their worth as poets in a hierarchical world. We also note differences between the poems (e.g., Lanyer's elegiac tone and Jonson's assertive confidence), and the issue of the extent to which differences are determined by gender inevitably arises in this initial discussion.

After the Lanyer-Jonson assignment, I divide the class into two groups that will then write papers for alternating class meetings: group A for each Tuesday, say; group B for each Thursday. When there are fewer papers on a day, we have time to discuss everybody's ideas, and students become increasingly willing to say, "I think my paper should probably come first in today's discussion," or, "Let me respond to your paper by reading mine." After five or six weeks, I rearrange the class into three groups, thus decreasing the frequency of writing assignments while the students are working on longer critical-research papers. Students do find so many short papers a daunting prospect, but the more they write about early modern texts, the more confident they become. As the weeks go by, they themselves note Philips's echoes of Donne; similarities and differences among Philips's, Bradstreet's, and Jonson's poems on the deaths of children; and various uses of pastoral motifs by Philips and Marvell. They become increasingly better readers of poetry (we often read poems aloud and comment on images, rhythmic patterns, and other poetic techniques). As we wrestle with ideas of class, religion, race, gender, and sexuality, we all reach an increasingly full understanding of the political and literary issues at stake among seventeenth-century writers; we also see how various are the attitudes with which different authors describe events such as the beheading of the king or cultural codes such as the dictate that women be chaste, silent, and obedient.

That Philips works for my students is indicated by the fact that in every class that has studied her, several students have chosen to write term papers on her. Some are critical of her class biases; others are eager to celebrate a woman writer whose wit and energy they admire. Most have focused on her friendship poems, though a few have used her writing in papers on themes such as female innocence, ambivalent politics, marriage poems, or children in seventeenth-century writing. Most rewarding for me, perhaps, is that when I teach an early modern period that includes women writers such as "the matchless Orinda," I feel I am teaching a period that is even more richly complicated, even more interesting than the early modern period (which we then called the Renaissance) that I studied when I was in school.

Anne Shaver

Margaret Cavendish, Duchess of Newcastle

For the last ten years I have included Margaret Cavendish's *Blazing World* in every course I could possibly fit it into: a surprising number, really. I teach it in the early British survey, right next to the Norton redaction of *Paradise Lost*, as an alternative notion of politics and paradise. I teach it as the first text in a course on feminist science fiction, where it begins the conversation on the estranging of gender. I teach it in variously designed seminars on early women writers, and once I created an entire honors seminar around the students' editing of some of Cavendish's plays—after we first got to know her by reading *Blazing World*.

Still, her works deserve an entire course to themselves. This course becomes possible as more of her works become generally available. In designing such a class, astonished English professors will find themselves called on to teach the history of seventeenth-century science, the conditions of Commonwealth and Restoration drama, modes of biography and autobiography, along with examples of poetry, fantasy, science fiction, essays, speeches, and personal letters that are both eccentric and expressive of their historical moment. One of Cavendish's main characteristics is the profusion of her output, the sheer amount of it, its generic variety, and the ways it challenges customary generic boundaries. No survey in which she can be granted only a few days or even a week or two can do justice to her energetic and original genius. She had a passion for singularity; in fact, the character who bears her name in *Blazing World* declares: "I endeavour [. . .] to be as singular as I can; for it argues but a mean nature to imitate others [. . .] my nature is such, that I had rather appear worse in singularity, then better in mode" (*Blazing World* [Lilley] 218).

To present her as she wanted to be known, the syllabus of an all-Cavendish course would need to include a good deal of her scientific writing, since she produced more of this than any other kind, putting her speculations into a variety of traditional and hybrid genres. Science—or natural philosophy, as it was then called—is the subject of her first two publications; those and her later scientific writings were the works she revised and reissued most often. The title of her first book, *Poems and Fancies* (1653), is misleading, because most of the poems are "fancies" based on scientific speculation. Her second work, also published in 1653, is *Philosophical Fancies*, greatly revised and republished as *Philosophical and Physical Opinions* in 1655 and 1663, then revised and retitled again as *Grounds of Natural Philosophy* in 1668. A study of the evolution of this work not only reveals her intellectual development but also reflects, often through her opposition to it, much that was going on around her as the seventeenth-century scientific community sought to define its modes and purposes. For example, Baconian experimental science, explicitly those parts of Robert Hooke's *Micrographia* dealing with the uses of the microscope, is the target of Cavendish's *Observations upon Experimental Philosophy, to Which Is Added, the Description of a New Blazing World* (1666). Help in understanding Cavendish's place in seventeenth-century science may be found in David F. Noble's *A World without Women: The Christian Clerical Culture of Western Science*, Patricia Phillips's *The Scientific Lady: A Social History of Women's Scientific Interests,*

1520–1918, and Linda Schiebinger's *The Mind Has No Sex? Women in the Origins of Modern Science*. An interesting alternative to a literary course might be a course on women in science, in which Cavendish's scientific texts are team-taught with a historian or philosopher of science.

In a course solely on Cavendish, however, judging her pride in them by the number of pages she published and the magnificence of the printed folios, her plays would also require several weeks of attention. She is the author of nineteen dramas, seven of them ten acts long, published in two volumes, *Plays* (1662) and *Plays Never Before Printed* (1668). Unlike her scientific writing, her plays were never reissued, and apparently she never tried to produce them. Although she was acknowledged as a playwright by some of her earliest critics, most scholars and biographers have dismissed this aspect of her work as least worthy of attention. In a recent article in *Criticism*, Marta Straznicky suggests that the negative attitude toward Cavendish's plays is due to "performance bias" on the part of critics (355), who are only recently beginning to realize the public intent and political uses of closet drama. But when Cavendish explains to the reader in copious epistles preceding *Playes* why she has chosen to publish her dramas without first having them performed, she does not claim that she wrote them only to be read; in fact, quite the opposite. Although she apologizes for their imperfections, she blames the current condition of the English theater for her choice, and in *Blazing World* the character named Duchess of Newcastle is a playwright who happily anticipates staging her own works in a world where they will be appreciated ([Lilley] 219–21). Cavendish's plays, idiosyncratic as they are, resemble prewar romances and Restoration comedies more than they do the classically structured closet drama of Elizabeth Cary or John Milton, and even Straznicky admits that Cavendish writes "as if" for performance (378).

Studying her plays would require less background work for most English majors than studying her science. Staged or simply seated readings done in class bring the dramas alive and make their structure and themes easily apparent. *Orations of Divers Sorts* might be taught in conjunction with the dramas, both thematically and as examples of another public mode made available for closet reading; their publication date, shared with *Playes*, suggests a strong intentional connection. Parts could be assigned to enact "Female Orations," in *Orations of Divers Sorts*, a debate about the nature, role, and worth of woman. It would be interesting, using evidence from the plays, to conjecture which of the several views propounded by the imagined female debaters seems closest to the author's. Help teaching Cavendish's plays may be found in publications by Jeffrey Masten; Linda R. Payne; Jacqueline Pearson; Straznicky; Sophie Tomlinson; and Susan Wiseman.

The short essays of *The World's Olio*; the gossipy, descriptive, opinionated epistles of *CCXI Sociable Letters*; and some of the expository writings in *Natures Pictures* connect with the persuasive style of the orations and also with many of the hortatory speeches made by suggestively autobiographical heroines in the plays. The connection invites study of the duchess's perceptions of the world she found herself inhabiting. These essays in several genres are the most firmly set in her present or recent experiences; for example, several of the *CCXI Sociable Letters* give a vivid picture of life in Antwerp, where the Cavendishes lived for most of their Commonwealth exile. Although the addressees of the *Letters* and the people discussed in them are putatively fictional, enough of them share some of Cavendish's actual experiences, and enough are introduced using variations on her and her husband's initials, to invite the reader to seek autobiographical information in them.

Of all the genres she wrote in, biography and to a lesser degree autobiography kept her name alive to literary history when all her other work was neglected. Though Samuel Pepys scorned it, her biography of her husband (*Life*) was generally acclaimed both when it appeared in 1667 and during the centuries that followed. It was published in a Latin translation by Walter Charleton in 1668 (*De Vita*), and the English version was reissued in 1675. Except for some anthologizing of her more whimsical poems, the biography and incidentally her own short memoir were the only works that nineteenth- and early-twentieth-century editors and scholars found worthy of their attention, and then primarily for their subject:

William Cavendish, the Cavalier Duke. "A True Relation of My Birth, Breeding, and Life," which first appeared as the last entry in the mostly fictional *Natures Pictures Drawn by Fancies Pencil to the Life* (1656; omitted in 1671), was republished in 1812 by William Cavendish's descendant Egerton Brydges and continued to appear as an appendix to the life of the duke in nineteenth- and twentieth-century editions, beginning with Mark Anthony Lower's in 1872. That the existence of these two narratives makes the lives and characters of the duchess and her duke more available to modern readers than those of almost any other writers and patrons of the seventeenth century is exactly what Cavendish had in mind.

Although both the biography and the memoir reflect her need that posterity acknowledge her worth and the honor of her hero-husband, and although some scholars think her account of Newcastle's financial losses is exaggerated, these works are essentially factual and position Cavendish as the appropriately adoring wife of such a noble man. But Cavendish was also a fiction writer whose short and not-so-short stories give some women—heroines based on her aspiring self—means to extraordinary self-realization. *Blazing World* and several of her plays, as well as *The Contract* and *Assaulted and Pursued Chastity*, the "other writings" in The Blazing World *and Other Writings*, edited by Kate Lilley, center on such women.

Thus, if the variousness of Cavendish's output threatens to send the syllabus into a scattering gyre, there are strong themes on which to center the course. Cavendish is a wavering feminist who accepts that men are superior to women but who finally locates that superiority in men's greater opportunities. She refuses to give up the excellences peculiar to "effeminate" women even as she imagines women who find ways to exercise their "masculine" abilities to rule, to fight, and to persuade. She is, however, an unwavering royalist. Recent scholars such as Catherine Gallagher and Anna Battigelli have connected her royalist politics both to her feminism and to her renunciation of the theory of atoms. Exercising the power of a duchess and negotiating her way around the powerlessness of women, she is a fascinating commentator on gender issues in her time.

Her time also comments vividly on her, in critical voices such as those of Dorothy Osborne, Mary Evelyn, Pepys, and John Stainsby (who is quoted in Douglas Grant's useful biography *Margaret the First*) and in voices of praise (whose sincerity varies) such as the letters collected and published as a memorial by the duke in *Letters and Poems in Honour of the Incomparable Princess, Margaret, Dutchess of Newcastle*. Until recently, subsequent voices, when they paid attention to Cavendish at all, were apt to be patronizing or even embarrassed, an attitude culminating finally in Virginia Woolf's famous image in *A Room of One's Own* of Cavendish's prolific writing as "a giant cucumber" that "spread itself over all the roses and carnations in the garden and choked them to death" (61–63). See Sandra Gilbert and Susan Gubar's reiteration of Woolf's discomfort with Cavendish's exuberance (*Madwoman* 65, 541–45). Although late-twentieth-century theories about women's different language offer a way through Woolf's reservations, even some of the most recent commentators seem not to be able to take Cavendish entirely seriously as a writer or a person. Part of the pleasure of teaching her work, then, is the sense of participating in a rescue of the reputation for which she was so ambitious.

The best Cavendish-centered class I have taught so far is one in which ten honors students actually produced an edition of four of her plays. I designed the course not so much to teach how to edit— indeed, I found myself learning the practicalities along with and often from my students—as to show how important editing is and how the attention of editors and reputable scholars can pave the way for a writer's entry into the classroom and thus into the broader culture. The course began with Aemilia Lanyer's *Salve Deus Rex Judaeorum*. We compared a photocopy of the 1611 book with Susanne Woods's 1993 edition for the Oxford University Press series Women Writers in English, 1330–1830. What was perhaps more important for the tone of the course, we read A. L. Rowse's introduction to his *Poems of Shakespeare's Dark Lady* next to Woods's introduction and Barbara Lewalski's chapter on Lanyer in *Writing Women in Jacobean England* (213–41; "Imagining Female Community: Aemilia Lanyer's Poems"). The disparities in the presentations were immediately apparent to the students: the difference between Rowse's voyeuristic interest in the person to the detriment of her poetry and the other two scholars' balanced attention to both and the difference in intent between Woods's mainly informational essay and Lewalski's more interpretative one. We went on to read Elizabeth Cary's *Mariam* in Barry Weller and Margaret W. Ferguson's edition (a more elaborate and expensive text than the Lanyer book) as well as Lewalski's chapter on Cary in *Writing Women*. We read Cavendish's *Blazing World* as edited by Lilley and felt the lack of Lewalski's validating attention (*Writing Women* covers exclusively women who wrote while James I was on the throne). Then, using photocopies of the original edition and a typescript of the text from the Brown Women Writers Project, the class divided into teams of two and rescued *The Convent of Pleasure,* one act to each pair. Their labor involved research into Cavendish's life and critical reputation as well as close attention to the text; each team wrote general introductions and critical comments for the act assigned to it. Having thus practiced, the student teams turned their work on *Convent* over to me to synthesize and set about rescuing the ten acts of *Loves Adventures*, the ten of *Bell in Campo*, and the five of *The Comedy Named the Several Wits.* Some class time was used for consulting about editorial decisions, but other sessions saw reports on scholarly essays and, toward the end of the semester, some excellently staged readings from the plays. The result, published by the college's office services and paid for by the honors program as a recruiting tool, is an anthology of the four plays, well glossed, each with an introduction composed by the student editors. We all contributed to a general introduction to Cavendish the person and the playwright.

Thus Cavendish offers riches for any number of courses on her work alone. Yet she should not be left out of a chronological survey; her work livens up the end of a *Beowulf*-to-Dryden course immensely. Unfortunately, the only standard survey anthology that includes any of her work, *The Norton Anthology of English Literature* (6th ed., vol. 1 [Abrams et al.]), contains no more than a slight introduction and one charming but hardly representative poem, "The Pastime of the Queen of Fairies" (1718–20). But other of her texts are available in various ways. These may be paired with works by other writers more usually found in anthologies and on survey syllabi; for example, Irene Dash has shown how to pair *The Convent of Pleasure* and *Love's Labour's Lost*, two plays that deal with single-sex retreats, one female, the other male. *Blazing World*, first published one year before Milton's *Paradise Lost*, presents a post-Restoration view of Eden very different from Milton's, and it imagines a scientific utopia from a gender perspective opposite that of Francis Bacon's *New Atlantis*. *Blazing World* can also be an early modern example in utopian fantasy and science fiction classes: the female singularity it celebrates is a provocative contrast with the communal world imagined in Charlotte Perkins Gilman's *Herland* (1915), while its uncommon genre mix of science writing, politics, and romance connects in interesting ways with Joanna Russ's *The Female Man* (1975) and Gerd Brantenberg's *Egalia's Daughters* (1978).

Enough affordable classroom texts are now available to create a viable course. To Kate Lilley's Penguin edition of *The Blazing World*, *The Contract*, and *Assaulted and Pursued Chastity* and to Paul Salzman's Oxford University Press *Anthology of Seventeenth-Century Fiction*, which includes *The Blazing World*, has recently been added Cavendish's *Sociable Letters*, edited by James Fitzmaurice for Garland Press, and an edition from Johns Hopkins University Press of four of her plays, *Loves Adventures*, *Bell in Campo*, *The Bridals*, and *Convent of Pleasure*, edited by me. There is also a selection of the *Letters* in *Major Women Writers of Seventeenth-Century England*, edited by Fitzmaurice, Josephine A. Roberts, Carol L. Barash, Eugene R. Cunnar, and Nancy A. Gutierrez. *Paper Bodies: A Margaret Cavendish Reader*, edited by Sylvia Bowerbank and Sara Mendelson, appeared in 2000. *CCXI Sociable Letters* (1969) and *Poems and Fancies* (1972) in Scolar Press facsimiles may be obtained through interlibrary loan. The Brown University Women Writers Project is constantly adding Cavendish texts to its collection of early women writers now available by subscription online. Most exhaustive is the University of Michigan's project to microfilm all books in the *English Short Title Catalogue*. The project includes an example of all but one of Cavendish's works, in most of their editions. Only

Philosophical Fancies, her first specifically scientific essay, is missing from the list. These microfilms can be found at most graduate-degree–granting institutions and may be copied for custom anthologies. Individual works have been filmed by other companies for specialized libraries—for example, *Orations of Divers Sorts* for the Kress Library of Economic Literature and both books of plays for the Readex series Three Centuries of English Drama. Most of the titles, including rare and modern books and various film versions, are recorded in OCLC, the Online Computer Library Center, and the list is growing.

Germaine Greer

Aphra Behn

Aphra Behn is one of the most exciting and mysterious characters in all English literature. She was working at a time when respectable, responsible publishing was being painfully born out of printing chaos, nurtured by exceptional publishers like the Jacob Tonsons and by businesslike authors like John Dryden. No systematic analysis of Behn's publishing career in its industrial context has ever been carried out; most accounts are distorted by twentieth-century assumptions about the social status of authors.

Behn scholars risk being sidetracked by the riddle of her biography. If Aphra Behn is the Eaffrey Johnson who was baptized at Harbledown near Canterbury on 14 December 1640, she was the daughter of a tradesman, later an innholder, and might have been expected to live and die in Kent, with no more literary skill than was necessary to cast her accounts and read her Bible. Perhaps young Eaffrey was taught French and introduced to French literature by the Huguenots sheltering in Canterbury from religious persecution over the water. Perhaps she went with an English royalist émigré

family to the Continent for the duration. Behn's use of French originals is a fundamental aspect of her literary contribution that remains
uninvestigated by students of comparative literature and largely misunderstood.

No documentary evidence can be found to link Eaffrey Johnson
with the Mrs. Behn who features in the state papers for 1666 as spying for the Crown on republican refugees in the Netherlands. If the
statements made by the young female narrator of Behn's novel
Oroonoko are true of Behn herself, in 1663 or so she and her family
were accompanying her father on his voyage to the West Indies to
take up the post of lieutenant governor, when he died, leaving them
to disembark in Surinam and wait for a passage home. Certainly
Behn was in Surinam at some time, for the English characters in her
novel are all real people who can be proved to have been there, and
details of the plantations and estates not to be found in contemporary writings about the colony are accurately described. Though
Oroonoko (published in 1688) was influential in its time and has inspired a mass of critical writing, its genre as a semifictional *histoire* is
still imperfectly understood.

How Aphra Behn came to the attention of the Stuart secret service in 1666, by which time she was evidently married, is not known.
Her job was to travel to Antwerp and report on the movements of
the republican William Scot, whom she had known in Surinam.
While she was in Antwerp, she witnessed the attempted execution of
Prince Tarquino, later to be the hero of another semifictional *histoire, The Fair Jilt,* based, she said, on "reality and matter of fact"
(*Oroonoko and Other Writings* 74). Her spying mission involved
her in considerable expense, but entreaties to her employers to cover
her liabilities went unanswered until long after she had returned to
England. In 1668 she was arrested at the command of her creditors,
but there is no record of her as an inmate of any prison.

We next hear of her as the author of a tragicomedy performed
by the Duke's Theatre. *The Forc'd Marriage* opened on 20 September 1670 and ran for six nights. As the author received the proceeds
of every third night, Behn had succeeded at her first attempt in an
honorable if precarious way of earning a living. In January 1671 the

play was published, as by Mrs. A. Behn, with the epigraph "*Va mon enfant! prends ta fortune*" ("Go my child! try your fortune").

By that time Behn's second play, *The Amorous Prince*, was ready for production and apparently was successful. No one objected that the subject matter—the seduction of a friend's sister by the amorous prince, who also attempts to seduce the same friend's beloved, in an atmosphere of dense and amoral sexual intrigue—was hardly suitable for treatment by a respectable woman. The theatrical fare of the time was outspoken and bawdy; Behn had no choice but to follow the fashion, which she was to complain about in later life. Her next play too was tailored to prevailing taste, but, badly produced and worse acted, *The Dutch Lover* failed.

Our imperfect understanding of the economics of the seventeenth-century theater industry means that we cannot be sure that either of her successes brought Behn any measure of financial security. Playwrights were often paid in advance in order to secure new playscripts to meet the production schedule. If the proceeds of every third night, which went to the author, covered her debt to the company and left her a substantial margin to live on, Behn did unusually well. Her friend Thomas Otway died in penury within months of the staging of his most successful play. It seems that even in this relatively early stage in her career Behn was experiencing bouts of illness so severe that she did not expect to survive.

The reality behind the notion that after the failure of *The Dutch Lover* Behn was commissioned to edit a miscellany is that she collected copies of prologues, epilogues, songs and ballads from friends and contacts in the Covent Garden milieu of theaters and coffeehouses to sell for publication as a miscellany. Strangely, *Covent Garden Drolery* contained little verse deriving from the Duke's Theatre, for which Behn wrote, and much from the opposition, the Theatre Royal, which was run by Thomas Killigrew, whom Behn knew, for she wrote to him in very familiar terms during her struggle to get payment from the Crown. *Covent Garden Drolery* connects Behn with a kind of publishing that is still not well understood. Much of the material that Behn selected for print was already available in scribal manuscript copies that could be ordered from a professional scriptorium where samples could be inspected. We know that women were employed in this copying trade, and there is some evidence that Behn was involved in it all her life. The same professional copyists were called on by the theaters, which may be the way that Behn was encouraged to try her hand at her own adaptations of older plays, which formed the staple of the weekly theatrical fare.

Behn's editorship of *Covent Garden Drolery* is still unproven; if she authored any plays in the interval before the appearance of her tragedy *Abdelazer* in the summer of 1676, they were performed and published as anonymous. *Abdelazer* and her following play, *The Town Fop*, were both successful; when they were published, they bore the name Mrs. A. Behn. (It is notable that Aphra Behn was seldom called by that name; she is more often Astraea or simply A. Behn. Contemporary habitués of the theatrical milieu usually filled in her Christian name on their copies as Anne.) Her next theatrical effort, her masterpiece, *The Rover*, was initially neither performed nor printed as hers. The prologue refers to the author as young, a man, and a beginner.

A good deal of work remains to be done on the precise relation between *The Rover* and the much longer play on which it is based and from which it borrows and paraphrases whole interchanges, Killigrew's *Thomaso*. The printed version of *The Rover* appeared with an equivocating postscript in which Behn both denied plagiarism and directed readers to her source. One way to interpret this bravado is that Behn was actually claiming not only *The Rover* but also *Thomaso* as her work. From the role of Killigrew as Behn's intimate friend in 1666, his contributions to *Covent Garden Drolery* in 1672, and his failure to claim *The Rover* as indebted to his 1677 work, we must conclude that there is more to his relationship with Behn than has yet been understood. There is the possibility, argued but not proven, that Behn was one of the amanuenses on whom Killigrew relied because he never learned to read or write or perhaps because he was dyslexic.

When the first copies of John Amery's printing of *The Rover* came off the presses, they did not bear Aphra Behn's name; then the presses were stopped and the words "A Comedy" added to the title page; at a third stage, three words were added to the postscript to reveal the sex of the author, and the title page was canceled for one bearing the words "Written by Mrs. A. Behn." When Behn's next play, *Sir Patient Fancy*, was published, it was attributed to "Mrs. A. Behn, the Author of the Rover." Within a year, she followed this with *The Young King*, *The Feign'd Curtizans*, and *The Second Part of the Rover*, another play drawn from Killigrew's *Thomaso*. During the ferment surrounding the exposure of the feigned Popish Plot, Behn cast her lot with the court party and produced two plays burlesquing the opposition, *The Roundheads* and *The City Heiress*, as well as *The False Count*, a version of Molière's *Le bourgeois gentilhomme*. It would seem that Behn was identified as a Tory writer—if a lone woman could afford political loyalties—for besides writing "Tory farce and doggerel" (her own words, in "A Letter to Mr. Creech" [Oroonoko *and Other Writings* 244]) for Whitehall she also accepted commissions from the trimmer earl of Mulgrave and the Whig earl of Dorset. Though she was a hired pen, she could still be held to account for what she wrote. On 12 August 1682, a warrant was issued for the arrest of "Mrs. Aphaw Behn" on the grounds that she had "made abusive reflections upon persons of Quality" (Duffy, *Shepherdess* 216). The person of quality she had dared to impugn, in a prologue and epilogue she had supplied for an anonymous play called *Romulus and Hersilia*, was the king's illegitimate son, the duke of Monmouth. Once more she seems to have escaped imprisonment, though she disappeared from the theater.

She was at work on her most underrated achievement, the thousand-page novel *Love Letters between a Nobleman and His Sister*. By some accounts this work is indebted to French sources, but no debt is as striking as the novel's extraordinary originality. It was published in three parts in 1684, 1685, and 1687 without Behn's name. She was not to be acknowledged its author in her lifetime. The novel too is semifictional, for it relies on the real-life elopement of Ford Lord Grey and his sister-in-law, Henrietta Berkeley, and on its context, the Whig conspiracies to prevent the succession of James II. *Love Letters* was probably commissioned, perhaps by Sir Roger L'Estrange, and written to order.

At the same time that she was toiling over part 1 of this novel, Behn was preparing a miscellany to be published by Tonson, to whom she wrote begging for a better price for it in terms that suggest that she was as short of money as she had ever been: "I have been without getting so long that I am just on the poynt of breaking. [. . .] I want extreamly or I would not urge this" (*Works* 1: xxi). When *Poems on Several Occasions with a Voyage to the Isle of Love* was published, a few weeks after part 1 of *Love Letters*, it carried a copious selection of commendatory poems, none of them signed by a well-known figure unless we count "T. C.," Thomas Creech. If Tonson had expected much new material, he was to be disappointed, for most of the poems had been printed before, in Behn's plays, in *Covent Garden Drolery*, or elsewhere. Three of the best known had appeared in 1680, as by Rochester, in *Poems on Several Occasions* by the "Right Honourable the E. of R."—and are to be found in many of the manuscripts associated with Rochester, another association that demands scholarly investigation. Half the volume consisted of a free adaptation of the abbé Paul de Tallemant's *Voyages de l'isle de l'Amour*. The volume cannot have sold well, for in 1697 the sheets printed in 1684 were bound up with those of Behn's later collection, *Lycidus*, and sold as a new edition.

In February 1685 all professional writers were at work penning poems on the death of Charles II. Behn's took the form of a Pindaric ode and ended with a section acclaiming the succession of James II; Behn then addressed a poem in heroic couplets to Catherine of Braganza and apparently got hold of the order of service in advance so she could produce *A Pindaric Poem on the Coronation* of James II and Mary of Modena in time for the event. These efforts would have earned her the usual emolument, a couple of guineas for each, but further royal patronage was not forthcoming. Instead she was forced to undertake, in addition to finishing *Love Letters*, a series of crushing literary labors of the least lucrative kind. She put together another *Miscellany*, for the printer J. Hindmarsh. It contains one of her finest poems, *Ovid to Julia: A Letter*, written in the person of the earl of Mulgrave, who was expelled from his court offices in 1682 for having dared to make love to a lady in the direct line of succession, the Julia of the title, Princess Anne. As Behn must have had this poem to hand when she prepared her collected verse for publication by Tonson, it seems she decided to split her collection between two publishers and so earn two payments. In both cases the volume was plumped out by a French translation, this time of the maxims of de la Rochefoucauld, which she called "Reflections on Morality; or, Seneca Unmasqu'd." Within a year yet another printer published another translation by Behn from the French, of *La montre* by Balthasar de Bonnecorse.

Heavy as the workload of these months must have been, Behn lost nothing of her characteristic lightness of touch, which is the more astonishing because she was also in chronic pain and virtually disabled by inflammation of her joints. She managed to adapt *Arlequin empereur dans la lune*, a stock entertainment of the French commedia dell'arte, for successful performance as *The Emperour of the Moon*, at the Queen's Theatre, and wrote an almost entirely original play, *The Luckey Chance*, for performance by the same company a few weeks later. At the same time she was working on an adaptation of the *Second Voyage de l'Isle de l'Amour of de Tallemant*, which was published as *Lycidus; or, The Lover in Fashion*. She then published the first in a series of *histoires*: a translation of *Agnes de Castro, nouvelle portuguaise*, "Written in French by a Lady of Quality," namely, Mademoiselle S. B. de Brillac, and only just published. Within weeks she had completed another translation, of the *Histoire des oracles* by Bernard le Bovier de Fontenelle, first published in 1686; the English translation appeared without the name of either author or translator. At about the same time Behn was asked to prepare potted versions of 110 of Aesop's fables to feature as new captions for the plates engraved by Francis Barlow, for their republication in 1687.

Behn had not given up hopes of finding a rich and powerful patron by publishing panegyric odes in broadside. She celebrated the appointment of the duke of Albemarle to the governorship of Jamaica with a fulsome Pindaric and the announcement of the pregnancy of Mary of Modena in September 1687 with *A Congratulatory Poem to Her Most Sacred Majesty on the Universal Hopes of All*

Loyal Persons for a Prince of Wales. When the child was born on 10 June 1688, Behn was ready with *A Congratulatory Poem to the King's Most Sacred Majesty on the Happy Birth of the Prince of Wales*, only to find herself ridiculed by John Baber in *To the King upon the Queen's Being Deliver'd of a Son* as one of those who would give the queen a son before her time. She replied with a furious lampoon *Upon the Poet Bavius* and had it published in broadside at her own expense. She then addressed herself to L'Estrange, congratulating him for exonerating the Catholics from suspicion of having murdered Sir Edmund Berry Godfrey. These publications earned her little beyond the distrust of the powerful opposition to their Catholic majesties. More successful perhaps were the two new short novels, *The Fair Jilt* and *Oroonoko*, that Behn was preparing for William Canning, who issued them both separately and bound up with *Agnes de Castro*, as *Three Histories*.

When James II and his family fled to France, Behn's hopes of any kind of preferment went with them. She was by this time so ill that Gilbert Burnet, who made a specialty of attending the deathbeds of repentant Restoration rakes, began asking after her. She replied with a dry Pindaric "on the honour he did [her] of Enquiring after [her] and [her] Muse" (*Oroonoko and Other Writings* 265; "A Pindaric Poem on the Reverend Dr. Burnett"). Though she rejected Burnet's implied suggestion that she seek favor by hymning William and Mary, when Mary arrived in England in February 1689, Behn had a poem ready, celebrating her as the "illustrious daughter of a king" (*Works* 1: 305; "A Congratulatory Poem to [. . .] Queen Mary") in terms that might be thought to remind the great lady rather too vividly that she was usurping her father's throne. Mary cannot have responded graciously to this, for Behn sold her Pindaric to Burnet for printing as a broadside a month later. Within days, on 16 April 1689 she was dead, her end hastened by "an unskilfull physician" (Duffy, *Shepherdess* 285). As more of her contemporaries died as a consequence of medical practice than were saved by it, we might question the precise meaning of these words, which derive from a most unreliable source, namely, Charles Gildon, who was to exploit and counterfeit Behn's oeuvre all his venal and ignominious life. The truth is that Behn's ceaseless toil in the last years of her life would hardly have been equal to the astronomical apothecaries' bills incurred by anyone being treated for chronic illness. By the kind offices of the literary Bishop Thomas Sprat she was buried in the cloisters of Westminster Abbey.

Behn's death did little to check the flow of publication of works attributed to her. New novels appeared. *The Lucky Mistake*, published by Richard Bentley, who also published her last Pindarics, is certainly by Behn; the genuineness of the other novellas is to be questioned. Behn plays appeared in print for the first time. *The Younger Brother*, in a rifacimento by Gildon, failed. *The Widdow Ranter* was printed by James Knapton but without the prologue and epilogue by Dryden, which belonged to Tonson, who had published nothing by Behn since she shortchanged him with her *Poems on Several Occasions*. Tonson now chose to issue them under his own imprint.

Taste had changed radically since the days of the merry monarch Charles II; after her death Aphra Behn's life and work were epitomized as sensational and obscene. Her very name became a bugbear to frighten young women away from literary endeavor. Behn's hope for her literary reputation was expressed in one of the multifarious labors of the last year of her life, her 1,740-line versification of the English translation of *Sylvia*, part 6 of Abraham Cowley's Latin poem *Of Plants*, which was in press when she died. The poet addresses the laurel:

> Let me with *Sappho* and *Orinda* be
> Oh ever sacred Nymph, adorn'd by thee;
> And give my Verses Immortality.
> (*Works* 1: 325; lines 592–94)

No study of women's literature, women's poetry, the genesis of the novel, the rise of the literary establishment, the history of the British stage, the advent of Whiggism (the development of the moral double standard in life and literature), libertinism, postcolonial literature, the desexualization of the female, autobiography, female literary identity, or literary relations between England and the Continent can afford to ignore the powerful and enigmatic figure of Aphra Behn.

In view of the advances made in early modern scholarship every year, care should be taken to see that students are aware of the status of Behn texts selected for study, whether translations, adaptations (acknowledged or unacknowledged), or original works—of which *Oroonoko* and *Love Letters between a Nobleman and His Sister* are the most important. Very few individual poems can be securely attributed and should be studied in the context of the publications in which they appeared.

Part III

Models for Teaching

Introduction

An increasing number of teachers have found that bringing early modern women writers into the classroom creates excitement for both the students and the instructor. It shows students how cultural constructions of gender are formed and resisted, offers instructors the opportunity to encounter and contribute to new knowledge that transforms what had seemed a well-tilled academic field, and suggests to both how various might be the discourse worth preserving and studying. One result is a creative atmosphere for teaching and learning, producing many good ideas that refresh the study of literature and open windows into related areas of knowledge, including history, theory, philosophy, and art.

The essays in this section offer a sampling of successful teaching practices and provide models for new teachers to help them spark their creativity. Limits on space and format meant that we could publish only a few essays derived from the many excellent suggestions we received. This short introduction allows us to list some of those other suggestions, each a valuable contribution to pedagogy.

Several suggestions involved pairing women's texts with men's in unusual and illuminating ways. Fran Murphy Zauhar at the College of Saint Vincent combines selections from women and men authors around certain themes, using, for example, Queen Elizabeth's "Doubt of Future Foes" with sections from Philip Sidney's *Arcadia* and Anne Dowriche's *French Historie* to examine different views of kingship. Jo Eldridge Carney of the College of New Jersey assigns papers in which her students compare Aemilia Lanyer's and Edmund Spenser's dedications, Isabella Whitney's and Ovid's epistles, and Mary Wroth's sonnets with others in the period. Lisa Low at Pace University compares Lanyer's "Cookeham" not only with Ben Jonson's "To Penshurst" but also with William Wordsworth's "Tintern Abbey." Gail Cohee at Siena College pairs Katherine Philips with Andrew Marvell and An Collins with George Herbert. Lisa Hopkins at Sheffield-Hallam University uses the figure of Cleopatra as she appears in various texts (beginning with Mary Sidney's *Antonius*) to raise issues of gendered discourse, particularly in drama.

We also received notice of some creative techniques that emerge from teaching early modern women. Mary Sue Ply of Southwestern Louisiana University uses role-playing, assigning individuals or groups the voices of authors or characters, to encourage students to reach for cultural attitudes alien to them. Lisa Blansett of Florida International University organizes her early British literature survey around historical maps and has students consider how authors' literary cartography compares to maps, garden and architectural plans, and paintings, with the Ditchley portrait of Queen Elizabeth I (used on the cover of part 1 of the *Norton Anthology of English Literature* [Abrams et al.]) as a starting point. Margarette R. Connor of Fu Jen Catholic University of Taiwan uses Aphra Behn and Katherine Philips to teach English as a second language; those authors' direct attack on conventional expectations of female behavior becomes a way to discuss cultural (as well as gender) expectations.

The essays that follow begin with some general approaches—first, with the relation of theory to the teaching of early modern women— and move to focused attention on specific authors and works.

Theoretical Issues

Gary F. Waller

Teaching the Writings of Early Modern Women from a Theoretical Perspective

Students of early modern women's writing cannot be immune to issues of sexuality, gender, to relational and identity politics raised by feminism or by the connections of these issues to writing. And these are pressing issues for our students in their own lives as well as in their studies. Why have there been so few women writers? Why, as it is often assumed, have men writers been historically better than women? Why is so much men's writing about or for women? What struggles did women writers have to find their voices? Are those voices recognizably women's voices? Why do so many women writers write under the shadow of men(tors)?

All these questions are theoretically informed—that is, they cannot be answered by reference just to the supposed transparency of the text—as well as part of the fabric of our students' individual and collective lives. Therefore we must be pedagogically sensitive to the enormous emotional task we may be setting before our students when we ask them, within a patriarchal society, to confront themselves as sexed and gendered (and writing) beings. As my colleague

Kim Christensen posed it to me, "This identification with one's (oppressed) gender is painful . . . there is no way that a woman student
can take these texts seriously until she confronts these hard facts.
How can she look clearly at the stifled lives of women in the early
modern period without confronting the forces which stifle her
own?" (E-mail). As teachers, we need to create spaces for students
to grapple with these issues. Many teachers of this material will be
women themselves. It is important that their own involvement in
the sex- and gender-related issues be a part of the mix of discussion
and discovery. And what of the male teacher? Does a man too readily impose a reading of history that is centered on activities predominately coded "male" and that ignores a woman writer's place in an
alternative, subversive history that takes as its landmarks activities
more associated with women? I recall a moment in the early 1970s
when a woman student asked me whether what Stella might have
felt about Astrophil's posturings might be relevant to our understanding of *Astrophil and Stella*. There didn't seem, she said, to be a
"space" for a woman in that text.

The best guides to opening up the most powerful and relevant
questions for understanding women writers are not most standard
literary histories of the period—which traditionally avoid both
women writers and theory—but the philosophers and psychologists
like Sigmund Freud, Julia Kristeva, Jessica Benjamin, or Judith Butler, whose work can help our students pose these crucial questions of
gender, sexuality, and writing. Contemporary political and intellectual life has benefited immeasurably from this area of theory; our
students are in its power, and whether they know it or not, theory
sets part of their emotional and intellectual agendas, helping make
both writing and living more understandable and bearable. As
teachers, we need to help students foreground their own experiences and articulate them better. The links among literature, theory,
and their lives can be the source of topics for group discussion: part
of paper brainstorming or focused class presentation. Because students need us to provide a vocabulary—or, better, varied vocabular-
ies—we may prescribe one or more theoretical essays alongside and
in dialogue with the texts. I have often used Louise Kaplan's treat-

ment in *Female Perversions,* of a woman's "forbidden masculine wishes" (174), to raise questions about Wroth's being drawn to, envious of, and determined to emulate the literary achievements of her family. Butler's considerations of the "troubling" nature of gender and sexuality are powerful (*Gender Trouble*). Freud's essay on the "family romance" is a useful way into the complex personal and literary relationships in the Sidney family. None of these works are explicitly about the early modern period or even about writing—but they are helpful in formulating the questions we need to ask. Suzanne Kessler's critiques of genitality as the West's primary marker of gender are also particularly provocative (Kessler; Kessler and McKenna).

Theory enables a class to raise the intriguing question, for instance, of the universality of women's experience. Did early modern women's subordination make for inner and outer worlds constructed differently from those of men? If potentially we all have qualities that our society defines as masculine and feminine, how is it that in the dominant assumptions of the period, femininity becomes linked to passivity, even to masochism, or that women overwhelmingly seek to have their desires recognized and recognizable through the subjectivity of an other? Or: Are there areas of autonomy or agency that were being carved out in opposition to the dominant by women and women writers? What collective fantasies can we cite as evidence of emergent aspirations or practices in women's lives? To what extent were women's desires acted on? Did those desires make material differences? What of the largely silenced power of women's sexuality? What of writing as an area of agency? What psychological and ideological dynamics were involved in being a writing woman? Was it emulation? rivalry? the conscious or unconscious rejection of the mother in favor of the power of the father?

We can ask other questions that are at once theoretical and yet intensely material and deeply relevant to students' experiences of early modern women's writing and to students' own sexual and gendered senses. Today's popular, and theoretical, fashion for gender b(l)ending and cross-dressing also can be made relevant: writing itself was so predominately a gender-specific activity—and, it could be

argued, not dissociated with sexuality—that our contemporary fasci-
nation with cross-gendered and bisexual experience is a powerful
way into the dynamics of the work and careers of writers like Wroth
and Behn, who explicitly raise issues of sexuality as well as challenging gender stereotypes. "Womanspace" is another useful focus in a
course on women's writing (see Bassin). Kristeva speaks eloquently
of women's "inner solitude" as a woman's first move toward such
autonomy (242). Jessica Benjamin argues that "the significance of
the spatial metaphor for a woman is likely to be just this discovery of
her own, inner desire, without fear of impingements, intrusions, or
violation" (128). The Freudian tradition has tended to see the fantasy of a productive inner space rooted in women's bodily organization and instinctual needs. Donna Bassin argues that the metaphor
of a woman's inner space should be regarded as equivalent to—
though, historically, it has never attained the dominant position of—
"phallic activity and its representations" (198). An important part of
women's fantasy life in patriarchal culture has been, as Benjamin
puts it, "for a holding other whose presence does not violate one's
space but permits the experience of one's own desire" (128). Those
teachers who feel uncomfortable with contemporary feminist theory
or with the tendency to essentialism implicit in some psychoanalytic
models of women's experience may prefer linking such issues to historical details in the early modern period—for instance, to the gradual architectural changes in the houses of the aristocracy that start to
allow more privacy and that are the subject of many references in
Wroth's writings. There are recurring scenes in *Urania* of inner
spaces, private chambers and gardens, as fervently desired and pro-
tected places for women's self-contemplation without onlookers, especially without other members of the family, though such private
space is not incompatible with a sense of autonomy if it is shared
with a chosen friend, especially another woman. Another inner space
is that afforded by fantasy and story, connecting directly with the activity of writing itself.

Theory, especially as (to some extent, necessarily) simplified for
the classroom, has a tendency to universalism and therefore may en-

courage the avoidance of the historical particular that materially produced women and women writers. Matters of class, economic and legal constraints, and access to education are all concrete historical details that call into question the seeming ahistorical nature of theory. One powerful critique of any universalist approach to women's writing might focus on the historical emergence of sexuality and gender as critical issues in both the early modern period and our own. The tensions within the patriarchal and the early modern family have been much commented on by social historians and recent feminist and materialist critics. To place women's writing within the details of early modern social history is to open valuable classroom debate. Are there transhistorical issues of sexuality, gender, and gender politics? Or are sex and gender both culturally produced? Such issues can be cast, at least initially, within the historicist-versus-universalist debate and then made more complex so that no injustice is done to either side.

But to restrict the influence of these writings to historical considerations in the sense of *antiquarian* seems to me to blunt their pedagogical force. Many of our students (and maybe not a few teachers), after all, are very actively caught in their own struggles of individuation and differentiation. I have learned that my students reverberate to these preoccupations and that they challenge me to go beyond explaining away limitation or lack of identity by historical excuses. "That is just what it was like back then" sounds hollow, especially if it comes from a male teacher. The goal of theoretically informed teaching is, finally, not just to acquire knowledge but also to understand and help change our own histories. Knowledge of the historical reality of literary production indicates that situations we imagine as uniquely ours are not ours at all, that we are never fully aware of the range of possibilities—as sexed and gendered beings, not just as readers and writers—from which we might choose. The role of the teacher becomes, therefore, that of making students cognizant of how these writings are historically produced both then and now. To discover the histories of women writers and writing is one of the great obligations of the present—and it is imposed not by sentimentality or guilt but by the fact that these marginalized lives and the broader theoretical issues they raise have had significant impact on the present. That the polarized sexual and gender stereotypes of Western patriarchy went largely unchallenged, in official records and practices at least, has left deep scars—psychological, social, historical—on our sense of our sexuality. We need a more flexible and healing conception of gender roles and a less polarized and destructive society. If that statement sounds moralistic, it is not because history itself is moral but because agendas to change and direct history can and should attempt to be moral. The dominant early modern ideologies of men and women remain so deeply ingrained in today's assumptions that we must ask repeatedly what alternatives we might have had, what different histories (and herstories) we might construct from what is apparently there in the records, and therefore what might be more richly and justly constructed in the future.

Studying the writings of Wroth and her contemporaries, then, necessarily involves theoretical issues of great pedagogical usefulness. Within the broader cultural patterns emerging from early modern England, the writings of women articulate, however fitfully, what Raymond Williams terms "pre-emergent" (104) signs of an articulated femininity that, in later centuries, has become less marginal and that we are now starting to use to rewrite the history of the ideologies and material practices of our culture. In the past decade we have put the writings and lives of these women into our classrooms; in the decade of the quincentennial celebrations of Columbus's voyage, we might usefully emphasize the irony of the New World's exploration as a work of masculinist domination. That work—conquering, destroying, pillaging, populating—precluded what might have been a different opening up in the history of Western men and women: the expansion of the frontiers of bodily freedom and ego formation through the exploration of sexuality, which (perhaps because it was historically and ideologically centered in the female) proved so much more gradual and had to wait a few centuries. In the writings of these women, we can sense the first stirrings of that expansion. This is not an insignificant discovery for the students in our classes—or for ourselves.

Paula Loscocco

Theory in the Teaching of Early Modern Women Writers

I am a scholar whose training was in its own brilliant way rigorously skeptical of literary and cultural theory, and I am still often dubious about the wisdom of bringing undergraduate students to early modern writing by means of current theoretical formulations. But my experience of teaching women writers over the past several years has convinced me that theory—particularly reception history, feminist and gender-based analysis, and poststructuralist formulations of subjectivity (or identity)—is integral to the project of introducing students to early modern women writers.

When I began teaching, I incorporated several women— Elizabeth I, Elizabeth Cary, Aemilia Lanyer, Mary Wroth, Rachel Speght, Anna Trapnel, Katherine Philips, Margaret Cavendish, Margaret Fell, Aphra Behn—into a variety of courses, and I did so without reference to theory. This teaching was not ineffective, especially when I introduced only a few women into survey courses whose primary concerns were literary, historical, religious, and political. Students were fascinated by how men as well as women used gender in their work, and they were grateful for women's perspectives on contemporary issues. The difficulty arose when we focused on women as their own topic: inevitably, a wave of distorting essentialism would sweep the class, committing all male writers to the dustbin of sexist history and making prescient saints out of such pro-woman writers as Elizabeth at Tilbury, Lanyer in her defense of Eve, Cavendish in what she calls her "effeminate" manifestos (*Poems and Fancies* Aa–Aa[v], after p. 160), and Behn in her apologies for female sexuality. These discussions troubled me, not only for their reductive characterization of the two sexes but also for their lack of interest both in female writings that did not explicitly advocate for women and in the troubling inconsistencies of even the most polemical pro-woman texts. Attuned as my students were to popular notions of twentieth-century feminism, according to which disenfranchised women require of the patriarchal powers that oppress them equal rights and responsibilities, they had difficulty hearing anything else.

These concerns came to an unfortunate head the first time I taught the senior seminar Women in the English Renaissance. To my dismay, I found that the course's very title fixed students' attention on precisely those topics—women, gender, and (inevitably) sex—most likely to prohibit thoughtful or complex discussion. The problem was exacerbated by the fact that few of our many female-authored texts—which we read in their entirety and which represented a broad range of topics and genres, from scriptural translation to philosophical argument—responded with the kind of feminist spit and fire that students had glimpsed in the cameo appearances women had made in their earlier survey courses. On the contrary, most of the women we studied had chosen, in Ann Jones's word ("Introduction"), to "negotiate" with the texts and institutions of their patriarchal culture, adhering to terms and topics deemed proper for their sex and interrogating existing norms in much less confrontational ways than my students could easily admire. Finally, the reception history and cultural theory that I did provide, outlining centuries of suppression both of women writers and of their literary history and asserting a feminist revolution of recovery in early modern studies, only made a bad situation worse. I

supplied this theoretical reading on its own and at the start of the semester: not surprisingly, students initially found it dry and incom-
prehensible, and finally deemed it both unhappily accurate (i.e.,
women's writings had been suppressed, but for good reason) and
deeply misleading (i.e., feminist claims for this material were ideological in origin and overstated in fact). Resonating to the feminist
rhetoric of what were for them the most recognizable and so most
compelling of their theoretical readings, my students felt betrayed
by early modern texts whose merely sporadic interrogations of patriarchal authority seemed tame and compliant and whose evident investment in the institutions of patronage, property, and religious
and secular power confused and at times alienated them.

The next time I taught this seminar, needless to say, I went back
to the drawing board, completely reconceiving the course and eventually realizing that the theoretical materials that had done me such
disservice the first time around were the essential components of a
successful course, could I but learn to use them effectively.

I began reconstruction by organizing the course into a series of
two-week units: the first week was devoted to a significant early
modern topic and a related array of (excerpted) historical and literary texts, mostly by men; the second week to a single woman writer
whose (unabridged) work emerged from these various con-texts.
The emphasis on historical situation, literary history, and men
proved effective: it shifted our focus from women as an abstract category to their particular social and cultural circumstances in early
modern England, it rendered male writers much more accurately
complex than they could appear in simple male-female pairings, and
it therefore allowed us to approach women's texts with enough
information to appreciate their several origins, ambitions, and
achievements.

In the course segment entitled Church and State, for example,
we prepared for Cary's *The Tragedy of Mariam* first by examining
such prescriptive writings as Juan Vives's *Instruction of a Christen
Woman*, the Church of England's marriage ceremony and homily
on matrimony (Klein 3–25), and *The Lawes Resolution of Women's
Rights* and then by exploring how William Shakespeare's *Othello*

highlights the limited opportunities and devastating vulnerabilities of the social and legal worlds implied by the preceding trio of authoritative texts. The unit on the *querelle des femmes* brought a different set of writings to bear on the featured works of Speght (*A Mouzell for Melastomous* and *Certaine Quaeres*) and Fell (*Womens Speaking Justified*): placing Joseph Swetnam's provoking *Araignment of Lewd, Idle, Froward, and Unconstant Women* in historical line with the apprentice Janekin's violently misogynistic anthology in Geoffrey Chaucer's Wife of Bath's Prologue, Christine de Pisan's ideal female community in *The Boke of the Cyte of Ladys*, and William Barton's biblical *Catalogue of Vertuous Women* (*Six Centuries*) enabled students to see how Speght and Fell use the resources of late English Protestant humanism to argue for the pro-woman nature of Christian scriptural exegesis. And when we explored the Reformation as a political (in addition to theological) movement, in the Radicals and Reformers sequence devoted to Katharine Evans and Sarah Cheevers's *A Short Relation of Cruel Sufferings*, our preliminary readings in John Foxe's *Acts and Monuments*, Anne Askew's *Examinations*, John Bunyan's *Pilgrim's Progress*, and the marquis of Winchester's *The Gallery of Heroick Women* made students acutely sensitive both to the pressure that historical events can exert on all kinds of writing and to the fact that the spoken and written word— as it is communicated, interpreted, revised, and rewritten—can itself effect and indeed constitute profound historical change.

At least as important as this reorganization of primary materials, however—or, more accurately, informing and so generating this reorganization—was a muted but sustained focus on twentieth-century literary and cultural theory. Each week, students supplemented their primary readings with short, sequentially ordered essays on reception history, feminist theory, and poststructuralism. I had two goals in providing these essays: (1) to guide students from simplistic assumptions of repression to complex expectations of expression, in ways that corresponded both to their intellectual development during the semester and to advances in scholarly awareness and understanding of early modern women's writing during the twentieth century, and (2) to develop pairings of primary and secondary texts whose internal dialogue and mutual illumination would valuably complicate and challenge the progressivist model implied by my motivated sequence of theoretical readings.

Our discussion of reception history began with Virginia Woolf, who at the start of the twentieth century imagined, in *A Room of One's Own*, only silence and madness for early modern women writers. It proceeded after a few weeks to Joan Kelly-Gadol, who much later came to the same conclusions as Woolf, answering her own provocative question, "Did women have a Renaissance?," with a deflating "No." And it ended well after midterm with Margaret Ezell (*Writing Women's Literary History*), who responds affirmatively to Kelly-Gadol's query by proving that women produced many different kinds of texts, if we have the eyes to see and the ears to hear. We followed a similar trajectory in our readings on gender and subjectivity, beginning with Catherine Belsey's claims for female silence (or speech fractured by radical self-alienation), proceeding after a few weeks to Hélène Cixous's bid for a "female" poetics, and finally arriving at Teresa de Lauretis's analysis of identity as an ongoing process in which "subject-positions" (including gender identities) are both imposed and chosen.

As presented, both narratives—of the twentieth century's reception of early women writers and of feminist theory as it relates to these writers—appealed to students and so proved pedagogically effective, because both describe developments in the students' own thinking. Like Woolf and Belsey, students began the semester convinced of the tragic nature of women's (non)writing; as they became better read, they stirred to the siren song of Kelly-Gadol's (despairing) and Cixous's (idealistic) essentialist feminism, according to which women have—and have lost access to—a distinctive voice of their own; by term's end, they had acquired enough knowledge to appreciate the more complex models for female expression provided by Ezell and de Lauretis.

Complicating and challenging the progressivist momentum asserted by these sequential readings, however—a momentum that, transferred from theoretical to primary texts, would likely have re-sulted in a disastrous reinscription of Woolf's assessment of Behn as England's first woman writer—was the crucial fact of weekly inter-sections of postmodern and early modern readings. These were in-tersections in which the several anxieties, insights, stages, and structures of twentieth-century feminist and poststructuralist theory served as valuable models for thinking about the always different but provocatively parallel anxieties, insights, stages, and structures of sixteenth- and seventeenth-century women's writing. Bringing twentieth-century theory, with all its considerable (and by now partly historical) diversity and conflict, to bear on early modern writ-ing opened up that writing in remarkable ways, enabling students not only to discern, understand, and appreciate an array of women's texts and textual strategies otherwise sealed from their perception but to do so with an imaginative and critical sophistication far be-yond what an instructor might normally expect from undergradu-ates. Indeed, it was my students who taught me to regard the development of theory in the twentieth century with something other than smug appreciation for current sophistication: if so many of the inevitably limited, necessarily partial, and always speculative moments in twentieth-century theoretical history still serve as viable and valuable models for discovering early modern constructions of self and society, my students insisted, then our own deployment of these several models extended a retrospective and resuscitative bless-ing over the entire history of theoretical formulation.

My students' acquired ability to use theory both to make imag-inative and critical sense of early women's writing and dispassion-ately to assess the limitations and value of theory itself achieved fullest expression in the elegantly historical and textual analyses of individual women's writings that they submitted at term's end. It is from these essays that I draw my closing comments on the mutually illuminating relations that can come to exist between theory and early modern female writing.

Theory works in the classroom when it enables students to move quickly to the heart of a primary text; it does so most readily when there is a demonstrable if necessarily analogical match—in genre, discourse, motive, or reception—between the signifying structures identified in the theoretical text and those informing the historical or literary one. This ideal situation prevails when I use Jones (*Currency*) and Cixous to teach Lanyer's *Salve Deus Rex Judaeorum*. Jones's outline of female responses to male traditions within patriarchal culture is accessible and adaptable; its particular value to Lanyer lies in its ability to lay bare those aspects of her writing—specifically, its interrogations of key Anglican and humanist texts—otherwise hidden from student perception. When we then consider Cixous's claims for wandering and repetitive writing by women as coherent and polemical, reflecting a peculiarly female engagement with language, Lanyer's sprawling masterpiece comes into sudden focus, and we can make expansive sense of apparently isolated details. Lanyer's defense of Eve (as the sinless partner of a sinning Adam), for example, radically reconfigures the theological underpinnings of her entire Passion narrative: if only men sinned, only men require redemption—and so only men are responsible for Christ's death.

Similarly effective pairings of theoretical and primary texts include de Lauretis with Wroth and Linda Alcoff with Cavendish. De Lauretis's description of subjectivity as an ongoing process shaped both by individual efforts at self-consciousness and by powerful social and cultural forces only dimly perceived has poignant pertinence to Wroth's sonnet cycle, remarkable for its flashes of self-objectifying brilliance against a background of dark and self-imprisoning interiority. And Alcoff's synopsis of the tension between what she identifies as "essentialist feminism" and poststructuralism encourages students to see the gendered self-obsession of Cavendish's female heroics as the source of both her triumphs and her tragedies. From a feminist perspective, Cavendish makes her gender a source of self-coherence and what she calls public "fame," first by identifying herself entirely with femininity and then by portraying femininity as absolutely heroic. From a poststructuralist perspective, however, she is undermined by her own essentialist doctrine: at best, her efforts to redefine what her culture means by femininity are intermittent and inflated; at worst, her insistence on her status as a woman (or "effeminate spirit") sabotages her own protofeminist ambitions, marked as women were, in her culture and herself, by patriarchal contempt.

My students come away from the Alcoff-Cavendish pairing appreciative of its relevance to their own academic endeavors. Young women studying female writers, they end up alert to the inevitability of personal investment in intellectual work and to the distorting and self-glorifying consequences of feminist identification with particular authors and epochs. But they also see such identification as an exhilarating and necessary source of empowerment and vision, enabling ultimate accomplishment. Their final dedication to a sober sympathy with early women writers, as generous in its insights as it is rigorous in its methodological restraint, is a model for their older but little wiser colleagues.

Kim F. Hall and Gwynne Kennedy

Early Modern Women Writing Race

The discourses through which early modern women writers claimed and exercised the authority to speak in public arenas, constructed subjectivities, and asserted the worth of their experiences and ideas were not only gender-inflected but also racialized. It is thus crucial to chart the histories of both modern racism and sexism as interlocking systems of oppression (Combahee River Collective 16; Margaret Ferguson, "Juggling" 209; hooks, "Reflections"; Lorde; Pharr 53–64) in early modern texts, including those by women. This charting is particularly important if our goal as scholars and teachers of women writers is to develop an inclusive, complex assessment of their historical and modern significance without replicating the deficiencies of either white mainstream feminism, which has generally ignored issues of race, or much critical work on early modern authors, which has often neglected both gender and race. Women-authored texts routinely construct a specifically fair English subject regardless of whether a dark other is present. For this reason, a conversation about race can and must be carried on when teaching women writers of the period. In this essay, we suggest some ways to sustain a classroom conversation about race and early modern texts by women and outline our underlying theoretical, political, and personal concerns about the study of race.

What do we mean by race, and when were race and racism first conceptualized? For us, studying early modern constructions of race means questioning (if not overturning) the traditional view that race and racism in their modern forms began with the biological notions of race that developed with nineteenth-century science. We agree with Stuart Hall that one must talk instead about a discursive logic of race:

> [R]acial discourses produce, mark and fix the infinite differences and diversities of human beings through a rigid binary coding. That logic establishes a chain of correspondences [. . .] between the physical and the cultural [. . .] it gives legitibility to a social system in which it operates; it allows us to decipher different signifiers from the racial fixing of the signifier "race"; and through that reading it organizes, regulates and gives meaning to social practices through the distribution of symbolic and material resources between different groups and the establishment of racial hierarchy.   (290)

This definition poses race as a dynamic construct that is deeply imbricated with other categories such as gender, class, and sexuality, a construct that implicates everyone (Uttal 43).

Recent work on race interrogates the idea of race itself and recognizes that the category includes color, ethnicity, colonialism, religion, geography, family, nationality, travel, reproduction, speech, and physiognomy. We cannot emphasize enough that race can be the subject of articulation without drastically changing one's syllabus. For instance, the confluence of race, gender, class, and economics in the Petrarchan language of beauty (K. Hall 63–73) is a useful entry into texts by Aemilia Lanyer, Elizabeth Cary, Mary Wroth, and Mary Sidney. In our experience, a recognition of the interconnectedness of race and gender oppressions is gradual and cumulative. Students are initially puzzled by our significant attention to race in surveys or courses not explicitly devoted to the subject; it takes a while to point out the recurring issues, tropes, and nuances of fairness and darkness that help the class see that this racialized discourse is a pervasive feature of early modern women's texts. Successive encounters with such discourses collectively produce an early modern pre-text for works, like Aphra Behn's *Oroonoko*, that at first seem to mirror modern notions of race yet trouble students' assumptions about racism and racial identity.

Race can also be incorporated rather easily by thinking broadly about what constitutes racial discourse. If race is often rooted in the physical, it is not simply about color. One way of exploring or uncovering heretofore invisible discourses of race is to focus on certain body parts (e.g., descriptions of breasts, beards, birthmarks) or on ornamentation and rites of the body (e.g., cosmetics, clothing, tattoos, circumcision), which can be key signifiers of difference. In addition, since *race* in the period had a primary meaning of family (Hendricks, "Managing" 183–85; Liu 565), one might also investigate how allusions to family and reproduction are used as signs of inclusion and exclusion in many women's texts. Problems of family and the marked body are linked, for example, in the manuscript continuation of Wroth's *Urania*, where birthmarks identify characters' destined mates. While not about color per se, this system of indelible, visible markers is clearly linked to Wroth's very hierarchical notions of family and class. One might further pressure certain genres, such as romance and epic, that connect family origins, foreignness, travel, and master-servant relations—topics that become key components of modern racial ideologies.

Indispensable to a conversation about race and early modern women is the recognition that whiteness is a racial identity, "*coproduced* with other colors, usually alongside blackness, in symbiotic relation" (Fine 58). In Western discourse whiteness is most often the signifier of superiority and dominance. Moreover, whiteness is meant to be invisible and seems natural to those who benefit from the advantages of white supremacy (Grillo and Wildman 46–47; hooks, "Overcoming"; Russo 309; Winant). For this reason, individuals privileged by whiteness often have difficulty seeing whiteness as a race or seeing racism as an institutionally and discursively produced system of domination and not simply as the personal beliefs of certain people (Christensen, "With Whom" 621–22; McIntosh 80–81). Like modern readers, early modern women writers use racialized language to describe themselves and the world, sometimes consciously and sometimes not.

One can trace how whiteness, often coded as fairness, works across moral, social, class, aesthetic, and racial registers as a signifier of superiority in many women's texts. As numerous readers have observed, Cary's *The Tragedy of Mariam, the Fair Queen of Jewry* questions the parameters of wifely submission, notably a wife's right to integrity and authoritative speech. To do so, the play constructs white privilege by aligning beauty, virtue, high rank, and white skin as superior qualities all signifiable by fairness. The dominant register is moral, as the pattern of pure-spotted imagery underlines, and the play reveals that built into white female subjectivity is the assumption of merit or desert—and (at minimum) moral neutrality—while nonwhite others (not just Salome and Cleopatra) are constructed as morally deficient. Yet the play displays the arbitrariness of this logic when Herod cannot determine whether Mariam is a "fair fiend" (4.4.213) or his "fair and spotless" wife (5.1.19) as well as when he calls his sister, Salome, "a sun-burned blackamoore" (4.7.105) without implicating his own racial position. In Wroth's *Urania*, fairness and whiteness function more pervasively as signifiers of class superiority than of moral virtue. Here women's self-worth is largely defined by their value as objects of male desire and eventual marriage partners. Noble rank and beauty frequently collapse in a single signifier of fairness (K. Hall 199). At various points in *Urania*, Wroth's female characters invoke or challenge this monolithic notion of fairness to wrest some interpretive control from men. In addition, Wroth's romance calls attention to another feature of whiteness: its concern with boundaries and self-control. The power to establish boundaries is often linked with dominant groups (Dyer 51), and whiteness is frequently associated with "order, rationality, rigidity, qualities brought out by the contrast with black disorder, irrationality and looseness" (Dyer 48; Weis, Proweller, and Centrie 214). A viligant self-monitoring of emotional, verbal, and physical expression is a central and desirable feature of the constant, noble, and fair female subject. In Wroth's character Pamphilia, we witness the privileging of a female self-control coded as white and thus denied to women with darker complexions or lower social positions.

We emphasize whiteness because it is paradoxically omnipresent yet seemingly invisible; however, we are aware of the traps of reinstating white identity as the central subjectivity and forgetting about the very real burdens racism imposes on people of color (Grillo and Wildman 47; Haney-Lopez 193–94). Students must also be encouraged to pay attention to seeming evasions of race in texts and in critical practice. Since discussion of race is often easily avoided, it is important to notice such displacements. For example, in *The Blazing World*, when Cavendish portrays peoples of "several complexions," including green, purple, and azure, she consciously marks her escape from the more racially vexed colors, "white, black, tawny, olive or ash" (*Blazing World* [Salzman] 261; see also Nussbaum; Greene 146–49).

Making race visible in these texts is for us an important aspect of our feminist work. We both routinely teach core women's studies courses, and our commitment to a feminism that will liberate all women means that a key part of our methodology and pedagogy is making students aware of the interlocking nature of categories of oppression. We strive to keep ourselves and our students from grasping one discourse as *the* primary discourse and thus from thinking of issues of race or class as outside of or additive to the study of women and gender (Margaret Ferguson, "Juggling" 209–13; Wing, "Killing Rage" 30–31). A historically grounded study of race in early modern women's texts is vital to give students a sense not only of the wide effects of the tropes and discourses of oppression but also of its surprisingly limited repertoire. This realization can allow for critique, coalition, and social change.

Strategies

Betty S. Travitsky and Anne Lake Prescott

Juxtaposing Genders:
Jane Lead and John Milton

There is, as we know, a gap between research and pedagogy, between recovery and the classroom. In recent years, as feminist scholars have recovered increasing numbers of early modern women writers—as a number of Judith Shakespeares have been shown to have existed—teaching tools have incorporated a few of these voices. Since early modern women, as we also know, were discouraged from writing, these tools continue to reflect the predominance of male authors in the period and thus fail to reflect the fact that women, in Constantia Munda's 1617 phrase, are and were "half humankind" (B4v). The result is what seems a sort of tokenism. To compound the distortion, women writers are often presented as an add-on unit, as another type of early modern voice to be remembered. Minimizing and ghettoizing women, however, is a disservice to both scholarship and pedagogy, since early modern women did not exist to write in isolation from men and since their voices, when sounded, intermingled with the voices of their male contemporaries. Whether their writings attracted scorn or approval, they were part of a more complex early modern melody than we have distinguished until recently.

One method for better integrating women's voices into the early modern scene or symphony, one that we have employed on a large scale in our forthcoming anthology, *Female and Male Voices in Early Modern England*, is to pair women's writings with those by early modern men. Doing so—that is, foregrounding gender by juxtaposing pairs of female and male writers—reminds students that most of the voices they have hitherto heard as human are also male and therefore assists the sounding of both female and male voices more resonantly, as embodied voices with gendered social roles to play. Admittedly, such pairing is not a representation or reflection of reality; rather, it is a hermeneutic and pedagogical tool, more techne than mimesis. It is a useful and dramatic method for encouraging students to think about a range of questions—for example, about the different attitudes that can result from different social positions (as witness Thomas Whythorne's description of his vain pursuit of an elusive widow and Elizabeth Egerton's condemnation ["Of Marriage and of Widdowes"] of the remarriage of widows) or about sometimes complicated and shifting gender roles (as in the homoerotic poems of Richard Barnfield and the seemingly lesbian ones by Katherine Philips).

The possibilities for textual pairing are limited only by the imagination of the instructor. Some pairings that work effectively are Francis Bacon's and Mary Astell's (or Egerton's) reflections on marriage; Aphra Behn's satirical "The Disappointment," on a gentleman's embarrassing bout with impotence, and several swaggering if amusingly indecent poems by John Suckling and by Thomas Carew (Thomas Nashe's "Choice of Valentines" would also do, but some students might find it too obscene); An Collins's religious lyrics and those of Henry Vaughan; passages from Mary Sidney's psalms and lyrics by George Herbert that match them well in tone and rhythms. Among the most intriguing pairing is a poem by John Milton and a poem by Jane Ward Lead (1624–1704).

After becoming a widow, Lead joined the household of John

Pordage, head of a nonconformist congregation. With Dr. Francis Lee, who was later her son-in-law, she founded the Philadelphian Society, a group based on the principles of the famous German mystic Jakob Böhme. She wrote "Solomon's Porch; or, The Beautiful Gate to Wisdom's Temple," a long prefatory poem to her *Fountain of Gardens* (1697–1701), well after Milton's death, but her verses are so much in the manner of his "On the Morning of Christ's Nativity" (1629) that the two texts go together beautifully (although teachers pressed for time or with a tight photocopying budget may need to excerpt Lead's impressive but repetitive poem). Lead ecstatically imagines not Christ's birth but his eventual marriage to his Church—the traditional female body of all believers who await the coming of the divine bridegroom. In exalted language often recalling Milton's meters and imagery, Lead's epithalamion summons muses, the bride's and groom's attendants, and the groom's mother, who seems in this poem to merge with Sophia, or Wisdom. Touchingly, Lead tells of the effect of this triumphant apocalyptic wedding on the earth itself: the planet that in *Paradise Lost* has its axis tilted by God's angels, a crookedness that memorializes Adam's sin while causing the heat and cold unknown to temperate Eden, is now righted. "Hitched in her poles," she can "through the liquid ether dance, / And on her axle spin, / In an harmonious round / Breathing substantial, dense, embodied sound" (F4v). Once again in tune with perfectly harmonious spheres, she even shines, being no longer dark and opaque but "one transparent, vast, self-moving wheel / Of liquid crystal, open to reveal / Her rich innumerable stores" (G1).

In teaching this poem, one might need to explain that Christians traditionally read the erotic and densely metaphoric Song of Solomon, quoted on Lead's title page, as allegorizing the marriage of God and humanity, Christ and his Church. (The headnote to the Geneva Bible's translation of the Song is useful here, available in a facsimile edition by Lloyd E. Berry.) Once this explanation is made, two other issues are particularly fruitful when Lead's seldom discussed text is paired with Milton's famous Christmas poem. First, even more than Milton, Lead evokes such female figures as Sophia, that Holy Wisdom about whom Solomon wrote and who was regularly, of course, imagined as a woman. The universe of "On the Morning" resounds less audibly with specifically feminine voices.

Just as apt to produce discussion is a passage in which Lead summons Milton and then quotes him. Students who are puzzled that she calls "On the Morning" a sonnet can be reminded that the word once applied to any lyric.

> Now harmless through the sky
> Let the sweet, whisking, treble lightnings fly.
>> Full base from shore to shore
>> Shall in deep thunders roar
> Not death, not horror now, but melody.
> Now, mighty bard, sing out thy sonnet free,
>> Nor doubt it true shall be.
>> Come thou and join
>> Thy loud prophetic voice with mine.
>> "Ring out ye crystal spheres,
>> "Now bless our humane ears,
> "For ye have power to touch our senses so.
>> "Now shall your silver chime
>> "Move in melodious time
> "And the deep base of heaven's great orb shall blow."
>> From the bright zenith high
> Of the clear, boundless, empyrean sky
>> From the all-radiant throne of God
> Down to earth's inmost, central, deep abode—
>> Nothing but pure consent and unity.
>
>   (F4–F4v)

It is worth telling students that these lines need not be called a "borrowing" or a "debt," for they perform a deliberate gesture of what one can loosely call intertextuality. But what sort of gesture, and how does it relate to voice and gender? Is this an homage to an earlier, greater poet? Or, on the contrary, is it an appropriation? Or both? Lead, who follows Milton in both time and style, first asks the "bard" to join his voice to hers, although in one sense he has already had his say, and then forces the issue by absorbing his voice into her own. Are the words still his? Still Milton's and still male?

As our readers will have noticed, moreover, Lead *mis*quotes Milton. His lines, as he published them, read:

Ring out ye Crystal spheres,
Once bless our human ears,
  (If ye have power to touch our senses so)
And let your silver chime
Move in melodious time;
  And let the Bass of Heav'n's deep Organ blow.
                                    ("Morning" 158)

Skeptical students may dismiss Lead's treatment of these lines as a mere error, due probably to her quoting from memory, but that begs the question of why she would misremember a poem she so evidently admires. Milton himself, students can be reminded, misremembered his Spenser, wrongly reporting that *The Faerie Queene's* Sir Guyon has his trusty guide with him as he visits the House of Mammon. Even without interpreting such misreadings as oedipal aggression meant to exploit but slay a powerful predecessor, we can still take Lead's misquotation as a strong refusal to let Milton have his own uninflected words. Perhaps what seems a mistake is intentional, for Lead changes what is tentative or wishful in Milton to the confident and predictive. Christmas, Lead may have thought, only begins our redemption: she therefore sings of the day when Milton's desires are realized. The Bride's triumph is hers, too.

Although Lead wrote late in the age of John Dryden, her style recalls an older manner: ecstatic, soaring, allegorical, lyric, baroque, biblical. She was not alone in writing such verse on the brink of the Augustan age (Dryden's own "Hymn for St. Cecelia" has lines in this style), but for the most part her poem looks back. Did being a woman, and hence in some degree out of the literary system, free her to follow her taste? Did religious topics still seem more appropriate for her sex? Milton himself remained a superstar despite shifts in the literary landscape—so did Lead hope to imp her wing on his even as she invaded (colonized?) his poem and made off with a part of it? Both her datedness and her originality invite a less teleogical and linear view of literary narrative than the one sometimes adopted by a culture believing, as ours often does, that forward motion is always better.

Erna Kelly

Portraits: Self and Other

The approach outlined below could be presented as a coherent seg
ment within a traditional seventeenth-century literature course or
divided into parts and used at appropriate points throughout such a
course. I use it as part of Studies in Women's Literature: Our Literary Foremothers, which I teach at the University of Wisconsin, Eau
Claire. Rather than apologize for its preoccupation with the "merely
personal," in this course segment I use life writing (e.g., biography,
autobiography, journal, diary) to expand traditional concepts of
canon and genre as well as to question the assumptions of Renaissance humanism. Life writing's relative lack of literary precedent and
its less public stance—when compared with epic, elegy, ode, or
drama—worked in women's favor. Lack of literary precedent meant
that women, even those without formal education, were on equal
footing with men when writing in this genre. Additionally, the
genre's personal nature kept women's restricted access to the public
sphere from being a disadvantage.

Life writing raises some very important questions about Renaissance humanism. In following the development of this genre from its inception, students are led to note the ways in which some genres have gained status while others have remained marginalized. They are thus guided toward questioning the assumptions of Renaissance humanism about the priority of epic and ode, for example, and toward seeing how categories as ostensibly neutral as literary genres become aligned with issues of public versus private, national versus domestic, civic versus familial, and so on, issues that inevitably polarize into male versus female. Students of life writing thus discover firsthand that the personal is indeed political. Furthermore, life writing, because its boundaries are so fluid, can open up discussions about the notion of genre itself. For example, within its realm lie not only biographies, autobiographies, letters, journals, diaries, and memoirs but also autobiography within poems, plays, novels, and even literary criticism. Criticism can lead students back to a consideration of gender, since as Nancy K. Miller demonstrates in *Getting Personal*, women are drawn more than men to "personal criticism," that is, embedding "autobiographical performances" in literary criticism. Students read excerpts from Miller's book, reflect on its ramifications, and then are encouraged to practice "personal criticism" as they write about the autobiographies, diaries, poems, and so on that they are reading for this class. They thus not only practice a nontraditional form of literary criticism as they study nontraditional forms of literature but also experience firsthand the empowering effects of autobiography.

This course segment includes painted as well as written portraits, allowing students to explore boundaries among disciplines as well as among genres, traditional hierarchies among disciplines, and discipline-related gender issues. Although not as high on the hierarchy of Renaissance genres as the epic or ode, life writing flourished in seventeenth-century England. Portraiture flourished as well. Considered a sister art during the Renaissance, painting fits in a course on early modern women writers, especially since a number of women—Anne Killigrew, for example—were known for their talent in the visual as well as the literary arts. After students encounter the Renaissance commonplace that painting is inferior to writing and the common explanation for this attitude, they are not surprised to find another generally held truth: the pencil suited women better than did the pen. Nor are students surprised to find that women who wrote and painted were often better known for their painting. By examining written and painted portraits by women who practiced both arts, students can consider if a given artist was better known for one of the two forms because of her talent or because of gendered cultural expectations.

This course segment begins with Anne Bradstreet, showing her awareness of traditional genres, her struggles with these genres, how she transforms them by introducing the personal, and how eventually she abandons them. Students are introduced to her *Quaternion*, its ambitious scheme (to delineate the four ages of man, the four seasons, the four elements, and the four humors), her *The Four Monarchies*, and her admiration for Guillaume du Bartas's epic-length *The Divine Weeks*. They then read carefully "Childhood," a subsection of *Quaternion*'s "The Four Ages of Man" (the irony of the title is usually noted by students) as well as Thomas Overbury's definition of a Theophrastan character. Overbury not only helps students understand the genre and thus the influence of another traditional form on Bradstreet but also highlights the course's central concern, portrait, since Overbury describes a character as "a picture [. . .] quaintlie drawne in various colours" (92). Comparing Bradstreet's "Childhood" with John Earle's character of "A Child" allows students to see how her use of *occupatio*, a traditional rhetorical figure, enables her to bring in female concerns and, to a degree, subvert the genre. Likewise, poems such as "A Letter to Her Husband, Absent upon Public Employment" and "To My Dear and Loving Husband" can be compared with several of John Donne's poems, among them "A Valediction Forbidding Mourning," to show how Bradstreet uses metaphysical conceits and yet brings something different to the genre of love poetry. Reading Celeste Schenck's essay "All of a Piece: Women's Poetry and Autobiography" at this point helps students focus on the autobiographical facets of Bradstreet's lyrics. The section on Bradstreet concludes with "The Prologue," which gives insight to the difficulties Bradstreet encountered being a writer of the wrong sex. Students should be able to see it as an example of "personal criticism" as well as a defense of her poetry.

The course then shifts to Anne Clifford's diary to show the conflict she has between prescribed female behavior and her concept of what is rightfully hers. Here students can be led to observe that rights and ownership are categorical outgrowths of the humanist concept of self. Clifford's diary is followed by Margaret Cavendish's autobiography ("True Relation"), which illustrates a more self-conscious grasp of humanist ideals, an awareness of the obstacles that society has created for women who aspire to these ideals, and a subconscious conflict between a desire to fit society's notion of the ideal woman and a desire to experience the humanist ideal of self. In addition to reading the writings of both these women, the class studies the painted and engraved portraits that these writers commissioned of themselves.

Although known as a poet today, Killigrew was probably better known during her lifetime for her painting. Among the poems read are "On a Picture by Her Self," "Upon the Saying That My Verses Were Made by Another," and "Herodias' Daughter Presenting to Her Mother St. John's Head." Her self-portrait as well as John Dryden's "To the Pious Memory of [. . .] Anne Killigrew" are also examined. Instead of learning about Killigrew through Dryden, students learn about Dryden after they know Killigrew: they see that his is just one possible reading of her. Her readings of herself and the students' readings of her are some of the other possibilities.

At the end of this course segment I like to reverse the approach I have used above to show students that literature does not have to be seen as the stronger of the two sister arts. Mary Beale works well for this purpose. Both a poet and a painter, she apparently thought her painting strong enough to train her son in that field. Samuel Woodforde, who published two of her poems, wrote that she had made "Painting and Poetrie [. . .] to be really the same" (qtd. in Fraser 342). Excerpts from her husband's detailed journals of her activities as well as selections of her poems can be examined against her portraits, especially her portraits of her husband, of the poet Abraham Cowley, and of herself. As a coda for a course segment that challenges traditional boundaries and hierarchies, I introduce Artemisia Gentileschi. Although she was not a British subject, Charles I owned several of her portraits, including the striking "Self-Portrait of the Artist as the Allegory of Painting." Mary Garrard's essay on Gentileschi in Domna Stanton's *The Female Autograph* is a good starting point for students.

A topic for a paper that has worked well in my class is comparing and contrasting Lucy Hutchinson's autobiographical fragment with Cavendish's autobiography; for a longer paper the two writers' biographies of their husbands could be compared and contrasted. Students have also compared and contrasted the memoirs of Alice Thornton, Anne Halkett, or Ann Fanshawe with Cavendish's autobiography or Clifford's diaries. Another successful assignment asks students to read John Berryman's "Homage to Mistress Bradstreet," construct their own verbal portraits, and then speculate on what might account for any discrepancies between his portrait and theirs.

On its own, the approach outlined above might be used for an interim period class or expanded to fill a semester. In an expanded version, the writers mentioned in the sample paper topics could be added. Another way to expand is to add excerpts from religious autobiography by women such as Anna Trapnel, Susanna Parr, and Sarah Davy (see Graham et al.). Selections from Dorothy Osborne's letters could be used also, especially those that describe local characters or comment on writing style, as well as the two letters that comment on Margaret Cavendish.

Ann Hurley

Archival Studies: Retrieving the "Nonexistent" Women Writers of the English Renaissance

As a specialist in Renaissance studies with an interest in British women writers of the early modern period in particular, I have been distressed when my students assume that there were no women writers in sixteenth- and seventeenth-century England. To address both this piece of misinformation and the paucity of available modernized texts that underlies it, I designed a course titled Archival Studies: Retrieving the "Nonexistent" Women Writers of the English Renaissance. The course raises the question why certain texts, especially those written by women, are alleged to be nonexistent or are in fact in short supply, and the course situates answers in the development of the archival skills needed to address that question.

The method of the course is to allow each student to select a manuscript or rare book from a previously compiled list of texts by Renaissance women writers. (I prepare the list in advance, checking the location of each text, so that I know that students will be able to find what they are searching for rather than leave them to search fruitlessly.) The student is then responsible for locating and describing the manuscript or book; for obtaining it either in facsimile or in paper copies from microfilm of the original manuscript; for situating it in the circumstances of its times; for noting in particular how female authorship does or does not affect it; and for giving several brief presentations on it, which all culminate in one final paper. The students are introduced to the techniques of locating manuscripts or rare books through such research tools as the *National Union Catalog* and the *English Short Title Catalogue* (*ESTC*) and their online equivalents. They are instructed in the skills of descriptive bibliography (formats, collation, signings, paper, printing processes, etc.) so that they can understand the information they will receive from the institution holding the original. They each trace the material history of their respective text—its contemporary references, its current and previous locations, its appearance in booksellers' lists or in earlier collections, both private and institutional. There are two reading lists for the course: one on women's studies in the early modern period and one on the technicalities of working with manuscripts and rare books. Group and individual assignments regularly direct students to working with each set of readings. Students are encouraged to raise questions about problems they encounter, to circulate information and discoveries, and to share possible solutions through weekly meetings that alternate workshops with an occasional formal presentation.

Among the scholarly and theoretical objectives of the course are to develop skills in research, descriptive bibliography, and attention to the material nature of texts and to create a directly engaged understanding of the problematic nature of what emerges in traditional courses and how it emerges. The course concludes by reminding students of its original objective: to examine some of the alleged causes behind the scarcity of texts by early modern women writers and to generate some collective conclusions about their validity or bias. Students also make the discovery that their experience has inverted the procedure of a standard literature course, because, instead of being handed a text already authorized by period, genre, and typical characteristics of its author, they have been privy to the very sources of that authority as these play through the texts they have selected. In short, they are not handed authority; they generate it themselves.

Those conclusions I anticipated, but teaching the course yielded a variety of unexpected discoveries as well, both for me and for my students. From the start we were all somewhat uneasy when the delivery of the course inevitably moved us away from the familiar. One consequence of that uneasiness was an ongoing interrogation of the usual classroom procedures. We quickly discovered that the normal lecture-and-discussion format did not serve us well, that the standard classroom was too inflexible for our purposes. Class time quickly evolved into workshop time, and meeting places invariably shifted around the campus and often away from the campus. I have taught this course in two different settings, at Skidmore College and, more recently, at Wagner College in New York City. At Skidmore, we met in the research area of the library, in the rare-book room where Skidmore's small collection of Renaissance texts was housed, in the computer lab to search institutional holdings using Gopher, and off campus at the home of a local book collector. We traveled to Albany to view the State University of New York's rare-book holdings and to Cornell University for a full day's exploration of Cornell's rare-book and manuscript collection. Our experience at Cornell was intensified by the fact that one student was working with the manuscript of Elizabeth Polwhele's play *The Frolicks* (1671), which is located there. At Wagner, we had the additional excitement of presentations by curators at the Pierpont Morgan Library and the Rare Book Collection at New York University.

At both Skidmore and Wagner, we discovered that the course content worked against the usual assumption that the professor is the center of authority. Rare-book librarians, the local book collector, a specialist on bindings, and a visiting scholar on researching Renaissance women artists all became sources of information and insight. More pertinent, students began to find themselves empowered by their growing mastery of a body of research that few scholars had access to. Thus, not only did the students find themselves corresponding directly with the limited number of scholars who had done what little secondary scholarship pertained to their respective authors, they also found themselves correcting misleading information in sources as respected as the *Dictionary of National Biography* or at institutions like the Newberry Library, where one Skidmore student was able to demonstrate that a holding there was being cited in current scholarship as an original edition when in fact it was a facsimile. At Wagner, another student discovered a misquotation of Anne Finch, by Virginia Woolf no less, and then published a brief essay on that discovery for a Woolf journal.

One concern I had in designing the course originally was that it might be too specialized, depriving students of the necessary broad overview of the Renaissance, its commonplaces, its theological and cosmological outlook, its specialized terminology. But I discovered that the term *humanist* gained new relevance when, as students began to notice and comment on our unusual classroom procedures, I was able to point out that much of what we take for granted in the average college classroom is derived from humanist formats of lecture and discussion when people brought the new discoveries of ancient Greece and Rome to places like early-sixteenth-century Oxford. We take for granted the practice of reading lectures out loud, which is a consequence of the rhetorical inheritance of humanism; the emphasis on academic competition in classroom discussions, which is a result of the humanist emphasis on public debate; the shared attention to a single text, because classical materials were transcribed and disseminated; the orator-lecturer as the central figure, which derives from attitudes such as that expressed by Quintilian: "There would be no eloquence if each talked to one's peers only" ("Non esset in rebus humanis eloquentia [. . .]." [*Institutio Oratoria* 1.2.31]). As my students searched out texts, made transcriptions, described their findings to one another in lively detail, they identified much more closely with early humanist textual endeavors than they could have through any lecture or dictionary definition of the term. They also noted, however, that this format's clear emphasis on mastery and dependence on a series of major authors marginalized female writers and manuscript (as opposed to print) circulation. Their efforts to contextualize the works they were studying independently of one another led them not only to put together a body of knowledge but also to share it. Thus the student working with An Collins's poetry did considerable research on Calvinism and the seventeenth-century religious lyric in general and on the meditative tradition specifically. Her reports proved useful to students working with royalist writers (like Anne Killigrew), whose verse, while less obviously religious, was nonetheless marked by non-Calvinist attitudes in need of clarification. I was also reassured to discover that "major" figures like Philip Sidney, Edmund Spenser, and William Shakespeare also received attention, albeit from a rather different direction and with different emphasis. Thus the student involved with Mary Wroth's *Urania* was quickly led to Sidney's *Arcadia*, and neither writer was diminished, although the student had reversed the usual procedure, learning about Sidney by way of Wroth rather than about Wroth by way of Sidney.

Finally, because students worked largely with primary materials, they emerged from the course with strongly expressed emotions about the specific texts they worked with and about the authors who had produced them. The one common experience of the course, articulated repeatedly in class discussions and in final essays, had to do with students' acute awareness of how entering the canon inevitably inscribes one in its assumptions, many of which are counterproductive for the study of women writers. Not only had they gained this awareness, they also had gained some of the skills essential in addressing it. For me the greatest pleasure was seeing a group of individuals who had entered a classroom as students emerge from it as genuine scholars.

Types of Courses

Carole Levin

Illuminating the Margins of the Early Modern Period: Using Women's Voices in the History Class

Even with the blurring of interdisciplinary boundaries, so that literature is taught as a primary text in history courses, and there is now a much wider range of genres—letters, speeches, diaries, and so on—that are taught as literature, history courses and literature courses obviously still have different goals and methodology. In my area of specialty, early modern England, the literature is rich indeed. For history classes, literature is not only of value for its own sake but also works well as a primary source. While one cannot always expect literature to present us with the "factual" truth, it can tell us a great deal about the deeper truth of how people of an era felt and believed.

Some, but not all, of the courses that I teach deal specifically with women. I offer a survey course, Women in European History, that covers chronologically the period from the Middle Ages to the present, and a more specialized course, Saints, Witches, and Madwomen, that specifically examines women on the margins and the labeling of women in the same time coverage. But in all my courses I am committed to including women's experience. So I also address women and gender issues in European History through Biography, which centers on case studies from England and France from the twelfth through the sixteenth century, and Power and Gender in Early Modern England, which is a thematically designed Tudor-Stuart course.

I am also committed to the use of a wide range of primary sources; the voices of early modern women are therefore an integral part of many of my courses. Students respond powerfully to the voices of women with whom they are already somewhat familiar, such as Lady Jane Grey, the "nine days queen," and Elizabeth I, but they also greatly appreciate and become very excited about other women, such as Anne Askew and Elizabeth Young, whose examinations appear in John Foxe's *Acts and Monuments*. I prefer to refer to these sources as women's voices rather than as their writing. Young, for example, did not write; what we have is, rather, a recording of her speeches during her trials. My students also read a number of speeches by women who wrote, including Grey and Elizabeth I.

In my courses I address certain themes that are significant to the use of early modern English women's writing and speaking. I often interrogate the subject with questions about how women obtained power and autonomy in the early modern period and how their voices speak out at the intersection of religion, politics, and nationalism. Religious conviction was empowering to early modern women; it gave them inner strength and allowed them the ability to publicly articulate their beliefs; it was also the cause of great danger to many women.

A discussion of the readings and assignments in Power and Gender in Early Modern England, which originally had the generic title England 2 (1485–1688), may demonstrate how a history class can be redefined thematically to make such issues as gender and power central.

One of the ways that I include a variety of sixteenth- and seventeenth-century Englishwomen's voices in this class is to give each student, on the first day, a card with the name of an interesting but less politically significant person. After the first two weeks I have one or two names scheduled for each class period; students will do a five-minute presentation on the person assigned to them, giving birth and death dates (when known) and one or two events in the person's life. I ask each student to have a one-page handout for the class on the person. It can be an illustration, a paragraph of information, an outline, or anything useful and relevant, but it must include a brief selection from a primary text, which is usually, though not always, the person's own words (in some cases it is a contemporary description). On the same day as the presentation, a short essay on the person is due; the essay includes the above information and gives at least one secondary source and at least one primary source. More than half the cards handed out have the names of women on them, including Margaret More Roper, Elizabeth Barton, Askew, Catherine Willoughby, Arbella Stuart, Frances Howard (first Lady Essex, then Lady Somerset), Henrietta Maria, the accused witch Elizabeth Southerns (also known as Old Demdike), Margaret Fell (Fox), Aphra Behn, and Nell Gwyn. *Acts and Monuments*, which should be available in any undergraduate library, is a fine source for a number of the sixteenth-century women. The editions in the Women Writers in English series are also extremely useful, particularly those of Askew and Stuart. (In European History through Biography, one of my students did his intensive research essay and presentation on Askew. During his report he and a woman student read aloud the examiner's questions and Askew's responses; it was a very powerful moment in the class.) The students say this is their favorite assignment, and they end the semester with a folder filled with primary sources on interesting women and men of early modern England. As the semester progresses, the students attempt to outdo one another in the elaborateness of their handouts.

A number of the readings assigned to the entire class have the voices of early modern women. I have on reserve the collection of primary texts *Complaint and Reform in England*, edited by William Dunham and Stanley Pargellis. For the section on the 1553 succession crisis and the beginning of Mary I's reign, the class reads (from *Acts and Monuments*) Lady Jane Grey's debate with Master Fecknam, which took place shortly before her execution; her letter to her former tutor, Master Harding, on his conversion to Catholicism; her letter to her sister Katherine the night before her death; and her speech at her execution. Grey's forthright Protestant voice, which does not falter even in the face of death, is impressive to the students, especially when they realize that at the time she wrote these works she was even younger than they are. Grey is one of the best known women of the sixteenth century. For Mary's reign I also assign from Foxe a little known woman, Young, who showed great spirit in her examinations for heresy in 1558. Young was so courageous and articulate that one of her examiners believed that she was a man in woman's clothes. Young is also a good counterpart to Grey, as she is not one of Foxe's martyrs; she survives until Elizabeth becomes queen, when it is safe to be forthright about Protestant beliefs. Though we have to acknowledge that the women's voices as represented in Foxe come to us through the men who wrote down what they said, they still provide us with an immediacy that is a powerful tool for working with undergraduates.

The reserve reading, *Complaint and Reform in England*, includes three of Elizabeth's speeches to Parliament (from 1585, 1593, and her "Golden Speech" in 1601). It also reprints the entire letter from Leonel Sharp to the duke of Buckingham, which contains her famous speech at Tilbury. We discuss what it means for Elizabeth to proclaim, "Though I may have the body of a weak and feeble woman, I have the heart and stomach of a king," and her willingness metaphorically to be her soldiers' general. I especially appreciate that this volume includes the rest of Sharp's letter, which is valuable background for a discussion in that, while this text is the traditionally accepted version, the letter that contains it was actually written in the 1620s, more than thirty years after the event. I also distribute to the class other variants of the speech, which can lead to a useful discussion about how to evaluate sources.

In my English history course as well as in my women's history courses, we also evaluate sources about beliefs in witchcraft and magic, and testimony from sixteenth-century trials allows our students to know the voices not only of famous women like Elizabeth but also of women whose names have been all but lost. My assigned reserve reading from *Complaint and Reform in England* includes the section on witchcraft: the 1563 statute against witchcraft and examples from several sixteenth-century chapbooks about witches. For example, the students read the confession of a condemned witch, Elizabeth Frances, who tells how she cursed a woman for refusing to give her food. In a typical form of accepted evidence, mischief following anger, the cursed woman developed a severe pain in her head.

I have a special place in my heart for my women's history classes. But I derive particular satisfaction from making women's voices so integral a part of what was once a conservative and traditional English history course. Their voices indeed illuminate the margins of early modern English history.

Bernadette Andrea

Teaching (Early Modern Women's) Writing

Teaching early modern women's writing to first-year students? To nonhumanities majors? As a writing seminar? These were the challenges I faced as I formulated Shakespeare's Sister; or, Did Women Have a Renaissance? for Cornell University's John S. Knight Writing Program, which offers freshmen writing seminars across the university curriculum (my seminar was one of 170 sections from more than 30 departments). The seminars are small, with a cap at seventeen students. The writing requirements are rigorous, including eight to fourteen formal assignments totaling at least thirty pages of writing and many more pages of in-class writing and revision. These seminars teach writing by introducing students to the prose and problematics of a specific discipline rather than by teaching composition per se. My seminar straddled the disparate fields of early modern studies and women's studies to articulate the emerging field of early modern women's studies.

As its title suggests, Shakespeare's Sister addressed a pivotal question for early modern women's studies by examining texts not only about but also by early modern women, including poetry, drama, religious writing, political treatises, witchcraft documents, and travel narratives. In addition, the seminar frequently extended beyond the textual: we considered late-sixteenth-century portraits of Elizabeth I of England and other aspects of early modern visual culture; we viewed an early-twentieth-century film featuring Greta Garbo as Queen Christina of Sweden and analyzed (mis)representations of witches in late-twentieth-century popular culture. Moreover, though the course focused on early modern Englishwomen's writing, it ranged beyond England (to consider Queen Christina) and beyond Europe (to consider Ottoman and Native American women). The seminar's interdisciplinary and cross-cultural approach thus not only addressed the complexity of the question of whether or not early modern women had a Renaissance but also provided a variety of cognitive avenues for students to engage material that often seemed intimidating in its unfamiliarity.

When I met my class of seventeen students—an academically and culturally diverse group of young women and men—I discovered they had only the vaguest (if any) idea of what "the Renaissance" connoted, but they did wonder ("Now that you mention it") why no woman writer ranked among canonical master(piece)s such as Shakespeare. (I generated this response through my first in-class writing assignment, which asked, "How would you describe, define, or date the period in European history commonly referred to as 'the Renaissance'? When you consider 'the Renaissance,' what images come to mind? What associations? What stereotypes? What objections?") The course took shape around Joan Kelly's foundational essay "Did Women Have a Renaissance?" (Kelly-Gadol) and Virginia Woolf's provocative fiction in *A Room of One's Own* of "Shakespeare's sister." We then turned to images of women in books written by men, analyzing selections from Walter Ralegh's *Discovery of Guiana*, William Gouge's *Of Domesticall Duties*, and John Milton's *Paradise Lost*. Subsequent units focused on early modern queens, including Elizabeth I, Queen Christina, and the Ottoman Queen Mother Safiye (Skilliter); witches and mystics, ranging from Margaret Ferneseede (*Arraignment*) to Margaret Fell; and New

World women, such as Anne Bradstreet, Sor Juana (Inés de la Cruz), and Doña Marina / La Malinche (see Díaz). Though I assigned two anthologies, Charlotte Otten's *English Women's Voices, 1540–1700* and Katherine Henderson and Barbara McManus's *Half Humankind: Contexts and Texts of the Controversy about Women in England, 1540–1640*, the bulk of our reading came from a photo-copied course packet I prepared using both seventeenth-century and twentieth-century editions of early modern texts. Seventeenth-century editions, while difficult to decipher (a process we eased through paraphrase and role-playing), exposed students to material dimensions of early modern textual production from formating to graphemes. The eccentric physical features of early modern editions, which posed an initially daunting challenge to students accustomed to standardized texts, ultimately enabled these students to respect the pastness of the past rather than collapse the early modern period into their own.

Integrating the content and the writing components of the course posed a further challenge, a common characteristic of writing seminars that attempt to introduce students to historically or discursively unfamiliar material. We productively broke down the content-composition dichotomy in class by using pertinent secondary sources to exemplify fundamental writing principles. For instance, students were introduced to Kelly's essay in the context of an exercise that required them to identify syntactic elements in a key passage for early modern women's studies, which begins by questioning "accepted schemes of periodization" and ends with the paradigm-shifting statement that "there was no renaissance for women—at least, not during the Renaissance" (19). I encouraged students to cite such secondary sources in their essays, thereby providing them with critical contexts they might not have otherwise pursued as well as with stylistic models they could readily employ.

Concomitantly, I stressed how early modern women used sophisticated structural, rhetorical, and stylistic techniques to shape their writing. For instance, I framed our study of radical sectarian women with this in-class exercise: "Spend the next five minutes or so responding to the following question: What rhetorical and political strategies did the women petitioners use to represent themselves? (Include at least one balanced sentence in your response.)" Subsequent exercises, focusing on Fell and Anna Trapnel, similarly integrated writing instruction and course content. In our unit on witches and mystics I reinforced these exercises with a library assignment that dwelled on specific personalities, political movements, and religious sects associated with the English Revolution; students prepared a one-page summary of their findings and circulated this material in class. We thus created a collective archive of historical sources for our study of mid-seventeenth-century women's writing.

This sequence of short assignments culminated in an essay assignment that asked students to respond to one of four questions:

1. Compare the rhetorical and political strategies of the early modern queens we studied with those of the women petitioners. Note the examples, symbolism, logic, and stereotypes these distinct classes of women used to negotiate a space for female (feminine? feminist?) speech and action in a male-dominated society.

2. Compare the rhetorical and political strategies of women petitioners and prophet figures. In making this comparison, focus on precedents, symbols, logic, and stereotypes. You may conclude by speculating about the effect these strategies had on the ability of Englishwomen en masse to participate in the public sphere of church and state government.

3. Trace similarities and note differences among the representations and reception of female witches, petitioners, and prophet figures. You may analyze both verbal and pictorial images to make your argument. Consider the dualistic paradigm of good woman versus bad woman when analyzing these representations.

4. Discuss the controversy surrounding the justification of women's speech in the Civil War period. Consider documents by women petitioners and prophet figures along with those of

Quaker controversialists. Again, focus on the details of symbolism, stereotypes, logic, and precedents to structure your argument. Also speculate about the effects of the displacement, rather than the replacement, of traditional antiwoman stereotypes characteristic of these documents.

I stressed the writing aims of this unit by consolidating in a final paragraph the features of coherence we had practiced over the past few weeks. Working through similar assignment sequences on early modern queens and New World women, students in this seminar learned to read analytically and critically by identifying writing techniques in early modern texts they could employ in their own writing.

In the end, these diverse students, who came to the course as unaware of "accepted schemes of periodization" (*pace* Kelly) that had left women out of the Renaissance as they were of early modern women's writing, proved to be enthusiastic readers of an impressive range of early modern women's texts. (Trapnel's *Report and Plea* was their favorite!) By reading early modern women's writing critically, historically, and rhetorically, these students learned to fashion pleasing and persuasive prose styles in the ongoing tradition of Shakespeare's sister.

Ramona Wray

Canons and Course Packs: Teaching Seventeenth-Century Women's Writing in Belfast

This essay describes a final-year module on seventeenth-century women's writing that I have taught at Queen's University, Belfast. The course aimed to instill in its twenty female students a broad sense of contemporary women's literary output.

The most immediate problem was accessing appropriate materials in Ireland, where no university library possesses the *STC*-Wing microfilm collections. Without such resources, it proved difficult to devise a course that reflected the generic range of contemporary text categories—without bankrupting the students. Individual editions proved, in the main, either inaccessible or overly expensive. Acquiring anthologies devoted only to an appreciation of a single genre seemed an unjustifiable indulgence, while the extracts printed in more generically diverse anthologies proved generally too short to employ constructively in assessment projects. *Her Own Life* (Graham et al.), with its varied textual selection, was invaluable, but letters, manuscript work, political pamphlets, and petitions still

271

remained absent from my course list. The solution was to supplement textbooks with transcriptions from manuscript sources,
printouts from the *Brown University Women Writers Project*, microfilm copies and photocopies from anthologies. After several days of
slaving over the photocopies, I finally nailed a twelve-week course
together.

The first week concentrated on thinking about the politics of
reading seventeenth-century women's writing in the late-twentieth-
century context. The second week situated the course texts in an
early modern historical environment. Following weeks looked at a
selection of women's poetry; Elizabeth Cary's drama and prose;
Lady Mary Wroth's *Urania*; and a group of diaries and memoirs.
Two weeks in the middle of the semester investigated women's writing produced during the Civil War. The final weeks focused on the
works of Margaret Cavendish, the conversion narratives of Hannah
Allen and Sarah Davy, and the plays and prose of Aphra Behn.

For students, this course differed in three ways from others they
had taken. First, they found it more demanding: their unfamiliarity
with many of the genres and subject matters meant that they had to
rethink many assumptions about reading and literature. Second,
working on texts that had attracted little or no critical attention, students were conscious of having to rely in a particularly crucial sense
on teamwork and class resources. Third, students felt a conviction
that their contributions to the course had "an importance" missing
from other modules.

In accounting for the critical neglect, the class had little hesita-
tion in arraigning a male academy that had chosen to overlook
women as worthy figures of scholarly inquiry. To stimulate students
to explore such assumptions in greater depth, I posed the question,
"What makes a text worthwhile?," and invited the class to make two
additional lists. First, students cataloged the criteria by which literary value is traditionally assessed ("artistic merit," "author status,"
"elevated genres," "stylistic self-consciousness," "serious subject
matter," etc.). Second, they detailed their own personal criteria,
which included "the joy of reading," "engaging with characters and
situations," "learning about other cultures," and "popular literary

genres." This exercise was useful in activating social interchange—
there was much hilarity as students revealed assorted penchants for
glossy magazines and soap operas. But it also had a more sober purpose: in juxtaposing the two lists, students were able to recognize
that evaluative terms are arbitrary and that one set of criteria is not
necessarily better than another. And, because the origins of this difference in our age and gender were specified, attention was drawn to
a more general observation—that what concerns us in texts is dependent on our positions as readers. This exercise, then, provided an
opportunity to encourage students to begin to develop and refine
their critical self-awareness. In a seventeenth-century women's writing course, such a movement is essential, since students who continue unthinkingly to utilize traditional literary criteria will find few
texts worthy of concentrated engagement.

To consolidate what had been learned, I circulated two poems,
one by George Herbert and one by An Collins. Both are addresses
to God in which the subjects lament their unworthiness. We broke
into groups to consider why only the Herbert poem has been the
object of literary acclaim. The exercise provided a means of reflecting on how our responses to poetry are often shaped, albeit uncon-
sciously, by traditional literary criteria and stylistic orthodoxies. It
was generally agreed that Herbert's "elaborate" language, confident
manipulation of literary tropes, and sophisticated imagery have been
seen to contrast with Collins's self-effacement and more unadorned
rhetorical appurtenances in a way unfavorable to the female poet
(my choice of poems was adapted from Healy's discussion of canon
formation, 49–51). The lack of ornament notwithstanding, the class
found much of interest in Collins's work. A discussion of what is lost
by reading only "literary" literary texts modified into speculation
about the material circumstances preventing women from joining
the ranks of the educated elite.

Drawing the threads of these various arguments together, I
asked the class what practical problems the construction of women's
writing as inferior might introduce. Considering my own position as
course convener allowed me to communicate to the students a sense
of the compromises that had to be made in order to package a

coherent module. Considering their positions as consumers of the course stimulated students to realize that the texts they encountered came to them free from the usual critical baggage—a prospect generally welcomed as a (challenging) positive. Casting ourselves in the role of adventurers embarking on a new expedition, we concluded the class with a discussion of our textual expectations.

Given the broad scope of the course, utilizing the resources of the group was a necessity, and week 2 (in which the historical position of women in the seventeenth century was addressed) developed necessary skills through class presentations. Each student focused on a different aspect of women's lives in the seventeenth century and, working from primary materials, prepared in advance a five-minute discussion and an accompanying handbook. Having put time and effort into the accessibility of the presentation, students were able to engage actively with other areas of debate. Few had taken the texts at face value, and most responded to the contradictions thrown up by different materials. Some had conducted additional research of both a primary and secondary nature. As the later course questionnaires made clear, the conscientiousness of the students was directly related to their recognition of the cooperative nature of this project. In return for a student's presentation and handout, the student received nineteen others, all of which were differently pertinent. The conclusion of a wide-ranging discussion—that, to understand texts by seventeenth-century women adequately, a close attention to issues of context is essential—reverberated through our course as a whole.

This principle received forceful emphasis when we looked at material produced by women during the Civil War. Once again, we used the presentation format, although this time building further on the collaborative atmosphere achieved. Students broke into groups of three to prepare, again in advance of class, Civil War materials that I had grouped under seven headings: "Warnings, Admonitions, Lamentations" included the pamphlets of Priscilla Cotton (Cotton and Cole) and Margaret Fell; "Petitions" encompassed collectively authored works as well as individual remonstrances; "Spiritual Autobiographies and Conversion Narratives" extended to texts by Mary

Simpson and Jane Turner; "Prison Writings" embraced texts by Mary Overton and Anna Trapnel; "Memoirs" included Lucy Hutchinson and Isabella Twysden; "Utopian Writing" read Mary Cary alongside Cavendish; and "Epistolary Genres" looked at Lady Brilliana Harley and Mary Howgill.

Apart from the texts reprinted in *Her Own Life*, the materials for these sessions took the form of photocopies from microfilm. On questionnaires, students positively referred to their use of these materials, professing themselves invigorated by reading "the real text." An additional stimulus was the texts' actual content. Instead of being bored or mystified by the religio-political material, students were activated to locate in the texts deeper motivations. Possibly part of this response is due to the fact that Northern Irish students are themselves implicated in a civil war situation. Certainly, they were fascinated by the notion that a period of social and political strife can be enabling for women, and they drew explicit parallels between the start of the modern Troubles in Northern Ireland and the rise of the local women's movement. Familiar, too, with the notion of religion as the organizing principle of social and cultural life, students drew on their personal, politicized experiences to enhance an understanding of the turbulent Civil War decades.

Enthusiasm was reflected in the high quality of presentation work. All the groups had met outside class to agree on a common strategy. Several began outlining for their colleagues a sense of the genre in which their writers were participating, enabling a consideration of the possibilities involved in women's inscription of themselves in a discrete literary practice. Often such consideration was followed with a practical example of how a particular woman's text creates a discursive speaking position. The overall sense was of Civil War women who, despite living in a culture inimicable to female creativity, took advantage of opportunities to appropriate, intervene in, and in some cases radically transform their chosen genres.

Another strength of the class presentations, both internally and culminatively, was that they exposed the divisions of class, religion, and political persuasion among the writers studied. At one end of the social spectrum, it was noted, are the memoirs of Twysden and the letters of Harley. At the other are spiritual autobiographies and political pamphlets written by women of the servant and laboring classes, such as Turner.

These presentations highlighted a nuanced appreciation of the enormous diversity and generic inventiveness both of women writing and of women's writing. We found ourselves concluding the Civil War sessions with a discussion of the female canon. Many students lamented the fact that the texts they had studied were not in print and pondered the consequences of a feminist concentration on literary genres. I was struck by how far we had come from our opening discussions of the male-centered canonical phenomenon. Despite the limitations of the local library resources, together we had settled on new ways of investigating a still unfolding territory.

Teaching Specific Texts

Patricia Brace

Teaching Class: Whitney's "Wyll and Testament" and Nashe's "Litany in Time of Plague"

The marginalization of women's writing presents a theoretical and pedagogical problem to the teacher of early modern women writers in a survey of sixteenth- and seventeenth-century British literature, a problem that I hope this discussion of Isabella Whitney and Thomas Nashe helps address. I think that the ghetto effect is perhaps more acute in literary surveys than in courses focused on women writers of the period, because in focused courses, writing by women is the entire object of study and thus becomes the center. Clustering writings by women in a survey frames them as different from the writings of men and, in the eyes of canonically aware students, as expendable, even if the grouping makes it possible to trace patterns of women's literary and social concerns. In order to combat this tendency and to naturalize the position of women writers in the bounds of a survey course, I have found it useful to place women's texts in units on specific social and literary issues. These texts then come to represent a piece of a larger pattern of interactions between class and gender in sixteenth- and seventeenth-century writing.

In my survey of sixteenth- and seventeenth-century poetry and prose, a section composed largely of sonnets traced shifts in class and the social and literary concerns attached to this change. It examined courtly sonnets by Thomas Wyatt, Surrey (Henry Howard), Philip Sidney, Mary Wroth, and Mary Stuart, followed by Shakespeare as an example of the movement of sonnets out of a courtly class. We discussed the social space marked out by social settings and economies in the poems, as well as the problem of the presence of the love object and the body of the speaker. Two key moments were identifying a relation between a restricted class and a restricted gender through the idea of the stigma of print (W. Wall 35–36) and showing the way Shakespeare's sonnets shift the social location to a more mercantile world and argue in favor of the availability of the body of the beloved. Finally, a class on Whitney's "Wyll and Testament," from her *Sweet Nosgay* (for an easily available modern edition of this will, see "Manner"), and Nashe's "Litany in Time of Plague," from *Summer's Last Will and Testament*, explored concerns generated by the idea of the city as a middle-class, economically oriented space. Both these writers represent complex class positions—Whitney as a minor "gentlewoman" in service to a high-ranking lady (Schleiner 7) and Nashe as one of the educated "university wits" attempting to make his living in the print market while seeking favor from the aristocracy (Wright 313)—in which social identity and fiscal reality are at odds. This last class was a collaborative effort, as I developed the theoretical framework, while Louise Noble, a teaching assistant for the course, came up with creative methods for conducting it.

Both Whitney and Nashe locate themselves in the context of city life: Whitney through her representation of the mercantile area of London around Saint Paul's and Nashe through his evocation of the devastation of plague. The poems are interesting in generic terms because they perform literary acts that belong to everyday life and locate individuals in community. Whitney's will is a personal statement that builds her community with the naming of each beneficiary, while Nashe's use of the liturgical form of the litany places the moment in a community of worshipers. To develop these ideas of community and to examine types of communities and class relations within them, Noble used two strategies. The first was to have the class map Whitney's London from the places she mentions in the "Wyll and Testament" and compare it to a contemporary map of London, and the second was to perform Nashe's "Litany" to simulate the experience of communal worship and petition. I intoned the petitions of the litany, while the class made the response, "Lord have mercy on us." For the Whitney exercise, the most useful and readily available sixteenth-century views of London are Georg Braun and Franz Hogenberg's "Londinum Feracissimi Anglize Regni Metropolis" (Fisher 3; Barker and Jackson 12–13; Glanville 76–77) and the "Civitas Londinum" (the Agas view; Fisher 4–10; Barker and Jackson 18). Ralph Agas's view has the advantage of including more street names, while Braun and Hogenberg's is of a more manageable size.

By collaboratively mapping Whitney's streets, buildings, and businesses on an overhead transparency and comparing her version of London with the maps, the class developed a clear idea of her sense of place. They noticed first the tight focus of her neighborhood on the south-west quadrant of the city, reflecting, in part, the fact that it had to be traversed on foot. The sense of the smallness of the community was conveyed by her familiarity with the locations of specific shops and their relation to one another. For example, Whitney notes, "I Hose doo leave in Burchin Lane, / of any kynd of syse: [. . .] Bootes, shoes or Pantables good store, / St. Martins hath for you" (119–20, 123–24 [line references from "Wyll"]). The class also noted the primacy of economic concerns as a result, possibly, of the area's proximity to the Thames. Discussion of the centrality of spiritual life and its close relation to the economic developed from an examination of the centrality of Saint Paul's as a location for both worship and trade in books. From this examination of Whitney's representation of London as primarily economic emerged further discussion of Whitney's class-inflected relation to London. Students noted the prominence of services (baker, fish market, milliner, etc.) associated with the daily tasks of domestic service. The social and physical distance of this area from the centers of courtly power explored in the earlier unit on courtly sonnets was made clear by Whitney's lengthy account of the various prisons and workhouses for felons and debtors within its bounds. Whitney's ironic deployment of London as her own cultural property highlighted her class position, for, as one student put it, Whitney has "everything to give away and nothing at all."

Whitney's detailed representation of place, from a class- and gender-specific point of view, both contrasted with and supported Nashe's understanding of city issues in "Litany in Time of Plague." The spatial representation of Whitney's London gave the class an awareness of its crowdedness, which set up the idea of the plague as a problem especially of the city. We looked at Nashe's use of a very specific liturgical moment in a communal space occupied by a wide range of people as a way of broadening the view of the city, and of the range of class positions, from Whitney's version. By emphasizing the inexorability of plague through the list of qualities (including mercantile wealth, beauty, strength, wit, and degree) that will not help people withstand it and by using the refrain, "I am sick, I must die," Nashe creates a play of universal and individual, economic and spiritual more sweeping than Whitney's version. In Nashe, class positions are noted only to be elided.

Finally, taught together, Whitney's "Wyll and Testament" and Nashe's "Litany in Time of Plague" provided an effective means of examining ideas of city, questions of class, and the mingling of economic and spiritual so central to the cultures of sixteenth- and seventeenth-century England.

Lynette F. McGrath

Isabella Whitney and the Ideologies of Writing and Publication

Isabella Whitney (fl. 1565–75) may not seem the most obvious starting place for an introduction to sixteenth-century ideologies of writing and publication. Yet her poetry and the speculatively reconstructed circumstances of its printing can be made the pedagogical center of an exploratory venture that fans out to a number of intriguing, interconnected issues. For both undergraduate and graduate students in American universities at the turn of the twenty-first century, when the circumstances of composition and publishing practice are radically different from those in England in the sixteenth century, Whitney can informatively focus attention on these changes.

A simple list of ideological shifts in writing culture from the sixteenth to the twentieth century, pointed up by a study of Whitney, would include: communal composition changed to solitary composition; Renaissance admiration for the rhetorical accomplishments of *imitatio* and *copia* turned in the twentieth century to praise for freshness and originality, accompanied by legal outrage over plagiarism; the tentative beginnings of the commercialization of writing in the sixteenth century developed into competition and full-fledged modern capitalist profiteering in publication; the somewhat shame-faced status of publication and at least the proclaimed desirability of anonymity for early modern writers as against, in the twentieth century, the active pursuit of celebrity and publicity; and the seeking of aristocratic patronage by Renaissance writers turned to the modern habit of writers hiring literary agents to advance their career.

But apparent in Whitney's case and still adequately represented in the twentieth-century ideologies of writing and publication are gendered differences in publication experience and the recognition of, and response to, class and educational gradations of audience, most obviously (materially) evident in variations in the quality of book production.

Clearly, to establish these comparisons, the use of a number of representative twentieth-century texts is desirable. Although choices here can be left to the discretion of students and teachers, necessary comparative texts from Whitney and the sixteenth century are:

Isabella Whitney's poetry in either Richard Panofsky's facsimile edition (*Floures*) or on the *STC* microfilm. A modern spelling edition edited by Sara Jayne Steen's students at Montana State University and available through Kinko's, Bozeman, MT 59717, may be useful for students unused to reading black letter, but the original print versions are essential for some of the investigations I describe below.

The final poem from the late-sixteenth-century poetry anthology *A Gorgeous Gallerie of Gallant Inventions* (116; see also notes on 204). Several critics, most persuasively R. J. Fehrenbach, have speculated that this poem may also be Whitney's.

A version of Geffrey Whitney's *Choice of Emblemes*. The most accessible edition of this work, edited by Henry Green, is out of print, so photocopies of selected portions are the best alternative. The most useful sections for a comparison with his sister Isabella's work are his will (xciii), his dedication to the earl of Leicester, and his dedication, "To the Reader." Emblems dedicated to George Mainwaring and members of the Whitney family are also interesting.

Indispensable critical bridges are Wendy Wall's (*Imprint*) and Arthur Marotti's (*Donne*, *Manuscript*, "Patronage," and "Transmission") analyses of the gendering of publication and printing and the communal nature of composition in the sixteenth century. Also helpful is Louise Schleiner's discussion of women's reading groups (esp. ch. 1).

To consider the communal nature of composition in the sixteenth century, it is enlightening to observe how Isabella Whitney situates herself in relation to other writers: T. B. (Thomas Berrie); the bachelor W. G. (William Gruffith?); and the other bachelor, R. Witc., who, with W. G. answers her letter to an unconstant lover (I. Whitney, *Copy*); immediate family members (her brothers, Geffrey and Brooke; her sisters, who are Anne and two younger sisters whose names we do not know), some of whom also respond poetically to her *Epistles* (in *Sweet Nosgay*); her cousins (F. W. and G. W.); and her friends C. B. and T. L. The collaborative nature of her association with her printer, Richard Jones, in the construction of her published texts is discussed by Paul A. Marquis (316). An interesting discussion on the end product of writing can be stimulated by this evidence and supported by reference to Schleiner and Marotti.

Anonymity and publication as gendered issues can be raised by the absence of Whitney's name on her publications (although, since the first three pages are missing, we cannot be sure about *A Sweet Nosgay*) and by the likelihood that at least one other anonymous poem in the *Gorgeous Gallery* is by her, and possibly one or more anonymous poems in other contemporary anthologies. Green speculates (doubtfully, I think) that a commendatory poem by I. W. to *A Plaine and Easie Introduction to Practicall Musicke* may also be hers, although the volume's late date (1597) would raise interesting questions about a possibly representative woman's writing career that went underground and anonymous, but did not cease, over a period of some thirty years. By comparison, her brother Geffrey's name is clearly affixed to his publication.

Issues of patronage and gendered influence in publication circles are also raised by Whitney's dedication of the *Nosgay* to an old family friend, Mainwaring, and Geffrey's dedication to Robert, earl of Leicester, who apparently urged him to publish his *Choice of Emblemes*. Geffrey dedicates one of his emblems to Mainwaring, but his access to a man of Leicester's station makes Mainwaring, in Geffrey's sphere, comparatively small potatoes.

In this context of different spheres of power influencing both gendered social status and print circulation, the elaborate and expensive presentation of Geffrey's *Choice of Emblemes*, with its beautiful and varied print fonts and elaborate illustrations, compared with the simple presentation of Isabella's poems, in a sometimes broken print that suggests the use of old or worn typeface, is also indicative. The popular nature of Isabella's publications compared with Geffrey's, assignable to differences in gender, wealth, social station, patronage, and education, is evident in the material quality of the texts themselves as well as in their content.

Both Isabella's "Auctor to the Reader" and Geffrey's dedication "To the Reader" justify Wall's assertion that publication had a dubious quality for both men and women. Both Isabella and Geffrey apologize for their entry into print, both proclaim their insufficient skill, and both refer to others to justify their action. However, Geffrey fills his dedication with references to the classics, establishing his authority in this educational context, whereas Isabella claims that she has had to give up reading such heavy works because they "mazed" her "muse" and "bruised" her "brain" (Avii). Probably in both cases the proclaimed humility is conventional, but Geffrey puts his name to his publication; Isabella does not. In any case, Isabella, as a woman, must potentially face a more intensely disapproving social response for her temerity.

To discuss gendered differences of property—imaginative and material—a useful comparison can be made between Isabella's poetic "Wyll and Testament" and Geffrey's legal will. He has valuable material property (as well as some debts) to distribute among his friends and relatives. Clues in his writing, including the emblem he dedicates to his brother, Brooke, together with Isabella's *Epistles* to Brooke and her two younger sisters, indicate that Geffrey's inheritance of all that was available of the family property left his siblings relatively impoverished. As the eldest son, Geffrey inherited the family possessions and had a university education; a public, political career; and an aristocratic patron. Brooke seems not to have inherited much of the family property, and Isabella and her two younger sisters became serving maids in London. Isabella's introductory poems and addresses to her readers indicate her constant impoverishment and her possible bankruptcy and indebtedness. Her "Wyll and Testament" tells us that she had to be rescued by friends (possibly from prison) and was forced to leave London. Her "Wyll" is in the nature of an imagined legacy, not a real one. She writes from a situation of deprivation. Wall's discussion of the emerging genre of women's legacies and women's legal marginalization in terms of owning or willing material property is a valuable enrichment of this material.

Finally, the similar but subtly different attitudes evident in Geffrey's and Isabella's comments on their borrowings from other writers highlight interesting issues of *imitatio* and plagiarism. All but 16 of Geffrey's 248 emblems are lifted from Continental sources: Andreus Alciatus, John Sambacus, Claude Paradin, and so forth. Geffrey expresses his indebtedness and gratitude but seems to have no sense that his use of these materials will be taken amiss. Rather, he expects some degree of admiration for his skill in newly rendering these examples. Perhaps Isabella also is working within the tradition of *imitatio* and *copia*, but her narrative of her borrowing from Hugh Plat's *Floures of Philosophie* contains a more heart-felt concern that he might feel that her renderings have damaged his flowers and "say in rage were she a man, / that with my flowers doth brag, / She well should pay the price, I wolde / not leve her worth a rag" (Cvii). Even if the tone here is witty, it is also more anxious than Geffrey's calm assumption of his right to borrow.

Ultimately, all these textual examples offer a fascinating glimpse into the gradual changes taking place in England between the advent of print culture and the end of the seventeenth century, from manuscript circulation of texts to publication, from anonymity to authoritative and possessive authorship, marking the slow emergence of writing as a materially lucrative profession.

Elizabeth Patton

Seven Faces of Cleopatra

"Dost thou not see my baby at my breast, / That sucks the nurse asleep?" whispers Cleopatra, quieting her stricken maidservant in the final scene of Shakespeare's play (*Ant.* 5.2.309–10). The metaphor's reversal of agency typifies shifting perspectives on Cleopatra's behavior and public image that occur within and among an array of early modern texts. Those discussed here are Mary Sidney's *Antonius* (1592), Elizabeth Cary's *Tragedy of Mariam* (1602–04), Shakespeare's *Antony and Cleopatra* (1607), Aemilia Lanyer's *Salve Deus Rex Judaeorum* (1610), Samuel Daniel's *Tragedie of Cleopatra* (1611), Katherine Philips's *Pompey. A Tragedy* (1663), and Sir William Davenant's farce in act 5 of *The Play House to Be Let* (c. 1663). These texts were read as part of a two-semester seminar on Renaissance women writers for first-year students. Although the course was of necessity at an introductory level, it was also designed to introduce the sixteen students to various aspects of scholarly research.

Since such year-long teaching opportunities are rare, for one-semester courses I suggest as a short list the plays by Shakespeare and Sidney, along with Cary if at all possible. We in fact read her play earlier and then reviewed it during our discussion of Cleopatra; we did the same with Lanyer's poetry. Cary deals only tangentially with Cleopatra: Mariam's mother, envious of the "brown Egyptian," tells her daughter that if circumstances had been different, Mariam herself might have been "in a Roman's chariot set / in place of Cleopatra" (lines 190, 195–96). Besides being the only original play by a woman on our list, *The Tragedy of Mariam* has the added advantage of drawing on Jewish historical sources rather than on the ubiquitous life of Antony by Plutarch.

The remaining works can be read in excerpted form or presented to the class through student reports. Daniel's *Tragedie of Cleopatra*, for example, dedicated to the countess of Pembroke (Mary Sidney), has many points of intersection with her translation of Robert Garnier's *Marc Antoine* (1592): in one instance, Pembroke plays on meanings of the word *still* in the concluding chorus of act 1 just as Daniel plays on the word *rest* at the end of act 2, both reflecting on Egypt's lack of stability from a stoic perspective. A class report on Philips's *Pompey, A Tragedy* (a translation of Corneille's 1644 *La Mort de Pompée* and intended, like Shakespeare's version, for the public stage) not only highlighted Cleopatra's earlier life, including her relations with her brother, Ptolemy, and with Julius Caesar, but also introduced us to the character of Cornelia, whom we would encounter again in Davenant's farce. Our required reading included a recent *Smithsonian* article by Barbara Holland, "Cleopatra: What Kind of Woman Was She, Anyway?" This illustrated survey of the Cleopatra image in popular culture separates popular icon from historical entity, suggesting a politically astute Cleopatra who, rather like Dido before the arrival of Aeneas, bases her actions on pragmatic concerns for Egypt's present needs and future agenda. The combination of clearly stated opinions with a lack of scholarly apparatus (this lack a feature of the magazine, not of the writer) was in fact a useful pedagogical tool in that students needed to find independent sources of confirmation for points they wished to cite.

Cleopatra's relations with Pompey, then with Julius Caesar, and finally with Mark Antony earn her the suspicion of shifting loyalties expressed in Shakespeare's epithet "triple-turned whore" (4.12.13). But in the world of the play this is a Roman rather than an Egyptian assessment, a distinction that we found to be a key one. While Shakespeare's Roman characters are imbued with sixteenth-century England's behavioral expectations for women and judge Cleopatra accordingly—specifically for seducing Antony, "the triple pillar of the world" (1.1.12)—when the characters are in the play's Egyptian mode, Cleopatra remains surprisingly free of such explicitly gender-linked criticisms.

Antony, who moves between both worlds, can think in either mode. Despite his own (Roman) awareness that "present pleasure, / By revolution low'ring, does become / The opposite of itself" (1.2.125–27), in his Egyptian persona he can simply dismiss the great revolving fortune's wheel of military victories and defeats: "Let Rome in Tiber melt, and the wide arch / Of the ranged Empire fall. Here is my space" (1.1.33–34). This space of "present pleasure" and sensual timelessness later resolves to "the very heart of loss" (4.12.29), and later still to the center of the tomb in which Cleopatra must play out her destiny when, for her, "the crown of the earth" melts with Antony's death (4.15.63).

In a short, early essay assignment, we began our analysis of the critical question of agency by evaluating whether or not Cleopatra had really "packed cards with Caesar" and plotted to save her skin rather than fight to the finish in the pivotal battle of Actium, as Shakespeare's Antony (again in his Roman mode) accuses her (4.12.9–29). In retrospect, students felt that this initial, written assessment of Cleopatra's motivations was an essential preparation for our later examination of her long, introspective soliloquies in Sidney's play, which opens with Antony's leveling of a very similar charge, and in Daniel's. (In keeping with the attention to classical unities characteristic of their French sources and models, these neo-Senecan tragedies deal entirely with events from Shakespeare's final episodes: Sidney opens with Antony raging about his defeat at Actium, while in Daniel's opening scene Cleopatra has already buried Antony and the action occurs entirely inside her monument.)

Additionally, students had learned to follow Shakespeare's shifts between Roman and Egyptian perspectives and were now quick to identify pairs of opposites such as time and timelessness, change and stasis, future fame and "present pleasure," a skill that was to prove helpful in discussions of stoic overtones in the neo-Senecan dramas of Sidney and Daniel.

Running alongside stoic themes such as self-reliance and stead-fastness in these plays (as well as in Cary's *Mariam*) is the early mod-ern assessment of the daughters of Eve as emotionally labile and dangerously persuasive. In Sidney's play, for example, the character of Antony assesses Cleopatra's behavior at Actium from this per-spective. "In wanton love a woman thee misleads," he tells himself, then quickly assumes a stance of stoic acceptance: "But ah, by nature women wavering are; / Each moment changing and rechanging minds" (1.120, 145–46). Later in the play he completes the thought with a short panegyric on the steadfastness of male friend-ships (3.117–30). And while Sidney's Cleopatra seems able to dis-tance herself somewhat from female emotions, at least in a maternal sense, by focusing entirely on Antony rather than on her children's welfare (2.318–30), she accepts the entire blame for the defeat at Actium as a "fearful woman" (2.194–220). Daniel's Cleopatra seems able to accept her fate in an even more stoic fashion—"I have both hands and will, and I can die" (2.1.423)—but spends most of the play using her feminine resources to manipulate men who may help her protect her children. And she speaks as a woman, not a woman-as-soldier, when she concludes a long self-analysis by admit-ting that the tug of worldly fame led her into an error evocative (to us) of Eve's sin of pride in the Garden of Eden:

> Am I the woman whose inventive pride
> Adorned like Isis scorned mortality?
> Is it I would have my frailty so belied,
> That flattery could persuade I was not I? (2.1.402–05)

These self-assessments, almost perversely contradictory at times, fit well into our ongoing discussions of agency, and in this context I also found it useful to draw on two apparently contrasting references to Cleopatra in Lanyer's *Salve Deus Rex Judaeorum*. Here, Cleopatra's two appearances flank Lanyer's central defense of Eve (lines 761–72). Initially, Lanyer identifies excessive beauty as a lure that brings about the downfall of men and that also leads Cleopatra to commit the sin of taking her own life (213–32). Later in the poem, however, Cleopatra's suicide is paradoxically termed "glorious" because it was done out of love—even though the earthly attachment of "the Blacke Egyptian" can in no way be commensurate with spiritual love for Christ (1407–48). As in Shakespeare's shifting modes, widely varying assessments are here applied to the same event.

Another significant variant in these texts is Cleopatra's skin color. Lanyer's "Blacke Egyptian" (line 1431) echoes Cary's reference to the "brown Egyptian" mentioned above; Cleopatra is a "black gypsy" in Davenant, as well as a "brown damsel" (95, 97); and she appears as a tawny-fronted Gypsy in Shakespeare's opening lines. We found Cary's image to be particularly intriguing in that the negative reference comes from a character who is herself of Mediterranean origin. On the other end of the color scale, on one occasion in Daniel's play it is reported that Cleopatra "blusht, and then was pale" (5.1.1549); Philips calls her "fair and fierce" (1.4.112); and Sidney describes her in full-blown Petrarchan language, calling her skin "marble" and "alabaster," her breast "fair," her lips "coral," and her hair "fine and flaming gold" (2.477–97). Our discussions of Cleopatra's variegated coloring were greatly assisted by readings from Kim F. Hall's *Things of Darkness: Economies of Race and Gender in Early Modern England*, particularly her investigation of "the appearance of dark/light pairs of women" in cases where early modern women writers "represent their own oppression and will-to-power in the intersections of gender, race, and empire formed by the language of Petrarchan beauty" (179).

We read Davenant's farce last. Students chose to act it out (taking about twenty minutes of class time) and soon recognized, beneath its bawdy surface humor, the same behavioral codes that had become familiar to them from other readings, which included diaries, correspondences, and conduct books. In that light, they heard the insult Cleopatra hurls at Cornelia, "You want a Tarquin to make you a Lucrece," as indicative of her own ultimate fate. In the eyes of an English audience, Cleopatra commits suicide not because, as she asks in Daniel, "Is th'honor, wonder, glory, pompe, and all / Of Cleopatra dead, and she not dead?" (2.1.379–80) or because of her "glorious" love for Antony, as praised in Lanyer. Rather, Cleopatra must die because, as a "triple-turned whore," she has more than exhausted her available social options. Tracking her ability to act independently of such judgments, as she does in the Egyptian world created by Shakespeare, was one of the most rewarding aspects of our study of the many faces of Cleopatra.

A note on editions: The plays by Sidney and Cary are included in *Renaissance Drama by Women*, edited by S. P. Cerasano and Marion Wynne-Davies, a collection rich with primary and secondary sources. References to Philips are from *Pompey*; the text is also available from the Brown University Women Writers Project (Box 1841, Brown University, Providence, RI 02912; www.wwp.brown .edu). I used Susanne Woods's edition of *The Poems of Aemilia Lanyer*. "Tragedy Travestie," the fifth act of Davenant's *The Play House to Be Let*, is available in his *Dramatic Works*.

Mary V. Silcox

Aemilia Lanyer and Virtue

One of the most puzzling and yet most important aspects of Aemilia
Lanyer's work for twenty-first-century students is the crucial role of
virtue. Students reading from a twentieth-century feminist perspective often become impatient with her complicity in her culture's
dominant prescriptions of what it is to be a woman, that is, the centrality of virtue to her definition. Using Lanyer's poetry and biography as a jumping-off point, we discuss the cultural shaping of
women in seventeenth-century England and, coincidentally, in our
own society.

Cultural doctrine generally described women as intellectually
and morally flawed, and women were constrained in the home, the
church, and the law courts to an inferior status. The virtuous
woman was held to an almost superhuman standard of conduct,
continually exhorted to chastity, modesty, obedience, and silence. In
spite of such difficulties, compounded in many cases by an inferior
education and the heavy burdens of childbearing and domestic duty,
women did write, but their works—in persona, choice of subject,

attitude toward it, and rhetorical strategies—were influenced and shaped (limited) by women's cultural environment. This influence meant, for most women, the writing of pious works that could justify their literary endeavors and prove them to be virtuous rather than shrewish women who were stepping beyond their proper limits. Lanyer takes this ideological anxiety about women's virtue and the activities suitable to a virtuous woman, always submerged in women's writings of the early seventeenth century, and raises it to be, not just in plain view, but her subject of subjects and her source of defiance. It is essential for students to recognize that her preoccupation with demonstrating that women achieve—indeed, actively realize—virtue in their own lives as well as historically through Christ's story turns what we would see as a restriction into a source of power and pride. A sense of moral superiority has its serious cultural uses.

Lanyer is representative of women writers in her addressing a female audience and thus typically lessening the public nature of her speaking, but she is quite extraordinary in her extended construction and praise of a veritable society of virtuous women, not just in her numerous dedications but in "Salve Deus Rex Judaeorum" and "The Description of Cooke-ham" as well. Because of time restrictions I generally discuss only her longest and central dedication, addressed to an illustrious female poet and patron of literature, "The Authors Dreame to the Ladie Marie, the Countess Dowager of Pembroke." This elaborate and complex tribute, in the form of a dream vision, is valuable for an understanding of the range of virtue's meaning for Lanyer. What is most notable in Pembroke (Mary Sidney) as a writer, what raises her to be esteemed beyond her brother Sir Philip Sidney, "For virtue, wisdom, learning, dignity" (28), is that her poetry enlightens others spiritually. Even more, the genre of dream vision comes into play as the poem and my class explore how Pembroke is not a dream only but also a living woman, reinforcing Lanyer's central point that learning and virtue do exist in women in actuality, not just in idealization.

I teach two passages from "Salve Deus Rex Judaeorum," lines 745–848 and 921–1016, which contain "The Passion of Christ,"

"Eves Apologie," "The Teares of the Daughters of Jerusalem," and the beginning of "The Sorrow of the Virgin Marie." I introduce these passages with the final prefatory address before "Salve Deus" itself, the prose "To the Vertuous Reader." Here Lanyer sets up the intimate relation among women, virtue, and Christ that forms the basis of her argument in "Salve Deus," beginning with her startling identification of men who defame women with "they that dishonoured Christ his Apostles and Prophets, putting them to shamefull deaths" (48–49) and going on to surround Christ with women. By associating the "Vertuous Reader," explicitly addressed as female, with Christ's virtue and the virtue of biblical heroines such as Deborah, Hester, and Judith, Lanyer constructs all women's virtue as an active, courageous endeavor rather than merely a passive state.

In my first selection from "Salve Deus" students discover how Lanyer's rhetorical strategies are themselves a part of the message, which here deals with the role of virtuous women in religion, learning, and ultimately society. I ask them to consider what the effects are of her composing "Eves Apologie" in the form of an argument. Lanyer does not stand in opposition to what her society considers verities about women's weakness as daughters of Eve. Instead she argues that those verities can be interpreted aslant, turned toward asserting women's goodness and thus made to justify women's independence. In my second passage from "Salve Deus," Lanyer changes to narrative strategies that strongly contrast men's and women's roles in Christ's Passion. The usual interpretation of Christ's marked association with women was that by doing so he was ministering to the lowliest, but in Lanyer's description of the Passion and women's reactions to Christ's suffering he is instead seen as being supported by women as his morally fittest followers.

Virtue is similarly central to "The Description of Cooke-ham" though explored through the relation among the countess of Cumberland, her female companions, and nature. As a country-house poem "Cooke-ham" is composed as a praise of the estate, but we discover that nature's virtue lies in its responsiveness to the countess, creating an ideal society cut off, for a time, from man-made society. The countess, a vessel for God's grace, sanctifies the landscape, but when she withdraws, a world of death and desolation is left behind. The question of the place of women's virtue in this fallen world permeates the poem and shapes its elegiac tone.

Lanyer's poetry is valuable for many reasons, but one of its primary values is to show students how a writer can work within her culture's ideology, in this instance her culture's need for virtue in a woman, and yet use that ideology to challenge the restrictions placed on women.

Josephine A. Roberts

Diabolic Dreamscape in Lanyer and Milton

One of the most distinctive features of Aemilia Lanyer's *Salve Deus Rex Judaeorum* (1611) is the dramatic monologue of Pilate's wife, who narrates her dream warning against her husband's involvement in Christ's crucifixion. Although biblically based (Matt. 27.19), the dream was described in more graphic detail in apocryphal writings and dramatized at length in several of the medieval cycle plays in England and on the Continent. Of the surviving English mystery plays, three present imaginative reenactments of the dream of Pilate's wife. In the *N———Town Plays* (formerly known as the *Ludus Coventriae*), Satan suddenly realizes that he must block the Crucifixion or risk losing dominion over mankind and thus chooses to send a dream to Pilate's wife, so that she will intervene with her husband. A similar episode occurs in the Cornish *Ordinalia*, where Beelzebub appears to Pilate's wife in a dream to warn her that severe reprisals will be inflicted on her husband and children if Christ is put to death. Alarmed at the danger awaiting her family, she sends a messenger to Pilate after the acts of torture have already begun.

A slightly different motivation occurs in the York plays, where Satan tells Pilate's wife that her riches will be taken away and her power will be destroyed if Christ is crucified. Her characterization is the most fully developed in the York cycle, where she is portrayed as an extremely vain woman, proud of her position as the governor's wife: she openly boasts that she is a "welle of all womanhede [. . .] wittie and wise" (*York Plays* 272). The York play also departs from the other English cycle dramas in using her proper name (Procula or Procla) and in providing several comic elements. When the Beadle insists that Procula should go home before dark, she disagrees, and they have a drink together shortly before she receives Satan's dream. When she awakens, she sends her boy to confront Pilate with the news.

Despite their differences, the English cycle plays uniformly agreed in presenting the dream of Pilate's wife as demonic, inspired by Satan's desperation. When Lanyer began fashioning her own account of Pilate's wife, she had a rich dramatic tradition that was in living memory of many of her readers; the cycle plays had continued to be performed annually until the late 1560s. Yet Lanyer radically alters the presentation of the dream by making clear that it is divinely inspired and guided by the purest motives, to save Christ's life and Pilate's soul: "Condemne not him that must thy Saviour be" (84; line 757). In the larger context of the poem, Lanyer links the dream of Pilate's wife to the idea of divinely inspired poetry in the dedicatory verses to Mary Sidney, the countess of Pembroke ("The Authors Dreame"), in which the persona describes how while sleeping she received a vision in which she heard "the heavenli'st musicke [. . .] / That ever earthly eares did entertaine" (27; lines 129–30). Upon awakening, she vows to present her poem, described as a "Dreame" (31; line 205), to her patron. Lanyer's final address "To the Doubtfull Reader" describes the entire work *Salve Deus Rex Judaeorum* as a divinely inspired vision, whose title came to her in sleep long before she had completed the poem.

Lanyer thus repeatedly denies an association between women and demonic dreams, in the account of Pilate's wife as well as in her own defense of authorship. In describing Eve before the fall, Lanyer also specifically excludes any references to a Satanic dream, a highly significant omission since the idea of Eve's temptation through dreams had a long tradition in England extending back to the Anglo-Saxon poem *Genesis B* (lines 564–67; 600–16). Lanyer's absolute exclusion of the Satanic dream may be contrasted with Milton's treatment of the highly controversial and much discussed episode of Eve's dream in *Paradise Lost* (5.38–121; in *Complete Poems*).

Milton anticipates the episode of the dream with his vivid depiction of Satan, who sat "squat like a Toad, close at the ear of *Eve*" (4.800). But the figure Eve sees in her dream appears angelic, "one shap'd and wing'd like one of those from Heav'n" (5.55). Nearly every detail of Eve's dream reveals Satan's cunning duplicity in presenting a pleasing visual image and ventriloquizing Adam's voice. Much of the previous critical debate on this passage has addressed the question of whether or not Eve actually tastes the fruit that Satan holds up to her mouth. Some critics (such as Irene Samuel [441–44] and Stanley Fish [222–25]) deny that she eats and argue that her refusal demonstrates that she is untainted by Satan's dreamscape temptation. Other critics believe that she does taste the fruit, but they differ as to whether the dream strengthens her resolve to behave virtuously (Lewalski, *Writing Women* 230–32; McColley 63–109) or whether it renders her more vulnerable and susceptible through the experience (Radzinowicz, "Eve" 170).

What is significant is that in her dramatic monologue Milton's Eve cannot verbalize the act of disobedience. In the climactic moment, she describes how "the pleasant savory smell / So quick'n'd appetite, that I, *methought*, / Could not but taste" (5.84–86; emphasis mine). As Eve contemplates the dream (superimposing present over past), she halts her description in mid line, refusing to give words to the forbidden act. Her present resistance is, I would argue, even more important than what may have actually occurred in the unbidden dream. Her refusal to describe the act of disobedience means that at this stage she is unwilling to sin; in contrast with the medieval examples of women who receive diabolic dreams, Milton's Eve refuses to become Satan's verbal instrument.

Adam's response reinforces the view that the dream does not imply Eve's weakness but, rather, her strength in responding to temptation. His observation that in dreams evil "may come and go, so unapprov'd, and leave / No spot or blame behind" (5.118–19) is important in denying the misogynist connection between weak women and diabolic dreams. In fact, in *Paradise Regained*, Milton describes how Christ is beset by satanic dreams yet remains without sin (4.397–431). Despite the reassurance Adam gives his wife, he misunderstands the nature of her dream, thinking that it is a *somnium animale*, composed of disjoined parts of their conversation from the previous day. Although neither partner has fallen, as Milton specifically emphasizes in his account before Satan's final speech in the garden ("thus *Eve* yet sinless" [9.659]), both have difficulty in understanding the enormity of the danger they confront.

In creating Eve's dream, Milton broke decisively with medieval traditions that would establish a direct link between frail womankind and demonic dreams. Although Lanyer and Milton are often contrasted in their treatments of Eve, on the issue of diabolic dreamscape the two authors seem to be aligned in reacting against the misogynist tradition. Lanyer's response is more radical, by replacing the demonic dream with a divinely inspired vision. Milton retains the diabolic dream but modifies it to show Eve's act of resistance. He also counterbalances the satanic dream in book 4 with the vision that Eve receives in book 12 (599–600).

Editor's Note

Josephine Roberts wrote this description of an approach to Lanyer and Milton in anticipation of expanding it for an MLA convention session on Milton and women writers. Because of her untimely death, the piece was never expanded, but the editors believe it is useful and important in its present form for this volume.

Stephen C. Behrendt

Teaching Aphra Behn's "The Disappointment"

In undergraduate survey courses in earlier English literature, one is always hard pressed to find works that engage students even as they illuminate the contemporary cultural milieu. This is especially true when the course includes significant numbers of nonmajors, who are especially susceptible to the anxiety and incomprehension that may be produced by the peculiar otherness of premodern British literature and culture. The difficulties are in some ways further multiplied when one includes women in the course materials, for the vexed position of women in this culture indicated by contemporary references to them, to their work (whether literary or domestic), and to the socially coded gender expectations that governed such references—including the typically slighting or derisive remarks of male writers about the characters of women—may encourage students to be similarly dismissive. Rather than chide students for their understandable impercipience, however, many of us have found in recent literary history's recovery of previously marginalized women's literary voices a wonderful array of textual sites for challenging these traditionally received, gendered notions. But one need not turn only to "new" women's voices in the field of discourse; even so historically canonized a figure as Aphra Behn offers often unsuspected opportunities for student discoveries, especially when one focuses on her unexpectedly sharp sense of humor.

Behn's brief pastoral "The Disappointment" always works with my students, including those who find her more extended works like *Oroonoko* (1688) or plays like *The Rover* (1677) or *The Lucky Chance* (1687) more than they can handle. For one thing, the pastoral is short, which makes it a manageable reading experience, especially early in a term. Second, its clearly identifiable pastoralism enables students (and their teachers) to situate it in a literary tradition whose conventions provide convenient points of comparison. Third, its rollicking humor—which hesitant, anxious students are often slow to discover—provides an occasion to examine not just humor in literature but also the more sharply focused subject of literary (and cultural) satire; this examination allows students and instructors to pursue another fruitful line of comparative analysis that places the work in a generic context at the same time that it focuses on the work's features in their own right. Most important, however, the poem presents a site at which students can organize profitable—often highly revealing—discussions relating specifically to women, to women's writing, to women's experience, and to socially conditioned expectations about women's behavior—including sexual behavior.

While there are many ways to approach a text like "The Disappointment," I have found that having students undertake a substantial writing assignment serves many useful purposes, one of which is to immediately foreground a woman's work in courses that have historically been dominated by male voices. I call mine a "working paper," which I define for my students as a directed or guided critical essay. While these essays are personal and therefore student-centered, they nevertheless pose several interrelated questions with which the students are required to wrestle in composing their essays. This type of assignment allows me to direct students' attention to key issues that they might not otherwise see—or that they might notice but be too insecure in their perceptions to explore. ("Is she really talking about sex?") The students take a week or so to read, reflect, and write; when they submit their papers, we devote that class period to a concentrated discussion, for which the writing process has prepared them well. By the time the discussion reaches the fun that Behn demonstrably has with sexual conduct and role reversals, the students are usually irrepressible in their enthusiasm to elaborate on their perceptions. Sex does sell, apparently.

In the latest incarnation of this assignment, I asked students to begin by examining the poem's overall tone, since many tend to be satisfied simply to read for content (which usually means narrative content). This examination of course involves asking student readers to be sensitive to a variety of forms of humor, an important point with students who tend for the most part to be largely unresponsive to humor in literature or, alternatively, to be undiscriminating about varieties of humor generally. (Since many of my students use the generic word *sarcastic* indiscriminately to denote irony, satire, burlesque, or other gradations of tone and intent, "The Disappointment" also opens up this ancillary topic.) Identifying the evidence for what they perceive as indicators of Behn's tone encourages my students to explore not just matters of humor but also issues like ambiguity, ambivalence, polyvalence, and both implicit and explicit contradiction in language.

Most important, though, is the poem's efficacy in the classroom for raising issues of gender. That Behn would take up a pastoral boy-meets-girl, boy-pursues-girl subject comes as little surprise to my students, and they confess to being initially bored with yet another iteration of this subject but nevertheless curious about how a woman will handle the pursuit (already a good sign of an initial openness to gender issues). They are indeed astonished, though, to see where Behn takes her oh-so-conventional subject, and they are not a little hesitant to believe that they are reading what in fact they are reading. That is, the poem's substitution of (male) sexual conquest and (male) sexual satisfaction (with or without a concomitant female fulfillment) with male impotence, male frustration, and female anger at thwarted sexual satisfaction leaves many quite literally disbelieving. Once reassured that they have not been deceived in their interpretation, and once they get beyond their initial delight (shared by many—but never all—of the male students) in the explicit sexuality (e.g., in Behn's figuring of Lysander's penis as the "weeping" "Insensible" [56; line 90] that "now wants the art to live" [55; line 83] or the "Snake" that Cloris's groping hand encounters [56; line 110]), students become increasingly voluble. Moreover, they invariably begin exploring the ingenious ways in which Behn turns the conventions of pastoral love-conquest poems against themselves by first reversing the roles of shepherd and shepherdess, seducer and seduced (or predator and prey), and then detailing with acute psychological insight both Lysander's shame and rage at his inability to perform and Cloris's righteous indignation over that same failure. At the same time, exploring these reversals reinforces for the students the fact that satire depends on author and audience's sharing the same vocabulary or expectations and therefore on the existence of an implicit (and often explicit) code of social and literary behavior by which the actions of literary characters—no less than the literary and rhetorical behaviors of the authors who bring them to life—are governed and evaluated.

This point of code inevitably leads us to a discussion of readership: for whom did Behn intend the poem? For female readers who would chuckle knowingly at this pointed deflation of male priapic pomp? For male readers who would find it hilarious so long as they assured themselves that Lysander could not possibly be them? For a mixed readership, in which case one must posit both a more risqué and a more various sort of readership than the undergraduate student (stereo)typically associates with earlier literature? Discussing the matter of intended and actual readerships generally leads students to be curious about the circumstances surrounding publication in the period. And this avenue of inquiry opens up yet another site for discussion of gender issues, in this case relating both to the production of literary texts (whether for private circulation or public sale) and to the reception of women's writing by variously constituted readerships. The lessons that students learn (and I encourage them to conduct further research, by providing a brief bibliography on the subject) in relation to Behn's text carry over to other authors (and audiences) whom we consider later in my course. Once this subject gets opened up in the context of "The Disappointment," I find that students revert to it with other authors. The same holds true with the issues of humor, literary tradition and convention, and gender politics: "The Disappointment" foregrounds these matters for students in ways that are clearly compelling, for students return to them time and again in the course, frequently invoking as a measuring stick the poem that in the process they come to know better and better as a result of these variously contextualized revisitings. That the poem—and the issues it raises—retains a real hold on student curiosity is apparent from the fact that since I have begun teaching it in the way described here, I have witnessed a remarkable shift in student research projects toward Behn, toward women writers, and toward issues of gender. Among the projects was a remarkable honors thesis that focused squarely on "The Disappointment." We have all come a long way.

Robin Ikegami

Teaching Aphra Behn's *The Rover*

As an introduction to Restoration comedy, an example of early modern feminism, or an insightful critique of the commodification of sexuality, Aphra Behn's 1677 play *The Rover* is a rich and entertaining text that engages students at a variety of levels. Following the adventures of the poor but otherwise carefree libertine Willmore, *The Rover* presents a series of parallel characters and dramatic situations, employing standard stage effects (masquerade, mistaken identity, etc.) to question traditional constructions of gender and class; to undermine the moral, economic, and social foundations of marriage as an institution; and to expose the fluidity of the boundary between respectable and scandalous society. Bringing students to a recognition and understanding of these issues, however, can pose something of a challenge, for students often become distracted by the business (and busyness) of the play: the variety of characters presented, the even larger number of real and assumed identities, the comic wordplay and miscues. Having taught this play in both a course on women writers and a survey of Restoration and eighteenth-century literature, I find that approaches that transform students from passive readers into active participants work best.

Rather than have students read the play out loud or perform the entire play in class, I divide them into groups and assign parallel scenes. One group assumes the roles of Angellica, Willmore, and Moretta in act 2, scene 2, where the three characters discuss the terms of Angellica's hire. Another group performs the scene in which Blunt is swindled out of his clothing and money by Lucetta (3.3). A third group acts the parts of Willmore and Angellica as they confront each other in act 4 (2.126–414), while a fourth takes the roles of Blunt and Florinda as Blunt tries to exact vengeance on womankind (represented in the body of Florinda) for Lucetta's trickery (4.5).[1] Finally, a fifth group performs lines 208 to 355 in act 5, Angellica's attack on Willmore with a pistol. When students perform these scenes in tandem, they are better able to recognize and appreciate Behn's use of gender-role reversal and her critique of mercenary lovers. They begin to identify the various alignments and cross-identifications. Angellica and Lucetta are both prostitutes, yet Angellica is cheated out of five hundred crowns and her sense of pride when Willmore tricks her into falling in love with him, while Lucetta (in the more conventional scenario) cheats Blunt out of his possessions when she tricks him into falling in love with her. Angellica and Blunt are both dupes, and both seek revenge as a result, but both are thwarted in the attempt and remain free to pursue their old ways, more cynical and guarded than before. Willmore and Lucetta are successful rogues, but each is tempered by the influence of an equal in love and trickery, for Willmore meets his match in the witty and ever-masquerading Hellena, and Lucetta has a companion in Philippo. The acting of parallel scenes avoids the passiveness many students assume when asked to read aloud and gives every student a role to play, thus forcing them to become active interpreters not only of their scene but also of the others. They want to figure out why I've chosen these five scenes, and participating in this kind of enactment leads them to look for connections they might not otherwise have seen or even suspected.

I sometimes also have students perform the scenes of conversation between Hellena and Willmore to get at conventional views of marriage, critiques of those views, and constructions of gender within the institution of marriage. To set the stage for Hellena, I begin with an enactment of her discussion of marriage with her sister, Florinda, in act 1, scene 1. Reminding students that Hellena is supposed to be destined for a nunnery—a fact easily forgotten, given her views and personality—I assign the following passages: 1.2.130–203; 3.1.136–283; 4.2.223–380; 5.396–576 (act 5 is not divided into scenes). What emerges from this comparison is an appreciation for Restoration wit and a celebration of female wit in particular. My students often initially see Hellena's pursuit of Willmore as misguided, even stupid, because he is after all a rover, a man who views women as sexual prey and hunts them at every turn. After performing these scenes, however, students feel more respect for Hellena and begin to consider the possibility that this novice-turned-lover has the upper hand over Willmore, for she knows his character and expresses little hope of changing his ways. Rather, she brings the fortune to the relationship and, as though to differentiate her love for Willmore from Angellica's, warns him that she is "Hellena the Inconstant" (5.488). Willmore will have to work to keep her love.

As we make our way through the play, students inevitably ask about Angellica's form of advertising herself, the posting of her portrait outside her residence. This picture of love for sale finds a parallel in the picture Florinda gives Belvile as a confirmation of their betrothal. I ask students to consider not only Behn's implicit commentary on the marriage market and the marketing of women generally but also modern-day parallels to such a practice. As we discuss commercials for 900-numbers, descriptions offered in personal ads, the significance of engagement rings, the exchanging of graduation photos, et cetera, students begin to recognize the radical implications of Behn's work in her own time and in ours. To help students appreciate more profoundly the implications of these forms of marketing, I sometimes ask them to create their own pictures: how would they sell themselves? This exercise gets students to ask questions such as these: What is revealed in the alignment of marriage and market? What is at stake in the marketing of self? And what are the alternatives?

In addition to analytic papers on the student's choice of topic, I also assign, by lottery, background reports at the beginning of the semester. For *The Rover*, I assign one report on Thomas Killigrew's *Thomaso; or, The Wanderer* (1654), on which *The Rover* is loosely based; one report on *The Second Part of the Rover* (1681), Behn's sequel; and one report on Behn's life and literary reputation. The three students with these assignments then give a ten-minute presentation to the class on their respective topics and turn in their papers to me. I find that these background reports offer historical, literary, and biographical context for the assigned reading in a way that decenters authority in the classroom and empowers students not only as facilitators but also as inquisitors, for they seem to feel freer to ask questions (either of me or the presenter) in the presentation format than in a lecture format. This kind of assignment also gives presenters valuable experience in doing library (sometimes archival) research; in properly documenting their findings; and in putting together a clear and concise oral presentation that is interesting, informative, and observant of time constraints.

The Rover is witty, entertaining, and revealing of both its culture and ours. It is a play that opens itself up to a variety of critical and pedagogical approaches because of its wordplay, its colorful and plentiful characterizations, and its rather surprisingly modern sensibilities. It is a play that investigates the nature of love and relationships between men and women of both equal and unequal abilities. It is a play, finally, that demands active engagement to be fully appreciated. Close reading alone does not do justice to Behn's wit and skill as a playwright, nor does it adequately challenge the analytic powers of students. When students have the opportunity to augment their careful reading of the play with a selective acting of it as well as with considerations of modern-day parallels, the play comes to life for them. Consequently, their insights become keener, their understanding stronger, and their appreciation finer.

Note
1. I use the Broadview Press edition of *The Rover*, edited by Anne Russell.

Part IV

Resources for Further Study

Georgianna Ziegler

Lost in the Archives?
Searching for Records of
Early Modern Women

Joyse Jeffreys, Sarah King, Eliza St. George, and Dorothy Wylde—
not household names, perhaps, but these women have several things
in common. They lived in seventeenth-century England, they each
owned at least one important book in which they wrote their names,
and all these books made their way to the Folger Library. Joyse,
Eliza, and Dorothy staked their claims by writing "her boke" along
with their names; Eliza added the date 1682, Dorothy 1645, and
Sarah 1662. Joyse's book was Lucan's *Pharsalia* (1614); Eliza's was
Elizabeth Joscelin's *The Mothers Legacie* (1624); Dorothy owned
Philip Sidney's *Arcadia* (1593); and Sarah the Second Folio of
Shakespeare's plays (1662). While most of the names appear in the
expected places—inside front cover, flyleaf, title page—Joyse wrote
her name boldly at the top of the page with the dedication of the
Pharsalia to Lucy, countess of Bedford. The names have been there
for a very long time for anyone to see, but only recently have they
been noted. None of the names appears in the Folger's Provenance
File of former owners, nor do they appear on the catalog cards for

these volumes. These women have effectively been silent for three hundred years.

I begin with this example to make a point about engaging in research on early modern women. Even if you look in the places where you would expect to find traces of them, they have often remained invisible through omission. This omission exists in bibliographies and book indexes as well as in library catalogs. Tracking early modern women in the printed books and manuscripts of history takes patience, imagination, and, above all, ingenuity. In the annotations to the bibliography that follows, I try to indicate where women appear, whether overtly or covertly, and how to discover their traces. I include material on Continental archives and writers. Many English families traveled on or had political business dealings with the Continent; a number of Englishwomen translated Continental works; and books themselves passed back and forth as part of an international exchange of humanistic ideas. In addition, many courses on women writers also deal with their lifestyles, addressing such topics as art, music, embroidery, and collecting, and these courses are often comparative, asking students to read the works of French, German, or Italian women writers with their English counterparts. During the past twenty years, there have been a number of fine publications on early modern women. With some exceptions, however, the main focus of this bibliography is on those reference works that provide access to primary and secondary materials rather than on works of criticism or individual biographies.

General Reference

Bibliographic Index: A Cumulative Bibliography of Bibliographies. New York: Wilson, 1937– .
   This useful periodical, published several times a year and as an annual cumulative volume, covers bibliographies published separately or in books or other periodicals (it monitors 2,600 English and foreign language journals). The annual subject index is extremely detailed, with many entries under "Women."

Bibliographie internationale de l'humanisme et de la Renaissance. Genève: Librairie Droz, 1965– .

This important annual periodical is usually several years behind, but it provides a wealth of references to secondary material and to modern editions of primary material (e.g., a new edition of *Mémoires et autres écrits* of Marguerite de Valois, published in 1987) published in the United States and abroad. The first part is a general index of persons, listing works about them; the second part is a subject-country bibliography, covering a wide range of subjects, including literature, history, religion, philosophy, theater, the arts, and sciences. The bibliography contains material on a number of early modern women such as Marie de Bourgogne, Teresa de Avila, Gaspara Stampa, Vittoria Colonna, Katherine Parr, Isabeau de Baviere, and Louise de Coligny. A CD-Rom version of the bibliography, retrospective to 1965, is also available.

General History

Printed Records

Great Britain

Royal Historical Society. *Writings on British History.* 1901–33; 1934–45. London: Cape, 1937–60; 1968–70. Cont. by *Writings on British History*, 1946–74. U of London. Inst. of Historical Research, 1973–86.

Royal Historical Society. *Annual Bibliography of British and Irish History.* Surrey: Harvester, 1976–87; Oxford UP, 1988– .
These volumes provide the standard current bibliography for British history from the fifth century. They are divided chronologically and include author and subject indexes.

Read, Conyers, ed. *Bibliography of British History, Tudor Period, 1485–1603* [. . .]. 2nd ed. Oxford: Clarendon, 1959.

Davies, Godfrey, and Mary Frear Keeler, eds. *Bibliography of British History, Stuart Period, 1603–1714.* 2nd ed. Oxford: Clarendon, 1970.
These basic bibliographies, issued under the auspices of the American Historical Association and the Royal Historical Society of Great Britain, are two volumes in the *Bibliography of British History*. They form a comprehensive survey of the earlier secondary literature.

Catalogue of the Pamphlets, Books, Newspapers and Manuscripts Relating to the Civil War, the Commonwealth, and Restoration, Collected by George Thomason, 1640–1661. 2 vols. London: British Museum, 1908.
Known familiarly as "the Thomason tracts," this collection provides a wealth of information about middle-class life in mid-seventeenth-century England. The two volumes cover 1640–52 and 1653–61; an index in the second volume includes entries under "Women" for general

works pertaining to them. Otherwise, one needs to look up individual women by name. The information about women is rich and varied, as shown in these brief examples: 1654: "Severall Circumstances to prove that Mrs. [sic] Jane Berkeley and Sr. William Killigrew have combined together to defraud me [Richard Lygon] of an estate"; 1654: "Strange and wonderful Newes from Whitehall, or, the mighty visions proceeding from Mistris Anna Trapnel"; and 1657: "Mistris Shawe's Tomb-Stone. Being remarkable passages in the life and death of Dorothy Shaw, who slept in the Lord 10 Dec." These tracts are available on a set of microfilm produced by UMI, 1981.

A Centenary Guide to the Publications of the Royal Historical Society, 1868–1968, and of the former Camden Society, 1838–1897. By Alexander Taylor Milne. London: Royal Historical Soc., 1968.

This work provides a detailed list and index of all publications issued by the Royal Historical Society and the Camden Society. Women can be searched by name in the general index, or material concerning women may be gleaned from the descriptive contents of the volumes. It is important to distinguish in the index between early modern women (names in small type) and modern women writing articles (names in large caps). One example of the kind of material made available in these antiquarian volumes are the letters (1625–43) of Lady Brilliana Harley (mother of Sir Edward Harley, founder of the Harleian Library). Another example is *The Diary of Henry Machyn* (1550–63); Machyn, a London merchant, records the goings-on of common folk: "The iii day of May dyd ryd in a care a-bowt London a woman that dwelt at Quen-heysse at the hott howsse, for a bawde." This kind of material is not specifically indexed by the *Centenary Guide*, but it provides a reference to Machyn's *Diary.* It is up to researchers to use their imagination in mining such sources.

Mullins, E. L. C. *Texts and Calendars: An Analytical Guide to Serial Publications.* London: Royal Historical Soc., 1958, 1983. 2 vols.

This work is described as "an analytical guide to printed texts and calendars relating to English and Welsh history issued in general collections or in series by a public body or private society before the end of March 1957." The first volume lists publications issued between 1802 and 1957; the second, from 1957 to 1982. The issuing bodies are the Public Record Office; Irish and Scottish Record Offices; the Catholic Record Society; Hakluyt, Harleian, and Huguenot Societies, et cetera; and various local record societies. Each volume contains a detailed index of names and some subjects. Other than looking up personal names, you might retrieve matter relating to women by looking under such topics as letters and diaries (both divided chronologically), wills, Catholics, Jews, and place-names.

France

Bibliographie annuelle de l'histoire de France: Du cinquième siècle à 1958.
Paris: Centre National de la Recherche Scientifique, 1975– . Continues
Bibliographie annuelle de l'histoire de France: Du cinquième siècle à 1939
and *à 1945.*
This excellent annual bibliography surveys thousands of monographs,
collected essays, and periodical literature for the period of French history
from the fifth century to 1958. It is divided into general topics, and
under each the references are given chronologically. The large topics
cover general historiography (including archives, bibliographies, and libraries); political, economic, social, religious, and local history; the history of institutions, of overseas French, and of civilization. Beginning in
the issue for 1989, a very useful chronological index breaks down the
subjects for each historic period. Under "*Société*" for the seventeenth
century, for example, are the subheadings "*Famille*," "*Femme et enfant*,"
"*Sexualité*," and "*Vie quotidienne*." Another index by subject clusters
the references chronologically. It is therefore possible to look up
"*Femmes*" and to isolate easily the references to the sixteenth through
eighteenth centuries.

French 17: Bibliography of French Seventeenth-Century Studies. Ed. J. D.
Vedvik. Fort Collins: Colorado State U, for the Seventeenth-Century
French Division of MLA, 1953– .
This annual descriptive bibliography covers books, articles, and work in
progress in literature, bibliography, linguistics, politics, philosophy, soci-
ety, science, and religion.

Hauser, Henri. *Les sources de l'histoire de France XVIe siècle (1494–1610).*
4 vols. Paris: Picard, 1906–15.
Hauser's volumes are divided chronologically (vol. 1: 1494–1515; vol.
2: 1515–59; vol. 3: 1559–89; vol. 4: 1589–1610). In each volume, the
material is organized by subject. His aim is to direct the researcher to primary source material, both in original and later editions. Hauser also
provides useful historical and biographical commentary. Under "Marguerite de Valois," for example, we learn that her *Memoires* were first
published in Paris in 1628 but written between 1585 and 1605 at
Usson. He then lists other editions from 1648 to 1858.

Bourgeois, Emile, and Louis André. *Les sources de l'histoire de France, XVIIe*
siècle (1610–1715). 8 vols. Paris: Picard, 1913–35.
Covering a shorter time span than the Hauser bibliography, these volumes are divided by subject only but have a similar aim of providing references to primary source material. The last volume has what is primarily
a name index; there is no entry under "*Femmes*." Anyone researching

women, therefore, needs to be creative and to explore general areas that look promising. Under the section "*Histoire des localités et livres de raison*," for example, there is an entry for Madeleine des Porcellets, comtesse de Rochefort, who in 1706 published a diary, *Journal de tout ce que j'ai fait depuis le 17 mai 1689, jour du départ de M. le comte de Rochefort.* An explanatory note says that the journal gives details of the countess's busy life, including the farm work and financial difficulties, while her husband was at war. Excerpts were published in an 1889 edition.

Germany

Dahlmann, Friedrich Christoph. *Dahlmann-Waitz Quellenkunde der deutschen Geschichte: Bibliographie der Quellen und der Literatur zur deutschen Geschichte.* 10th ed. Stuttgart: Hiersemann, 1965– .
Originally by Friedrich Dahlmann and Georg Waitz, this standard bibliography of German history to the end of World War II has more recently been edited by Hermann Heimpel and Herbert Geuss at the Max-Planck-Institut. The work is still in progress, with fascicles continuing to appear, but the general organization is as follows: volumes 1–4: general section; volumes 5–7: individual historic periods. Four index volumes, 1985–91, provide access by author, subject, and personal and geographic names. Volume 6 covers the Middle Ages through the Reformation and begins the period 1618–48; volume 7 completes that period and also covers 1648–1792. Besides political and religious history, the bibliography covers the sciences, literature, theater, arts and music, and social science (including women and children).

Schottenloher, Karl. *Bibliographie zur deutschen Geschichte im Zeitalter der Glaubensspaltung, 1517–1585.* 7 vols. Stuttgart: Hiersemann, 1956–66.
This bibliography provides a comprehensive listing of books and articles on the Reformation, both original and secondary modern sources. It is organized by broad subject areas, as follows: volumes 1–2: individuals (A–Z) and towns and provinces; volume 3: nobility and rulers and the German states; volume 4: the Reformation itself; volume 5: addenda and supplements; volume 6: a combined author-title index for sixteenth-century works; volume 7: writings on the Reformation from 1938 to 1960. Again, the researcher must use imagination in looking for women, but they can certainly be found by name. For example, under the German territory "Pfalz" appears Maria, daughter of Kasimirs von Brandenburg-Kulmbach and wife of Friedrich III. Two sixteenth-century works dealing with her are listed, as well as a late-nineteenth-century biography.

Manuscripts

The following select grouping of printed manuscript catalogs provides entree to the major holdings of British and some European manuscript collections in libraries in the United States and abroad. This list does not intend to be exhaustive; it merely points to some of the major sources. It was impossible to include other equally useful sources, such as the various printed catalogs for the libraries at Oxford and Cambridge. When you visit an archive, it is also a good idea to ask what other guides might be available on-site. Most libraries and archives have their own catalogs and finding aids for manuscript collections, many of which are still in-house.

Scholars should also be aware of a new resource in development, offered through the Research Library Group (RLG). Libraries with a subscription will soon be able to search and retrieve archival finding aids for a number of manuscript collections around the world. This means that some of the in-house finding aids mentioned above are now encoded and searchable online. Ask your local college or university library for more information.

Beal, Peter. *Index of English Literary Manuscripts.* Vol. 1: 1450–1625; vol. 2: 1625–1700. London: Mansell, 1980–87.
The *Index* provides access to "the extant manuscripts of literary works by a select number of British and Irish authors who flourished between 1450 and 1700." It includes corrected proof sheets, diaries, notebooks, and marginal notes in printed books (1.1.13). While there are no women authors in the first volume, and only Aphra Behn and Katherine Philips make it into the second, it is possible to find material about women in the family papers of the male authors.

Beinecke Library. Yale University. *Catalogue of Medieval and Renaissance Manuscripts in the Beinecke Rare Book and Manuscript Library, Yale University.* Ed. Barbara A. Shailor. 2 vols. Binghamton: Medieval and Renaissance Texts and Studies, 1984–92.
Each volume has a very detailed general index that includes people, topics ("Proverbs on Women," recipes, prayers), as well as an extraordinarily detailed subindex of illuminations (allegorical and religious figures, special topics such as "Utensils, Household," "Wife and Husband at Home," "Woman with Mirror," etc.). A provenance index provides information on former owners of the manuscripts, some of whom were women.

Bibliothèque Nationale (France). *Catalogue générale des manuscrits français* [. . .]. Ed. Henri Omont et al. 18 vols. Paris: Leroux, 1868–1902.
Though not an easy catalog to use, this work is nevertheless a major resource. The manuscripts are divided into groups ("Anciens fonds," "Ancien supplément français," "Ancien Saint-Germain français," etc.) and in each group are listed by number with a brief survey of contents. The last volume in each of the groups contains an index to names and general subjects in the beginning and, except for "Nouvelles acquisitions françaises," a classification at the end of the manuscripts according to general subject matter. Among the most relevant of these classifications are "Arts divers," "Prosateurs français," Poètes français," "Théâtre," and other subheadings under "Belles-lettres."

Bibliothèque du Roi. *Les manuscrits françois de la Bibliothèque du Roi*. Ed. Paulin Paris. 7 vols. Paris: Techener, 1836–48.
The manuscripts are listed by number with a brief physical description and a longer description of contents for each in the personal style of Paris. Each volume has an index of titles and of places and persons. The material is varied and includes letters, verse, and dramatic pieces. Examples of entries are "Quatre épistres escriptes par quatre damoyselles à quatre gentilshommes de diverses affections," a group of rhyming letters by ladies at the court of Charles IX; a set of verses between Catherine de Médicis and Isabel, queen of Scotland; and a number of rhyming letters between Catherine de Médicis and her daughter, Elizabeth.

British Library. Department of Manuscripts. *Index of Manuscripts in the British Library*. 10 vols. Cambridge, Eng.: Chadwyck-Healey, 1984–86.
These volumes index all the major manuscript collections at the British Library, primarily by personal names, corporate names, or place-names. Some subjects may be listed under names. It's best, however, if you have names to work from, though you can find women by browsing under, for example, "London. Muscovy Co. (letters to Anne, countess of East Friesland)" and "London. Wills."

De Ricci, Seymour, and W. J. Wilson. *Census of Medieval and Renaissance Manuscripts in the United States and Canada*. 3 vols. and supp. New York: Wilson, 1935–40.
This still-important census includes British and European manuscripts. In addition to a general index of names, titles, and headings there are indexes of scribes, illuminators, and cartographers, and of previous owners.

Folger Shakespeare Library. *Catalog of Manuscripts of the Folger Shakespeare Library*. 3 vols. Boston: Hall, 1971.
The catalog reproduces in photo-facsimile the cards from the Folger

manuscript catalog, giving author-title-subject entries. Other than searching under their names, you can find material by early modern women especially under "Commonplace Book," "Cookery," "Costume," and "Inventories." In addition, the Folger, like many other research libraries, has calendars of large manuscript collections. At the Folger, these include the papers of the sixteenth- and seventeenth-century Bacon-Townshend, Bagot, Bennet, and Cavendish-Talbot families. There are a number of letters by women in the Bagot and Bacon papers, and many letters in the Cavendish-Talbot papers are directed to Elizabeth, countess of Shrewesbury.

Historical Manuscripts Commission. *A Guide to the Reports on Collections of Manuscripts of Private Families, Corporations and Institutions in Great Britain and Ireland.* London: HMSO, 1914–38.
Part 1 is a topographical index; part 2, in two volumes, is an index of persons. This early work covers reports issued 1870–1911. It is succeeded by *Guide to the Reports of the Royal Commission on Historical Manuscripts, 1911–1957* (London: HMSO, 1966–73). Again, part 1 is a topographical index; part 2, in three volumes, is an index of persons. The indexes are quite detailed. An entry under "Beale, Eadithe," for example, turns up two references in the papers from Hatfield House; one of these records is a letter from Beale to Sir Robert Cecil, dated 11 July 1601, asking for his favor in her suit to the king "for a fee farm to the value of 30*l.* yearly, for the relief of herself and her fatherless children."

Houghton Library. Harvard University. *Catalogue of Manuscripts in the Houghton Library, Harvard University.* 8 vols. Alexandria: Chadwyck-Healey, 1986–87.
These volumes reproduce the contents of the card catalog, filed under main entries, as of 1985. Individually described collections are listed in *The Houghton Library, Manuscripts and Drawings: A Handlist of Finding Aids with a List of Published Guides* (Cambridge: Office of the Univ. Publisher, 1985).

Huntington Library. *Guide to Medieval and Renaissance Manuscripts in the Huntington Library.* Ed. C. W. Dutschke et al. 2 vols. San Marino: Huntington Lib., 1989.
The second volume has a number of indexes that provide access to owners, scribes, artists, iconography, saints, and so on. Under "Iconography" are listings for owner portraits, some of which include women.

Women's History

The field of women's studies is now well served with a variety of bibliographic tools, and while most of these focus on the nineteenth and twentieth centuries, they do include material about earlier women. Pioneering in this area was the Office of the Women's Studies Librarian-at-Large at the University of Wisconsin, which continues to publish a variety of periodicals such as *Feminist Periodicals* (covering over 100 publications), and *New Books on Women and Feminism* ("a subject-arranged, indexed bibliography of new titles in women's studies listing books and periodicals"). Other standard reference tools are *Women Studies Abstracts, Studies on Women Abstracts,* and *Women and Society: A Critical Review of the Literature.* The *Bibliographic Guide* to the microforms in *The Gerritsen Collection of Women's History, 1543–1945* contains only 55 imprints dated 1543–1700 among some 5,000 titles (4,000 at the University of Kansas, the rest at the University of North Carolina, Greensboro). With the limitations of these kinds of reference tools in mind, however, the scholar of early modern women can find some useful materials. In addition, there are sources, not strictly in women's studies, that do focus on the early modern period. The selection that follows highlights some of the most useful items from both groups.

British Women's History: A Bibliographical Guide. Comp. June Hannam, Ann Hughes, and Pauline Stafford. Manchester: Manchester UP, 1996.

History of Women: A Comprehensive Microfilm Publication. New Haven: Research, 1975–77.
This microfilm collection reproduces monographs, pamphlets, periodicals, manuscripts, and selected photographs from the most important library collections on women's history until 1920. The core collections are those at Smith College and the Schlesinger Library at Radcliffe College, but also included is material from the New York Public Library and from the private collection of Miriam Y. Holden on medieval and western European women. A printed guide with an extremely detailed index accompanies this collection.

A History of Women in the West. Ed. Georges Duby and Michelle Perrot. Cambridge: Belknap–Harvard UP, 1992–94. Vol. 2: *Silences of the Mid-*

dle Ages. Ed. Christiane Klapisch-Zuber. 1992. Vol. 3: *Renaissance and Enlightenment Paradoxes.* Ed. Natalie Zemon Davis and Arlette Farge. 1993.

This women's history project brings together the work of a number of international scholars in different fields who contribute essays in their particular areas of interest. Each volume contains extensive bibliographic information.

Hufton, Olwen. *The Prospect before Her: A History of Women in Western Europe, 1500–1800.* New York: Knopf, 1996.

In addition to the bibliographic footnotes to each chapter, Hufton supplies an extensive bibliographical essay at the end, which lists books and articles under a wide variety of topics and includes other reference works.

King, Margaret L. *Women of the Renaissance.* Chicago: U of Chicago P, 1991.

This good introductory volume has an extensive bibliography.

Wiesner, Merry E. *Women and Gender in Early Modern Europe.* Cambridge: Cambridge UP, 1993.

In this excellent overview of the topic, each chapter deals with different areas of women's cultural, economic, and religious lives and contains a useful discursive bibliography that surveys the major work in that area.

Women in Western European History: A Select Chronological, Geographical, and Topical Bibliography. 2 vols. Comp. and ed. Linda Frey, Marsha Frey, and Joanne Schneider. Westport: Greenwood, 1982; 1st suppl., 1986.

The first volume covers the period from antiquity to the French Revolution and references monographs and articles available in at least ten American libraries; no rare editions, obscure periodicals, primary or literary sources are included.The bibliography moves from the general to the specific with a very detailed historical outline and topical guide as a table of contents. Major figures such as Bess of Hardwick, Elizabeth I, Marguerite de Valois, and Catherine de Médicis are singled out with their own sections. The supplement updates the first volumes.

Women's History Sources: A Guide to Archives and Manuscript Collections in the United States. 2 vols. Ed. Andrea Hinding et al. New York: Bowker, 1979.

This enormous work is based on an exhaustive survey of collections of family and personal papers, photographs, papers of organizations related to women, correspondence, diaries, and so on in American archives. While much of it is material from the nineteenth and twentieth centuries, there are valuable pockets of earlier items. The lack of a chronological

index makes it difficult to identify quickly collections that might be relevant, but a little imaginative use of the personal name index and the
geographic organization of the book can yield rewarding results. For
example, looking at state archives in the earliest colonies such as Pennsylvania, New York, Massachusetts, and Rhode Island may reveal
seventeenth-century material. The Historical Society of Pennsylvania contains papers of the Logan family dating back to the mid-
seventeenth century, papers from an English Quaker minister, Elizabeth
Kendall (1685–1765), and papers of Frances Logan that include correspondence of Elizabeth Webb of Rhode Island (1698–1712).

Specialized Works

Aresty, Esther B. *The Delectable Past: The Joys of the Table from Rome to the
Renaissance* [. . .]. New York: Simon, 1964.
Aresty herself was a collector of cookbooks. Chapters discuss cooking in
different eras, including Elizabethan England and seventeenth- and
eighteenth-century England and France. There is a bibliography of early
cookbooks.

Ballard, George. *Memoirs of Several Ladies of Great Britain: Who Have Been
Celebrated for Their Writings or Skill in the Learned Languages, Arts,
and Sciences.* Ed. with introd. Ruth Perry. Detroit: Wayne State UP,
1985.
Originally published in 1752, this book contains an index and a 42-page
bibliography.

Berriot-Salvadore, Evelyne. *Les femmes dans la société française de la Renaissance.* Genève: Librairie Droz, 1990.
This history contains a useful list of works published by French women
from 1497 to 1626, plus another large bibliography of primary manuscript and printed sources, and of secondary sources.

Erdmann, Axel. *My Gracious Silence: Women in the Mirror of Sixteenth-
Century Printing in Western Europe.* Luzern: Gilhofer, 1999.
Part 1 is a catalog of books on and for women, arranged by subject; of
books by women writers; and of books printed by women. Part 2 contains several bibliographies: books printed on and for women; women
writers given alphabetically and by country, with the first editions of their
works; books with music by women; books with illustrations by women;
women in the book business; and secondary literature with a subject
index. There is also a general index of authors, printers, and subjects.

Gibson, Wendy. *Women in Seventeenth-Century France.* New York: St. Martin's, 1989.
Gibson provides an overview of women's family, work, political, and religious life in the period. There is a very useful and extensive bibliography of primary sources, arranged by topics such as travel literature, memoirs, biographies, medicine, and novels.

Hansen, Marlene R. *The Fair Sex: Writing by and about Women in the British Isles, 1600–1800: A Bibliographical Study of Material in the Royal Library, Copenhagen, with a Biographical Index.* Copenhagen: Dept. of English, U of Copenhagen, 1988.

Kelso, Ruth. *Doctrine for the Lady of the Renaissance.* Urbana: U of Illinois P, 1956.
This classic study reviews the British and Continental conduct literature for women and contains a lengthy bibliography of early conduct books.

Knaster, Meri. *Women in Spanish America: An Annotated Bibliography from Pre-Conquest to Contemporary Times.* Boston: Hall, 1977.
The bibliography is divided into many subjects, including the arts; literature; magic, religion, and ritual; biography and autobiography; and history. History itself is subdivided into four areas, including preconquest (before the sixteenth century) and conquest and colony (sixteenth through eighteenth centuries). There are also lists of unpublished theses and author and subject indexes.

Mendelson, Sara, and Patricia Crawford. *Women in Early Modern England, 1550–1720.* Oxford: Clarendon, 1998.
The excellent bibliography includes early printed books as well as a large list of manuscript collections with material about women.

Perry, Mary Elizabeth. *Gender and Disorder in Early Modern Seville.* Princeton: Princeton UP, 1990.
The useful bibliography includes "Archival Manuscripts" and "Writings of the Period and Published Primary Sources."

Timmermans, Linda. *L'accès des femmes à la culture (1598–1715): Un débat d'idées de Saint François de Sales à la Marquise de Lambert.* Paris: Champion, 1993.
This thorough discussion includes chapters on women writers, women and religion, mysticism, and the *querelle des femmes.* There is a very extensive bibliography of primary and secondary literature.

Utley, Francis Lee. *The Crooked Rib: An Analytical Index to the Argument about Women in English and Scots Literature to the End of the Year 1568.* Columbus: Ohio State UP, 1944.
The first and major part of the book is an analytic index based on first lines of poems and prose works. Part 2 is an index by title; part 3 lists the locations of manuscripts and the *STC* numbers for printed books. There is also a general index of names at the end.

Wiesner, Merry E. *Gender, Church, and State in Early Modern Germany: Essays.* London: Longman, 1998.
This book has an extensive bibliography.

Witchcraft: Catalogue of the Witchcraft Collection in the Cornell University Library. Ed. Martha J. Crowe. Introd. Rossell Hope Robbins. Index by Jane Marsh Dieckmann. Millwood: KTO, 1977.

Woods, Jean M., and Maria Fürstenwald. *Schriftstellerinnen, Künstlerinnen und gelehrte Frauen des deutschen Barock: Ein Lexikon.* Stuttgart: Metzler, 1984.
The book covers literary, artistic, and learned women from seventeenth- and early-eighteenth-century Germany.

Wunder, Heide. *He Is the Sun, She Is the Moon: Women in Early Modern Germany.* Trans. Thomas Dunlap. Cambridge: Harvard UP, 1998.
Wunder's book contains a number of contemporary pictures of early modern women and an extensive bibliography.

Women and Art

Borzello, Frances. *Seeing Ourselves: Women's Self-Portraits.* New York: Abrams, 1998.
The first chapters provide information on women artists from the early modern period.

Chadwick, Whitney. *Women, Art, and Society.* 2nd ed. London: Thames, 1997.
This book includes an excellent bibliography on women artists in general and on particular artists.

Dixon, Laurinda S. *Perilous Chastity: Women and Illness in Pre-Enlightenment Art and Medicine.* Ithaca: Cornell UP, 1995.
In addition to a bibliography of primary and secondary sources, this

book includes a listing of medical dissertations on female hysteria, 1575–1740.

Ellet, Elizabeth Fries Lummis. *Women Artists in All Ages and Countries.* New York: Harper, 1859.
Ellet, an American writer interested in documenting the role of women in history, also understood how art can be found in what are considered female employments, such as spinning and weaving.

Franits, Wayne E. *Paragons of Virtue: Women and Domesticity in Seventeenth-Century Dutch Art.* Cambridge: Cambridge UP, 1993.
This book contains extensive bibliographies of primary and secondary source materials.

Harris, Ann Sutherland, and Linda Nochlin. *Women Artists, 1550–1950.* Los Angeles County Museum of Art. New York: Knopf, 1976.

Matthews Greico, Sara F. M. *Ange ou diablesse: La représentation de la femme au XVIᵉ siècle.* Paris: Flammarion, 1991.
This study explores the depiction of women in thousands of emblems and engravings of the period.

Petersen, Karen, and J. J. Wilson. *Women Artists: Recognition and Reappraisal, from the Early Middle Ages to the Twentieth Century.* New York: Harper, 1976.

Petteys, Chris, et al. *Dictionary of Women Artists: An International Dictionary of Women Artists Born before 1900.* Boston: Hall, 1985.

Piland, Sherry. *Women Artists: An Historical, Contemporary, and Feminist Bibliography.* 2nd ed. Metuchen: Scarecrow, 1994.

Slatkin, Wendy. *Women Artists in History: From Antiquity to the Present.* 3rd ed. Upper Saddle River: Prentice, 1997.

Tinagli, Paola. *Women in Italian Renaissance Art: Gender, Representation and Identity.* Manchester: Manchester UP, 1997.
This book includes bibliographical references.

Tufts, Eleanor. *Our Hidden Heritage: Five Centuries of Women Artists.* New York: Paddington, 1974.

Women and Literature

Arbour, Roméo. *L'ère baroque en France: Répertoire chronologique des éditions de textes littéraires.* Genève: Librairie Droz, 1977–85. Vol. 1: 1585–1615; vol. 2: 1616–28; vol. 3: 1629–43; vol. 4: supp.
The books are listed by year of publication. The supplement volume contains indexes of personal names and of titles of anonymous works.

Beilin, Elaine V. *Redeeming Eve: Women Writers of the English Renaissance.* Princeton: Princeton UP, 1987.
This important early study contains bibliographic notes and a list of works by women, 1521–1624.

Bibliography of Women and Literature. Ed. Florence Boos et al. 2 vols. New York: Holmes, 1989.
This work is primarily a bibliography of secondary literature. Volume 1 covers articles and books printed in 1974–78; volume 2 in 1979–81, including dissertations.

The Cambridge Guide to Women's Writing in English. Ed. Lorna Sage et al. Cambridge: Cambridge UP, 1999.
This volume is mainly useful for quick reference. Though it has entries for works as well as authors, there are no bibliographies and no chronological listing of authors.

Cioranescu, Alexandre. *Bibliographie de la littérature française du dix-septième siècle.* 3 vols. Paris: Centre National de la Recherche Scientifique, 1965–67.
This standard reference work for French authors of the seventeenth century gives place of origin, dates, and lists of works by and about each author. The large general bibliography in volume 1 contains sections on religious history, intellectual milieu, literary genres, literary exchange with other countries, the theater, and various literary themes. There are author and subject indexes in the third volume. See also *Bibliographie de la littérature française du seizième siècle*, ed. Cioranescu and V.-L. Saulnier, Paris: Klincksieck, 1959.

Davis, Gwenn, and Beverly A. Joyce. *Drama by Women to 1900: A Bibliography of American and British Writers.* Toronto: U of Toronto P, 1992.

Davis, Gwenn, and Beverly Joyce. *Poetry by Women to 1900: A Bibliography of American and British Writers.* Toronto: U of Toronto P, 1991.

De La Porte, Joseph, and Jean François de la Croix. *Histoire littéraire de femmes françoises* [. . .] . *Contenant un précis de la vie, & une analyse* [. . .] *des ouvrages des femmes qui se sont distinguées dans la littérature française.* 5 vols. Paris: Lacombe, 1769.

In their preface to this history, the compilers write that "the list of those [women] who have successfully occupied themselves with agreeable arts and serious studies will astonish our Readers." The first volume begins with Héloïse and includes pieces on a number of sixteenth- and seventeenth-century writers to Mme de Maintenon. A brief account of each and a bibliography is provided. This work is available on microfiche in the Gerritsen Collection, no. E1625.

The Feminist Encyclopedia of French Literature. Ed. Eva Martin Sartori et al. Westport: Greenwood, 1999.

Authors as well as subjects, such as abortion, convents, and didactic literature are covered in this useful encyclopedia. A chronological listing of French women writers by century shows a hundred names from the Middle Ages through the seventeenth century. Each author entry comprises a brief biography followed by a bibliography of primary and secondary texts.

The Feminist Encyclopedia of Italian Literature. Ed. Rinaldina Russell. Westport: Greenwood, 1997.

This encyclopedia has entries on subjects as well as authors, and a useful appendix organizing the entries by period and subject. Under "Renaissance and Early Modern," for example, Petrarchism, the courtesan, and women's publishing are discussed.

Hull, Suzanne W. *Chaste, Silent, and Obedient: English Books for Women, 1475–1640.* San Marino: Huntington Lib., 1982.

Now a classic of its kind, Hull's book provides a bibliography of English books for women printed in the *STC* period.

Italian Women Writers: A Bio-bibliographical Sourcebook. Ed. Rinaldina Russell. Westport: Greenwood, 1994.

Each writer is discussed in an essay that comprises a biography, major themes, a survey of criticism, and a bibliography. Twenty-three early modern writers are included.

Quentin-Bauchart, Ernest. *Les femmes bibliophiles de France (XVIᵉ, XVIIᵉ & XVIIIᵉ siècles)*. 2 vols. Paris: Damascène Morgand, 1886. Geneva: Slatkine, 1993.
This very useful illustrated study provides lists of books and manuscripts belonging to various famous women.

Scott, Mary Augusta. *Elizabethan Translations from the Italian*. Boston: Houghton, 1916.
This useful work begins with a listing of titles divided according to literary type (prose romances, poetry, plays, etc.), with their translators. Bibliographic description and commentary for each work then follow, with a detailed name-title index. There is much useful information concerning women and books about women, translated by women, or dedicated to women. We learn, for example, that the 1608 edition of *The Historie of Aurelio and of Isabell*, printed in Brussels, is dedicated to Margaret Volschaten, whose woodcut portrait appears on the verso of the title page, and that Anna Hume, daughter of the scholar David Hume, translated Petrarch's *Triumphs* and published them in Edinburgh in 1644 in an edition dedicated to "the Princesse Elisabeth, Eldest daughter to the King of Bohemia."

Smith, Hilda L., and Susan Cardinale. *Women and the Literature of the Seventeenth Century: An Annotated Bibliography Based on Wing's* Short-Title Catalogue. New York: Greenwood, 1990.
Another classic, this volume complements the one by Hull (above). It is divided into parts dealing with works by women and works for and about women (1641–1700). In addition there are lists of women printers, publishers, and booksellers and chronological and general indexes. The general index has subjects such as humor, marriage, childbirth, and prostitutes, as well as proper names.

Vaganay, Hugues. *Le sonnet en Italie et en France au XVIᵉ siècle*. Lyon: au Siège des Facultés Catholiques, 1902–03.
This very useful bibliography, arranged by year of publication, provides access to hundreds of editions of sonnets published during the sixteenth century. The index of names records authors whose works appear in collections as well as primary authors. Thus we find a Venice 1554 edition of *Rime* by the well-known Gaspara Stampa, but also one poem by the obscure Anne Begat in a general anthology published at Lyon in 1594, and eight or so women contributing to a large collection in memory of Irene delle Signore di Spilimbergo in 1561.

Walker, Kim. *Women Writers of the English Renaissance*. New York: Twayne, 1996.
This book provides a good introduction to a number of women writers, plus a useful bibliography.

Women in the Renaissance: Selections from English Literary Renaissance. Ed. Kirby Farrell et al. Amherst: U of Massachusetts P, 1990.
This volume contains the important bibliographies "Recent Studies in Women Writers of Tudor England" by Elizabeth H. Hageman, "Recent Studies in Mary Sidney" by Josephine A. Roberts, and "Recent Studies in Women Writers of the English Seventeenth Century, 1604–1674" by Hageman. For updates, see "Recent Studies in Women Writers of Tudor England, 1485–1603 (1990 to mid-1993)" by Georgianna Ziegler and "Recent Studies in Women Writers of the Seventeenth Century, 1604–1674 (1990 to mid-1993)" by Sara Jayne Steen in *English Literary Renaissance* 24 (1994): 229–74. Further updates are scheduled for future issues of *English Literary Renaissance*.

Women and Music

Adkins Chiti, Patricia. *Donne in musica*. Rome: Armando, 1996.
This book includes a bibliography and illustrations.

Beredes, Jane L. *Women Musicians of Venice: Musical Foundations, 1525–1855*. Rev. ed. Oxford: Clarendon, 1996.

Hixon, Donald L., and Don A. Hennessee. *Women in Music: An Encyclopedic Biobibliography*. 2nd ed. 2 vols. Metuchen: Scarecrow, 1993.

Women and Music: A History. Ed. Karin Pendle. Bloomington: Indiana UP, 1991.
This book has bibliographic references and a discography.

Biography

Those of us who work in the early modern period know how difficult it often is to find biographical information on women. They are frequently hidden under their husband's names in the standard articles of the *Dictionary of National Biography*, and if the woman was married more than once, it may take some searching to discover under which family name she is listed. The works selected below should help take some of the mystery out of the search.

British Biographical Index. Ed. David Bank and Anthony Esposito. 4 vols. London: Saur, 1990.

Index biographique français. Ed. Helen Dwyer and Barry Dwyer. 4 vols. London: Saur, 1993.

One of the most comprehensive series of biographical indexes has been published by the Saur company to accompany a massive microfiche set composed of hundreds of biographical reference works. The British index lists over 170,000 persons referenced in biographical sources published between 1601 and 1929, while the French index lists about 140,000 persons referenced in 180 biographical sources published between 1647 and 1986. There are similar volumes for Italian, German, and Spanish-Portuguese biographies. Though most libraries will not be able to afford the microfiche set, the accompanying index volumes may be used alone quite usefully. Under each name is listed the biographical sources in which that person appears, and those may be found more widely in research libraries. Variant names, cross-references, dates, and other identifying information are also provided. Typical entries are "Marguerite, d'Autriche, duchesse de Savoie (1480–1530), gouvernante des Pays-Bas, femme de lettres—*Coste*; *Depery*; *Feller*; *Hoefer*; *Dezobry*; *Dufay*" and "Marguerite, de Bohême (dite Maultasche, Gueule de Sac ou la Grande Bouche) (v. 1316–1369)—*Gal. Versailles.*"

Besides the venerable *Dictionary of National Biography* for Great Britain, other standard national biographical dictionaries are *Allgemeine Deutsche Biographie*, 56 vols., 1875–1912; rpt. 1967–71; *Deutsches Literatur-Lexikon*, 1968– , 18 vols; Michaud's *Biographie universelle ancienne et moderne* [. . .] *nouvelle édition*, 1854–65, 45 vols.; Hoefer's *Nouvelle biographie générale* [. . .], 1853–66, 46 vols.; *Dizionario biografico degli italiani*, 1960– , 51 vols.

Specialized Biographical Resources

Aldis, H. G., et al. *A Dictionary of Printers and Booksellers in England, Scotland and Ireland, and of Foreign Printers of English Books, 1557–1640.* London: Bibliographical Soc., 1968.

Other volumes cover 1641–67, 1668–1725, and 1726–75. The volume for the earliest period, *A Century of the English Book Trade* by Gordon Duff, covers 1457–1557. A number of women were booksellers or owners of printing establishments in early modern England. They are listed here under their husband's name (as Joyce, the wife of Matthew Lawe, who inherited all his property after his death) or under their own name (as Joan Broome, who in 1591 entered three plays by John Lyly in the *Stationers' Register*).

Bainton, Roland H. *Women of the Reformation in France and England.* Minneapolis: Augsburg, 1973.

———. *Women of the Reformation in Germany and Italy.* Minneapolis: Augsburg, 1971.

Along with Pearl Hogrefe (see below), Bainton was a pioneer in discovering and publishing information about women's lives in early modern Europe.

Bandini Buti, Maria Ferrari. *Poetesse e scrittrici.* 2 vols. Roma: Tosi, 1941–42.

These volumes form series 6 of the *Enciclopedia biografica e bibliografica italiana.* They provide short biographies of women writers with (usually brief) bibliographic references and a number of illustrations.

Beach, Cecilia. *French Women Playwrights before the Twentieth Century: A Checklist.* Westport: Greenwood, 1994.

A Biographical Dictionary of English Women Writers, 1580–1720. Ed. Maureen Bell et al. Boston: Hall, 1990.

This very useful biobibliographic dictionary supplies references to modern editions of works, where available, including items that are anthologized.

British Women Writers: A Critical Reference Guide. Ed. Janet Todd. New York: Unger, 1989.

This excellent book begins with an alphabetic list of writers and their dates, allowing the reader to find early authors. The substantial entries by specialists provide information about an author's life and writings as well as brief listings of selected works and references.

Contemporaries of Erasmus: A Biographical Register of the Renaissance and Reformation. 3 vols. Ed. Peter G. Bietenholz and Thomas B. Deutscher. Toronto: U of Toronto P, 1985–87.

Here may be found short biographies of women in the Reformation, including Margaret More (Roper), other women of More's family, Catherine of Aragon, Margaret Beaufort, and Mary Tudor.

A Dictionary of British and American Women Writers, 1660–1800. Ed. Janet Todd. Totowa: Rowman, 1985.

Entries cover the lives and work of over five hundred women writers— "aristocratic, middle, and working class"—from this period but do not include bibliographies.

Dictionary of British Portraiture. Ed. Richard Ormond and Malcolm Rogers. 4 vols. New York: Oxford UP, 1979–81.

Volume 1, compiled by Adriana Davies, covers "the Middle Ages to the early Georgians: historical figures born before 1700." This valuable reference tool "provides a listing of the portraits (with birth–death dates and descriptive epithet) of some 5,000 famous figures in British history that are in the galleries, institutions or collections accessible to the public."

Emerson, Kathy Lynn. *Wives and Daughters: The Women of Sixteenth Century England*. Troy: Whitston, 1984.
In spite of some historical inaccuracies in the entries, this early book provides much useful information, including a cross-listing of women's family names, making it easier to look them up in other sources.

An Encyclopedia of British Women Writers. Ed. June Schlueter and Paul Schlueter. Revised and expanded ed. New Brunswick: Rutgers UP, 1998.
This book contains lengthy biographical articles written by specialists. Each entry ends with a list of the writer's works and a short bibliography of secondary material.

Eroine, Ispiratrici e Donne di Eccezione [. . .]. Ed. Francesco Orestano. Milano: Istituto Editorale Italiano B.C. Tosi, 1940.
A companion volume to the one by Maria Bandini Buti listed above, it is series 7 of the *Enciclopedia biografica e bibliografica italiana*. The biographies here are of heroines and other exceptional women from Italian history and legend. Again, there are short bibliographies for each entry and a number of illustrations.

The Feminist Companion to Literature in English: Women Writers from the Middle Ages to the Present. Ed. Virginia Blain et al. New Haven: Yale UP, 1990.
This book, one of the best general one-volume surveys of the subject, contains a useful chronological index of names at the end, so that one can look up writers born or active during the periods 1401–1500, 1501–1600, 1601–50, and 1651–1700.

Ferri, Pietro Leopoldo. *Biblioteca femminile italiana* [. . .]. Padova: Crescini, 1842.
Ferri's bibliography is arranged by author name and includes many early imprints and anthologized pieces. A typical entry is one listing Giulia de Braccali-Ricciardi as having sonnets in *Rime diverse*, edited by Lodovico Domenichi (Lucca, 1559) and *rime* in *Rime di cinquanta illustri poetesse* [. . .] (Napoli, 1695). The one drawback is Ferri's failure to include birth and death dates for the authors, so that we can be sure only from imprint dates which authors are early. Individual authors, however, can be searched in Maria Bandini Buti's *Poetesse e scrittrici* (see above).

French Women Writers: A Bio-bibliographical Source Book. Ed. Eva Martin Sartori and Dorothy Wynne Zimmerman. New York: Greenwood, 1991. Fourteen of the fifty-two entries cover women writers from the *trobairitz* through the seventeenth century. The scholarly essay on each writer includes a biography, major themes in her work, and a survey of criticism, followed by a bibliography of books by and about her.

Hogrefe, Pearl. *Tudor Women: Commoners and Queens.* Ames: Iowa State UP, 1975.
———. *Women of Action in Tudor England.* Ames: Iowa State UP, 1977. Hogrefe was one of the first scholars in our time to do serious work on early modern women, and her books still contain much valuable information and good bibliographies.

Juncker, Christian. *Schediasma Historicum de Ephemeridibus sive Diariis Eruditorum, in Nobilioribus Europae Partibus Hactenus Publicatis.* Liepzig: Gleditsch, 1692.
The book contains an appendix, "Exhibetur Centuria Foeminarum Eruditione et Scriptis Illustrium [. . .]," with brief biographical information and bibliographic references to where writers are mentioned and to their works. It includes a number of more obscure writers, going back into the Middle Ages. The work is available in the microfilm series History of Women, reel 47, no. 305.

La Croix du Maine, François Grudé, and Antoine Du Verdier. *Les bibliothèques françoises de La Croix du Maine et de Du Verdier* [. . .]. 6 vols. Rev. ed. Paris: Sailliant, 1772–73.
La Croix du Maine and Du Verdier were sixteenth-century French bibliographers who compiled lists of all the authors they knew about who had written in or been translated into French. Their remarkable works were reedited with some errors in the eighteenth century in an edition that is more easily accessible. They record an astonishing number of women writers, not all of whom were published in print but whose skills were known at the time.

Major Tudor Authors: A Bio-bibliographical Sourcebook. Ed. Alan Hager. Westport: Greenwood, 1997.
This book covers British and some major Continental (male) authors of the period. Women writers included are Anne Askew; Elizabeth Cary; Elizabeth I; Aemilia Lanyer; Mary, Queen of Scots; Katherine Parr; Mary Sidney; and Lady Mary Wroth. Each entry comprises a biography, consideration of major works, themes and critical reception, and a brief bibliography of primary and secondary sources.

Mann, David D., and Susan Garland Mann. *Women Playwrights in England, Ireland, and Scotland, 1660–1823.* Bloomington: Indiana UP, 1996.
The book is really a little encyclopedia, not only of the playwrights but also of the plays, providing useful plot summaries for a number of plays that are not always easy to find. Useful appendices list the writers and their works and provide a year-by-year list of all their plays from 1662 to 1854.

Rinascimento al femminile. Ed. Ottavia Niccoli. Roma: Laterza, 1991.
Contains substantial scholarly essays with bibliographies on seven Italian Renaissance women from different walks of life: Isotta Nogarola, humanist; Paola Antonia Negri, nun; Beatrice De Luna Mendes, Jewess; Ginevra Gozzadini dall'Armi, gentlewoman; Gostanza da Libbiano, healer and witch; Camilla la Magra, prostitute; and Angela Vallerani, widow.

Shattock, Joanne. *The Oxford Guide to British Women Writers.* New York: Oxford UP, 1993.
Entries cover more than four hundred writers from the medieval period to the present. Each brief but densely packed entry provides information on the writer's life and works, with some attempt to contextualize her among her contemporaries. Since the entries are alphabetical, a chronological cross-listing would have been useful.

Todd, Janet. *The Sign of Angellica: Women, Writing, and Fiction, 1660–1800.* New York: Columbia UP, 1989.
Todd provides a useful survey of early fiction from Mary Astell to Fanny Burney, along with extensive bibliographies of primary and secondary works.

Ungherini, Aglauro. *Manuel de bibliographie biographique et d'iconographie des femmes célèbres.* Turin: Roux; Paris: Nilsson, 1892. Supp. 1900, 2nd supp., 1905.
This older but valuable biobibliography gives reference sources (including primary material) under the names of women, followed by a bibliography of books on women by country and a bibliography by portrait sources. It includes a number of interesting early resources, for example H. de Coste, *Eloges et vies des roynes, princesses, dames et damoiselles illustré en piété, courage et doctrine*, Paris, 1630 and M. U. Briquet-Bernier, *Dictionnaire historique, littéraire et bibliographique des françaises et des étrangères naturalisées en France*, Paris, 1804. There is a cumulative index to the whole work.

Women Writers of Germany, Austria, and Switzerland: An Annotated Bio-bibliographical Guide. Ed. Elke Frederiksen. New York: Greenwood, 1989.

Women Writers of Spain: An Annotated Bio-bibliographical Guide. Ed. Carolyn L. Galerstein and Kathleen McNerney. New York: Greenwood, 1986. Both these books have an appendix that lists the authors by birth date, thus providing names that can be looked up in the general alphabetic listing. Each author entry includes biographical information and a list of works with publication information.

Online Resources

Computerized indexes and the Internet are quickly becoming important resources for the study of early modern women. Some of the sites are offered by subscription only, but a number are publicly accessible. The following list is highly selective but should provide an introduction to the kinds of resources available.

BCMSV (Brotherton Collection of Manuscript Verse) "is a database of information about the individual items of English poetry contained in the seventeenth- and eighteenth-century manuscripts in the Brotherton Collection of Leeds University Library." Much of the information is culled from miscellanies and commonplace books that have never before been indexed. There are currently about 5,150 records from 300 different manuscripts in the database, which is searchable over 17 fields, including author, title, date, and content. A search just on *woman* produced 753 records, the term appearing in a variety of contexts. Address: www.leeds.ac.uk/library/spcoll/bcmsv/intro.html.

The *Brown University Women Writers Project* (WWP) has created an online, searchable text base of writings in English by women, 1400–1850. Known as *Women Writers Online*, the text base is available to institutions or individuals only by a modestly priced subscription. A subset of this text base, *Renaissance Women Online*, still in development, will provide a hundred texts with scholarly introductions and contextual essays. In addition, printed paper copies of many of these texts are available and may be ordered from the Web site. The site also provides a complete bibliography of all texts, including those still being edited. The related WWP-L discussion group of about three hundred scholars fields questions about teaching and researching women writers, offers information on conferences, calls for papers, discusses new books and articles, and updates WWP's latest projects. Instructions for joining may be found on the Web site (www.wwp.brown.edu/wwp_home.html).

A Celebration of Women Writers is a cross-cultural site with some nice features maintained by Mary Mark Ockerbloom. It provides multiple references to the same author under variant names and allows browsing by century. The site "provides a comprehensive listing of links to biographical and bibliographical information about women writers, and complete published books written by women." Online editions of older, out-of-copyright materials are also being added. Address: digital.library .upenn.edu/women/.

Digital Librarian: A Librarian's Choice of the Best of the Web, maintained by Margaret Vail Anderson of Courtland, New York, is a rich source for women's resources on the Web. Included in her site are connections to other sites that provide materials for the study of early modern women. These include *Celebration of Women Writers* (see above); *Diotima: Materials for the Study of Women and Gender in the Ancient World*, maintained by Ross Scaife and Suzanne Bonefas at the University of Kentucky; and the *International Alliance for Women in Music*, from Abilene Christian University in Texas, maintained by Sally Reid, with an annotated list of women composers born before 1750 and an annotated discography of early women composers. Address: www.servtech.com/public/mvail/women.html.

EMW is the Web site maintained by Sheila ffolliott at George Mason University, for the Society for the Study of Early Modern Women, an interdisciplinary group that sponsors sessions on women writers, artists, and patrons at a number of conferences, offers annual rewards for the best articles and books in the field, and supports an electronic discussion group. The Web site also lists upcoming events and fellowship opportunities. Address: http://chnm.gmu.edu/emw/.

The *English Short Title Catalogue (ESTC)* of books printed in Britain and on the Continent in English between 1473 and 1800 now has over 400,000 bibliographic records and is growing daily. It is a file accessed by subscription through the Research Libraries Group and can be searched over a variety of fields. Not only are women authors represented but also women printers, booksellers, and books about women. Author, title, subject, note word, imprint date, and language are only a few of the fields that can be used to narrow a search. (Subject searching is limited to that part of the database covering pre-eighteenth-century materials.) Smith and Cardinale in *Women and the Literature of the Seventeenth Century* (see above, under "Women and Literature") provide a list of women printers, publishers, and booksellers whose wares can be searched under their names on this database. Most of the items in the database are available on microfilm in the *STC I*, *STC II*, and Eighteenth-Century series from University Microfilms.

The Institute of Historical Research in London has a Web site that provides access to many online resources for the study of history, both British and European. Included are links to archives, national sources for illustrations, an introduction to manuscript sources for British history, European library catalogs, the Netherlands Historical Data Archive, and much more. Address: www.ihr.sas.ac.uk.

ITER. This large, important bibliography of Renaissance studies, sponsored by the Renaissance Society of America, the Centre for Reformation and Renaissance Studies, the University of Toronto, and the Arizona Center for Medieval and Renaissance Studies, covers about 250,000 articles and reviews from more than 400 medieval and Renaissance journals. It adds over 60,000 records annually. Individual or institutional subscriptions are available from the Renaissance Society of America. Address: http://iter.library.utoronto.ca/iter/index.htm.

Literary Resources on the Net, maintained by Jack Lynch at Rutgers University, has established itself as one of the top sites providing access to a rich variety of Web literary resources covering periods from antiquity to the modern. While focusing on English literature, the site also provides links to literary materials in other languages, notices of conferences, calls for papers, and a list of literary discussion groups and how to subscribe. There are also the sections "Women's Literature and Feminism" and "Bibliography and History of the Book." Address: newark.rutgers.edu/~jlynch/Lit/.

Medieval Feminist Index, a useful Web site maintained by Margaret Schaus, a librarian at Haverford College, provides an online bibliography to "journal articles, book reviews, and essays in books about women, sexuality, and gender during the Middle Ages" (450–1500) in Europe, North Africa, and the Middle East. It monitors more than three hundred journals and many essay collections. Address: www.haverford.edu/library/reference/mschaus/mfi/mfi.html.

The Orlando Project is a Canadian initiative that complements the Brown University Women Writers Project. It is developing a comprehensive scholarly history of British women's writing that will appear in five printed volumes, divided chronologically. Volume 1 will cover writers to 1830. In addition, a searchable electronic text base will include all the material in the printed volumes. Address: www.ualberta.ca/ORLANDO/.

Voice of the Shuttle: Web Page for Humanities Research is a megasite maintained by Alan Liu at the University of California, Santa Barbara. It organizes many other sites under a host of subjects that include art history; history; literature (English and other); music; and women, gender, and queer studies. Because there are so many sites under this umbrella, the individual addresses are sometimes out-of-date, but that is to be expected in the volatile world of the Web. Address: vos.ucsb.edu/index.html.

Editions of Works by and about Early Modern Women

Great strides have been made in recent years to provide accessible modern editions of texts by and about early modern women in printed and machine-readable form. Most notable for its efforts is

the Women Writers Project at Brown University, directed by Allen
Renear, with the text base editor Julia Flanders and Elizabeth H.
Hageman, chair of the Advisory Board. See the entry on the WWP
above, under "Online Resources."

Another project creating machine-readable texts by early modern women is
MARGOT, organized by Hannah Fournier, Delbert Russell, and Peter
Marteinson at the University of Waterloo. The project has produced a
database of works by early Frenchwomen and a selection of their Latin
sources. Available texts include *Les advis [. . .]* (1641) and *L'ombre [. . .]*
(1626) of Marie de Gournay; *Les jumeaux martyrs* of Mme de Saint-
Balmon; *Les sonets spirituels* of Anne de Marquets; and Latin works by
Cicero, Horace, Vergil, Ovid, Terence, Sallust, Suetonius, and Quintilian.
Other authors whose texts are in the works are Marie de Pech de Calages,
Mlle Cosnard, Mme de Pringy, Mme de Sennecterre, Marie de Coste-
blanche, and Mme de Gomez. Address: arts.uwaterloo.ca/FREN/
margot/.

Emory Women Writers Resource Project, directed by Sheila Cavanagh,
mounts edited and nonedited texts by women writing in English from
the seventeenth through the nineteenth century. There is good coverage
of seventeenth-century works by such writers as Aphra Behn, Judith
Boulbie, Margaret Cavendish, Elizabeth I, Mary Evelyn, Margaret Fell
Fox, Sarah Jinner, Anna Trapnell, Mary Waite, and Hannah Wolley. Address: chaucer.library.emory.edu/wwrp/.

Perdita, organized by Elizabeth Clarke, Martyn Bennett, and Victoria
Burke at Nottingham Trent University is a project producing a database
guide to about 400 manuscript miscellanies and commonplace books by
British women from the sixteenth and seventeenth centuries. The guide
will offer bibliographic information and detailed descriptions of contents. Address: human.ntu.ac.uk/perdita/.

The Early Modern Englishwoman: A Facsimile Library of Essential Works is
an important new series edited by Betty Travitsky and Patrick Cullen and
published by Ashgate Press. So far, ten volumes have been published,
providing high-quality photographic facsimiles made from the best available early copies of the texts.

The University of Chicago Press is publishing a series titled The Other
Voice in Early Modern Europe. The press provides editions and translations of (mainly) early modern Italian works by and about women. Titles
in print so far are Laura Cereta, *Collected Letters of a Renaissance Feminist*; Tullia d'Aragona, *Dialogue on the Infinity of Love*; Cecilia Ferrazzi,
Autobiography of an Aspiring Saint; Moderata Fonte, *The Worth of
Women*; Veronica Franco, *Poems and Selected Letters*; Antonia Pulci, *Flo-
rentine Drama for Convent and Festival: Seven Sacred Plays*; Anna Maria

van Schurman, *Whether a Christian Woman Should Be Educated*; and Henricus Cornelius Agrippa, *Declamation on the Nobility and Preeminence of the Female Sex.*

Defiant Muse is the title of a series of bilingual anthologies of poetry by women from the Middle Ages to the present, published by the Feminist Press of the City University of New York (1986–98). It includes volumes of French, German, Hispanic, Italian, and Dutch and Flemish poems.

A general online site that includes full-text material by women is *ARTFL Project.* Maintained at the University of Chicago, it is a full database offering thousands of French and Italian works of literature to educational institutions for a modest subscription fee. Texts range from the twelfth to the twentieth century, with special groups of Provençal and Old French items. The Italian part of the database has over 1,300 vernacular texts from before 1375. Address: humanities.uchicago.edu/ARTFL.html.

Athena is a Swiss site providing links to hundreds of texts online in a variety of subjects and languages. Address: hypo.ge-dip.etat-ge.ch/athena/html/athome.html.

The following brief listing of books that provide often hard-to-find texts by early modern women is limited to anthologies containing works by more than one woman.

Convents Confront the Reformation: Catholic and Protestant Nuns in Germany. Ed. Merry Wiesner-Hanks. Milwaukee: Marquette UP, 1996. This anthology contains facing-page German and English texts of works by four women: Katherine Rem, Ursula of Münsterberg, Anna Sophia of Quedlinburg, and Martha Elisabeth Zitter.

Deutsche Dichterinnen vom 16. Jahrhundert bis zur Gegenwart. Ed. Gisela Brinker-Gabler. Frankfurt: Fischer, 1978. A general anthology of poetry in German by women from the sixteenth century to the present.

Dichtungen schlesischer Autorinnen des 17. Jahrhunderts: Eine Anthologie. Ed. Mirosława Czarnecka. Wrocław: Wydawnictwo Uniwersytetu Wrocławskiego, 1997. An anthology of poetry by Silesian women writers of the seventeenth century.

Distaves and Dames: Renaissance Treatises for and about Women. Facsim. reproductions. Introd. Diane Bornstein. Delmar: Scholars' Facsims. and Rpts., 1978. Contains *The Gospelles of Dystaves* [n.d.], *The Northern Mother's Blessing* (1597), *The Boke of the Cyte of Ladyes* (1521), and *The Instruction of a Christen Woman* (1529).

English Women's Poetry: Elizabethan to Victorian. Ed. R. E. Pritchard. New York: Continuum, 1993.

English Women's Voices, 1540–1700. Ed. Charlotte F. Otten. Miami: Florida Intl. UP, 1992.

Female Playwrights of the Restoration: Five Comedies. Ed. Paddy Lyons and Fidelis Morgan. London: Dent, 1991. Contains plays by Aphra Behn, Mary Pix, Ariadne, and Susannah Centlivre.

The Female Spectator: English Women Writers before 1800. Ed. Mary R. Mahl and Helene Koon. Bloomington: Indiana UP; Old Westbury: Feminist, 1977. Selections of works by twenty authors, from Dame Julian of Norwich to Anna Seward, are represented.

Female Wits: Women Playwrights on the London Stage, 1660–1720. Ed. Fidelis Morgan. London: Virago, 1981. The book is divided into two parts. The first part provides a background discussion of early women playwrights, beginning with Katherine Philips and Aphra Behn, while the second part gives the texts of five plays, by Behn, Trotter, Manley, Pix, and Centlivre. A checklist of dramatic and nondramatic works by seventeenth- and eighteenth-century women forms a useful appendix.

First Feminists: British Women Writers, 1578–1799. Ed. Moira Ferguson. Bloomington: Indiana UP; Old Westbury: Feminist, 1985.

Gaspara Stampa e altre poetesse del '500. Ed. Francesco Flora. Milan: Nuova Accademia, 1962. Accompanied by a record.

Her Own Life: Autobiographical Writings by Seventeenth-Century Englishwomen. Ed. Elspeth Graham et al. London: Routledge, 1989.

Kissing the Rod: An Anthology of Seventeenth-Century Women's Verse. Ed. Germaine Greer et al. London: Virago, 1988.

"Lay By Your Needles Ladies, Take the Pen": Writing Women in England, 1500–1700. Ed. Suzanne Trill, Kate Chedgzoy, and Melanie Osborne. New York: St. Martin's, 1997.

Love and Thunder: Plays by Women in the Age of Queen Anne. Ed. Gillian Murray Kendall. London: Methuen Drama, 1988. Contains plays by Susannah Centlivre, Mary Pix, Catharine Trotter, and Jane Wiseman.

The Lunatic Lover *and Other Plays by French Women of the Seventeenth and Eighteenth Centuries.* Ed. Perry Gethner. Portsmouth: Heinemann, 1994. Contains plays by Françoise Pascal, Marie-Catherine Desjardins, Anne de la Roche-Guilhen, Catharine Bernard, Marie-Anne Barbier, and Françoise d'Issembourg d'Happoncourt de Graffigny.

Major Women Writers of Seventeenth-Century England. Ed. James Fitzmaurice et al. Ann Arbor: U of Michigan P, 1997. At close to 400 pages, this is a major anthology including writers such as Lanyer, Cary, Wroth, Cavendish, Philips, Behn, Finch, Speght, and Sowernam.

Le miroir des femmes. Ed. Arlette Farge. Paris: Montalba, 1982. An anthology of texts from 1698 to 1832.

Œuvres poétiques [by Louise Labé and] *Rymes* [by Pernette du Guillet]. Ed. Françoise Charpentier. Paris: Gallimard, 1983. This volume also contains a useful collection, "Blasons du corps féminin," by a variety of (mostly male) authors.

The "Other" Eighteenth Century: English Women of Letters, 1660–1800. Ed. Robert W. Uphaus and Gretchen M. Foster. East Lansing: Colleagues, 1991.

The Paradise of Women: Writings by Englishwomen of the Renaissance. Ed. Betty Travitsky. Westport: Greenwood, 1981.

The Plays of Mary Pix and Catharine Trotter. Ed. Edna L. Steeves. 2 vols. New York: Garland, 1982.

Poesía femenina en los cancioneros. Ed. Miguel Angel Pérez Priego. Madrid: Castalia, 1990. Contains early Spanish poems to 1500.

Popular Fiction by Women, 1660–1730: An Anthology. Ed. Paula R. Backscheider and John Richetti. New York: Oxford UP, 1996. The anthology offers eight works by seven writers. The two earliest are *The History of the Nun* (1689) by Aphra Behn and *The Secret History of Queen Zarah and the Zarazians* (1705) by Delariviere Manley.

Renaissance Drama by Women: Texts and Documents. Ed. S. P. Cerasano and Marion Wynne-Davies. New York: Routledge, 1996. This book contains the following play texts: the fragment of a translation from Seneca attributed to Elizabeth I; *The Tragedie of Antonie* by Mary Sidney; *The Tragedie of Mariam* by Elizabeth Cary; Robert White's masque, *Cupid's Banishment*, performed by the gentlewomen of Queen Anne's court; *Love's Victory* by Mary Wroth; and *The Concealed Fancies* by Elizabeth Brackley and Jane Cavendish. Selections from contemporary documents about women and the theater follow the plays.

Renaissance Women: The Plays of Elizabeth Cary: The Poems of Aemilia Lanyer. Ed. Diane Purkiss. London: Pickering, 1994.

Rime di tre gentildonne de secolo XVI: Vittoria Colonna, Gaspara Stampa, Veronica Gambara. Facsim. ed. Preface by Olindo Guerrini. Milano: Sonzongno, 1882.

Three Women Poets, Renaissance and Baroque: Louise Labé, Gaspara Stampa, and Sor Juan Inez de la Cruz. Ed. and trans. Frank J. Warnke. Lewisburg: Bucknell UP, 1987.

Tras el espejo la musa escribe: Lírica femenina de los Siglos de Oro. Ed. Julián Olivares and Elizabeth S. Boyce. Madrid: Siglo Veintiuno de España, 1993.

Tudor and Stuart Women Writers. By Louise Schleiner. Bloomington: Indiana UP, 1994. Contains useful translations by Connie McQuillen and Lynn E. Roller from Latin and Greek writings by English women writers.

The Whole Duty of a Woman: Female Writers in Seventeenth-Century England. Ed. Angeline Goreau. Garden City: Dial, 1985.

Women Poets of the Italian Renaissance: Courtly Ladies and Courtesans. Ed. Laura Anna Stortoni. Trans. Stortoni and Mary Prentice Lillie. New York: Italica, 1997.

Women Poets of the Renaissance. Ed. Marion Wynne-Davies. London: Dent, 1998.

Women's Acts: Plays by Women Dramatists of Spain's Golden Age. Ed. Teresa Scott Soufas. Lexington: UP of Kentucky, 1997. Contains plays by Angela de Azevedo, Ana Caro Mallén de Soto, Leonor de la Cueva y Silva, Feliciana Enríquez de Guzmán, and María de Zayas y Sotomayor.

Women's Writing in Stuart England: The Mothers' Legacies of Dorothy Leigh,

Elizabeth Joscelin, and Elizabeth Richardson. Ed. Sylvia Brown. Stroud: Sutton, 1999.

Women Writers in Renaissance England. Ed. Randall Martin. New York: Longman, 1997. Includes dedicatory material from works by Margaret Tyler, Anne Dowriche, Rachel Speght, and Elizabeth Joscelin.

The Controversy about Women: Works Mostly by Men about Women

These books reprint a variety of early works, for and against women, that formed part of what is generally known as the *querelle des femmes.*

The Cultural Identity of Seventeenth-Century Woman: A Reader. Comp. and ed. N. H. Keeble. London: Routledge, 1994. Contains selections from works by male and female writers.

The Feminist Controversy of the Renaissance. Facsim. reproductions. Introd. Diane Bornstein. Delmar: Scholars' Facsims., 1980. Contains Guillaume Alexis, *An Argument betwyxt Man and Woman* (1525); Sir Thomas Elyot, *The Defence of Good Women* (1545); Henricus Cornelius Agrippa, *Female Pre-eminence* (1670).

La femme dans la littérature française et les traductions en français du XVIième siècle. Comp. and ed. Luce Guillerm-Curutchet et al. Lille: Université de Lille III, 1971.

Le grief des femmes. Vol. 1: "Anthologie de textes féministes du Moyen Age à la Seconde République." Ed. Maïté Albistur and Daniel Armogathe. Paris: Hier et Demain, 1978.

Half Humankind: Contexts and Texts of the Controversy about Women in England, 1540–1640. Ed. Katherine Usher Henderson and Barbara F. McManus. Urbana: U of Illinois P, 1985.

Her Immaculate Hand: Selected Works by and about the Women Humanists of Quattrocento Italy. Ed. Margaret L. King and Albert Rabil, Jr. Binghamton: Center for Medieval and Early Renaissance Studies, 1983.

Le miroir des femmes [. . .]. Ed. Luce Guillerm et al. Vol. 1: "Moralistes et polémistes au XVI^c siècle"; vol. 2: "Roman, Conte, Théâtre, Poésie au XV^{c}siècle." Lille: Presses Universitaires, 1983, 1984. These volumes contain excerpts about women from texts mostly by men. A chronological table (1530–1600) in volume 2 places the texts with other writings of the period.

Satires on Women: Love Given O're *[Robert Gould, 1682];* The Female Advocate *[Sarah Fige, 1687];* The Folly of Love *[Richard Ames, 1691].* Introd. Felicity A. Nussbaum. Augustan Reprint Soc. 180. Los Angeles: U of California for the William Andrews Clark Memorial Lib., 1976.

"Three Early Renaissance Treatises on Women." By Conor Fahy. *Italian*

Studies 11 (1956): 30–55. The article describes treatises by Bartolomeo Gogio, Mario Equicola, and Agostino Strozzi and includes a useful "List of Treatises on the Equality or Superiority of Women Written or Published in Italy during the Fifteenth and Sixteenth Centuries."

The Women's Sharp Revenge: Five Women's Pamphlets from the Renaissance. Ed. Simon Shepherd. New York: St. Martin's, 1985. Contents: *Jane Anger Her Protection for Women*; *A Mouzell for Melastomus* by Rachel Speght; *Ester Hath Hang'd Haman* by Ester Sowernam; *The Worming of a Mad Dogge* by Constantia Munda; *The Women's Sharpe Revenge* by Mary Tattle-Well and Joan Hit-Him-Home.

Note

I would like to thank three historians and friends whose collective insight has been especially valuable: Judith Bennett and Cynthia Herrup, for their most helpful suggestions in getting me started on this bibliography, and Carole Levin, for reading it through near the end.

Suzanne W. Hull

Traditional Studies of Early Women Writers

Interest in early women writers has exploded since 1980, but the groundwork for this revolution was laid decades, even centuries, earlier, when the subject began intriguing the occasional scholar or publisher. In the twentieth century, several literary and social historians, writing before 1980, have given more than passing attention to early modern women of letters.

One, Myra Reynolds, devoted most of one book to them. Her *The Learned Lady in England, 1650–1760* is a rich resource of biographical essays on many women writers. Her emphasis is on eleven decades, 1650–1760, but she leads up to them with several pages on classical, medieval, and Renaissance writers. Dozens of now familiar authors command from half a page to multipage essays: Christine de Pisan, Anne Clifford, Katherine Philips, Margaret Cavendish, Aphra Behn, Bathsua Makin, Hannah Woolley, Margaret Fell Fox, Jane Sharp, and Lady Jane Grey as well as a number of less well known writers. She missed a few. Among them are Isabella Whitney, Margaret Hoby, and Elizabeth Grymeston. But *The Learned Lady* still offers a good jumping-off point. Especially useful are her bibliography, more than a dozen portraits, and an extensive index.

Ada (Mrs. Graham) Wallas wrote four long biographical essays in her *Before the Bluestockings*, but she covered only Hannah Woolley, Damaris Cudworth Masham (a friend of John Locke's, to whom her early work was attributed), Mary Astell, and Elizabeth Elstob.

Two early PhD dissertations, Ruth Willard Hughey's "Cultural Interests of Women in England, from 1524 [to] 1640, Indicated in the Writings of the Women" and Charlotte Kohler's "The Elizabethan Woman of Letters: The Extent of Her Literary Activity," continued the general subject; each provides a list of early writers. (Kohler, a faculty member of the University of Virginia, replaced the male editor of the *Virginia Quarterly Review* in World War II and continued in that position for some three decades, though her name stood alone as editor on the masthead for only the last eleven years.)

Two well-known male academics weave women writers into their early modern histories. In 1935 Louis B. Wright, the prolific historian of both England and America, published what became a basic tool for the study of Renaissance society, *Middle-Class Culture in Elizabethan England*. Entries under the heading "Women" fill half a page in the index, yet there is no subheading "Writers" or "Authors." Wright spends several pages on women's reading (103–18) and books published for and about women, but he examines only a few female writers: Margaret Tyler (116–17), Esther Sowernam (if that pseudonym indeed represents a woman), Constantia Munda, and Rachel Speght (488–90).

Carroll Camden expressed enough interest in early modern female writing to note, in his *The Elizabethan Woman*, "Over fifty women wrote some eighty-five compositions during the years from 1524 to 1640. Fifty-eight of these books were printed separately, while the others appeared in anthologies, liturgies, and other collections" (58). Current research is extending that list. Camden mentions only a few of the authors: Elizabeth Carew, Jane Anger, Anne Dowriche, Christine de Pisan (du Castel), Mary Fage, and Rachel Speght.

The greatest value of both Camden's and Wright's work is

setting the social and cultural scene in which women writers found themselves during the English Renaissance.

Ruth Kelso made a strong contribution to the history of female accomplishments in her *Doctrine for the Lady of the Renaissance.* This lengthy work treats not only English but also French and Italian women in the period 1400–1600. Kelso uses long, direct quotations from many original sources and summarizes and condenses others. English female authors mentioned include Jane Anger (again, the sex of that author is uncertain); Dorothy Leigh; Esther Sowernam; Rachel Speght; Hannah More; Margaret Tyler; Mary, Queen of Scots; Christine de Pisan (du Castel); and Elizabeth Joscelin. The book has extensive indexes, bibliography, and notes.

The British scholar Doris Mary Stenton is touted in a catalog blurb on her 1957 book, *The English Woman in History,* as the first historian who "has ever undertaken a survey of this kind before." Lady Stenton devotes four chapters to women in the Renaissance and the Reformation (120–245). Like Wright and Camden, she provides background material on early modern women, and her biographies of writers make interesting reading, but she provides few quotations. Recent scholarship expands and corrects some of her work.

A more specialized study is the poet Ann Stanford's *The Women Poets in English: An Anthology.* Following a lengthy introduction, Stanford sets out short biographical essays and samples of work for dozens of poets, from Anglo-Saxon time to the present. About twenty are female poets of the early modern period.

When women's historians cried out for new material in the late 1970s, Pearl Hogrefe rushed into print, perhaps too fast, with two books. *Tudor Women: Commoners and Queens* is the more valuable, with chapters on women in business and as officeholders. (Another book with a similar title, Alice Plowden's *Tudor Women: Queens and Commoners* [New York: Atheneum], appeared in 1979. Plowden was a popular historian.) The chapter "Women as Literary Patrons and as Writers" is heavily slanted to patronage, not writing. *Women of Action in Tudor England: Nine Biographical Sketches* concentrates on royal women or noblewomen and has little that is new about

Mildred Cooke Cecil, Lady Burghley; Anne Cooke, Lady Bacon; Bess of Hardwick, countess of Shrewsbury; Catherine Willoughby, duchess of Suffolk; Mary Sidney, countess of Pembroke; Margaret Beaufort, countess of Richmond and Derby; Queen Catherine of Aragon; Queen Katherine Parr; and Queen Elizabeth I. Hogrefe includes short paragraphs about any authorship of the biographees.

Mary R. Mahl and Helene Koon were also in the vanguard with *The Female Spectator: English Women Writers before 1800*, an anthology of material in the Huntington Library. This limitation is not as narrow as it may sound, since the Huntington collection contains almost 40,000 early modern English books.

Well before the twentieth century, other books devoted to women writers appeared. George Ballard's *Memoirs of Several Ladies of Great Britain Who Have Been Celebrated for Their Writings or Skill in the Learned Languages, Arts and Sciences*, published in 1752 and reprinted in 1985, was the first. Ballard started with Julian of Norwich, Julian Barnes (Berners), and Margery Kempe and worked chronologically through Mary Astell. His work is valuable as an early look at women writers but is hardly all-inclusive.

In the next century, the Reverend Alexander Dyce wrote *Specimens of British Poetesses: Selected and Chronologically Arranged*. He says in the preface that he is putting together this work because "the productions of women have been carefully excluded" from collections of English poets (iii), but he spoils his good intentions by writing, "It is true that the grander inspirations of the Muse have not been often breathed into the softer frame. [. . .] The tremendous thoughts [. . .] have not proceeded from woman" (iv).

Louisa Stuart Costello published in 1844 the first two volumes of what became her four-volume *Memoirs of Eminent Englishwomen*. Not all her eminent women were writers, but there are enough to give her work value, if only to compare her analyses (and excerpts) with those of later critics. She described the duchess of Newcastle as "insufferable" (2: 316) and her many books "the nuisance of the time" (3: 211).

George W. Bethune edited *The British Female Poets: with Biographical and Critical Notices*, an 1848 anthology that went into a dozen printings by the end of the century, proof that female poetry had a large and loyal audience by that time.

Jane Williams wrote *The Literary Women of England, Including a Biographical Epitome of All the Most Eminent to the Year 1700 and Sketches of the Poetesses to the Year 1850 with Extracts from Their Works*. The 1861 publication has an interesting introduction in which Williams discusses the value of women's writing. Of the more than ninety "authoresses noticed in this essay" (vii), at least half are early modern writers, though their listings are short in comparison with the later poets.

Compilers' views of early modern women writers evolved over time. The changing evaluations, found in these pre-1980 anthologies and biographies (and continuing today), invite further study.

For bibliographies of other resources on early modern women writers, see Elizabeth H. Hageman's fine bibliographies in *English Literary Renaissance* ("Recent Studies [. . .] Seventeenth Century" and "Recent Studies [. . .] Tudor England") and Rosemary Masek's "Women in an Age of Transition, 1485–1714."

Traditionally, women did not write for publication, particularly not their personal diaries, journals, and letters. With the exception of sensational writing like the journal of the martyr Anne Askew, whose story was "headline" news at the time of her death, autobiographical material was rarely published or mentioned until years or even centuries after the author's death. In some cases this silence was the fault of descendants who kept private papers within the family. In others it was the descendants themselves who brought the material to light. According to Elaine Hobby, "Many diary manuscripts were discovered and printed in private editions in the nineteenth century" (*Virtue* 214). Not much of this autobiographical material has yet found its way into anthologies or traditional studies. But personal literature, hidden in manuscript form for many generations and beginning to emerge in the nineteenth century, is finally getting the recognition it deserves in late-twentieth-century reprints. The different versions and critiques of this literature, published in different time periods, offer a rich base for comparative studies by students and scholars of social history, English literature, and women's studies.

Some of the English book clubs led the way in printing this genre. These were usually small print runs, often no more than 250 copies. Several examples follow.

The horrifying *Examinations of Anne Askew* (1521–46), originally edited and expanded on by John Bale and printed on the Continent right after Askew's burning, and printed as part of John Foxe's *Acts and Monuments* in 1563, was reprinted by the Parker Society in 1849. Several editions have appeared since. Derek Wilson's 1972 biography with excerpts is useful, as are the Scolar Press facsimile and Elaine Beilin's edition, both in 1996.

The Camden Society printed the *Letters of the Lady Brilliana Harley* (1600–43) in 1854, when they were made available by one of her descendants. Lady Brilliana writes to her husband and her son about the terrors she faced while trying to protect their estate against royalist sympathizers and troops during the Civil War.

The Autobiography of Mrs. Alice Thornton (1627–1707) was "for the first time given to the world" by the Surtees Society in 1875 (2). The editor, touching on the controversy over publishing female memoirs, says some people would argue, "The autobiography [. . .] touches upon matters of domestic concern [. . .] trivial subjects [. . . that] ought not to be brought out into the full glare of day." The editor believed however that "works like the present, for their intrinsic merit have a right to be considered public as well as privati juris" (2). This journal, like Lady Brilliana's, deserves more study and reprinting.

A biography of Anne, Lady Halkett had been included in a 1701 publication of her devotional works, but *The Autobiography of Anne, Lady Halket* (1622–99) was first published by the Camden Society in 1875. A recent version, *The Memoirs of Anne, Lady Halkett and Ann, Lady Fanshawe*, edited by John Loftis, was published in 1979. Lady Halkett, a royalist, reputedly helped with the escape to France of the duke of York, later James II.

The Roxburghe Club published part of the diaries of Lady Anne

Clifford (1590–1676) in 1916; other editions, notably one intro-duced by Victoria (Vita) Sackville-West in 1924 and a 1990 version edited by D. J. H. Clifford, are more complete. Lady Anne's jour-nals describe domestic activities in a large, noble household as well as long-standing battles with relatives over land she claimed was hers.

The book clubs helped bring these early writings to public view, but individual scholars and editors also began to uncover and pub-lish such manuscripts. One of the earliest known female diarists was Lady Margaret Hoby (1571–1633). Her *Diary*, edited by Dorothy M. Meads, was published in 1930. Though Lady Margaret was re-lated to many of the leading aristocratic families, her diary is rather dull, heavily devotional in tone but with little of interest about per-sonal lives or contemporary events.

The unpublished reminiscences of Grace Sherrington, Lady Mildmay (c. 1552–1620), came to light in an article by Rachel Weigall, "An Elizabethan Gentlewoman: The Journal of Lady Mild-may." Lady Mildmay left recipes for medicinal cures as well as in-sight into her Puritan household.

Lady Cecilie Goff's *A Woman of the Tudor Age* (1930) is a bi-ography of Catherine Willoughby, duchess of Suffolk (1520–80); it intersperses her letters with those of others. In another biography, Evelyn Read's *Catherine, Duchess of Suffolk: A Portrait* (1962), the duchess (fourth wife, after Mary Tudor, of Charles Brandon) was described as a Puritan, an ex-Catholic, and a correspondent of polit-ical leaders.

One of the most entertaining collections of letters was written by Dorothy Osborne (1627–95) to her future husband, Sir William Temple. Civil war and opposing sympathies postponed the Temples' union but did not dull Lady Temple's wit and charm. Haphazard excerpts from her letters were printed as a "Supplement" to the two-volume *Life of Sir William Temple* by Thomas Peregrine Courtenay in 1836. Courtenay was criticized for relegating the letters to an ap-pendix. Edward A. Parry, editor of the 1888 edition of the Osborne letters, a more complete collection, says of Courtenay, "We can never quite forgive the apologetic paragraph with which he relegates

Dorothy Osborne's letters to the mouldy obscurity of an Appendix" (*Letters from Dorothy Osborne* 2). Parry reproduced some of the letters in an article, "Dorothy Osborne," in *English Illustrated Magazine* in 1886. Other editions appeared in 1903, 1928, 1959, and 1987.

Letters by Lady Temple's sister-in-law, Lady Martha Giffard (1638–1722), who lived with the Temples and wrote about her brother, are considered sequels to the Osborne collection. They were published in 1911, coattailing on the popularity of the Osborne letters; they do not match Osborne's entertaining style.

When women wrote about, or to, their husbands, such work tended to get early recognition—for example, writing by Margaret Cavendish, Ann Fanshawe, and Lucy Hutchinson. Margaret Cavendish, duchess of Newcastle (1623–73), was famous in her day for both her writing (in several genres) and her eccentricities. Among the many manuscripts published during her lifetime was an autobiographical chapter, "A True Relation of My Birth, Breeding, and Life," published at the end of *Natures Pictures Drawn by Fancies Pencil to the Life* (1656) and also in her *Life of the Thrice Noble [. . .] William Cavendishe* (1668). The biographical material, writing that attracted popular interest and reprints, was reprinted in 1872 as *The Lives of William Cavendishe, Duke of Newcastle, and of His Wife, Margaret, Duchess of Newcastle.*

The *Memoirs of Lady Fanshawe* was published originally by a family member in 1829. *The Memoirs of Ann Lady Fanshawe, Wife of the Right Honorable Sir Richard Fanshawe, Bart [. . .]* appeared in 1907. John Loftis edited another version in 1979 (Halkett). Lady Fanshawe (1625–80) produced babies almost annually (most of whom died), traveled with her diplomat husband, and wrote about her experiences in the many countries where he was assigned.

The Correspondence of Anne, Viscountess Conway (1631–79), edited by Marjorie Hope Nicolson, published in 1930 and reprinted in 1979 (Finch), includes a biographical account of the viscountess, who wrote philosophical and scientific treatises as well as personal letters.

Hughey, who wrote the unpublished dissertation mentioned

above, published *The Correspondence of Lady Katherine Paston, 1603–27* in 1941. After Lady Katherine's husband became ill in 1618, Lady Katherine (1578–1629) handled considerable business correspondence, leading Hughey to say she "furnishes [an] excellent picture of the ability and interests of an early seventeenth-century woman" (Paston 15).

Lucy Hutchinson (b. 1620) wrote *Memoirs of the Life of Colonel Hutchinson*; Colonel Hutchinson, her husband, was a Parliamentarian in the Civil War. First published in 1806 and reprinted in 1973, it is valuable as biography, autobiography, and English Civil War history. The first editor said of the memoirs, "The ladies will feel that it carries with it all the interest of a novel, strengthened with the authenticity of real history" (xiv).

Another entertaining and useful journal was that kept by the inveterate traveler Celia Fiennes (1662–1741), whose journeys around England were gathered and published as *Through England on a Side Saddle in the Time of William and Mary* by a kinswoman in 1888. The journal is now considered a valuable reference to late-seventeenth-century travel and country life, and several more reprints have appeared, including an illustrated edition in 1982.

Interesting patterns emerge in these publications. Most appeared in public from one to three centuries after they were written. Most have been reprinted during the mid to late twentieth century. Hidden in the various editions—and in the comments of biographers and editors—are valuable clues about changing attitudes toward women and their writing. Within these works, then, is grist for future, less traditional, women's studies.

Sara Jayne Steen

"My Bookes and Pen I Wyll Apply": Recent Studies of Early Modern British Women Writers

The joy of composing an essay like this one is being reminded how many early modern British women writers did, like Isabella Whitney, apply their pens and how many fine scholars have authored articles and books on those writers since 1980. Teachers now can choose, as they could not, even a decade ago, from numerous well-designed editions that can be carried proudly next to a paperback of the works of Edmund Spenser. A substantial body of criticism allows students to enter an exciting and ongoing conversation about the shape of early modern literature and culture, a conversation that includes women from Katherine Parr to Jane Barker. In fact, and wonderful to recognize, so much research has appeared that I could not in these pages offer a full bibliography. For that, readers should consult more comprehensive sources, including the list of works cited at the end of this volume.

This essay is intended to introduce teachers planning to integrate women writers into their courses to the editions and studies published since 1980. As a result, I have focused on books rather than journal articles, have concentrated on critical volumes that treat many women writers or in which a significant portion of the volume is devoted to women as writers, and have omitted reprints of previously published work. Since teachers may be preparing survey, genre, period, author, topics, or entirely new interdisciplinary courses, I have attempted to allow for multiple directions by beginning with general materials and becoming increasingly specific. Although some scholars have argued rightly that emphasis on traditional literary genres has led us to misunderstand the richness of early modern literary culture, and although many women wrote in a number of forms and thus cannot be easily classified, enough courses are grounded in genre that it seemed helpful to include brief discussions of genres. Teachers coming to the field for the first time may want to choose an anthology and a background study that are congenial, then move to specific authors or works that seem engaging and suitable for their courses and students. I hope that they, as well as teachers experienced with these writers, will find much here to incorporate into their classes.

Background Studies

Among broadly based works treating women across Europe that are useful contextual introductions is the historian Joan Kelly-Gadol's *Women, History, and Theory* (1984), with her essays "Did Women Have a Renaissance?" and "Early Feminist Theory and the *Querelle des Femmes*, 1400–1789." Margaret L. King's *Women of the Renaissance* (1991) explores women in the contexts of the family, the church, and high culture. Merry E. Wiesner's *Women and Gender in Early Modern Europe* (1993) examines women's lives from 1500 to 1750, with sections on the body, mind, and spirit, summarizing recent research so that students can see how the field has developed. Natalie Zemon Davis and Arlette Farge's collection *Renaissance and Enlightenment Paradoxes* (1993), volume 3 of *A History of Women in the West*, provides essays by many scholars on topics such as medicine, witches, and protesters. In volume 1 of *The Prospect be-*

fore Her (1996), Olwen Hufton considers the texture of women's lives from 1500 through 1800, placing gender issues in social and economic contexts. More specific is Joy Wiltenburg's *Disorderly Women and Female Power in the Street Literature of Early Modern England and Germany* (1992), in which Wiltenburg compares English and German attitudes toward women in works such as ballads and broadsides.

Other studies focus on England. Retha M. Warnicke's *Women of the English Renaissance and Reformation* (1983) examines changes in women's lives from generation to generation. In *The Weaker Vessel* (1984), Antonia Fraser compares the theory of the weaker vessel with the lives seventeenth-century Englishwomen actually led. Margaret George's *Women in the First Capitalist Society* (1988) highlights middle-class women's experiences during the social transformations of the seventeenth century. Anthony Fletcher's *Gender, Sex, and Subordination in England, 1500–1800* (1995) considers the gender system and its alteration over time. In *Women according to Men* (1996), Suzanne W. Hull explores early modern men's prescriptions about how Tudor-Stuart women should live. More specific are Hull's *Chaste, Silent, and Obedient: English Books for Women, 1475–1640* (1982), an analysis of printed books directed toward a female audience, and Frances E. Dolan's *Dangerous Familiars* (1994), an examination of popular literature on domestic crimes such as husband or wife murder.

Volumes providing early modern works to which students can refer are Kate Aughterson's *Renaissance Woman* (1995), an anthology of texts by women and men on topics such as theology, sexuality, education, and work; N. H. Keeble's *The Cultural Identity of Seventeenth-Century Woman* (1994), a similar collection focusing on seventeenth-century texts; Joan Larsen Klein's *Daughters, Wives, and Widows: Writings by Men about Women and Marriage in England, 1500–1640* (1992), an anthology offering humanist and Puritan perspectives; and *The Flower of Friendship: A Renaissance Dialogue Contesting Marriage*, edited by Valerie Wayne (1992), Edmund Tilney's humanist text on marriage.

Multigenre Anthologies and Series

Several multigenre anthologies of works by early modern women
have appeared since 1980, each quite distinct.[1] The earliest, and still
widely used, collection is *The Paradise of Women*, edited by Betty
Travitsky (1981; rpt. 1989). Travitsky includes old-spelling excerpts
of works written between 1500 and 1640, categorized as religious
compositions, familial and personal writings, and secular writings,
with separate sections on Anne Askew, Mary Stuart, and Elizabeth
Cary. British writers from the late sixteenth through the eighteenth
century are anthologized in *First Feminists*, edited by Moira Ferguson (1985). Ferguson traces the evolution of feminist thought
through old-spelling excerpts of works by women. *The Whole Duty
of a Woman*, edited by Angeline Goreau (1985), explores the social and educational circumstances that affected seventeenth-century
women's writing, with sections on women's duty (excerpts of works
largely by men), on the debate about women, and by women on
their work. *English Women's Voices, 1540–1700*, edited by Charlotte
F. Otten (1992), excludes fictional writing and draws on diaries, letters, petitions, health manuals, autobiographies, and biographical
poems to demonstrate how Renaissance women described their
lives. Modernized texts are divided into topics such as politics, marriage, and health care.

Two literary anthologies intended for undergraduates or general readers appeared in 1997. *Major Women Writers of Seventeenth-
Century England*, edited by James Fitzmaurice, Josephine A. Roberts,
Carol L. Barash, Eugene R. Cunnar, and Nancy A. Gutierrez, contains chapters on and modernized works by frequently taught figures: Aemilia Lanyer, Elizabeth Cary, Mary Wroth, Margaret
Cavendish, Katherine Philips, Aphra Behn, and Anne Finch.
Women Writers in Renaissance England, edited by Randall Martin,
provides modernized editions of works by many sixteenth- and
early-seventeenth-century writers. Works are loosely categorized
into prose, prose autobiography, and verse.

Sections on English writers appear in two anthologies dedicated
to European women writers. *Women Writers of the Renaissance and*

Reformation, edited by Katharina M. Wilson (1987), offers studies and excerpts of the writings of Margaret More Roper, Mary Sidney, Elizabeth I, Mary Wroth, and Katherine Philips. *Women Writers of the Seventeenth Century*, edited by Katharina M. Wilson and Frank J. Warnke (1989), provides similar materials on Bathsua Makin, Margaret Cavendish, and Aphra Behn.

Two series provide important resources. Oxford University Press publishes Women Writers in English, 1350–1850 (general editors Susanne Woods and Elizabeth H. Hageman); its texts are aimed at the student or informed nonspecialist. (The series is discussed in a special issue of *South Central Review* edited by Margaret J. M. Ezell [*Creating*].) Ashgate Press publishes The Early Modern Englishwoman: A Facsimile Library of Essential Work: Printed Writings, 1500–1640 (general editors Betty S. Travitsky and Patrick Cullen). Each volume contains a brief introduction and a facsimile of the best available early modern printed copy.

Writings by early modern women also are available from the *Women Writers Project*, a computer project originally directed by Susanne Woods and now managed by Julia Flanders. For the text list, consult the project's home page (http://www.wwp.brown.edu/) or write the Women Writers Project, Box 1841, Brown University, Providence, RI 02912. A related initiative, *Renaissance Women Online*, will provide approximately one hundred texts for electronic delivery. The *Women Writers Project* home page contains links to other online editions.

General Studies

Three volumes explore female authorship in relation to genre and forms of literary production. In *The Patriarch's Wife* (1987), Margaret J. M. Ezell contends that emphasis on publication devalues women's participation in an intellectual world where manuscript circulation was an acceptable means of acquiring readership. She extends her thesis in *Writing Women's Literary History* (1993), maintaining that a restrictive model of literary history has led critics to diminish the achievements of early modern women whose writings do not fit traditional categories. In *The Imprint of Gender* (1993), Wendy Wall investigates connections among authorship, gender, and publication, considering ways in which writers such as Isabella Whitney, Aemilia Lanyer, and Mary Wroth created new models of authorship as they entered the world of print.

Other scholars examine authorial voice in relation to dominant ideologies of womanhood. Elaine V. Beilin's *Redeeming Eve* (1987) explores how thirty Tudor and Stuart writers "redeemed Eve" by allying women with virtue; she emphasizes Mary Sidney, Elizabeth Cary, Aemilia Lanyer, and Mary Wroth. In *Oppositional Voices* (1992), Tina Krontiris investigates strategies by which women voiced opposition to dominant gender beliefs; she focuses on Isabella Whitney, Margaret Tyler, Mary Sidney, Elizabeth Cary, Aemilia Lanyer, and Mary Wroth. Barbara Kiefer Lewalski's *Writing Women in Jacobean England* (1993) considers nine Jacobean women who "rewrote the major discourses of their era in strikingly oppositional terms"; Lewalski includes chapters on Queen Anne, Princess Elizabeth, Arbella Stuart, Lucy Harington Russell, Anne Clifford, Rachel Speght, Elizabeth Cary, Aemilia Lanyer, and Mary Wroth. In *Tudor and Stuart Women Writers* (1994), Louise Schleiner suggests that reading and writing circles allowed women from the 1560s through the 1630s to develop and sustain authorial voices. Kim Walker's *Women Writers of the English Renaissance* (1996) explores the context in which women wrote between 1560 and 1640 and how they established themselves as writers. Megan Matchinske's *Writing, Gender, and State in Early Modern England: Identity Formation and the Female Subject* (1998) considers the construction of female identity in relation to emerging English statehood, focusing on Anne Askew, Ester Sowernam, and Eleanor Davies; and Eve Rachele Sanders's *Gender and Literacy on Stage in Early Modern England* (1998) investigates how gender identity was taught with literacy and how the theory compared to actual writings by women such as Mary Sidney and Anne Clifford.

Among scholars who focus on the later seventeenth century, Elaine Hobby, in her *Virtue of Necessity* (1988), examines the wide range of genres in which women expressed themselves in writing—prophecy, religious writing, autobiography, prose fiction, drama, poetry, skill books on subjects such as housewifery and medicine, and educational tracts—and how these writers transformed limitations into opportunities. In *Reason's Disciples* (1982), Hilda L. Smith considers the prose and poetry of fifteen women writers, such as Margaret Cavendish, Katherine Philips, Mary Astell, and Mary, Lady Chudleigh, as she argues that during the later 1600s a feminist ideology emerged in England. In *The Mental World of Stuart Women* (1987), Sara Heller Mendelson employs the writings of Margaret Cavendish, Mary Rich, and Aphra Behn to investigate seventeenth-century women's mental universe. Marilyn L. Williamson's *Raising Their Voices: British Women Writers, 1650–1750* (1990) discusses the degree to which later women drew on seventeenth-century writers such as Margaret Cavendish, Katherine Philips, and Aphra Behn.

Essay Collections

Many useful collections of essays have appeared since 1980. Among volumes treating both the sixteenth and seventeenth centuries, *Women and Literature in Britain, 1500–1700*, edited by Helen Wilcox (1996), is a comprehensive introduction to the context in which women wrote, with separate chapters on courtly writing, poetry, autobiographical writing, prose, and drama. *Voicing Women*, edited by Kate Chedgzoy, Melanie Hansen, and Suzanne Trill (1996), explores the cultural conditions under which women wrote, with essays treating writers from Mary Sidney to Aphra Behn. *English Literary Renaissance* has published three special issues on women in the Renaissance (1984, 1988, 1994) containing texts, critical studies, and bibliographies; some articles from the first two issues are reprinted, with additional essays, in *Women in the Renaissance*, edited by Kirby Farrell, Elizabeth H. Hageman, and Arthur F. Kinney (1990). *Privileging Gender in Early Modern England*, edited by Jean R. Brink (1993), explores gender in relation to texts by and about women. *Women in English Society, 1500–1800*, edited by Mary Prior (1985), contains pieces on widows, recusant women, and seventeenth-century women's diaries and published writings. *Women in the Middle Ages and the Renaissance*, edited by Mary Beth Rose (1986), has essays on Mary Sidney and women's autobiographies, and *Women in Scotland, c. 1100–c. 1750*, edited by Elizabeth Ewan and Maureen M. Meikle (1999), contains essays on women in the book trade and on highland women's songs.

Some collections are organized around topics, such as *Political Rhetoric, Power, and Renaissance Women*, edited by Carole Levin and Patricia A. Sullivan (1995), which, in examining women and politics, deals with women from Anne Boleyn to Aphra Behn, and *Gloriana's Face*, edited by S. P. Cerasano and Marion Wynne-Davies (1992), which explores the representations of sixteenth- and seventeenth-century Englishwomen and the interplay between women's public and private selves. In examining the nature of women's alliances, scholars in *Maids and Mistresses, Cousins and Queens*, edited by Susan Frye and Karen Robertson (1999), treat writers from Isabella Whitney to Aphra Behn. In *Attending to Women in Early Modern England*, edited by Betty S. Travitsky and Adele F. Seeff (1994), scholars consider the process of interdisciplinary study, public and private identities, visible and invisible women, and pedagogy; in a subsequent volume, *Attending to Early Modern Women*, edited by Susan D. Amussen and Adele Seeff (1998), the topics are our subjects and selves, women's places, placing women, and pedagogy. *New Ways of Looking at Old Texts*, edited by W. Speed Hill (1993), contains eight papers on editing women writers. *Shakespeare Quarterly* has published a special issue, *Teaching Judith Shakespeare*, edited by Elizabeth H. Hageman and Sara Jayne Steen (1996), in which teacher-scholars discuss ways to teach early modern British women writers in relation to Shakespeare, the Renaissance writer most often taught in the university curriculum.

Other collections focus on either the sixteenth or the seventeenth century. Among volumes emphasizing writers of the sixteenth and early seventeenth centuries are *Silent but for the Word*, edited by Margaret P. Hannay (1985), which examines how Tudor women spoke through patronage, religious writing, and translation, and *The Renaissance Englishwoman in Print*, edited by Anne M.

Haselkorn and Betty S. Travitsky (1990), which juxtaposes representations of women by Tudor and Stuart men with those by women. Collections featuring later writers include *Women, Texts and Histories, 1575– 1760*, edited by Clare Brant and Diane Purkiss (1992), which explores how "women's writings generate and negotiate speaking-positions in discourse," and *Women, Writing, History, 1640–1740*, edited by Isobel Grundy and Susan Wiseman (1992), which considers the interconnections among gender, writing, and historical situation in the era after print became a primary mode of literary production. *Women, "Race," and Writing in the Early Modern Period*, edited by Margo Hendricks and Patricia Parker (1994), examines the forms of difference, such as race, class, and gender, that shape seventeenth-century women's writings. Similarly, *Feminist Readings of Early Modern Culture*, edited by Valerie Traub, M. Lindsay Kaplan, and Dympna Callaghan (1996), investigates the "production of gendered subjects," with essays on writers such as Elizabeth Cary and Margaret Cavendish. Ann Rosalind Jones and Betty S. Travitsky were guest editors of a special issue of *Women's Studies* entitled *Women in the Renaissance: An Interdisciplinary Forum (MLA 1989)*, in which appear articles treating Mary Wroth, Quaker writers, Elizabeth Egerton, and Aphra Behn. *New Feminist Discourses*, edited by Isobel Armstrong (1992), offers essays on Aemilia Lanyer, prophetic writings, and Aphra Behn.

Autobiography

Her Own Life, edited by Elspeth Graham, Hilary Hinds, Elaine Hobby, and Helen Wilcox (1989), contains twelve modernized excerpts of autobiographical prose and poetry from seventeenth-century writers such as Anne Clifford and Mary Carleton. Volumes treating a single author include *The Examinations of Anne Askew*, edited by Elaine V. Beilin (1996), an old-spelling edition of Askew's record of interrogation and imprisonment, and Linda Pollock's *With Faith and Physic* (1993), a biography of Lady Grace Mildmay with modernized extracts from Mildmay's autobiography and spiritual meditations. (See also "Letters" below.)

The Debate about Women

Half Humankind, edited by Katherine Usher Henderson and Barbara F. McManus (1985), provides modernized excerpts of pamphlets from 1540 to 1640, including works attributed to Jane Anger, Ester Sowernam, Constantia Munda, and Mary Tattle-Well and Joan Hit-Him-Home. *The Women's Sharp Revenge*, edited by Simon Shepherd (1985), similarly offers modernized texts of five pamphlets attributed to women. *The Polemics and Poems of Rachel Speght*, edited by Barbara Kiefer Lewalski (1996), contains, in old-spelling, Speght's responses to Joseph Swetnam's *Araignment of [. . .] Women*.

Linda Woodbridge's *Women and the English Renaissance* (1984) emphasizes the role of literary convention in the controversy about the nature of women. In *Renaissance Feminism* (1990), Constance Jordan examines the debate across Europe, treating topics such as women and natural law. Pamela Joseph Benson's *The Invention of the Renaissance Woman* (1992) considers the degree to which texts in the debate from Italy and England are protofeminist.

Drama

Renaissance Drama by Women, edited by S. P. Cerasano and Marion Wynne-Davies (1996), provides modernized texts of plays translated or composed by Elizabeth I, Mary Sidney, Elizabeth Cary, Mary Wroth, and Elizabeth Brackley and Jane Cavendish, as well as documents about women and theater. Editions of Cary's works include *The Tragedy of Mariam, the Fair Queen of Jewry*, edited by Barry Weller and Margaret W. Ferguson (1994), which contains modernized texts of *Mariam* and the biography of Cary (*Lady Falkland*), and *Renaissance Women: The Plays of Elizabeth Cary, the Poems of Aemilia Lanyer*, edited by Diane Purkiss (1994), which offers modernized texts of *Mariam* and *Edward II*. The Convent of Pleasure *and Other Plays*, edited by Anne Shaver (1999), contains old-spelling texts of four plays by Margaret Cavendish. Old-spelling editions of Aphra Behn's plays compose volumes 5–7 of *The Works of*

Aphra Behn, edited by Janet Todd (1996); Jane Spencer's edition of *Aphra Behn:* The Rover *and Other Plays* (1995) provides modernized editions of four plays.

In *Women Playwrights in England, c. 1363–1750* (1980), Nancy Cotton supplies a biographical and critical introduction to playwrights from the medieval era through the mid-eighteenth century. Jacqueline Pearson, *The Prostituted Muse: Images of Women and Women Dramatists, 1642–1737* (1988), explores the context in which later women playwrights wrote, with chapters on women's roles in the post-Restoration theater, male playwrights' images of women, and women's dramas. *Curtain Calls*, edited by Mary Anne Schofield and Cecilia Macheski (1991), contains essays on playwrights such as Margaret Cavendish and Aphra Behn, as well as a checklist of women's plays staged and published between 1660 and 1820. *Readings in Renaissance Women's Drama*, edited by Cerasano and Wynne-Davies (1998), collects early commentaries on women's drama and provides both reprinted and newly written essays on cultural context and individual dramatists.

Letters

The Lisle Letters, edited by Muriel St. Clair Byrne (1981) in six volumes, contains modernized texts of letters by Honor Lisle, one of three primary correspondents; a one-volume abridgment appeared in 1983. *Two Elizabethan Women: Correspondence of Joan and Maria Thynne, 1575–1611*, edited by Alison D. Wall (1983), provides modernized texts of the correspondence of Joan Thynne of Longleat and the daughter-in-law she disliked. *The Letters of Lady Arbella Stuart*, edited by Sara Jayne Steen (1994), contains old-spelling texts of letters by this claimant to the English throne who defied King James to marry clandestinely. *Letters to Sir William Temple*, edited by Kenneth Parker (1987), supplies old-spelling texts of Dorothy Osborne's letters to Temple, the man who eventually became her husband. Patrick Thomas has edited *The Collected Works of Katherine Philips, the Matchless Orinda* (1990–92), volume 2 of which (*The Letters*) contains old-spelling texts of Philips's letters. *Women's Letters and Letter Writing in England, 1450–1700*, a collection of essays edited by James Daybell, is forthcoming.

Nonfiction Prose, including Prophetic Writing

Women Critics, 1660–1820, edited by the Folger Collective on Early Women Critics (1995), supplies old-spelling texts of critical writings by Margaret Cavendish, Aphra Behn, Jane Barker, Anne Finch, and Catherine Trotter Cockburn. *Prophetic Writings of Lady Eleanor Davies*, edited by Esther S. Cope (1995), contains old-spelling texts of thirty-eight tracts. Jane Sharp's *The Midwives Book*, edited by Elaine Hobby (1999), provides an old-spelling text of Sharp's manual, and *The Collected Works of Anne Vaughan Lock*, edited by Susan M. Felch (1999), supplies old-spelling texts of Lock's prose, translations, and poetry.

In *Visionary Women* (1992), Phyllis Mack explores how writings by seventeenth-century religious women, especially Quakers, changed over time. Hilary Hinds's *God's Englishwomen* (1996) examines, in relation to modern feminist criticism, the writings of seventeenth-century women who were members of radical religious sects. In *Handmaid of the Holy Spirit* (1992), Cope argues that Eleanor Davies was a seventeenth-century feminist who overcame persecution. In *Margaret Cavendish and the Exiles of the Mind* (1998), Anna Battigelli considers Cavendish's exploration of scientific and philosophical ideas. Ruth Perry's *The Celebrated Mary Astell* (1986) emphasizes Astell's intellectual life and includes significant excerpts of her prose, with appendices containing her letters and poetry. Frances Teague's *Bathsua Makin, Woman of Learning* (1998) provides a biography of Makin in the context of women's history and a modernized text of *An Essay to Revive the Antient Education of Gentlewomen*.

Poetry

Kissing the Rod, edited by Germaine Greer, Susan Hastings, Jeslyn Medoff, and Melinda Sansone (1988), offers old-spelling texts of poems by approximately fifty seventeenth-century women poets, and *Women Poets of the Renaissance*, edited by Marion Wynne-Davies (1999), contains modernized extracts of works by thirteen poets, from Isabella Whitney to Anne Bradstreet. *The Collected Works of Mary Sidney Herbert, Countess of Pembroke*, edited by Margaret P. Hannay, Noel J. Kinnamon, and Michael G. Brennan (1998), contains old-spelling texts of the countess's poems, translations, and correspondence. *The Poems of Aemilia Lanyer*, edited by Susanne Woods (1993), provides an old-spelling edition of Lanyer's poems in *Salve Deus Rex Judaeorum*, and *Renaissance Women: The Plays of Elizabeth Cary, the Poems of Aemilia Lanyer*, edited by Diane Purkiss (1994), supplies modernized texts of them. In *The Poems of Lady Mary Wroth* (1983; rpt. 1992), editor Josephine A. Roberts furnishes old-spelling texts of Wroth's poems. *Divine Songs and Meditacions*, edited by Sidney Gottlieb (1996), contains old-spelling texts of An Collins's poems. In *The Southwell-Sibthorpe Commonplace Book* (1997), editor Jean Klene provides a diplomatic transcription of Anne Southwell's manuscript. Volume 1 of *The Collected Works of Katherine Philips, the Matchless Orinda*, edited by Patrick Thomas (1990), includes old-spelling texts of Philips's poems. *The Poems and Prose of Mary, Lady Chudleigh*, edited by Margaret J. M. Ezell (1993), offers old-spelling texts of Chudleigh's work. *The Uncollected Verse of Aphra Behn*, edited by Germaine Greer (1989), contains old-spelling texts of Behn's poems, as does volume 1 of *The Works of Aphra Behn*, edited by Janet Todd (1992). *The Poems of Aphra Behn*, also edited by Todd (1994), is a selection from her complete edition. Katherine Philips's *Poems, Plays, and Letters*, edited by Elizabeth H. Hageman and Andrea Sununu, is forthcoming.

Ann Rosalind Jones, *The Currency of Eros* (1990), examines strategies by which lyric poets from 1540 to 1620 in England, France, and Italy negotiate places for themselves within gender ideologies and lyric traditions. In *English Women's Poetry, 1649–1714* (1997), Carol Barash discusses writers—especially Katherine Philips, Aphra Behn, Anne Killigrew, Jane Barker, and Anne Finch—who shaped the public sense of what women write and how they are written about. Margaret P. Hannay's *Philip's Phoenix: Mary Sidney,*

Countess of Pembroke (1990) explores how Mary Sidney overcame gender restrictions to become a powerful Protestant voice. In *Lanyer: A Renaissance Woman Poet* (1999), Susanne Woods examines Lanyer's work in relation to that of male poets of her era such as Shakespeare and Ben Jonson. *Aemilia Lanyer: Gender, Genre, and the Canon*, edited by Marshall Grossman (1998), is a collection of essays on Lanyer's life and writing.

Prose Fiction

An Anthology of Seventeenth-Century Fiction, edited by Paul Salzman (1991), contains works by women and men, including modernized texts of Mary Wroth's *Urania* (book 1) and Margaret Cavendish's *Blazing World*. Paula R. Backscheider and John J. Richetti's *Popular Fiction by Women, 1660–1730* (1996) includes modernized texts of Aphra Behn's *History of the Nun*, Delariviere Manley's *Queen Zarah*, and Jane Barker's *Love Intrigues*. Josephine A. Robert's edition of *The First Part of the Countess of Montgomery's Urania* (1995) provides an old-spelling text of this earliest known work of prose fiction by a woman; the text of Mary Wroth's unpublished manuscript of the second part has been edited by Roberts and completed by Suzanne Gossett and Janel Mueller (1999). Patrick Colborn Cullen's edition of Anna Weamys's *Continuation of Sir Philip Sidney's Arcadia* (1994) offers two versions of the romance, a modernized edition for students and a corrected reprint edition for scholars. The Blazing World *and Other Writings*, edited by Kate Lilley (1992; rpt. 1994), contains partially modernized texts of Margaret Cavendish's "The Contract," "Assaulted and Pursued Chastity," and *The Blazing World*. In *Margaret Cavendish: Sociable Letters* (1997), James B. Fitzmaurice provides old-spelling texts of Cavendish's fictional correspondence. Volumes 2 and 3 of *The Works of Aphra Behn*, edited by Janet Todd (1993 and 1995), comprise Behn's prose fiction; Todd also has edited Oroonoko, The Rover, *and Other Works* (1992). Further volumes of Behn's prose are Oroonoko *and Other Writings*, edited by Paul Salzman (1994), which offers modernized texts of six pieces as well as a selection of poetry, and *Oroonoko*, edited by Joanna Lipking (1997), which provides a modernized text, contextual materials, and critical essays. The Galesia Trilogy *and Selected Manuscript Poems of Jane Barker*, edited by Carol Shiner Wilson (1997), contains old-spelling texts of Barker's novels.

Janet Todd's *The Sign of Angellica* (1989) examines Restoration writers' self-presentations and portraits of women, emphasizing Margaret Cavendish, Aphra Behn, and Delariviere Manley. Critical volumes treating Mary Wroth at length are Mary Ellen Lamb's *Gender and Authorship in the Sidney Circle* (1990); *Reading Mary Wroth*, edited by Naomi J. Miller and Gary Waller (1991); Gary Waller's *The Sidney Family Romance* (1993); Kim F. Hall's *Things of Darkness* (1995); and Naomi J. Miller's *Changing the Subject* (1996).

Biographical and Bibliographic Resources

Maureen Bell, George Parfitt, and Simon Shepherd's *A Biographical Dictionary of English Women Writers, 1580–1720* (1990) furnishes brief entries on the lives and writings of over 550 women. Brief entries on the lives and works of many early modern women also appear in *The Feminist Companion to Literature in English*, edited by Virginia Blain, Patricia Clements, and Isobel Grundy (1990). Hilda L. Smith and Susan Cardinale's *Women and the Literature of the Seventeenth Century* (1990) lists and describes seventeenth-century publications by women, as well as books for and about women. Bibliographies of editions and studies of early modern women writers (through 1674) can be found in special issues of *English Literary Renaissance* (Kinney and Farrell; Kinney and Hageman; Kinney and Jones).

———

Much remains to be done. We need more editions (and editing is a process in which students are eager to participate); we need more studies, especially of earlier writers for which studies are so few; and we need to continue the discussions of pedagogy that have begun in sessions at conferences in North America and abroad, in online news groups, in the special issue of *Shakespeare Quarterly*, and in this volume. Nonetheless, the new editions and critical studies discussed here testify that much has been done. They argue the vibrancy of early modern literary studies and the vitality of early modern women writers.

Notes

The quotation in the essay title is from Isabella Whitney, "To Her Sister Misteris A. B.," in *Sweet Nosgay*.

1. General anthologies may be appropriate for some survey courses in British or women's literature or for some women's studies courses. Volume 1 of the *Norton Anthology of English Literature* (Abrams et al.) contains more work by women than did early editions, but of the nearly 1,400 pages of Renaissance literature, approximately 50 are dedicated to nine women writers. Considerably more space is allotted in the *Norton Anthology of Literature by Women* (Gilbert and Gubar) and *British Women Writers: An Anthology from the Fourteenth Century to the Present* (Spender and Todd); the scope of these volumes is still sufficiently broad, however, that early modern women constitute a small percentage of the whole. Depending on course constraints, instructors may prefer to adopt one or more of the texts described elsewhere in this essay.

Notes on Contributors

Bernadette Andrea is assistant professor of English at the University of Texas, San Antonio, and previously has taught at West Virginia and Cornell Universities. While at Cornell, she was honored with several teaching awards, including a Clark Distinguished Teaching Award. She has published articles on Mary Wroth's *Urania*, Ben Jonson's queen's masques, Ottoman mappings of the New World, and postcolonial readings of early modern women's writing. She is currently completing a book on cultural encounters between England and Islam in the early modern period.

Stephen C. Behrendt is George Holmes Distinguished Professor of English at the University of Nebraska, Lincoln. Among his books are *Shelley and His Audiences* (1989), *Reading William Blake* (1992), and *Royal Mourning and Regency Culture: Elegies and Memorials of Princess Charlotte* (1997). He edited *Approaches to Teaching Shelley's* Frankenstein (1990) and coedited *Approaches to Teaching British Women Poets of the Romantic Period* (1997). Current projects involve books on historically marginalized women writers of the Romantic period, especially the relations in their works of radical politics, social critique, and gender delineation.

Elaine V. Beilin is professor of English at Framingham State College and recipient of the 1999 Distinguished Faculty Award. She is the editor of *The Examinations of Anne Askew* and the author of *Redeeming Eve: Women Writers of the English Renaissance* and numerous articles on early modern women writers. She was the 1999 president of the Society for the Study of Early Modern Women and is currently working on a study of women as writers of history.

Pamela J. Benson is the author of *The Invention of the Renaissance Woman* (Penn State) and *Italian Tales from the Age of Shakespeare* (Everyman). She has written numerous articles on English and Italian Renaissance literature and culture. She is professor of English at Rhode Island College.

Patricia Brace is assistant professor of English at Laurentian University, Sudbury, Canada. She is currently editing Elizabeth Tyrwhit's *Morning and Euening Praiers* for the Ashgate Press series The Early Modern Englishwoman: A Facsimile Library of Essential Works.

Elizabeth Clarke is research lecturer at Nottingham Trent University, where she directs the British Academy–funded Perdita Project for Early Modern Women's Manuscript Compilations. She has published a book on George Herbert with Oxford University Press and coedited a book of essays with Danielle Clarke, *The Double Voice: Gendered Writing in Early Modern England* (Macmillan, forthcoming).

Frances E. Dolan is associate professor of English at Miami University, Ohio. She is the author of *Dangerous Familiars: Representations of Domestic Crime in England, 1550–1700* (Cornell, 1994) and the editor of The Taming of the Shrew*: Texts and Contexts* (Bedford, 1996). Her essay in this volume draws from her forthcoming book *Whores of Babylon: Catholicism, Gender, and Seventeenth-Century English Print Culture* (Cornell UP) and from her essay "Reading, Writing, and Other Crimes" (*Feminist Readings of Early Modern Culture: Emerging Subjects*, ed. Valerie Traub, M. Lindsay Kaplan, and Dympna Callaghan, Cambridge UP, 1996).

Susan M. Felch is associate professor of English at Calvin College. She is the editor of *The Collected Works of Anne Vaughan Lock* (RETS, 1999) and the author of articles ranging from sixteenth-century British writers to Mikhail Bakhtin.

Germaine Greer is professor of English and comparative studies at the University of Warwick. She is also director of Stump Cross Books, which publishes scholarly editions of early modern women's poetry.

Elizabeth H. Hageman, professor of English at the University of New Hampshire, Durham, is editing (with Andrea Sununu) an edition of the poems, plays, and letters of Katherine Philips. With Susanne Woods she is co–general editor of the Oxford University Press series Women Writers in English, 1350–1850. In 1996 she and Sara Jayne Steen compiled *Teaching Judith Shakespeare*, a special edition of *Shakespeare Quarterly* treating methods of teaching women writers with Shakespeare's texts.

Kim F. Hall teaches English and women's studies at Georgetown University, where she is associate professor. She is author of *Things of Darkness: Economies of Race and Gender in Early Modern England* and of multiple essays on racial formations in the Renaissance. She is currently working on a book, "A Taste of Empire: Women, Gender, and Material Culture," that examines the roles of women in the seventeenth-century sugar trade.

Margaret P. Hannay, professor of English literature at Siena College, has edited *The Collected Works of Mary Sidney Herbert, Countess of Pembroke* with Noel J. Kinnamon and Michael G. Brennan (Clarendon, 1998). She is the author of *Philip's Phoenix: Mary Sidney, Countess of Pembroke* (Oxford UP, 1990) and editor of *Silent but for the Word: Tudor Women as Patrons, Translators, and Writers of Religious Works* (Kent State UP, 1985).

Elaine Hobby has been researching seventeenth-century women's writing since 1978 and finds it even more wonderful, and stranger, as the years pass. She is the author of *Virtue of Necessity: English Women's Writing, 1649–1688* (Virago, 1988; U of Michigan P, 1989) and co-editor of *Her Own Life: Autobiographical Writings by Seventeenth-Century Englishwomen* (Routledge, 1989). She works very happily at Loughborough University, England.

Suzanne W. Hull is the author of two books on Tudor-Stuart women: *Chaste, Silent, and Obedient: English Books for Women, 1475–1640* (1982, 1988) and *Women according to Men: The World of Tudor-Stuart Women* (1996). She was the first woman appointed as one of the principal officers of the Huntington Library, Art Gallery and Botanical Gardens, where she also helped found the ongoing Women's Studies Seminar in 1984.

Ann Hurley is associate professor of English at Wagner College, where she teaches early modern literature. Her most recent publication is *So Rich a Tapestry: The Sister Arts and Cultural Studies* (Bucknell UP, 1995), and she is currently finishing "Donne's Poetry and

Visual Culture." She is also working on a critical edition of *The Frolicks; or, The Lawyer Cheated*, a seventeenth-century comedy by Elizabeth Polwhele.

Robin Ikegami teaches courses in eighteenth-century British literature and women's literature at Xavier University, Ohio, where she is associate professor. Her research interests vary, but right now she is focusing on the idea of the exotic in the British imagination.

Erna Kelly, professor of English at the University of Wisconsin, Eau Claire, has published essays on a range of topics, including emblem books, women's wit, and women's diaries and journals. Her current project is on rhetorical stances in the works of Margaret Cavendish.

Gwynne Kennedy is associate professor of English at the University of Wisconsin, Milwaukee, where she teaches early modern literature (including women writers) and women's studies courses. She has written articles on Elizabeth Cary, and her book, *Just Anger*, examines representations of women's anger in early modern texts by women.

John N. King is professor of English at Ohio State University, Columbus. Among his books are *English Reformation Literature: The Tudor Origins of the Protestant Tradition* (1982), *Tudor Royal Iconography: Literature and Art in an Age of Religious Crisis* (1989), and *Spenser's Poetry and the Reformation Tradition* (1990), all published by Princeton University Press. He serves as coeditor of *Literature and History*, literature editor of *Reformation*, and advisory board member for the British Academy project to edit John Foxe's *Acts and Monuments of the Christian Martyrs*.

Mary Ellen Lamb is the author of *Gender and Authorship in the Sidney Circle* (U of Wisconsin P, 1990) as well as numerous essays in such journals as *Criticism, English Literary Renaissance, Shakespeare Survey,* and *Shakespeare Studies.* She is currently working on a book-length project on the role of old wives' tales in the works of Sidney, Spenser, and Shakespeare.

Carole Levin is professor of history at the University of Nebraska, Lincoln. For a number of years she taught at the State University of New York, New Paltz, where she received the Chancellor's Award for excellence in teaching. She has published widely in sixteenth-century cultural history and women's history and is the author of *The Heart and Stomach of a King: Elizabeth I and the Politics of Sex and Power* (U of Pennsylvania P, 1994) and coeditor with Patricia Sullivan of *Political Rhetoric, Power, and Renaissance Women* (State U of New York P, 1995).

Barbara K. Lewalski is William R. Kenan, Jr., Professor of History and Literature and of English Literature at Harvard University. Her most recent books are *Writing Women in Jacobean England* (Harvard UP, 1993), Paradise Lost *and the Rhetoric of Literary Forms* (Princeton UP, 1985), and an edition of *The Polemics and Poems of Rachel Speght* (Oxford UP, 1996). She is an editor of the *Norton Anthology of English Literature* and is now finishing a critical biography of Milton.

Paula Loscocco is associate professor at Barnard College, where she teaches Renaissance and seventeenth-century English literature. She has written essays on Katherine Philips, John Milton, and Laurence Sterne and is currently completing a book entitled "Eikonoklastic Song: Milton and Royalist Poetics." She is also preparing a facsimile edition of Philips's 1667 *Poems*.

Lynette F. McGrath teaches English and women's studies courses at West Chester University. She has published widely in Renaissance literature, women's poetry, and feminist theory. She teaches graduate and undergraduate courses in early modern women's culture and writing. She is currently coordinator of the English graduate program. She has just completed a book, *Walking on the Ridge: Women's Poetry in Early Modern England.*

Naomi J. Miller is associate professor of English and women's studies at the University of Arizona. Her publications on early modern women writers and gender include a book-length study of Mary Wroth entitled *Changing the Subject* (UP of Kentucky, 1996); a collection of essays on Wroth entitled *Reading Mary Wroth* (U of Tennessee P, 1991); and various articles on Aemilia Lanyer, Elizabeth Cary, Shakespeare, and early modern conceptions of gender and maternity. She is currently working on a book on representations of maternity in early modern England and has coedited with Naomi Yavneh an interdisciplinary collection of essays entitled *Maternal Measures: Figuring Caregiving in the Early Modern Period* (Ashgate, 2000).

Janel Mueller is William Rainey Harper Professor of English and Humanities and dean of humanities at the University of Chicago. She has published critical essays on several Tudor and Stuart women writers—including Queen Katherine Parr, Elizabeth I, and Aemilia Lanyer—and is currently editing Parr's writings and correspondence. With Suzanne Gossett she completed the late Josephine Roberts's edition of *The Second Part of the Countess of Montgomery's Urania*, and with Leah Marcus and Mary Beth Rose she has edited the works of Queen Elizabeth (U of Chicago P, 2000).

Elizabeth Patton is a visiting assistant professor in the Humanities Center at Johns Hopkins University. Her research interests include women as writers and educators in early modern Europe. She has published articles on Juan Luis Vives as a proponent of women's education and is currently at work on a study of women's education in the early Renaissance, with particular regard to its problematic roots in the classical rhetorical tradition.

Anne Lake Prescott, who teaches at Barnard College and Columbia University, is the author of *French Poets and the English Renaissance* (Yale UP, 1978) and *Imagining Rabelais in Renaissance England* (Yale UP, 1998). She is coeditor with Hugh Maclean of the *Norton Critical Edition of Edmund Spenser*; with Thomas P. Roche, Jr., of *Spenser Studies*; and with Patrick Cheney of a collection of essays for the MLA, *Approaches to Teaching Shorter Elizabethan Poetry*. She and Betty Travitsky have recently completed an anthology juxtaposing texts by early modern women and men, *Female and Male Voices in Early Modern England* (Columbia UP, 2000).

Josephine A. Roberts was William A. Read Professor of English Literature at Louisiana State University until her tragic death in August 1996. She edited *The Poems of Lady Mary Wroth* (1983, 1992) and *The First Part of the Countess of Montgomery's Urania* (RETS/ MRTS, 1995) and had begun an edition of Wroth's Newberry MS completion of *Urania*, which was completed by Suzanne Gossett and Janel Mueller as *The Second Part of the Countess of Montgomery's Urania* (RETS/ MRTS, 1999).

Anne Shaver is Lorena Woodrow Burke Professor of English at Denison University. Her edition The Convent of Pleasure *and Other Plays* (Johns Hopkins UP, 1999) contains four of Cavendish's plays: *Convent, Loves Adventures Parts 1 and 2, Bell in Campo Parts 1 and 2,* and *The Bridals.*

Mary V. Silcox is associate professor at McMaster University, Ontario. Her major areas of scholarly interest are English emblem books and early modern English poetry. She has most recently published *The English Emblem Tradition*, volume 4, an ongoing series coedited with Peter M. Daly, and articles on Puttenham's *Arte of English Poesie* and Combe's *Theater of Fine Devices.*

Sara Jayne Steen, professor and chair of English at Montana State University, Bozeman, is the author of numerous books and articles on early modern women writers, Shakespeare, and drama. Most recently she published *The Letters of Lady Arbella Stuart* (Oxford UP, 1994) and, with Elizabeth H. Hageman, edited a special issue of *Shakespeare Quarterly* on teaching Shakespeare with early modern women writers. She has received her university's highest honors in both scholarship and teaching.

Betty S. Travitsky, of the Center for the Study of Women and Society, Graduate Center, City University of New York, is editor of *Paradise of Women: Writings by Englishwomen of the Renaissance*; coeditor of *The Renaissance Englishwoman in Print: Counterbalancing the Canon, Attending to Women in Early Modern England,* and *Female and Male Voices in Early Modern England*; and author of many articles and reviews. With Patrick Cullen she coedits, for Ashgate Press, The Early Modern Englishwoman: A Facsimile Library of Essential Works, 1500–1750, and Women and Gender in Early Modern England, 1500–1750, and she is preparing, for Cambridge University Press, *The Cambridge Critical Bibliography of English Women Writers, 1500–1640*.

Wendy Wall is associate professor of English literature at Northwestern University, where she teaches early modern English literature and culture (1500–1650). Author of *The Imprint of Gender: Authorship and Publication in the English Renaissance* (1993) and currently at work on a book tentatively entitled "In the Nation's Kitchen: Domesticity and Englishness in Early Modern Drama," she was recently appointed the Wender-Lewis Research and Teaching Professor.

Gary F. Waller is professor of literature and cultural studies and vice president for academic affairs at the State University of New York, Purchase College. He has published more than a dozen books and many articles, mainly on early modern literature. These include *The Sidney Family Romance: Mary Wroth, William Herbert, and the Early Modern Construction of Gender*; *English Poetry of the Sixteenth Century*; *Spenser: A Literary Life*; and *Mary Sidney, Countess of Pembroke*. He has edited works by Mary Sidney and Mary Wroth. He has published two collections of poetry. His study of gender crossing in Shakespeare is forthcoming.

Barry Weller has coedited *The Tragedy of Mariam* and *The Lady Falkland: Her Life* (U of California P, 1994) with Margaret Ferguson and Byron's dramas for *The Complete Poetical Works of Lord Byron* (Oxford UP) with Jerome McGann. He teaches Renaissance and nineteenth-century literature at the University of Utah; his essays in these and other fields have appeared in *New Literary History, English Literary History, Modern Language Notes, Kenyon Review,* as well as the recent collection *Novel-Gazing* and *The Columbia Companion to the Twentieth-Century American Short Story.*

Susanne Woods, provost and professor of English at Wheaton College, Massachusetts, founded the Brown University Women Writers Project. She has been professor of English and also served in academic administration at Brown University and Franklin and Marshall College. Her publications include *Natural Emphasis: English Versification from Chaucer to Dryden* (Huntington Lib., 1984) and *Lanyer: A Renaissance Woman Poet* (Oxford UP, 1999). With Elizabeth H. Hageman she is co–general editor of the Oxford University Press series Women Writers in English, 1350–1850, for which she edited *The Poems of Aemilia Lanyer* (1993).

Ramona Wray is a lecturer in English literature at the Queen's University of Belfast. She is the coeditor of *Shakespeare and Ireland: History, Politics, Culture* (Macmillan, 1997) and of *Shakespeare, Film, Fin de Siècle* (Macmillan, 2000). Also the author of *Women Writers of the Seventeenth Century* (Northcote, 2001), she is currently working on *Women, Writing, Revolution: An Anthology of Writing by Women during the English Civil War* for Blackwell.

Georgianna Ziegler is Louis B. Thalheimer Reference Librarian at the Folger Shakespeare Library in Washington, DC, where she does presentations on bibliographic searching. She has published on the depiction of women by Greene, Montaigne, and Shakespeare and on the calligrapher Esther Inglis. She is preparing an exhibition and catalog on Elizabeth I for the 400th anniversary, in 2003, of Elizabeth's death.

Works Cited

Abrams, M. H., et al., eds. *The Norton Anthology of English Literature.* 6th ed. 2 vols. New York: Norton, 1993.

Adams, Thomas. *Mystical Bedlam; or, The World of Mad-Men.* London, 1615.

Alcoff, Linda. "Cultural Feminism versus Post-structuralism." *Signs* 13 (1988): 405–36.

Alexander, Gavin. "Constant Works: A Framework for Reading Mary Wroth." *Sidney Journal* 14 (1996–97): 5–32.

———. "Five Responses to Sir Philip Sidney, 1586–1828." Diss. U of Cambridge, 1996.

Allison, A. F., and D. M. Rogers. *The Contemporary Printed Literature of the English Counter-Reformation between 1558 and 1640.* 2 vols. New York: Scolar, 1990–94.

Amussen, Susan Dwyer. *An Ordered Society: Gender and Class in Early Modern England.* Oxford: Blackwell, 1988.

Amussen, Susan Dwyer, and Adele Seeff, eds. *Attending to Early Modern Women.* Newark: U of Delaware P; London: Assoc. U Presses, 1998.

Anderson, Judith. *Biographical Truth: The Representation of Historical Persons in Tudor-Stuart Writing.* New Haven: Yale UP, 1984.

[Anger, Jane]. *Jane Anger Her Protection for Women.* London, 1589. *Women Writers Project.* 4 Apr. 2000 <http://www.wwp.brown.edu/texts/index.html>. Excerpted in Henderson and McManus 172–88.

Applegate, Joan. "Katherine Philips's 'Orinda upon Little Hector': An Un-recorded Musical Setting by Henry Lawes." *English Manuscript Studies, 1100–1700* 4 (1993): 272–80.

Armstrong, Isobel, ed. *New Feminist Discourses: Critical Essays on Theories and Texts.* London: Routledge, 1992.

The Arraignment and Burning of Margaret Ferneseede. 1608. Henderson and McManus 351–59.

Ascham, Roger. *The Schoolmaster.* 1570. Ed. Lawrence V. Ryan. Char-lottesville: UP of Virginia, 1967.

Askew, Anne. *The Examinations of Anne Askew.* Ed. John Bale. Marburg, 1546; London, 1547.

———. *The Examinations of Anne Askew.* Ed. Elaine V. Beilin. New York: Oxford UP, 1996.

Astell, Mary. *A Serious Proposal to the Ladies for the Advancement of Their True and Greatest Interest.* 1694, 1697. Excerpted in Goreau, *Whole Duty* 242–55.

Atkinson, Colin B., and Jo B. Atkinson. "Anne Wheathill's *A Handfull of Holesome (Though Homelie) Hearbs* (1584): The First English Gentle-woman's Prayer Book." *Seventeenth-Century Journal* 27 (1996): 659–72.

Aughterson, Kate, ed. *Renaissance Woman: A Sourcebook: Constructions of Femininity in England.* London: Routledge, 1995.

Aylmer, John. *An Harborowe for Faithfull and Trewe Subjectes.* London, 1559.

Backscheider, Paula R., and John J. Richetti, eds. *Popular Fiction by Women, 1660–1730.* Oxford: Clarendon, 1996.

Bacon, Francis. *The New Atlantis.* London, 1626–27.

———. *Of the Proficience and Advancement of Learning Divine and Hu-mane.* 1605. Ed. James Spedding. Boston: Taggard, 1863. Vol. 6 of *The Works of Francis Bacon.*

Baer, Cynthia Marie. "Wise and Worthier Women: Lady Mary Wroth's *Urania* and the Development of Women's Narrative." Diss. U of Wash-ington, 1993.

Ballard, George. *Memoirs of Several Ladies of Great Britain Who Have Been Celebrated for Their Writings or Skill in the Learned Languages, Arts and Sciences.* Oxford, 1752. Detroit: Wayne State UP, 1985.

Ballaster, Ros. "Aphra Behn and the Female Plot." Hutner 187–211.

Barash, Carol. *English Women's Poetry, 1649–1714: Politics, Community, and Linguistic Authority.* Oxford: Oxford UP, 1997.

Barker, Felix, and Peter Jackson. *The History of London in Maps.* London: Barry, 1990.

Barker, Jane. *The Galesia Trilogy and Selected Manuscript Poems of Jane Barker.* Ed. Carol Shiner Wilson. New York: Oxford UP, 1997.

Barton, William. *Six Centuries of Selected Hymns and Spiritual Songs, Col-lected out of the Bible: Together with a Catechism, the Canticles, and a*

Catalogue of Vertuous Women, by William Barton. 4th ed. London: Heptinstall, 1688.

Bassin, Donna. "Women's Images of Inner Space: Data towards Expanded Interpretive Categories." *International Review of Psychoanalysis* 9 (1982): 191–203.

Battigelli, Anna. *Margaret Cavendish and the Exiles of the Mind.* Lexington: UP of Kentucky, 1998.

Beck, Margaret. *The Reward of Oppression, Tyranny, and Injustice.* London, 1655.

Behn, Aphra. *Aphra Behn: The* Rover *and Other Plays.* Ed. Jane Spencer. Oxford: Oxford UP, 1995.

———. "The Disappointment." *The Other Eighteenth Century: English Women of Letters, 1660–1800.* Ed. Robert W. Uphaus and Gretchen M. Foster. East Lansing: Colleagues, 1991. 53–57.

———. *Love Letters between a Nobleman and His Sister.* Ed. Maureen Duffy. London: Virago, 1987.

———. Oroonoko *and Other Writings.* Ed. Paul Salzman. Oxford: Oxford UP, 1994.

———. Oroonoko, The Rover, *and Other Works.* Ed. Janet Todd. London: Penguin, 1992.

———. *The Poems of Aphra Behn: A Selection.* Ed. Janet Todd. New York: New York UP, 1994.

———. *The Rover.* Ed. Anne Russell. Peterborough, ON: Broadview, 1994.

———. *The Second Part of the Rover.* London, 1681.

———. *The Uncollected Verse of Aphra Behn.* Ed. Germaine Greer. Stump Cross, Eng.: Stump Cross, 1989.

———. *The Works of Aphra Behn.* Ed. Janet Todd. 7 vols. Columbus: Ohio State UP, 1992–96.

Beilin, Elaine V. Introduction. Askew, *Examinations* [Beilin] xv–xliii.

———. *Redeeming Eve: Women Writers of the English Renaissance.* Princeton: Princeton UP, 1987.

———. " 'Some Freely Spake Their Minde': Resistance in Anne Dowriche's *French Historie.*" Donawerth, Burke, Dove, and Nelson, *Women* 119–40.

———. "Winning 'the Harts of the People': The Role of the Political Subject in Wroth's *Urania.*" S. King 1–18.

———. "Writing Public Poetry: Humanism and the Woman Writer." *Modern Language Quarterly* 51 (1990): 249–71.

Bell, Maureen, George Parfitt, and Simon Shepherd. *A Biographical Dictionary of English Women Writers, 1580–1720.* Boston: Hall, 1990.

Belsey, Catherine. "Silence and Speech." *The Subject of Tragedy: Identity and Difference in Renaissance Drama.* London: Routledge, 1985. 149–91.

Benjamin, Jessica. *The Bonds of Love: Psychoanalysis, Feminism, and the Problem of Domination.* New York: Pantheon, 1988.

Benson, Pamela Joseph. *The Invention of the Renaissance Woman: The Challenge of Female Independence in the Literature and Thought of Italy and England*. University Park: Pennsylvania State UP, 1992.

Bentley, Thomas. *The Monument of Matrons*. London, 1582.

Bethune, George W., ed. *The British Female Poets: with Biographical and Critical Notices*. Philadelphia, 1848.

Bevington, David. "A. L. Rowse's Dark Lady." Grossman 10–24.

Blain, Virginia, Patricia Clements, and Isobel Grundy, eds. *The Feminist Companion to Literature in English: Women Writers from the Middle Ages to the Present*. New Haven: Yale UP, 1990.

Bloch, Chana. *Spelling the Word: George Herbert and the Bible*. Berkeley: U of California P, 1985.

Bossy, John. *The English Catholic Community, 1570–1850*. New York: Oxford UP, 1976.

Bowerbank, Sylvia, and Sara Mendelson, eds. *Paper Bodies: A Margaret Cavendish Reader*. Orchard Park: Broadview, 2000.

Bradstreet, Anne. *The Four Monarchies*. Bradstreet, *Works* 73–178.

———. "The Prologue." Bradstreet, *Works* 15–17.

———. *The Works of Anne Bradstreet*. Ed. Jeannine Hensley. Cambridge: Harvard UP, 1967.

Brant, Clare, and Diane Purkiss, eds. *Women, Texts and Histories, 1575–1760*. London: Routledge, 1992.

Brantenberg, Gerd. *Egalia's Daughters*. Trans. Louis Mackay with Brantenberg. Seattle: Seal, 1978.

Brennan, Michael G. *Literary Patronage in the English Renaissance: The Pembroke Family*. London: Routledge, 1988.

Brink, Jean R., ed. *Privileging Gender in Early Modern England*. Sixteenth-Century Essays and Studies 23. Kirksville: Sixteenth-Century Journal, 1993.

Brooke, Tucker. "Queen Elizabeth's Prayers." *Huntington Library Quarterly* 2 (1938–39): 69–77.

Browne, William. "An Elegy on the Countess Dowager of Pembroke." *Poems of William Browne of Tavistock*. Ed. Gordon Goodwin. London: Routledge, 1893. 249.

Burke, Victoria E. "Women and Seventeenth-Century Manuscript Culture: Miscellanies, Commonplace Books, and Song Books Compiled by English and Scottish Women, 1600–1660." Diss. U of Oxford, 1996.

Butler, Judith. *Gender Trouble: Feminism and the Subversion of Identity*. London: Routledge, 1990.

———. "Performative Acts and Gender Constitution: An Essay in Phenomenology and Feminist Theory." *Performing Feminisms: Feminist Critical Theory and Theatre*. Ed. Sue-Ellen Case. Baltimore: Johns Hopkins UP, 1990. 270–82.

Byrne, Muriel St. Clair, ed. *The Lisle Letters*. 6 vols. Chicago: U of Chicago P, 1981.

————. *The Lisle Letters: An Abridgement.* Selected by Bridget Boland. Chicago: U of Chicago P, 1983.

Camden, Carroll. *The Elizabethan Woman.* Houston: Elsevier, 1958.

Camden, William. *The History of the Most Renowned and Victorious Princess Elizabeth.* 1688. Ed. Wallace T. MacCaffrey. Chicago: U of Chicago P, 1970.

Carleton, Mary. *The Case of Madam Mary Carleton, Lately Stiled the German Princess.* London, 1663.

————. *An Historicall Narrative of the German Princess.* London, 1663.

Carrell, Jennifer Lee. "A Pack of Lies in a Looking Glass: Lady Mary Wroth's *Urania* and the Magic Mirror of Romance." *Studies in English Literature* 34 (1994): 79–107.

Cary, Elizabeth. *The Tragedy of Mariam, the Fair Queen of Jewry.* Weller and Ferguson, Tragedy 61–176.

Cary, Mary. "England's Fall from (the Mystical Babylon) Rome." 1648. Excerpt in Otten 100–03.

Cavanagh, Sheila T. *Wanton Eyes and Chaste Desires: Female Sexuality in The Fairie Queene.* Bloomington: Indiana UP, 1994.

Cavendish, Jane, and Elizabeth Brackley. *The Concealed Fancies.* Cerasano and Wynne-Davies, *Renaissance Drama* 127–54.

Cavendish, Margaret. *The Blazing World.* Salzman 249–348.

————. The Blazing World *and Other Writings.* Ed. Kate Lilley. London: Penguin, 1994.

————. *The Convent of Pleasure and Other Plays.* Ed. Anne Shaver. Baltimore: Johns Hopkins UP, 1999.

————. *The Description of a New World, Called the Blazing World.* London, 1668.

————. *De Vita et Rebus Gestis Nobilisseme Illustrissimique Principis, Guilielmi Ducis Novocastrensis, commentarii.* Trans. Walter Charleton. London, 1668.

————. *Divers Orations.* London, 1662.

————. *Grounds of Natural Philosophy.* London, 1668.

————. *The Life of the Thrice Noble, High, and Puissant Prince William Cavendishe, Duke, Marquess, and Earl of Newcastle.* London, 1667, 1675.

————. *The Lives of William Cavendishe, Duke of Newcastle, and of His Wife, Margaret, Duchess of Newcastle. Written by the Thrice Noble and Illustrious Princess, Margaret, Duchess of Newcastle.* Ed. Mark Antony Lower. London: Smith, 1872.

————. *Margaret Cavendish: Sociable Letters.* Ed. James B. Fitzmaurice. New York: Garland, 1997.

————. *Natures Pictures Drawn by Fancies Pencil to the Life.* London, 1656. *Early English Books, 1641–1700.* London, 1671.

————. *Observations upon Experimental Philosophy, to Which Is Added, the Description of a New Blazing World.* London, 1666.

————. *Orations of Divers Sorts.* London, 1662.

————. *Philosophical and Physical Opinions.* London, 1655.

————. *Philosophical Fancies.* London, 1653.

————. *Playes.* London, 1662.

————. *Plays Never Before Printed.* London, 1668.

————. *Poems and Fancies.* London, 1653. Menston, Eng.: Scolar, 1972.

————. "A True Relation of My Birth, Breeding, and Life." *Natures Pictures* [1656].

————. *CCXI Sociable Letters.* London, 1664. Menston, Eng.: Scolar, 1969.

————. *The World's Olio.* London, 1655.

Cavendish, William, ed. *Letters and Poems in Honour of the Incomparable Princess, Margaret, Dutchess of Newcastle.* London, 1676.

Cellier, Elizabeth. *Malice Defeated; or, A Brief Relation of the Accusation and Deliverance of Elizabeth Cellier.* London, 1680. Ed. Anne Barbeau Gardiner. Los Angeles: Clark Memorial Lib., 1988.

Cerasano, S. P., and Marion Wynne-Davies, eds. *Gloriana's Face: Women, Public and Private, in the English Renaissance.* Detroit: Wayne State UP, 1992.

————, eds. *Readings in Renaissance Women's Drama: Criticism, History, and Performance, 1594–1998.* London: Routledge, 1998.

————, eds. *Renaissance Drama by Women: Texts and Documents.* London: Routledge, 1996.

Chartier, Roger. "Reading Practices." *The Passions of the Renaissance.* Ed. Chartier. Cambridge: Harvard UP, 1989. 111–57. Vol. 3 of *A History of Private Life.*

Chedgzoy, Kate, Melanie Hansen, and Suzanne Trill, eds. *Voicing Women: Gender and Sexuality in Early Modern Writing.* Pittsburgh: Duquesne UP, 1998.

Christensen, Kimberly. E-mail to Gary Waller. May 1997.

————. " 'With Whom Do You Believe Your Lot Is Cast?' White Feminists and Racism." *Signs* 22 (1997): 617–48.

Christine de Pisan. *The Boke of the Cyte of Ladys.* Trans. Brian Anslay. London, 1521.

Chudleigh, Mary. *The Poems and Prose of Mary, Lady Chudleigh.* Ed. Margaret J. M. Ezell. New York: Oxford UP, 1993.

Cixous, Hélène. "Castration or Decapitation?" *Signs* 7 (1981): 41–55.

Clancy, Thomas H. *English Catholic Books, 1641–1700: A Bibliography.* Chicago: Loyola UP, 1974.

Clarendon, Edward. *The History of the Rebellion and Civil Wars in England Begun in the Year 1641, Re-edited from a Fresh Collacion of the Original Ms. in the Bodleian Library.* Ed. W. Dunn Macray. Oxford: Clarendon, 1888.

Clay, William Keating, ed. *Liturgical Services: Liturgies and Occasional Forms of Prayer Set Forth in the Reign of Queen Elizabeth.* Parker Soc. 30. Cambridge: Cambridge UP, 1848.

Clifford, Anne. *The Diaries of Lady Anne Clifford*. Ed. D. J. H. Clifford. Stroud, Eng.: Sutton, 1990.

———. *The Diary of Lady Anne Clifford with an Introductory Note by V. Sackville-West*. London: Heinemann, 1924.

———. *Lives of Lady Anne Clifford, Countess of Dorset, Pembroke and Montgomery and of Her Parents, Summarized by Herself*. Ed. J. P. Gilson. Roxburghe Club. London: Hazell, 1916.

Clifford, D. J. H. Introduction. A. Clifford, *Diaries* x–xv.

Clinton, Elizabeth. *The Countesse of Lincolnes Nurserie*. London, 1622. *Women Writers Project*. 4 Apr. 2000 <http://www.wwp.brown.edu/texts/index.html>.

Coiro, Ann Baynes. "Writing in Service: Sexual Politics and Class Position in the Poetry of Aemelia Lanyer and Ben Jonson." *Criticism* 35 (1993): 357–77.

Collins, An. *Divine Songs and Meditacions*. Ed. Sidney Gottlieb. Renaissance English Text Soc. / Medieval and Renaissance Texts and Studies. Tempe: Arizona Center for Medieval and Renaissance Studies, 1996.

Collinson, Patrick. "Windows in a Woman's Soul: Questions about the Religion of Queen Elizabeth I." *Elizabethan Essays*. London: Hambledon, 1994. 87–118.

Combahee River Collective. "A Black Feminist Statement." *All the Women Are White, All the Blacks Are Men, but Some of Us Are Brave*. Ed. Gloria T. Hull, Patricia Bell Scott, and Barbara Smith. New York: Feminist, 1982. 13–22.

Constantia Munda. *The Worming of a Mad Dogge; or, A Soppe for Cerberus the Jaylor of Hell. No Confutation but a Sharpe Redargation of the Bayter of Women*. London, 1617. Excerpted in Henderson and McManus 244–63.

Cope, Esther S. *Handmaid of the Holy Spirit: Dame Eleanor Davies, Never Soe Mad a Ladie*. Ann Arbor: U of Michigan P, 1992.

Costello, Louisa Stuart. *Memoirs of Eminent Englishwomen*. 4 vols. London: Bentley, 1844.

Cotton, Nancy. *Women Playwrights in England, c. 1363–1750*. Lewisburg: Bucknell UP, 1980.

Cotton, Priscilla, and Mary Cole. *To the Priests and People of England, We Discharge Our Consciences, and Give Them Warning*. 1655.

Crandall, Coryl, ed. Swetnam the Woman-Hater: *The Controversy and the Play*. Lafayette: Purdue UP, 1969.

Crane, Mary Thomas. *Framing Authority: Sayings, Self, and Society in Sixteenth-Century England*. Princeton: Princeton UP, 1993.

Crawford, Patricia. "The Construction and Experience of Maternity in Seventeenth-Century England." Fildes 3–38.

———. *Women and Religion in England, 1500–1720*. London: Routledge, 1993.

———. "Women's Published Writings." M. Prior 211–82.

Cressy, David. *Literacy and the Social Order: Reading and Writing in Tudor and Stuart England.* Cambridge: Cambridge UP, 1980.

Crosby, Christina. "Dealing with Differences." *Feminists Theorize the Political.* Ed. Judith Butler and Joan W. Scott. London: Routledge, 1992. 130–43.

Cruz, Anne J. "Chains of Desire: Luisa de Carvajal y Mendoza's Poetics of Penance." *Estudios sobre escritoras hispánicas en honor de Georgina Sabat-Rivers.* Ed. Lou Charnon-Deutsch. Madrid: Castalia, 1992. 97–112.

Daniel, Samuel. *Delia.* 1592. Rpt. as *Samuel Daniel and a Defence of Rhyme.* Ed. Arthur Sprague. Chicago: U of Chicago P, 1930.

———. *The Tragedie of Cleopatra.* London: Waterson, 1611.

Dash, Irene. "Single-Sex Retreats in Two Early Modern Dramas: *Love's Labor's Lost* and *The Convent of Pleasure.*" *Shakespeare Quarterly* 47 (1996): 387–95.

Davenant, William. *The Play House to Be Let.* Edinburgh: Paterson; London: Sotheran, 1873. Vol. 4 of *The Dramatic Works of Sir William D'Avenant.*

Davies, Eleanor. *Prophetic Writings of Lady Eleanor Davies.* Ed. Esther S. Cope. New York: Oxford UP, 1995.

Davies, John. *The Muse's Sacrifice.* London: Snodham, 1612.

Davis, Natalie Zemon. "Gender and Genre: Women as Historical Writers, 1400–1820." *Beyond Their Sex: Learned Women of the European Past.* Ed. Patricia H. Labalme. New York: New York UP, 1984. 153–82.

Davis, Natalie Zemon, and Arlette Farge, eds. *Renaissance and Enlightenment Paradoxes.* Cambridge: Belknap–Harvard UP, 1993. Vol. 3 of *A History of Women in the West.*

Daybell, James, ed. *Women's Letters and Letter Writing in England, 1450–1700.* London: Macmillan, forthcoming.

de Grazia, Margreta. *Shakespeare Verbatim: The Reproduction of Authenticity and the 1790 Apparatus.* Oxford: Oxford UP, 1991.

de Grazia, Margreta, and Peter Stallybrass. "The Materiality of the Shakespearean Text." *Shakespeare Quarterly* 44 (1993): 255–83.

Delany, Paul. *British Autobiography in the Seventeenth Century.* London: Routledge; New York: Columbia UP, 1969.

de Lauretis, Teresa. "The Technology of Gender." *Technologies of Gender.* Bloomington: Indiana UP, 1987. 1–30.

Díaz, Bernal. "Doña Marina's Story." *The Conquest of New Spain.* Trans. J. M. Cohen. Harmondsworth: Penguin, 1963. 85–87.

Diehl, Huston. *Staging Reform, Reforming the Stage: Protestantism and Popular Theater in Early Modern England.* Ithaca: Cornell UP, 1997.

Dolan, Frances E. *Dangerous Familiars: Representations of Domestic Crime in England, 1550–1700.* Ithaca: Cornell UP, 1994.

———. *Whores of Babylon: Catholicism, Gender, and Seventeenth-Century Print Culture.* Ithaca: Cornell UP, 1999.

Donawerth, Jane. "Women's Poetry and the Tudor-Stuart System of Gift Exchange." Donawerth, Burke, Dove, and Nelson, *Women.*

Donawerth, Jane, Mary Burke, Linda Dove, and Karen Nelson, eds.

Women, Writing, and the Reproduction of Culture in Tudor and Stuart Britain. Syracuse: Syracuse UP, 2000.

Donne, John. *John Donne's Poetry.* Ed. A. L. Clements. Norton Critical Ed. New York: Norton, 1966.

Dowriche, Anne. *The French Historie.* London, 1589.

Dryden, John. "To the Pious Memory of the Accomplisht Young Lady Mrs Anne Killigrew, Excellent in the Two Sister-Arts of Poesie, and Painting. An Ode." *The Works of John Dryden: Poems, 1685–1692.* Vol. 3. Ed. Earl Miner et al. Berkeley: U of California P, 1969. 109–15.

Dubrow, Heather, and Richard Strier, eds. *The Historical Renaissance: New Essays on Tudor and Stuart Literature and Culture.* Chicago: U of Chicago P, 1988.

Duffy, Maureen. Introduction. Behn, *Love Letters* v–xvii.

———. *The Passionate Shepherdess: Aphra Behn, 1640–89.* London: Cape, 1977.

Dunham, William Huse, Jr., and Stanley Pargellis, eds. *Complaint and Reform in England, 1436–1714.* New York: Octagon, 1968.

Dyce, Alexander. *Specimens of British Poetesses: Selected and Chronologically Arranged.* London: Rodd, 1825, 1827.

Dyer, Richard. "White." *Screen* 29 (1989): 44–64.

Early English Books, 1641–1700. Ann Arbor: UMI.

Egerton, Elizabeth Cavendish. "Of Marriage and of Widdowes." *Subordination and Authorship in Early Modern England: The Case of Elizabeth Cavendish Egerton and Her "Loose Papers."* Ed. and introd. Betty S. Travitsky. Tempe: Arizona Center for Medieval and Renaissance Studies, 1999. 191–92.

Eisenstein, Elizabeth. *The Printing Revolution in Early Modern Europe.* 2 vols. Cambridge: Cambridge UP, 1979.

Elizabeth I. *A Book of Devotions Composed by Her Majesty Elizabeth Regina, with Translations by the Reverend Adam Fox D.D. and a Foreword by the Reverend Canon J. P. Hodges.* Gerrards Cross: Smythe, 1970.

———. *Elizabeth I: Autograph Compositions and Foreign Language Originals.* Ed. Janel Mueller and Leah S. Marcus. Chicago: U of Chicago P, forthcoming.

———. *Elizabeth I: Collected Works.* Ed. Leah S. Marcus, Janel Mueller, and Mary Beth Rose. Chicago: U of Chicago P, 2000.

———. "The French Verses of Elizabeth I (Text)." Ed. Steven W. May and Anne Lake Prescott. *English Literary Renaissance* 24.1 (1994): 9–43.

———. *Letters of Queen Elizabeth and James VI of Scotland.* Ed. James Bruce. London, 1849.

———. *The Letters of Queen Elizabeth I.* Ed. G. B. Harrison. London: Cape, 1935. New York: Funk, 1968. Westport: Greenwood, 1981.

———. *The Poems of Queen Elizabeth I.* Ed. Leicester Bradner. Providence: Brown UP, 1964.

———. *The Public Speaking of Queen Elizabeth: Selections from Her Official Addresses.* Ed. George P. Rice, Jr. 1951. New York: AMS, 1966.

Elyot, Thomas. *The Boke Named the Gouernour.* London: Bertheleti, 1531.

Erickson, Amy Louise. *Women and Property in Early Modern England.* London: Routledge, 1993.

Erler, Mary C. "Davies's *Astraea* and Other Contexts of the Countess of Pembroke's 'A Dialogue.'" *Studies in English Literature* 30 (1990): 41–61.

Evans, Katharine, and Sarah Cheevers. *This Is a Short Relation of Some of the Cruel Sufferings for the Truths Sake of Katharine Evans and Sarah Chevers.* London, 1662.

Evelyn, John. *Kalendarium, 1650–1672.* Ed. E. S. De Beer. Oxford: Clarendon, 1955. Vol. 3 of *The Diary of John Evelyn.*

Evelyn, Mary. "Letter to Mr. Bohun." *Diary and Correspondence of John Evelyn.* Ed. William Bray. London, 1857. iv.

Ewan, Elizabeth, and Maureen M. Meikle, eds. *Women in Scotland, c. 1100–c. 1750.* East Linton, Eng.: Tuckwell, 1999.

Ezell, Margaret J. M., ed. *Creating a Literary Series.* Spec. issue of *South Central Review* 11.2 (1994): 1–130.

———. *The Patriarch's Wife: Literary Evidence and the History of the Family.* Chapel Hill: U of North Carolina P, 1987.

———. "'To Be Your Daughter in Your Pen': The Social Functions of Literature in the Writings of Lady Elizabeth Brackley and Lady Jane Cavendish." *Huntington Library Quarterly* 51 (1988): 281–96.

———. *Writing Women's Literary History.* Baltimore: Johns Hopkins UP, 1993.

Fanshawe, Ann. *The Memoirs of Ann, Lady Fanshawe.* Loftis 101–92.

Farrell, Kirby, Elizabeth H. Hageman, and Arthur F. Kinney, eds. *Women in the Renaissance: Selections from* English Literary Renaissance. Amherst: U of Massachusetts P, 1990.

Fehrenbach, R. J. "Isabella Whitney, Sir Hugh Plat, Geoffrey Whitney, and 'Sister Eldershae.'" *English Language Notes* 21 (1983): 7–11.

Fell, Margaret. *Womens Speaking Justified.* 1666. Otten 363–78.

Ferguson, Margaret W. "Juggling the Categories of Race, Class, and Gender: Aphra Behn's *Oroonoko.*" Hendricks and Parker 209–24.

———. "A Room Not Their Own: Renaissance Women as Readers and Writers." Koelb and Noakes 93–116.

———. "Running On with Almost Public Voice: The Case of 'E. C.'" *Tradition and the Talents of Women.* Ed. Florence Howe. Urbana: U of Illinois P, 1991. 37–67.

Ferguson, Margaret W., Maureen Quilligan, and Nancy J. Vickers, eds. *Rewriting the Renaissance: The Discourses of Sexual Difference in Early Modern Europe.* Chicago: U of Chicago P, 1986.

Ferguson, Moira, ed. *First Feminists: British Women Writers, 1578–1799.* Bloomington: Indiana UP, 1985.

Fienberg, Nona. "Mary Wroth and the Invention of Female Poetic Subjectivity." Miller and Waller 175–90.

Fiennes, Celia. *The Illustrated Journeys of Celia Fiennes, 1684–c. 1712.* London: Macdonald, 1982.

Fildes, Valerie, ed. *Women as Mothers in Pre-industrial England.* New York: Routledge, 1990.

Finch, Anne Conway. *Conway Letters: The Correspondence of Anne, Viscountess Conway, Henry More, and Their Friends.* Ed. Marjorie Hope Nicolson. London, 1930. New Haven: Yale UP, 1979.

Fine, Michelle. "Witnessing Whiteness." Fine, Weis, Powell, and Wong 57–65.

Fine, Michelle, Lois Weis, Linda C. Powell, and L. Mun Wong, eds. *Off White: Readings on Race, Power and Society.* London: Routledge, 1997.

Fish, Stanley. *Surprised by Sin.* London: Macmillan, 1967.

Fisher, John. *A Collection of Early Maps of London, 1553–1667.* London: Margary, 1981.

Fisken, Beth Wynne. "Mary Sidney's *Psalmes*: Education and Wisdom." Hannay, *Silent* 166–83.

———. " 'To the Angell Spirit . . .': Mary Sidney's Entry into the 'World of Words.' " Haselkorn and Travitsky 263–75.

Fitzmaurice, James. Introduction. Cavendish, *Margaret Cavendish* xi–xxi.

Fitzmaurice, James, et al., eds. *Major Writers of the Seventeenth Century.* New York: Oxford UP, 1997.

Fitzmaurice, James, Josephine A. Roberts, Carol L. Barash, Eugene R. Cunnar, and Nancy A. Gutierrez, eds. *Major Women Writers of Seventeenth-Century England.* Ann Arbor: U of Michigan P, 1997.

Fleming, Juliet. "The Ladies' Man and the Age of Elizabeth." Turner 58–181.

Fletcher, Anthony. *Gender, Sex, and Subordination in England, 1500–1800.* New Haven: Yale UP, 1995.

Flynn, Elizabeth, and Patrocinio Schweickart, eds. *Gender and Reading: Essays on Readers, Texts, and Contexts.* Baltimore: Johns Hopkins UP, 1986.

Folger Collective on Early Women Critics, ed. *Women Critics, 1660–1820: An Anthology.* Bloomington: Indiana UP, 1995.

Fox, Adam, ed. *A Book of Devotions Composed by Her Majesty Elizabeth Regina, with Translations by the Reverend Adam Fox D.D. and a Foreword by the Reverend Canon J. P. Hodges.* Gerrards Cross, Eng.: Smythe, 1970.

Foxe, John. *Acts and Monuments.* Ed. George Townsend. 8 vols. New York: AMS, 1965.

Foxton, Rosemary. *"Hear the Word of the Lord": A Critical and Bibliographical Study of Quaker Women's Writing, 1650–1700.* Melbourne: Bibliographical Soc. of Australia and New Zealand, 1994.

Fraser, Antonia. *The Weaker Vessel.* New York: Knopf, 1984.

Freer, Coburn. *Music for a King: George Herbert's Style and the Metrical Psalms.* Baltimore: Johns Hopkins UP, 1972.

Freud, Sigmund. "Family Romances." *The Standard Edition of the Works of Sigmund Freud.* Ed. and trans. James Strachey et al. Vol. 9. London: Hogarth, 1959. 237–41.

Friedman, Alice T. *House and Household in Elizabethan England*. Chicago: U of Chicago P, 1989.

Frye, Susan, and Karen Robertson, eds. *Maids and Mistresses, Cousins and Queens: Women's Alliances in Early Modern England*. New York: Oxford UP, 1999.

Gallagher, Catherine. "Embracing the Absolute: The Politics of the Female Subject in Seventeenth-Century England." *Genders* 1 (1988): 24–39.

Gallagher, Lowell. "Mary Ward's 'Jesuitresses' and the Construction of a Typological Community." Frye and Robertson 199–217.

Gambara, Veronica. *Le rime*. Ed. Alan Bullock. Italian Medieval and Renaissance Studies 6. Florence: Olschki, 1995.

Garman, Mary, Judith Applegate, Margaret Benefiel, and Dortha Meredith, eds. *Hidden in Plain Sight: Quaker Women's Writings, 1650–1700*. Wallingford: Pendle Hill, 1996.

Garrard, Mary. "Artemisia Gentileschi: The Artist's Autograph in Letters." *The Female Autograph*. Ed. Domna Stanton. Chicago: U of Chicago P, 1984. 81–95.

Gascoigne, George. *The Posies of George Gascoigne*. London, 1575.

The Geneva Bible: A Facsimile Edition. 1560. Ed. Lloyd E. Berry. Madison: U of Wisconsin P, 1969.

George, Margaret. *Women in the First Capitalist Society: Experiences in Seventeenth-Century England*. Urbana: U of Illinois P, 1988.

Giffard, Martha. *Martha, Lady Giffard, Her Life and Correspondence (1664–1722), a Sequel to the Letters of Dorothy Osborne*. Ed. Julia G. Longe. London: Allen, 1911.

Gilbert, Sandra, and Susan Gubar. *The Madwoman in the Attic*. New Haven: Yale UP, 1979.

———, eds. *The Norton Anthology of Literature by Women: The Tradition in English*. 2nd ed. New York: Norton, 1996.

Gilman, Charlotte Perkins. *Herland*. 1915. New York: Pantheon, 1979.

Glanville, Philippa. *London in Maps*. London: Connoisseur, 1972.

Goff, Lady Cecilie. *A Woman of the Tudor Age*. London: Murray, 1930.

Goreau, Angeline. *Reconstructing Aphra: A Social Biography of Aphra Behn*. New York: Dial, 1980.

———, ed. *The Whole Duty of a Woman: Female Writers in Seventeenth-Century England*. Garden City: Dial, 1985.

A Gorgeous Gallerie of Gallant Inventions. 1578. Ed. Hyder E. Rollins. Cambridge: Harvard UP, 1926.

Gouge, William. *Of Domesticall Duties*. London, 1622.

Graham, Elspeth. "Women's Writing and the Self." Wilcox 209–33.

Graham, Elspeth, et al., eds. *Her Own Life: Autobiographical Writings by Seventeenth-Century Englishwomen*. London: Routledge, 1989.

Grant, Douglas. *Margaret the First*. Toronto: U of Toronto P, 1957.

Green, Henry. Introduction. G. Whitney lxix.

Greene, Roland. "Petrarchism among the Discourses of Imperialism."

America in European Consciousness, 1493–1750. Ed. Karen Ordahl Kupperman. Chapel Hill: U of North Carolina P, 1995. 130–65.

Greer, Germaine. Introduction. Greer, Hastings, Medoff, and Sansone 1–31.

Greer, Germaine, Susan Hastings, Jeslyn Medoff, and Melinda Sansone, eds. *Kissing the Rod: An Anthology of Seventeenth-Century Women's Verse*. New York: Farrar, 1988.

Greville, Fulke. *Poems and Dramas of Fulke Greville*. Ed. Geoffrey Bullough. 2 vols. New York: Oxford UP, 1945.

Grillo, Trina, and Stephanie M. Wildman. "Obscuring the Importance of Race: The Implications for Making Connections between Racism and Sexism (or Other Isms)." Wing, *Feminism* 44–50.

Grossman, Marshall, ed. *Aemilia Lanyer: Gender, Genre, and the Canon*. Lexington: UP of Kentucky, 1998.

Grundy, Isobel. "Women's History? Writings by English Nuns." Grundy and Wiseman 126–38.

Grundy, Isobel, and Susan Wiseman, eds. *Women, Writing, History, 1640–1740*. Athens: U of Georgia P, 1992.

Grymeston, Elizabeth. *Miscelanea, Meditations, Memoratives*. London, 1604.

Guilday, Peter. *The English Catholic Refugees on the Continent, 1558–1795*. London: Longman, 1914. Vol. 1 of *English Colleges and Convents in the Catholic Low Countries, 1558–1795*.

Guillemeau, Jacques. *Child-birth; or, The Happy Deliverie of Women*. London, 1612.

Hackett, Helen. " 'Yet Tell Me Some Such Fiction': Lady Mary Wroth's *Urania* and the 'Femininity' of Romance." Brant and Purkiss 39–68.

Haec-Vir; or, The Womanish-Man: Being an Answre to a Late Booke Intituled Hic-Mulier, Exprest in a Brief Dialogue betweene Haec-Vir the Womanish-Man, and Hic-Mulier the Man-Woman. London, 1620.

Hageman, Elizabeth H. "The 'False Printed' Broadside of Katherine Philip's 'To the Queens Majesty on Her Happy Arrival.' " *Library* 17.4 (1995): 321–26.

———. "Making a Good Impression: Early Texts of Poems and Letters by Katherine Philips, the 'Matchless Orinda.' " *South Central Review* 11.2 (1994): 39–65.

———. "Recent Studies in Women Writers of the English Seventeenth Century (1604–1674)." *English Literary Renaissance* 18 (1988): 138–67.

———. "Recent Studies in Women Writers of Tudor England: 1. Women Writers, 1485–1603." *English Literary Renaissance* 14 (1984): 409–25.

Hageman, Elizabeth H., and Sara Jayne Steen, eds. *Teaching Judith Shakespeare*. Spec. issue of *Shakespeare Quarterly* 47 (1996): 353–496.

Hageman, Elizabeth H., and Andrea Sununu. "New Manuscript Texts of Katherine Philips, the 'Matchless Orinda.' " *English Manuscript Studies, 1100–1700* 4 (1993): 174–219.

Halkett, Anne. *The Memoirs of Anne, Lady Halkett*. Loftis 9–87.

Hall, Kim F. *Things of Darkness: Economies of Race and Gender in Early Modern England*. Ithaca: Cornell UP, 1995.

Hall, Stuart. "Subjects in History: Making Diasporic Identities." *The House That Race Built: Black Americans, U.S. Terrain*. Ed. Wahneema Lubiano. New York: Pantheon, 1997. 289–300.

Hampton, Timothy. *Writing from History: The Rhetoric of Exemplarity in Renaissance Literature*. Ithaca: Cornell UP, 1990.

Haney-Lopez, Ian. *White by Law: The Legal Construction of Race*. New York: New York UP, 1996.

Hannay, Margaret P. "Constructing a City of Ladies." *Shakespeare Studies* 25 (1997): 76–87.

———. "The Countess of Pembroke as a Spenserian Poet." S. King 41–62.

———. " 'House-Confined Maids': The Presentation of Woman's Role in the Psalmes of the Countess of Pembroke." *English Literary Renaissance* 24 (1994): 44–71.

———. "Incorporating Women Writers into the Survey Course: Mary Sidney's Psalm 73 and *Astrophil and Stella* 5." *Approaches to Teaching Shorter Elizabethan Poetry*. Ed. Patrick Cheney and Anne Lake Prescott. New York: MLA, 2000. 133–38.

———. *Philip's Phoenix: Mary Sidney, Countess of Pembroke*. New York: Oxford UP, 1990.

———, ed. *Silent but for the Word: Tudor Women as Patrons, Translators, and Writers of Religious Works*. Kent: Kent State UP, 1985.

———. " 'The Trial of True Curtesie': Teaching Book VI as Pastoral Romance." *Approaches to Teaching Spenser's* Faerie Queene. Ed. David Lee Miller and Alexander Dunlop. New York: MLA, 1994. 172–80.

———. " 'Unlock My Lipps': The *Miserere Mei Deus* of Anne Vaughan Lok and Mary Sidney Herbert, Countess of Pembroke." *Privileging Gender in Early Modern England*. Ed. Jean R. Brink. Sixteenth-Century Essays and Studies 23. Kirksville: Northern Missouri State U, 1993. 19–36.

———. " 'Your Vertuous and Learned Aunt': The Countess of Pembroke as a Mentor to Lady Wroth." Miller and Waller 15–34.

Harington, John. *The Letters and Epigrams of Sir John Harington*. Ed. Norman Egbert McClure. Philadelphia: U of Pennsylvania P, 1930.

———. *Nugae Antiquae: Being a Miscellaneous Collection of Original Papers, in Prose and Verse*. Ed. Harington and Thomas Park. 2 vols. London, 1804.

Harley, Brilliana Conway. *Letters of the Lady Brilliana Harley, Wife of Sir Robert Harley*. London: Camden Soc., 1854.

Harvey, Elizabeth D. *Ventriloquized Voices: Feminist Theory and English Renaissance Texts*. London: Routledge, 1992.

Haselkorn, Anne M., and Betty S. Travitsky, eds. *The Renaissance Englishwoman in Print: Counterbalancing the Canon*. Amherst: U of Massachusetts P, 1990.

Hayward, John. *Annals of the First Four Years of the Reign of Queen Elizabeth*. Ed. John Bruce. London, 1840.

Heal, Felicity. *Hospitality in Early Modern England*. Oxford: Clarendon P, 1990.

Heale, William. *An Apologie for Women*. Oxford, 1609.

Healy, Thomas. *New Latitudes: Theory and English Renaissance Literature*. London: Arnold, 1992.

Henderson, Katherine Usher, and Barbara F. McManus, eds. *Half Humankind: Contexts and Texts of the Controversy about Women in England, 1540–1640*. Urbana: U of Illinois P, 1985.

Hendricks, Margo. "Civility, Barbarism, and Aphra Behn's *The Widow Ranter*." Hendricks and Parker 225–39.

———. "Managing the Barbarian: *The Tragedy of Dido, Queen of Carthage*." *Renaissance Drama* ns 23 (1992): 165–88.

Hendricks, Margo, and Patricia Parker, eds. *Women, "Race," and Writing in the Early Modern Period*. London: Routledge, 1994.

Hibbard, Caroline M. "Early Stuart Catholicism: Revisions and Re-revisions." *Journal of Modern History* 52.1 (1980): 1–34.

Hic Mulier; or, The Man-Woman: Being a Medicine to Cure the Coltish Disease of the Staggers in the Masculine-Feminine of Our Times. Exprest in a Breif Declamation. London, 1620.

Higgins, Patricia. "The Reactions of Women, with Special Reference to Women Petitioners." *Politics, Religion, and the English Civil War*. Ed. Brian Manning. London: Arnold, 1973.

Hill, Christopher. *Puritanism and Revolution*. London: Mercury, 1962.

———. *Society and Puritanism in Pre-revolutionary England*. 2nd ed. New York: Schocken, 1967.

———. *The World Turned Upside Down: Radical Ideas during the English Revolution*. Harmondsworth: Penguin, 1975.

Hill, W. Speed, ed. *New Ways of Looking at Old Texts: Papers of the Renaissance English Text Society, 1985–1991*. Renaissance English Text Soc. / Medieval and Renaissance Texts and Studies. Binghamton: Center for Medieval and Early Renaissance Studies, 1993.

Hinds, Hilary. *God's Englishwomen: Seventeenth-Century Radical Sectarian Writing and Feminist Criticism*. Manchester: Manchester UP, 1996.

Hobby, Elaine. " 'Discourse So Unsavory': Women's Published Writings of the 1650s." Grundy and Wiseman 16–32.

———. " 'Oh Oxford Thou Art Full of Filth': The Prophetical Writings of Hester Biddle, 1629[?]–1696." *Feminist Criticism: Theory and Practice*. Ed. Susan Sellers. New York: Harvester Wheatsheaf, 1991. 157–69.

———. "The Politics of Women's Prophecy in the English Revolution." Wilcox et al. 295–306.

———. "Usurping Authority over the Man: Women's Writing, 1630–89." *An Introduction to Women's Writing from the Middle Ages to the Present*. New York: Prentice, 1998. 65–93.

―――. *Virtue of Necessity: English Women's Writing, 1649–1688*. London: Virago, 1988.

Hoby, Margaret. *Diary*. Ed. Dorothy M. Meads. London: Routledge, 1930.

Hogrefe, Pearl. *Tudor Women: Commoners and Queens*. Ames: Iowa State UP, 1975.

―――. *Women of Action in Tudor England: Nine Biographical Sketches*. Ames: Iowa State UP, 1977.

Holland, Barbara. "Cleopatra: What Kind of Woman Was She, Anyway?" *Smithsonian* 27 (1997): 56–62.

Holm, Janis Butler. "Struggling with the Letter: Vives's Preface to *The Instruction of a Christen Woman*." Logan and Rudnytsky 265–97.

"A Homilie of the State of Matrimonie." *The Seconde Tome of Homilies*. London, 1563. 253–63.

Hooke, Robert. *Micrographia*. 1665.

hooks, bell. *Ain't I a Woman: Black Women and Feminism*. Boston: South End, 1981.

―――. "Overcoming White Supremacy: A Comment." *Talking Back: Thinking Feminist, Thinking Black*. Boston: South End, 1989. 112–19.

―――. "Reflections on Race and Sex." *Yearning: Race, Gender, and Cultural Politics*. Boston: South End, 1990. 57–65.

Howard, Jean. *The Stage and Social Struggle in Early Modern England*. London: Routledge, 1994.

Howell, Thomas B., ed. *Cobbett's Complete Collection of State Trials*. 33 vols. London: Bagshaw, 1809–26.

Hufton, Olwen. *The Prospect before Her: A History of Women in Western Europe*. Vol. 1 (1500–1800). New York: Knopf, 1996.

Hughey, Ruth Willard. "Cultural Interests of Women in England, from 1524 [to] 1640, Indicated in the Writings of the Women." Diss. Cornell U., 1932.

Hull, Suzanne W. *Chaste, Silent, and Obedient: English Books for Women, 1475–1640*. San Marino: Huntington Lib., 1982.

―――. *Women according to Men: The World of Tudor-Stuart Women*. Walnut Creek: AltaMira, 1996.

Hunter, Lynette. "Women and Domestic Medicine: Lady Experimenters, 1570–1620." Hunter and Hutton 108–21.

Hunter, Lynette, and Sarah Hutton, eds. *Women, Medicine and Science 1500–1700*. Phoenix Mill, Eng.: Sutton, 1997.

Hutchinson, Lucy. *Memoirs of the Life of Colonel Hutchinson [. . .] with the Fragment of an Autobiography of Mrs. Hutchinson*. Ed. James Sutherland. Oxford: Oxford UP, 1973.

Hutner, Heidi, ed. *Rereading Aphra Behn: History, Theory, and Criticism*. Charlottesville: UP of Virginia, 1993.

Hyrde, Richard. Preface. Roper.

Inés de la Cruz, Juana. "The Reply to Sor Philothea." *A Sor Juana Anthology*. Trans. Alan S. Trueblood. Cambridge: Harvard UP, 1988. 205–43.

James, Susan E. *Kateryn Parr: The Making of a Queen*. Aldershot: Ashgate, 1999.

Jardine, Lisa. *Reading Shakespeare Historically*. London: Routledge, 1996.

———. *Still Harping on Daughters: Women and Drama in the Age of Shakespeare*. New York: Columbia UP, 1989.

Jones, Ann Rosalind. "Counter-attacks on 'the Bayter of Women': Three Pamphleteers of the Early Seventeenth Century." Haselkorn and Travitsky 45–62.

———. *The Currency of Eros: Women's Love Lyric in Europe, 1540–1620*. Bloomington: Indiana UP, 1990.

———. "Introduction: Imitation, Negotiation, Appropriation." Jones, *Currency* 1–10.

———. "Maidservants of London: Sisterhoods of Kinship and Labor." Frye and Robertson 21–32.

Jones, Ann Rosalind, and Betty S. Travitsky, eds. *Women in the Renaissance: An Interdisciplinary Forum (MLA 1989)*. Spec. issue of *Women's Studies* 19 (1991): 129–257.

Jones, Kathleen. *A Glorious Fame: The Life of Margaret Cavendish, Duchess of Newcastle, 1623–1673*. London: Bloomsbury, 1988.

Jones, Vivien, ed. *Women and Literature in Britain, 1700–1800*. Cambridge: Cambridge UP, forthcoming.

Jonson, Ben. "A Sonnet to the Noble Lady, the Lady Mary Wroth." *Ben Jonson*. Ed. Ian Donaldson. Oxford: Oxford UP, 1985. 349–50.

Jordan, Constance. *Renaissance Feminism: Literary Texts and Political Models*. Ithaca: Cornell UP, 1990.

———. "Renaissance Women and the Question of Class." Turner 90–106.

Joscelin, Elizabeth. *The Mothers Legacie to Her Vnborn Childe*. 1622. Ed. Jean Le-Drew Metcalfe. Toronto: U of Toronto P, 2000.

Kanner, Barbara, ed. *The Women of England: From Anglo-Saxon Times to the Present*. Hamden: Archon, 1979.

Kaplan, Louise. *Female Perversions: The Temptations of Emma Bovary*. New York: Doubleday, 1991.

Kay, Dennis. *Melodious Tears: The English Funeral Elegy from Spenser to Milton*. Oxford: Clarendon, 1990.

Keeble, N. H., ed. *The Cultural Identity of Seventeenth-Century Woman: A Reader*. London: Routledge, 1994.

Kelly-Gadol, Joan. "Did Women Have a Renaissance?" Kelly-Gadol, *Women* 19–50.

———. "Early Feminist Theory and the *Querelle des Femmes*, 1475–1789." *Signs* 8 (1982): 2–28.

———. *Women, History, and Theory: The Essays of Joan Kelly*. Chicago: U of Chicago P, 1984.

Kelso, Ruth. *Doctrine for the Lady of the Renaissance*. Urbana: U of Illinois P, 1956.

Kessler, Suzanne J. *Lessons from the Intersexed*. New Brunswick: Rutgers UP, 1998.

Kessler, Suzanne J., and Wendy McKenna. *Gender: An Ethnomethodological Approach*. Chicago: U of Chicago P, 1985.

Killigrew, Thomas. *Thomaso; or, The Wanderer*. London, 1654.

Killin, Margaret, and Barbara Patison. *A Warning from the Lord to the Teachers and People of Plimouth*. London, 1656.

King, John N. *English Reformation Literature: The Tudor Origins of the Protestant Tradition*. Princeton: Princeton UP, 1982.

———. "Patronage and Piety: The Influence of Katherine Parr." Hannay, *Silent* 43–60.

———. *Tudor Royal Iconography*. Princeton: Princeton UP, 1989.

King, Margaret L. *Women of the Renaissance*. Chicago: U of Chicago P, 1991.

King, Sigrid M., ed. *Pilgrimage for Love: Festschrift for Josephine A. Roberts*. Renaissance English Text Soc. / Medieval and Renaissance Texts and Studies. Tempe: Arizona Center for Medieval and Renaissance Studies, 2000.

Kinnamon, Noel J. "A Note on Herbert's 'Easter' and the Sidneian Psalms." *George Herbert Journal* 1 (1978): 44–48.

———. "Notes on the Psalms in Herbert's 'The Temple.'" *George Herbert Journal* 4 (1981): 10–29.

Kinney, Arthur F. "Sir Philip Sidney and the Uses of History." Dubrow and Strier 293–314.

Kinney, Arthur F., and Kirby Farrell, eds. *Women in the Renaissance*. Spec. issue of *English Literary Renaissance* 14 (1984): 249–444.

Kinney, Arthur F., and Elizabeth H. Hageman, eds. *Women in the Renaissance II*. Spec. issue of *English Literary Renaissance* 18 (1988): 1–168.

Kinney, Arthur F., and Ann Rosalind Jones, eds. *Women in the Renaissance III: Studies in Honor of Ruth Mortimer*. Spec. issue of *English Literary Renaissance* 24 (1994): 1–280.

Klein, Joan Larsen, ed. *Daughters, Wives, and Widows: Writings by Men about Women and Marriage in England, 1500–1640*. Urbana: U of Illinois P, 1992.

Klene, Jean. Introduction. A. Southwell xi–xliii.

Knox, John. *The First Blast of the Trumpet against the Monstruous Regiment of Women*. Geneva, 1558.

———. *A Notable and Comfortable Exposition of M. John Knoxes, upon the Fourth of Mathew*. London, 1583. *STC* 15068.

Koelb, Clayton, and Susan Noakes, eds. *The Comparative Perspective on Literature*. Ithaca: Cornell UP, 1988.

Kohler, Charlotte. "The Elizabethan Woman of Letters: The Extent of Her Literary Activity." Diss. U of Virginia, 1936.

Kramer, Annette. " 'Thus by the Musick of a Ladyes Tongue': Margaret Cavendish's Dramatic Innovations in Women's Education." *Women's History Review* 2 (1993): 57–79.

Kristeva, Julia. *The Kristeva Reader*. Ed. Toril Moi. New York: Columbia UP, 1986.

Krontiris, Tina. *Oppositional Voices: Women as Writers and Translators of Literature in the English Renaissance*. London: Routledge, 1992.

Kusunoke, Akiko. " 'Their Testament at Their Apron-Strings': The Representation of Puritan Women in Early Seventeenth Century England." Cerasano and Wynne-Davies, *Gloriana's Face* 185–204.

Labé, Louise. *Louise Labé's Complete Works*. Trans. and ed. Edith R. Farrell. Intro. C. Frederick Farrell, Jr., and Edith Farrell. Troy: Whitston, 1986.

The Lady Falkland: Her Life, by One of Her Daughters. Weller and Ferguson 183–275.

Lamb, Mary Ellen. "The Agency of the Split Subject: Lady Anne Clifford and the Uses of Reading." *English Literary Renaissance* 22 (1992): 347–68.

———. "The Cooke Sisters: Attitudes toward Learned Women in the Renaissance." Hannay, *Silent* 107–25.

———. "The Countess of Pembroke and the Art of Dying." Rose, *Women* 207–26.

———. *Gender and Authorship in the Sidney Circle*. Madison: U of Wisconsin P, 1990.

———. "Tracing a Heterosexual Erotics of Service in *Twelfth Night* and in the Autobiographical Writings of Thomas Whythorne and Lady Anne Clifford." *Criticism* 40 (1998): 1–25.

Lanyer, Aemilia. *The Poems of Aemilia Lanyer: Salve Deus Rex Judaeorum*. Ed. Susanne Woods. New York: Oxford UP, 1993.

Lasocki, David, with Roger Prior. *The Bassanos: Venetian Musicians and Instrument Makers in England, 1531–1665*. Aldershot: Scolar, 1995.

Latz, Dorothy L. *"Glow-worm Light": Writings of Seventeenth-Century English Recusant Women from Original Manuscripts*. Salzburg, Aus.: Institut für Anglistik und Amerikanistik, 1989.

Lead, Jane. "Solomon's Porch; or, The Beautiful Gate to Wisdom's Temple." *A Fountain of Gardens: Watered by the Rivers of Divine Pleasure, and Springing Up in All the Variety of Spiritual Plants; Blown Up by the Pure Breath into a Paradise*. London, 1687.

The Lawes Resolution of Women's Rights. London, 1632.

Leigh, Dorothy. *The Mother's Blessing*. London, 1616. Excerpted in Klein 291–302.

Levin, Carole, and Patricia A. Sullivan, eds. *Political Rhetoric, Power, and Renaissance Women*. Albany: State U of New York P, 1995.

Lewalski, Barbara Kiefer. "Female Text, Male Reader Response: Contemporary Marginalia in Rachel Speght's *A Mouzell for Melastomus*." Summers and Pebworth 136–62.

———. Introduction. R. Speght, *Polemics* xi–xxxvi.

———. *Protestant Poetics and the Seventeenth-Century Religious Lyric*. Princeton: Princeton UP, 1979.

————. *Writing Women in Jacobean England*. Cambridge: Harvard UP, 1993.

Lewis, C. S. *English Literature in the Sixteenth Century Excluding Drama*. Oxford: Clarendon, 1954. Vol. 3 of *The Oxford History of English Literature*.

Lewis, Jayne. *The Trial of Mary Queen of Scots: A Brief History with Documents*. Boston: Bedford–St. Martin's, 1999.

Lilley, Kate. "Blazing Worlds: Seventeenth-Century Women's Utopian Writing." Brant and Purkiss 102–33.

Ling, Nicholas. *Politeuphuia, Wit's Commonwealth*. London, 1597.

Liu, Tessie P. "Race." *A Companion to American Thought*. Ed. Richard Wrightman Fox and James T. Kloppenberg. Oxford: Blackwell, 1995. 564–67.

Lock, Anne [Prowse]. *The Collected Works of Anne Vaughan Lock*. Ed. Susan M. Felch. Renaissance English Text Soc. 21 / Medieval and Renaissance Texts and Studies 185. Tempe: Arizona Center for Medieval and Renaissance Studies, 1999.

————. *Of the Markes of the Children of God, and of Their Comforts in Afflictions, to the Faithfull of the Low Countrie. By John Taffin. Ouerseene Againe and Augmented by the Author, and Translated out of French by Anne Prowse*. 1590. Lock, *Collected Works* 74–189.

————, trans. *Sermons of John Calvin, upon the Songe That Ezechias Made after He Had Bene Sicke and Afflicted by the Hand of God*. London: Day, 1560.

Loewenstein, Joseph. "The Script in the Marketplace." *Representing the Renaissance*. Ed. Stephen Greenblatt. Berkeley: U of California P, 1988. 265–78.

Loftis, John, ed. *The Memoirs of Anne, Lady Halkett[,] and Ann, Lady Fanshawe*. Oxford: Clarendon, 1979.

Logan, Marie-Rose, and Peter L. Rudnytsky, eds. *Contending Kingdoms: Historical, Psychological, and Feminist Approaches to Literature of Sixteenth-Century England and France*. Detroit: Wayne State UP, 1991.

Lorde, Audre. "Age, Race, Class, and Sex." *Sister Outsider: Essays and Speeches*. Trumansburg: Crossing, 1984. 114–23.

Lorris, Guillaume de. *The Romance of the Rose*. Trans. Harry W. Robbins. Ed. Charles W. Dunn. New York: Dutton, 1962.

Love, Harold. *Scribal Publication in Seventeenth-Century England*. Oxford: Clarendon, 1993.

Lucas, Caroline. *Writing for Women: The Example of Women as Reader in Elizabethan Romance*. Philadelphia: Open UP, 1989.

Lucas, R. Valerie. "Puritan Preaching and the Politics of the Family." Haselkorn and Travitsky 224–40.

Mack, Phyllis. *Visionary Women: Ecstatic Prophecy in Seventeenth-Century England*. Berkeley: U of California P, 1992.

Mahl, Mary R., and Helene Koon. *The Female Spectator: English Women Writers before 1800*. Bloomington: Indiana UP, 1977.

Makin, Bathsua. *An Essay to Revive the Antient Education of Gentlewomen.* 1673. Ed. Frances Teague. Wilson and Warnke 285–304.

Markham, Gervase. *The English Housewife.* 1615. Ed. Michael R. Best. Montreal: McGill-Queen's UP, 1986.

Marotti, Arthur. "Alienating Catholics in Early Modern England: Recusant Women, Jesuits, and Ideological Fantasies." Marotti, *Catholicism* 1–34.

———, ed. *Catholicism and Anti-Catholicism in Early Modern English Texts.* New York: Macmillan, 1999.

———. *John Donne: Coterie Poet.* Madison: U of Wisconsin P, 1986.

———. *Manuscript, Print, and the English Renaissance Lyric.* Ithaca: Cornell UP, 1995.

———. "Patronage, Poetry, and Print." *Yearbook of English Studies* 21 (1991): 1–26.

———. "The Transmission of Lyric Poetry and the Institutionalizing of Literature in the English Renaissance." Logan and Rudnytsky 21–41.

Marquis, Paul A. "Oppositional Ideologies of Gender in Isabella Whitney's *A Copy of a Letter.*" *Modern Language Review* 90 (1995): 314–24.

Marriott, Richard. Advertisement. *Intelligencer* 18 Jan. 1664: 47.

Marshall, Sherrin, ed. *Women in Reformation and Counter-Reformation Europe: Private and Public Worlds.* Bloomington: Indiana UP, 1989.

Martin, Randall. "The Autobiography of Grace, Lady Mildmay." *Renaissance and Reformation / Renaissance et Réforme* 18 (1994): 33–81.

———, ed. *Women Writers in Renaissance England.* London: Longman, 1997.

Martz, Louis. *Poetry of Meditation.* New Haven: Yale UP, 1962.

Masek, Rosemary. "Women in an Age of Transition, 1485–1714." Kanner 138–82.

Masten, Jeffrey. *Textual Intercourse: Collaboration, Authorship and Sexualities in Renaissance Drama.* Cambridge: Cambridge UP, 1997.

Matchinske, Megan. "Gendering Catholic Conforming / Modeling Feminist Practice: The Politics of Equivocation in Elizabeth Grymeston's *Miscelanea.*" *Journal of English and Germanic Philology*, forthcoming.

———. *Writing, Gender, and State in Early Modern England: Identity Formation and the Female Subject.* Cambridge: Cambridge UP, 1998.

Matthew, Tobie. *The Life of Lady Lucy Knatchbull.* London: Sheed, 1931.

May, Steven M. *The Elizabethan Courtier Poets: The Poems and Their Contexts.* Columbia: U of Missouri P, 1991.

Mayer, Thomas F., and D. R. Woolf, eds. *The Rhetorics of Life-Writing in Early Modern Europe: Forms of Biography from Cassandra Fedele to Louis XIV.* Ann Arbor: U of Michigan P, 1995.

McColley, Diane. *Milton's Eve.* Urbana: U of Illinois P, 1983.

McCrea, Adriana. "Whose Life Is It, Anyway? Subject and Subjection in Fulke Greville's *Life of Sidney.*" Mayer and Woolf 299–320.

McCutcheon, Elizabeth. "Margaret More Roper." K. Wilson 477–80.

McGrath, Lynette. " 'Let Us Have Our Libertie Againe': Aemilia Lanier's Seventeenth-Century Feminist Voice." *Women's Studies* 20 (1992): 331–48.

McGregor, J. F., and B. Reay, eds. *Radical Religion and the English Revolution*. Oxford: Oxford UP, 1984.

McIntosh, Peggy. "White Privilege and Male Privilege: A Personal Account of Coming to See Correspondences through Work in Women's Studies." *Race, Class, and Gender: An Anthology*. Ed. Margaret L. Andersen and Patricia Hill Collins. Belmont: Wadsworth, 1992. 70–81.

McKeon, Michael. *Origins of the English Novel, 1600–1740*. Baltimore: Johns Hopkins UP, 1987.

McLaren, Margaret Anne. "An Unknown Continent: Lady Mary Wroth's Forgotten Pastoral Drama, 'Loves Victorie.' " Haselkorn and Travitsky 276–94.

Mendelson, Sara Heller. *The Mental World of Stuart Women: Three Studies*. Amherst: U of Massachusetts P, 1987.

Meres, Francis. *Palladis Tamia*. London, 1598. Excerpt in Rollins and Baker.

Mildmay, Grace. *Autobiography*. c.1617. Ms Northampton Central Lib. Extract in Martin, "Autobiography" 33–81.

Miller, Jacqueline. "Lady Mary Wroth in the House of Busirane." *Worldmaking Spenser: Exploration in the Early Modern Age*. Ed. Patrick Cheney and Lauren Silberman. Lexington: UP of Kentucky, 1999. 115–240.

Miller, Nancy K. *Getting Personal: Feminist Occasions and Other Autobiographical Acts*. London: Routledge, 1991.

Miller, Naomi. *Changing the Subject: Mary Wroth and Figurations of Gender in Early Modern England*. Lexington: UP of Kentucky, 1996.

Miller, Naomi, and Gary Waller, eds. *Reading Mary Wroth: Representing Alternatives in Early Modern England*. Knoxville: U of Tennessee P, 1991.

Milton, John. *Complete Poems and Major Prose*. Ed. Merritt Y. Hughes. New York: Macmillan, 1957.

———. "On the Morning of Christ's Nativity." *Paradise Regained and the Minor Poems and Samson Agonistes*. Ed. Merritt Y. Hughes. New York: Odyssey, 1937. 150–65.

More, Thomas. *Utopia*. Trans. Paul Turner. London: Penguin, 1984.

Mueller, Janel. Introduction. *Katherine Parr: Collected Writings*. Forthcoming.

———. "A Tudor Queen Finds Voice: Katherine Parr's *Lamentation*." Dubrow and Strier 15–47.

Muld Sacke; or, The Apologie of Hic Mulier: To the Late Declamation against Her. London, 1620.

Murray, Timothy. *Theatrical Legitimation: Allegories of Genius in Seventeenth-Century England and France*. Oxford: Oxford UP, 1987.

Mush, John. *Mr. John Mush's Life of Margaret Clitherow. The Troubles of Our Catholic Forefathers Related by Themselves*. Ed. John Morris. Vol. 3. London: Burns, 1877.

Nashe, Thomas. "A Litany in Time of Plague." *Summers Last Will and Tes-*

tament. Works. Vol. 3. Ed. R. B. McKerrow. London: Bullen, 1904–10. 282–84.

Newton, Richard C. "Jonson and the (Re-)Invention of the Book." *Classic and Cavalier: Essays on Jonson and the Sons of Ben.* Ed. Claude J. Summers and Ted-Larry Pebworth. Pittsburgh: U of Pittsburgh P, 1982. 31–55.

Noakes, Susan. "On the Superficiality of Women." Koelb and Noakes 339–55.

——. *Timely Reading.* Ithaca: Cornell UP, 1988.

Noble, David F. *A World without Women: The Christian Clerical Culture of Western Science.* New York: Knopf, 1993.

Norton, Thomas, and Thomas Sackville. *Ferrex and Porrex; or, Gorboduc.* London, 1570. Rpt. in *Tudor Facsimile Texts.* Ed. John S. Farmer. London, 1908.

Nussbaum, Felicity. " 'A Difference of Complexion': Women and Race." V. Jones.

Ong, Walter. "Latin Language Study as a Renaissance Puberty Rite." *Studies in Philology* 56 (1959): 106–24.

Orchard, M. Emmanuel. *Till God Will: Mary Ward through Her Writings.* London: Darton, 1985.

Orgel, Stephen. *Impersonations: The Performance of Gender in Shakespeare's England.* Cambridge: Cambridge UP, 1996.

——. "What Is a Text?" *Research Opportunities in Renaissance Drama* 2.4 (1981): 3–6.

Osborne, Dorothy. *Letters from Dorothy Osborne to Sir William Temple (1652–54).* Ed. Edward A. Parry. New York: Dodd, 1888.

——. *Letters to Sir William Temple.* Ed. Kenneth Parker. London: Penguin, 1987.

Otten, Charlotte F., ed. *English Women's Voices, 1540–1700.* Miami: Florida International UP, 1992.

Overbury, Thomas. *The Overburian Characters.* Ed. W. J. Paylor. Oxford: Blackwell, 1936.

Owen, Jane. *An Antidote against Purgatory.* London, 1634.

Owen, Susan J. "Sexual Politics and Party Politics in Behn's Drama, 1678–83." J. Todd, *Studies* 15–29.

Parry, Edward A. "Dorothy Osborne." *The English Illustrated Magazine.* London: Macmillan, 1886. 470–78.

Paston, Katherine. *The Correspondence of Lady Katherine Paston, 1603–1627.* Ed. Ruth Willard Hughey. Norfolk, Eng.: Norfolk Record Soc., 1941.

Patterson, Annabel. *Censorship and Interpretation: The Conditions of Writing and Reading in Early Modern England.* Madison: U of Wisconsin P, 1984.

Patton, Elizabeth A. "Mothers as Humanist Educators in Italy, Spain, and England." MLA Annual Convention. Toronto Convention Centre, Toronto. 29 Dec. 1997.

Payne, Linda R. "Dramatic Dreamscape: Women's Dreams and Utopian Vision in the Works of Margaret Cavendish, Duchess of Newcastle." Schofield and Macheski 18–33.

Pearson, Jacqueline. *The Prostituted Muse: Images of Women and Women Dramatists, 1642–1737.* New York: St. Martin's, 1988.

Pembroke, countess of. *See* Sidney, Mary

Pepys, Samuel. *Diary.* Ed. Robert Latham and William Matthews. 11 vols. Berkeley: U of California P, 1974.

Perry, Maria. *The Word of a Prince: A Life of Elizabeth I from Contemporary Documents.* Woodbridge, Eng.: Boydell, 1990.

Perry, Ruth. *The Celebrated Mary Astell: An Early English Feminist.* Chicago: U of Chicago P, 1986.

Peters, Henriette. *Mary Ward: A World in Contemplation.* Trans. Helen Butterworth. Leominster, Eng.: Gracewing, 1991.

Pettie, George. *A Petite Pallace of Pettie His Pleasure.* Ed. Herbert Hartman. London: Oxford UP, 1938.

Pharr, Suzanne. *Homophobia: A Weapon of Sexism.* Inverness: Chardon, 1988.

Philips, Katherine. *The Letters.* Ed. Patrick Thomas. Stump Cross, Eng.: Stump Cross, 1992. Vol. 2 of *The Collected Works of Katherine Philips, the Matchless Orinda.*

———. *Letters from Orinda to Poliarchus.* London, 1705.

———. *The Poems.* Ed. Patrick Thomas. Stump Cross, Eng.: Stump Cross, 1990. Vol. 1 of *The Collected Works of Katherine Philips, the Matchless Orinda.*

———. *Poems, by the Most Deservedly Admired Mrs. Katherine Philips, the matchless Orinda. To Which Is Added Monsiur Corneille's* Pompey *and* Horace, *Tragedies, with Several Other Translations out of French.* London, 1667.

———. *The Poems, Plays, and Letters of Katherine Philips.* Ed. Elizabeth H. Hageman and Andrea Sununu. New York: Oxford UP, forthcoming.

———. *Pompey. A Tragedy.* 1663. *The Translations.* Ed. G. Greer and R. Little. Essex, Eng.: Stump Cross, 1993. 2–91. Vol. 3 of *The Collected Works of Katherine Philips, the Matchless Orinda.*

Phillips, Patricia. *The Scientific Lady: A Social History of Women's Scientific Interests, 1520–1918.* New York: St. Martin's, 1990.

Pollak, Ellen. "Beyond Incest: Gender and the Politics of Transgression in Aphra Behn's *Love-Letters between a Nobleman and His Sister.*" Hutner 151–86.

Pollock, Linda. *A Lasting Relationship: Parents and Children over Three Centuries.* London: Fourth Estate, 1987.

———. *With Faith and Physic: The Life of a Tudor Gentlewoman: Lady Grace Mildmay, 1552–1620.* New York: St. Martin's, 1993.

Prescott, Anne Lake. "The Pearl of the Valois and Elizabeth I: Marguerite de Navarre's *Miroir* and Tudor England." Hannay, *Silent* 61–76.

Prescott, Anne Lake, and Betty S. Travitsky, eds. *Female and Male Voices in Early Modern England: An Anthology of Renaissance Writing*. New York: Columbia UP, 2000.

Primrose, Diana. *A Chaine of Pearle; or, A Memoriall of the Peerles Graces, and Heroick Vertues of Queene Elizabeth, of Glorious Memory*. London, 1630.

Prior, Mary, ed. *Women in English Society, 1500–1800*. London: Methuen, 1985.

Prior, Roger. "Emilia Bassano and Alphonso Lanier." Lasocki 101–13.

———. "Was Emilia Bassano the Dark Lady of Shakespeare's Sonnets?" Lasocki 114–39.

Prynne, William. *The Popish Royall Favourite*. London, 1643.

Purkiss, Diane, ed. *Renaissance Women: The Plays of Elizabeth Cary, the Poems of Aemilia Lanyer*. London: Pickering, 1994.

———, ed. *Three Tragedies by Renaissance Women*. London: Penguin, 1998.

Puttenham, George. *The Arte of English Poesie*. Ed. Gladys Doidge Willcock and Alice Walker. Cambridge: Cambridge UP, 1936.

Questier, Michael C. *Conversion, Politics, and Religion in England, 1580–1625*. Cambridge: Cambridge UP, 1996.

Quilligan, Maureen. "The Constant Subjects: Instability and Female Authority in Wroth's *Urania* Poems." *Soliciting Interpretation: Literary Theory and Seventeenth-Century English Poetry*. Ed. Elizabeth D. Harvey and Katharine Eisaman Maus. Chicago: U of Chicago P, 1990. 307–35.

———. "Lady Mary Wroth: Female Authority and the Family Romance." *Unfolded Tales: Essays on Renaissance Romance*. Ed. George M. Logan and Gordon Teskey. Ithaca: Cornell UP, 1989. 257–80.

———. "Spenser's Audience." *Milton's Spenser: The Politics of Reading*. Ithaca: Cornell UP, 1983. 179–208.

Quintilian. *The Institutio Oratoria of Quintilian, with an English Translation by H. E. Butler in Four Volumes*. Vol. 1. London: Heinemann; New York: Putnam, 1921.

Radzinowicz, Mary Ann Nevins. "Eve and Dalila: Renovation and the Hardening of the Heart." *Reason and the Imagination: Studies in the History of Ideas, 1600–1800*. Ed. J. A. Mazzeo. New York: Columbia UP, 1962. 155–81.

———. "Reading Paired Poems Nowadays." *LIT: Literature, Interpretation, Theory* 1 (1990): 275–90.

Ralegh, Walter. *The Discovery of Guiana*. 1596. Rpt. *Sir Walter Ralegh: Selected Prose and Poetry*. Ed. Agnes M. C. Latham. London: Athlone, 1965.

Rathmell, J. C. A. Introduction. Sidney and Sidney xi–xxxii.

Read, Evelyn. *Catherine [Willoughby], Duchess of Suffolk: A Portrait*. London: Cape, 1962.

Reid, W. Stanford. "The Battle Hymns of the Lord: Calvinist Psalmody of the Sixteenth Century." *Sixteenth Century Essays and Studies* 2 (1971): 36–54.

Reynolds, Myra. *The Learned Lady in England, 1650–1760.* Boston, 1920. Boston: Houghton, 1964.

Rhodes, Elizabeth. "Luisa de Carvajal's Counter-Reformation Journey to Selfhood (1566–1614)." *Renaissance Quarterly* 51 (1998) : 887–911.

Rhodes, J. T. "English Books of Martyrs and Saints of the Late Sixteenth and Early Seventeenth Centuries." *Recusant History* 22.1 (1994): 7–25.

Rich, Mary. *Autobiography of Mary Countess of Warwick.* Ed. T. Crofton Croker. London: Percy Soc., 1848.

Rienstra, Debra. "Aspiring to Praise: The Sidney-Pembroke Psalter and the English Religious Lyric." Diss. Rutgers U, 1995.

Ringler, William A. "The Myth and the Man." *Sir Philip Sidney: 1586 and the Creation of a Legend.* Ed. Jan Van Dorsten, Dominic Baker-Smith, and Arthur Kinney. Leiden: Brill, 1986. 3–15.

Roberts, Josephine, ed. *The First Part of the Countess of Montgomery's Urania.* Renaissance English Text Soc. / Medieval and Renaissance Texts and Studies. Binghamton: Center for Medieval and Early Renaissance Studies, 1995.

———. " 'The Knott Never to Bee Untide': The Controversy Regarding Marriage in Lady Mary Wroth's *Urania.*" Miller and Waller 109–32.

———. "Radigund Revisited: Perspectives on Women Rulers in Lady Mary Wroth's *Urania.*" Haselkorn and Travitsky 187–210.

———. "Recent Studies in Women Writers of the English Renaissance: Mary Sidney, Countess of Pembroke." Farrell, Hageman, and Kinney 245–58, 265–69.

———. " 'Thou Maist Have Thy *Will*': The Sonnets of Shakespeare and His Stepsisters." Hageman and Steen 407–23.

Roche, Thomas P., Jr. *Petrarch and the English Sonnet Sequences.* New York: AMS, 1989.

Roesslin, Encharias. *The Byrth of Mankynde.* London: Raynald, 1540.

Rollins, Hyder, and Herschel Baker, eds. *The Renaissance in England: Nondramatic Prose and Verse of the Sixteenth Century.* Boston: Houghton, 1956.

Roper, Margaret More, trans. *A Devout Treatise upon the Pater Noster.* London, 1526?

Rose, Mary Beth. "Gender, Genre, and History: Seventeenth-Century English Women and the Art of Autobiography." Rose, *Women* 245–78.

———. "Where Are the Mothers in Shakespeare? Options for Gender Representation in the English Renaissance." *Shakespeare Quarterly* 42 (1991): 291–314.

———, ed. *Women in the Middle Ages and the Renaissance: Literary and Historical Perspectives.* Syracuse: Syracuse UP, 1986.

Rostenberg, Leona. *The Minority Press and the English Crown: A Study in Repression, 1558–1625.* The Hague: Nieukoop, 1971.

Rowe, Elizabeth Singer. *The Poetry of Elizabeth Singer Rowe, 1674–1737*. Ed. Madeleine Forell Marshall. Lewiston: Mellen, 1987.

Rowlands, Marie B. "Recusant Women, 1560–1640." M. Prior 149–80.

Rowse, A. L. Introduction. *The Poems of Shakespeare's Dark Lady*. By Aemilia Lanyer. Ed. Rowse. London: Cape, 1978. 1–37.

Rueff, Jacob. *The Expert Midwife*. London, 1637.

Russ, Joanna. *The Female Man*. Boston: Beacon, 1986.

Russo, Ann. " 'We Cannot Live without Our Lives': White Women, Antiracism, and Feminism." *Third World Women and the Politics of Feminism*. Ed. Chandra Talpade Mohanty, Ann Russo, and Lourdes Torres. Bloomington: Indiana UP, 1991. 297–313.

Salzman, Paul, ed. *An Anthology of Seventeenth-Century Fiction*. Oxford: Oxford UP, 1991.

Samuel, Irene. "*Purgatorio* and the Dream of Eve." *Journal of English and Germanic Philology* 63 (1964): 441–49.

Sanders, Eve Rachele. *Gender and Literacy on Stage in Early Modern England*. Cambridge: Cambridge UP, 1998.

Saunders, J. W. "From Manuscript to Print: A Note on the Circulation of Poetic Mss. in the Sixteenth Century." *Proceedings of the Leeds Philosophical and Literary Society* (1951): 507–25.

———. "The Stigma of Print: A Note on the Social Bases of Tudor Poetry." *Essays in Criticism* 1 (1951): 139–64.

Schenck, Celeste. "All of a Piece: Women's Poetry and Autobiography." *Life/Lines*. Ithaca: Cornell UP, 1988. 281–305.

Schiebinger, Linda. *The Mind Has No Sex? Women in the Origins of Modern Science*. Cambridge: Harvard UP, 1989.

Schleiner, Louise. *Tudor and Stuart Women Writers, with Verse Translation from Latin by Connie McQuillen, from Greek by Lynn E. Roller*. Bloomington: Indiana UP, 1994.

Schofield, Mary Anne, and Cecilia Macheski, eds. *Curtain Calls: British and American Women and the Theater, 1660–1820*. Athens: Ohio UP, 1991.

Schurman, Anna Maria van. *The Learned Maid; or, Whether a Maid May Be a Scholar?* London: Redmayne, 1659.

Scoloker, Anthony. *Daiphantus; or, The Passion of Love*. London, 1606.

Scoufos, Alice-Lyle. Oral communication to the author. 30 Apr. 1979.

Shakespeare, William. *The Complete Works of Shakespeare*. 4th ed. Ed. David Bevington. New York: Longman, 1997.

———. *The Tempest*. Ed. Robert Langbaum. New York: Signet, 1987.

Sharp, Jane. *The Midwives Book*. Ed. Elaine Hobby. Women Writers in English, 1350–1850. New York: Oxford UP, 1999.

———. *The Midwives Book; or, The Whole Art of Midwifry Discovered, Directing Childbearing Women How to Behave Themselves in Their Conception, Breeding, Bearing, and Nursing of Children*. 1671. *Women Writers Project*. 4 Apr. 2000 <http://www.wwp.brown.edu/texts/index.html>.

Shaver, Anne. "A New Woman of Romance." *Modern Language Studies* 21 (1991): 63–77.

Shell, Alison. "Popish Plots: *The Feign'd Curtizans* in Context." J. Todd, *Studies* 30–49.

Shell, Marc, ed. *Elizabeth's Glass.* Lincoln: U of Nebraska P, 1993.

Shepherd, Simon, ed. *The Women's Sharp Revenge: Five Women's Pamphlets from the Renaissance.* London: Fourth Estate, 1985.

Sidney, Mary. *Antonius.* Cerasano and Wynne-Davies 19–42.

———. *Antonius and a Discourse of Life and Death.* 1592. Facsim. Introd. Gary F. Waller. Aldershot: Scolar, 1996.

———. *The Collected Works of Mary Sidney Herbert, Countess of Pembroke.* Ed. Margaret P. Hannay, Noel J. Kinnamon, and Michael G. Brennan. 2 vols. Oxford: Clarendon, 1998.

———. "A Dialogue between Two Shepherds, *Thenot* and *Piers,* in Praise of *Astrea.*" *A Poetical Rapsody Containing, Diverse Sonnets, Odes, Elegies, Madrigals, and Other Poesies, both in Rhyme, and Measured Verse.* Ed. Francis Davison. London, 1602. 297–313.

———. *A Discourse of Life and Death. Written in French by Philippe Mornay; Antonius: A Tragedy Written Also in French by Robert Garnier. Both Done in English by the Countess of Pembroke.* London: Ponsonby, 1592.

Sidney, Mary, and Philip Sidney. *The Psalms of Sir Philip Sidney and the Countess of Pembroke.* Ed. J. C. A. Rathmell. New York: New York UP, 1963.

Sidney, Philip. *The Defence of Poesy. Sir Philip Sidney.* Ed. Katherine Duncan-Jones. Oxford: Oxford UP, 1989. 212–50.

———. *The Defence of Poetry. Miscellaneous Prose of Sir Philip Sidney.* Ed. Katherine Duncan-Jones and Jan van Dorsten. Oxford: Clarendon, 1973. 59–121.

———. *The Poems of Sir Philip Sidney.* Ed. W. A. Ringler. Oxford: Clarendon, 1962.

Siebert, Frederick Seaton. *Freedom of the Press in England, 1476–1776: The Rise of Governmental Controls.* Urbana: U of Illinois P, 1952.

Silberman, Lauren. *Transforming Desire: Erotic Knowledge in Books Three and Four of* The Faerie Queene. Berkeley: U of California P, 1994.

Skilliter, S. A. "Three Letters from the Ottoman 'Sultana' Safiye to Queen Elizabeth I." *Documents from Islamic Chanceries.* Vol. 3. Ed. S. M. Stern. Oxford: Cassirer, 1965. 130–33, 138–40, 142–54.

Smith, Henry. *A Preparative to Marriage.* London, 1591.

Smith, Hilda L. "Humanist Education and the Renaissance Concept of Women." Wilcox 9–29.

———. *Reason's Disciples: Seventeenth-Century English Feminists.* Urbana: U of Illinois P, 1982.

Smith, Hilda L., and Susan Cardinale, comps. *Women and the Literature of the Seventeenth Century: An Annotated Bibliography Based on Wing's Short Title Catalogue.* New York: Greenwood, 1990.

Smith, Thomas. *Commonwelth of England*. London, 1583.

Southwell, Anne. *The Southwell-Sibthorpe Commonplace Book: Folger MS V b. 198.* Ed. Jean Klene. Renaissance English Text Soc. / Medieval and Renaissance Texts and Studies. Tempe: Arizona Center for Medieval and Renaissance Studies, 1997.

Southwell, Robert. *The Poems of Robert Southwell, SJ.* Ed. James H. MacDonald and Nancy Pollard Brown. Oxford: Clarendon, 1967.

Sowernam, Ester. *Ester Hath Hang'd Haman; or, An Answere to a Lewd Pamphlet, Entituled the Arraignment of Women. With the Arraignment of Lewd, Idle, Froward, and Unconstant Men, and Husbands. Divided into Two Parts. The First Presents the Dignity and Worthinesse of Women, out of Divine Testimonies. The Second Shewing the Estimation of the Foeminine Sexe, in Ancient and Pagan Times.* London, 1617. Excerpted in Henderson and McManus 217–43.

Speght, James. *A Brief Demonstration, Who Have, and of the Certainty of Their Salvation, That Have the Spirit of Christ.* London, 1613.

———. *The Day-Spring of Comfort. A Sermon Preached before the Lord Maior and Aldermen of London on Sunday the Sixth of January, Anno 1610 [1611] Being Also the Feast of Epiphanie.* London, 1615. Rpt. as *The Christian's Comfort. A Sermon Preached before the Lord Maior and Aldermen of London.* London, 1616.

Speght, Rachel. *Certaine Quaeres to the Bayter of Women. With Confutation of Some Part of His Diabolicall Discipline.* Appended to R. Speght, *Mouzell.*

———. *Mortalities Memorandum, with a Dreame Prefixed, Imaginarie in Manner; Reall in Matter.* London, 1621. R. Speght, *Polemics* 43–89.

———. *A Mouzell for Melastomus, the Cynicall Bayter of, and Foule Mouthed Barker against Evahs Sex.* London, 1617.

———. *The Polemics and Poems of Rachel Speght.* Ed. Barbara Kiefer Lewalski. New York: Oxford UP, 1996.

Spence, Richard T. *Lady Anne Clifford, Countess of Pembroke, Dorset and Montgomery, 1590–1676.* Phoenix Mill, Eng.: Sutton, 1997.

Spender, Dale, and Janet Todd, eds. *British Women Writers: An Anthology from the Fourteenth Century to the Present.* New York: Bedrick, 1989.

Spenser, Edmund. *Astrophel. A Pastoral Elegy upon the Death of the Most Noble and Valorous Knight, Sir Philip Sidney.* London: Ponsonby, 1595.

———. *Poetical Works.* Ed. J. C. Smith and E. DeSelincourt. 1912. Oxford: Oxford UP, 1991.

Spevack, Marvin, Michael Steppat, and Marga Munkelt, eds. *Antony and Cleopatra.* A New Variorum Edition of Shakespeare. New York: MLA, 1990.

Spufford, Margaret. *Small Books and Pleasant Histories.* Athens: U of Georgia P, 1981.

Stallybrass, Peter. "Patriarchal Territories: The Body Enclosed." Ferguson, Quilligan, and Vickers 123–44.

Stanford, Ann. *The Women Poets in English: An Anthology.* New York: Mc-Graw, 1972.

Steen, Sara Jayne. Introduction. Stuart 1–105.

———. "Textual Introduction." Stuart 107–11.

Steinberg, Theodore L. "The Sidneys and the Psalms." *Studies in Philology* 92 (1995): 1–17.

Stenton, Doris Mary. *The English Woman in History.* 1957. London: Allen, 1977.

Stock, Phyllis. *Better than Rubies: A History of Women's Education.* New York: Putnam, 1978.

Stortoni, Laura Anna, ed. *Women Poets of the Italian Renaissance: Courtly Ladies and Courtesans.* Trans. Stortoni and Mary Prentice Lillie. New York: Italica, 1997.

Straznicky, Marta. "Reading the Stage: Margaret Cavendish and Commonwealth Closet Drama." *Criticism* 37 (1995): 355–90.

Stuart, Arbella. *The Letters of Lady Arbella Stuart.* Ed. Sara Jayne Steen. New York: Oxford UP, 1994.

Stubbes, Philip. *A Crystall Glasse for Christian Women.* London, 1591.

Summers, Claude J., and Ted-Larry Pebworth, eds. *Representing Women in Renaissance England.* Columbia: U of Missouri P, 1997.

Sutcliffe, Alice. "Of Our Losse by Adam, and Our Gayne by Christ." *Meditations of Man's Mortalitie.* 1634. 141–200. Rpt. in Wynne-Davies 238–54.

Swain, Margaret. *The Needlework of Mary, Queen of Scots.* New York: Van Nostrand, 1973.

Swetnam, Joseph [pseud. Thomas Tel-troth]. *The Araignment of Lewde, Idle, Froward, and Unconstant Women; or, The Vanitie of Them, Choose You Whether.* London, 1615. Excerpted in Henderson and McManus 189–216.

———. *The Schoole of the Noble and Worthy Science of Defence.* London, 1617.

Swetnam the Woman-Hater. Arraigned by Women. A New Comedie, Acted at the Red Bull by the Late Queenes Servants. London, 1620.

Swift, Carolyn Ruth. "Feminine Identity in Lady Mary Wroth's Romance *Urania.*" *English Literary Renaissance* 14 (1984): 328–46.

———. "Feminine Self-Definition in Lady Mary Wroth's *Love's Victorie* (c. 1621)." *English Literary Renaissance* 19 (1989): 171–88.

Teague, Frances. *Bathsua Makin, Woman of Learning.* Lewisburg: Bucknell UP, 1998.

———. "Elizabeth I." K. Wilson 522–47.

———. "Queen Elizabeth in Her Speeches." Cerasano and Wynne-Davies, *Gloriana's Face* 63–78.

Thornton, Alice. *The Autobiography of Mrs. Alice Thornton of East Newton, Co. York.* Ed. Charles Jackson. Durham: Andrews, 1875.

Tilney, Edmund. *The Flower of Friendship: A Renaissance Dialogue Contesting Marriage (1573)*. Ed. Valerie Wayne. Ithaca: Cornell UP, 1992.

Todd, Janet, ed. *Aphra Behn Studies*. Cambridge: Cambridge UP, 1996.

——. *The Sign of Angellica: Women, Writing, and Fiction, 1660–1800*. New York: Columbia UP, 1989.

——. " 'Who Is Silvia: What Is She?' Feminine Identity in Aphra Behn's *Love-Letters between a Nobleman and His Sister*." J. Todd, *Studies* 199–218.

Todd, Richard. " 'So Well Atyr'd Abroad': A Background to the Sidney-Pembroke Psalter and Its Implications for the Seventeenth-Century Religious Lyric." *Texas Studies in Literature and Language* 29 (1987): 74–93.

Tomlinson, Sophie. "My Brain the Stage: Margaret Cavendish and the Fantasy of Female Performance." Brant and Purkiss 134–63.

Trapnel, Anna. *The Cry of a Stone; or, A Relation of Something Spoken in Whitehall*. London, 1654.

——. *Report and Plea*. 1654. Otten 64–78.

Traub, Valerie, M. Lindsay Kaplan, and Dympna Callaghan, eds. *Feminist Readings of Early Modern Culture: Emerging Subjects*. Cambridge: Cambrige UP, 1996.

Travitsky, Betty, ed. *The Paradise of Women: Writings by Englishwomen of the Renaissance*. 2nd ed. New York: Columbia UP, 1989.

Travitsky, Betty, and Adele F. Seeff, eds. *Attending to Women in Early Modern England*. Newark: U of Delaware P, 1994.

Trevett, Christine. *Women and Quakerism in the Seventeenth Century*. York: Ebor, 1991.

Trill, Suzanne. "Religion and the Construction of Femininity." Wilcox 30–55.

Trill, Suzanne, Kate Chedgzoy, and Melanie Osborne, eds. *"Lay By Your Needles, Ladies, Take the Pen": Writing Women in England, 1500–1700*. London: Arnold, 1997.

Trubowitz, Rachel. "Female Preachers and Male Wives: Gender and Authority in Civil War England." *Pamphlet Wars: Prose in the English Revolution*. Ed. James Holstun. London: Cass, 1992. 112–33.

Turner, James Grantham, ed. *Sexuality and Gender in Early Modern Europe: Institutions, Texts, Images*. Cambridge: Cambridge UP, 1993.

Tyler, Margaret, trans. *The Mirrour of Princely Deedes and Knighthood*, by Diego Ortunez de Calahorra. London, 1578.

Uttal, Lynet. "Inclusion without Influence: The Continuing Tokenism of Women of Color." *Making Face, Making Soul = Haciendo Caras: Creative and Critical Perspectives by Women of Color*. Ed. Gloria Anzaldúa. San Francisco: Aunt Lute, 1990. 42–45.

van Heertum, Cis. "A Hostile Annotation of Rachel Speght's *A Mouzell for Melastomus* (1617)." *English Studies* 6 (1987): 490–96.

Verbrugge, Rita. "Margaret Roper's Personal Expression in the *Devout Treatise upon the Pater Noster.*" Hannay, *Silent* 34–42.

The Victoria History of the Counties of England: Huntingdonshire. Vol. 2. London: Inst. of Historical Research, 1974.

Vives, Juan Luis. *Instruction of a Christen Woman.* Trans. Richard Hyrde. London, 1585.

Walker, Kim. *Women Writers of the English Renaissance.* New York: Twayne, 1996.

Wall, Alison D., ed. *Two Elizabethan Women: Correspondence of Joan and Maria Thynne, 1575–1611.* Devizes, Eng.: Wiltshire Record Soc., 1983.

Wall, Wendy. *The Imprint of Gender: Authorship and Publication in the English Renaissance.* Ithaca: Cornell UP, 1993.

Wallas, Ada. *Before the Bluestockings.* London: Allen, 1929.

Waller, Gary F. *Mary Sidney, Countess of Pembroke: A Critical Study of Her Writings and Literary Milieu.* Salzburg: U of Salzburg, 1979.

——. *The Sidney Family Romance: Mary Wroth, William Herbert, and the Early Modern Construction of Gender.* Detroit: Wayne State UP, 1993.

——. "Struggling into Discourse: The Emergence of Renaissance Women's Writing." Hannay, *Silent* 238–56.

Warnicke, Retha M. "Lady Mildmay's Journal: A Study in Autobiography and Meditation in Reformation England." *Sixteenth Century Journal* 20 (1989): 55–68.

——. *Women of the English Renaissance and Reformation.* Westport: Greenwood, 1983.

Watt, Tessa. *Cheap Print and Popular Piety, 1550–1640.* Cambridge: Cambridge UP, 1991.

Wayne, Valerie. " 'Some Sad Sentence': Vives' *Instruction of a Christian Woman.*" Hannay, *Silent* 15–29.

Weamys, Anna. *A Continuation of Sir Philip Sidney's Arcadia.* Ed. Patrick Colborn Cullen. New York: Oxford UP, 1994.

Weidemann, Heather L. "Theatricality and Female Identity in Mary Wroth's *Urania.*" Miller and Waller 191–209.

Weigall, Rachel. "An Elizabethan Gentlewoman: The Journal of Lady Mildmay." *Quarterly Review* 215 (1911): 119–38.

Weil, Rachel. " 'If I Did Say So, I Lyed': Elizabeth Cellier and the Construction of Credibility in the Popish Plot Crisis." *Political Culture and Cultural Politics in Early Modern England: Essays Presented to David Underdown.* Ed. Susan D. Amussen and Mark A. Kishlansy. Manchester: Manchester UP, 1995. 189–209.

Weis, Lois, Amira Proweller, and Craig Centrie. "Re-examining 'A Moment in History': Loss of Privilege inside Working-Class Masculinity in the 1990s." Fine, Weis, Powell, and Wong 210–28.

Weller, Barry, and Margaret Ferguson. Introduction. Weller and Ferguson, *Tragedy* 1–59.

——, eds. The Tragedy of Mariam the Fair Queen of Jewry *[by Elizabeth*

Cary], with The Lady Falkland: Her Life, by One of Her Daughters. Berkeley: U of California P, 1994.

Whately, William. A Bride-Bush; or, A Direction for Married Persons. London, 1616.

White, Elizabeth Wade. Anne Bradstreet, The Tenth Muse. New York: Oxford UP, 1971.

White, Micheline. "Recent Studies in Women Writers of Tudor England, 1485–1603 (mid-1993 to 1999)." English Literary Renaissance 29 (2000): forthcoming.

———. "Renaissance Englishwomen and Translation: The Case of Anne Lock's Of the Markes of the Children of God." English Literary Renaissance 29, forthcoming.

Whitehead, Lydia. "A Poena et Culpa: Penitence, Confidence and the Miserere in Foxe's Actes and Monuments." Renaissance Studies 4 (1990): 287–300.

Whitney, Geffrey. A Choice of Emblemes by Geffrey Whitney. 1586. Ed. Henry Green. New York: Blom, 1967.

Whitney, Isabella. The Copy of a Letter, Lately Written in Meeter, by a Yonge Gentilwoman: to Her Unconstant Lover. London, 1567.

———. The Floures of Philosophie (1572) by Hugh Plat and A Sweet Nosgay (1573) and The Copy of a Letter (1567) by Isabella Whitney. Ed. Richard Panofsky. Delmar: Scholars Facsims. and Rpts., 1982.

———. "The Manner of Her Will and What She Left to London." Martin, Women Writers 289–302.

———. A Sweet Nosgay, or Pleasant Posye: Contayning a Hundred and Ten Phylosophicall Flowers. London, 1573.

———. "Wyll and Testament." I. Whitney, Sweet Nosgay E2–E8v. Rpt. as "The 'Wyll and Testament' of Isabella Whitney." Ed. Betty Travitsky. English Literary Renaissance 10 (1980): 76–94.

Whythorne, Thomas. The Autobiography of Thomas Whythorne. Ed. James M. Osborn. New Haven: Yale UP, 1961.

Wiesner, Merry E. Women and Gender in Early Modern Europe. Cambridge: Cambridge UP, 1993.

Wilcox, Helen, ed. Women and Literature in Britain, 1500–1700. Cambridge: Cambridge UP, 1996.

Wilcox, Helen, et al., eds. Sacred and Profane: Secular and Devotional Interplay in Early Modern British Literature. Amsterdam: Vrije UP, 1996.

Willen, Diane. "Women and Religion in Early Modern England." Marshall 140–65.

Williams, Franklin. Index of Dedications and Commendatory Verses in English Books before 1641. London: Bibliographical Soc., 1962.

Williams, Jane. The Literary Women of England. London: Saunders, 1861.

Williams, Raymond. Keywords. London: Oxford UP, 1983.

Williamson, Marilyn L. Raising Their Voices: British Women Writers, 1650–1750. Detroit: Wayne State UP, 1990.

Wilson, Adrian. "The Ceremony of Childbirth and Its Interpretation." Fildes, *Women as Mothers* 68–107.

Wilson, Derek. *The Tudor Tapestry: Men, Women and Society in Reformation England.* London: Heinemann, 1972.

Wilson, Katharina M., ed. *Women Writers of the Renaissance and Reformation.* Athens: U of Georgia P, 1987.

Wilson, Katharina M., and Frank J. Warnke, eds. *Women Writers of the Seventeenth Century.* Athens: U of Georgia P, 1989.

Wiltenburg, Joy. *Disorderly Women and Female Power in the Street Literature of Early Modern England and Germany.* Charlottesville: UP of Virginia, 1992.

Winant, Howard. "Behind Blue Eyes: Whiteness and Contemporary U.S. Racial Politics." Fine, Weis, Powell, and Wong 40–53.

Wing, Adrien Katherine, ed. *Critical Race Feminism: A Reader.* New York: New York UP, 1997.

———. "Killing Rage: Brief Reflections toward a Multiplicative Theory and Praxis of Being." Wing, *Feminism* 27–34.

Wiseman, Susan. "Gender and Status in Dramatic Discourse: Margaret Cavendish, Duchess of Newcastle." Grundy and Wiseman 159–77.

Wolfe, Heather R. "The Scribal Hands and Dating of *Lady Falkland: Her Life.*" *English Manuscript Studies* 9 (1999): 187–217.

Woodbridge, Linda. *Women and the English Renaissance: Literature and the Nature of Womankind, 1540–1620.* Urbana: U of Illinois P, 1984.

Woods, Susanne. "Anne Lock and Aemilia Lanyer: A Tradition of Protestant Women Speaking." *Form and Reform in Renaissance England: Essays in Honor of Barbara Kiefer Lewalski.* Ed. Amy Boesky and Mary Thomas Crane. Newark: U of Delaware P, 2000. 171–84.

———. Introduction. Lanyer xv–xlii.

———. *Lanyer: A Renaissance Woman Poet.* New York: Oxford UP, 1999.

———. *Natural Emphasis: English Versification from Chaucer to Dryden.* San Marino: Huntington Lib., 1984.

Woolf, D. R. *The Idea of History in Early Stuart England: Erudition, Ideology, and 'the Light of Truth' from the Accession of James I to the Civil War.* Toronto: U of Toronto P, 1990.

Woolf, Virginia. *A Room of One's Own.* 1929. New York: Harcourt, 1989.

Woudhuysen, H. R., ed. *The Penguin Book of Renaissance Verse, 1509–1659.* London: Penguin, 1992.

Wright, Louis B. *Middle-Class Culture in Elizabethan England.* Ithaca: Cornell UP, 1935.

Wroth, Mary. *The Countess of Montgomeries Urania.* Introd. Josephine A. Roberts. The Early Modern Englishwoman: A Facsim. Lib. of Essential Works, Printed Writings, 1500–1640, pt. 1, vol. 10. Brookfield: Ashgate, 1996.

———. *The Countess of Mountgomeries Urania. Written by the Right Honourable the Lady Mary Wroath. Daughter to the Right Noble Robert Earle of Leicester. And Neece to the Ever Famous, and Renowned Sir Phillip Sidney Knight. And to the Most Exelent Lady Mary Countesse of Pembroke Late Deceased.* London: Marriott, 1621.

———. *The First Part of the Countess of Montgomery's Urania.* Ed. Josephine A. Roberts. Renaissance English Text Soc. / Medieval and Renaissance Texts and Studies. Binghamton: Center for Medieval and Early Renaissance Studies, 1995.

———. *Lady Mary Wroth's* Love's Victory: *The Penshurst Manuscript.* Ed. Michael G. Brennan. London: Roxburghe Club, 1988.

———. "Mary Sidney: Lady Wroth." Ed. Margaret P. Hannay. K. Wilson 548–65.

———. *The Poems of Lady Mary Wroth.* Ed. Josephine A. Roberts. Baton Rouge: Louisiana State UP, 1992.

———. *The Second Part of the Countess of Montgomery's Urania.* Ed. Josephine A. Roberts. Completed by Suzanne Gossett and Janel Mueller. Renaissance English Text Soc. / Medieval and Renaissance Texts and Studies. Tempe: Arizona Center for Medieval and Renaissance Studies. 2000.

Wynne-Davies, Marion, ed. *Women Poets of the Renaissance.* London: Routledge, 1999.

York Plays: The Plays Performed by the Crafts or Mysteries of York on the Day of Corpus Christi. Ed. Lucy Toulmin Smith. New York: Russell, 1963.

Zim, Rivkah. *English Metrical Psalms: Poetry as Praise and Prayer, 1535–1601.* Cambridge: Cambridge UP, 1987.

Index